3/2015

D1737883

Health and Education in Early Childhood

Health and Education in Early Childhood presents conceptual issues, research findings, and program and policy implications in promoting well-being in health and education in the first five years of life. Leading researchers in the multidisciplinary fields of early learning and human capital formation explore the themes of the integration of health and education in promoting young children's well-being; the timing of influences on child development; and the focus on multiple levels of strategies to promote healthy early development. Through this, a unique framework is provided to better understand how early childhood health and education predictors and interventions contribute to well-being at individual, family, community, and societal levels and to policy development. Key topics addressed in the chapters include nutritional status, parenting, cognitive development and school readiness, conduct problems and antisocial behavior, obesity, and well-being in later childhood and adulthood.

ARTHUR J. REYNOLDS is a professor at the Institute of Child Development and co-director of the Human Capital Research Collaborative at the University of Minnesota.

ARTHUR J. ROLNICK is a senior fellow at the Humphrey School of Public Affairs and co-director of the Human Capital Research Collaborative at the University of Minnesota.

JUDY A. TEMPLE is an associate professor at the Humphrey School of Public Affairs and the Department of Applied Economics at the University of Minnesota.

Health and Education in Early Childhood

Predictors, Interventions, and Policies

Edited by

Arthur J. Reynolds
University of Minnesota

Arthur J. Rolnick
University of Minnesota

and

Judy A. Temple
University of Minnesota

CAMBRIDGE
UNIVERSITY PRESS

University Printing House, Cambridge CB2 8BS, United Kingdom

Cambridge University Press is part of the University of Cambridge.

It furthers the University's mission by disseminating knowledge in the pursuit of education, learning and research at the highest international levels of excellence.

www.cambridge.org
Information on this title: www.cambridge.org/9781107038349

© Cambridge University Press 2014

First published 2014

Printed in the United States of America by Sheridan Books, Inc.

A catalogue record for this publication is available from the British Library

Library of Congress Cataloguing in Publication data
Health and education in early childhood : predictors, interventions, and policies / edited by Arthur J. Reynolds, Arthur J. Rolnick, Judy A. Temple.
    p. ; cm.
Includes bibliographical references and index.
ISBN 978-1-107-03834-9
I. Reynolds, Arthur J., editor of compilation.   II. Rolnick, Arthur J., 1944–
editor of compilation.   III. Temple, Judy A., editor of compilation.
[DNLM: 1. Early Intervention (Education) – United States.   2. Health Services
Accessibility – United States. 3.   Child – United States.   4. Child Welfare –
United States. 5. Health Policy – United States.   6. Health Status – United States.
7. Socioeconomic Factors – United States. WA 320 AA1]
HQ778.5
362.7–dc23

                                                                    2014002314

ISBN 978-1-107-03834-9 Hardback

Contents

Figures

Tables

Contributors

JEAN MARIE ABRAHAM University of Minnesota

CATHERINE AYOUB Harvard Medical School

JESSICA DYM BARTLETT Harvard Medical School

KAREN L. BIERMAN Pennsylvania State University

PAULA A. BRAVEMAN University of California, San Francisco

ROBERT H. BRUININKS University of Minnesota

FRANCES A. CAMPBELL University of North Carolina at Chapel Hill

RACHEL CHAZAN-COHEN George Mason University

PEGGY CHEN RAND Corporation

ALYSSA CRAWFORD Johns Hopkins Bloomberg School of Public Health

KATINA D'ONISE University of South Australia

CELENE E. DOMITROVICH Pennsylvania State University

GREG J. DUNCAN University of California, Irvine

SUSAN EGERTER University of California, San Francisco

MICHELLE M. ENGLUND University of Minnesota

TEMITOPE O. ERINOSHO University of North Carolina at Chapel Hill

KEVIN D. FRICK Johns Hopkins Carey Business School

MICHAEL K. GEORGIEFF University of Minnesota

SCOTT D. GEST Pennsylvania State University

BERNARD GUYER Johns Hopkins Bloomberg School of Public Health

MOMOKO HAYAKAWA University of Minnesota

ARIEL KALIL University of Chicago

PINAR KARACA-MANDIC University of Minnesota

SAMUEL A. KLEINER Cornell University

NARAYANA KOCHERLAKOTA Federal Reserve Bank of Minneapolis

JOHN W. LYNCH University of Adelaide

SAI MA Johns Hopkins Bloomberg School of Public Health

LAURIE T. MARTIN RAND Corporation

ROBYN A. MCDERMOTT University of South Australia

ROBIN E. MOCKENHAUPT Robert Wood Johnson Foundation

ROBERT L. NIX Pennsylvania State University

HELEN RAIKES University of Nebraska

ARTHUR J. REYNOLDS University of Minnesota

ARTHUR J. ROLNICK University of Minnesota

SHARON ROLNICK HealthPartners Institute of Education and Research

LAWRENCE J. SCHWEINHART HighScope Educational Research
    Foundation

AMY SUSMAN-STILLMAN University of Minnesota

JUDY A. TEMPLE University of Minnesota

JIM THORP University of Minnesota

DIANNE S. WARD University of North Carolina at Chapel Hill

JANET A. WELSH Pennsylvania State University

BARRY WHITE University of Minnesota

SUNG J. CHOI YOO University of Minnesota

KATHLEEN M. ZIOL-GUEST University of New York

Foreword: Health, education, and early childhood development

In 2010, the Minneapolis Fed served as host in partnership with the University of Minnesota for a conference on health and early childhood development. The presentation and discussion sessions were designed to lead to a deeper understanding of the impact that early childhood health has on later education and health outcomes, as children progress through school and into adulthood. The presentations and discussions led to this volume, which features several conference participants.

The Minneapolis Fed hosts conferences on a number of topics, including economic research, community development, and economic and financial education. And this wasn't the first time it hosted a conference on early childhood issues. In 2003, researchers gathered for a one-day conference titled "The Economics of Early Childhood Development: Lessons for Economic Policy." After the Minneapolis Fed joined the University of Minnesota to form the Early Childhood Research Collaborative, the precursor to the HCRC, the Fed hosted a two-day conference in 2007 on "Critical Issues in Cost Effectiveness in Children's First Decade."

So why is the Federal Reserve interested in early childhood development issues? After all, the Fed's primary mission is to conduct monetary policy as the nation's central bank. It also regulates banks and provides fiscal services for the US Treasury. At first glance it seems that early childhood development is a bit far from the Fed's core responsibilities. However, the Federal Reserve is also charged with promoting employment and economic growth, and education is a key – if not the primary – component of growth and jobs. Here is what Federal Reserve Chairman Ben Bernanke had to say about early childhood education in a 2007 speech:

Although education and the acquisition of skills is a lifelong process, starting early in life is crucial. Recent research – some sponsored by the Federal Reserve Bank of Minneapolis in collaboration with the University of Minnesota – has documented the high returns that early childhood programs can pay in terms of subsequent educational attainment and in lower rates of social problems, such as teenage pregnancy and welfare dependency. The most successful early childhood programs appear to be those that cultivate both cognitive and non-cognitive skills and that engage families in stimulating learning at home.

In other words, one need look no further than the first two words in the HCRC acronym, "human capital." One of the key ingredients to sustained economic growth is the development of human capital. That is, economies with highly educated and skilled workers have higher levels of productivity, which supports economic growth, including higher earnings for workers. For example, in the US economy, the median earnings for a worker age 25 to 34 with a college degree was about 70 percent more than for a worker with only a high school diploma in 2011. Twenty years earlier, the earnings differential was 56 percent. Furthermore, during this past recession, employment deteriorated less for workers with higher levels of education than for workers with lower levels of education. Over the long run, the US economy will continue to demand more highly educated and skilled workers.

As this volume emphasizes, human capital development begins early. Research by Nobel laureate economist James Heckman reveals that skill acquisition is a cumulative process that works most effectively when a solid foundation has been provided in early childhood. As children get off to a good start, they are more likely to succeed in school and later in the workforce. Moreover, as articulated by Art Rolnick during his time as research director at the Minneapolis Fed, many of the benefits of early investments, particularly those that target at-risk children, accrue to the general public – for example, in the form of reduced crime costs.

This volume is designed to reach many audiences, including policy-makers, researchers, students, practitioners, and interested citizens. The discussions inspired by the following chapters can lead to better practice and policy in early health and education and to a better quality of life for the nation's children.

NARAYANA KOCHERLAKOTA
President, Federal Reserve Bank of Minneapolis

References

Baum, Sandy, Ma, Jennifer, and Payea, Kathleen (2013). *Education pays 2013: the benefits of higher education for individuals and society*. College Board. http://trends.collegeboard.org/sites/default/files/education-pays-2013-full-report.pdf.
Bernanke, Ben S. (2007). The level and distribution of economic well-being. Comments before the Greater Omaha Chamber of Commerce, Omaha, Neb., February 6, 2007. www.federalreserve.gov/newsevents/speech/bernanke20070206a.htm.

Heckman, James J., and Masterov, Dimitriy V. (2007). The productivity argument for investing in young children. *Applied Economic Perspectives and Policy*, 29(3), 446–493.

Rolnick, Arthur, and Grunewald, Rob (2003). Early childhood development: economic development with a high public return. *The Region*, 17(4) Supplement (December), 6–12.

Acknowledgements

This volume is a product of the Human Capital Research Collaborative (HCRC), a partnership of the University of Minnesota and the Federal Reserve Bank of Minneapolis devoted to understanding the determinants of well-being and the effects of social programs on improving health and well-being. Many individuals, centers, and organizations made contributions to make this volume possible. We want to thank in particular the Federal Reserve Bank of Minneapolis for their support of the work of the Human Capital Research Collaborative.

Introduction and overview

1 Early childhood health and education: policies and interventions to promote child well-being

Arthur J. Reynolds, Arthur J. Rolnick, and Judy A. Temple

Introduction

The early years of childhood represent a crucial window of opportunity for investments in skills or capabilities that can place children on the path to well-being in adulthood. Many recent studies in the last decade have focused on the importance of early human capital investments in academic and social skills for promoting long-term educational and economic success. The chapters in this volume explicitly examine the role of health – another type of human capital – in promoting children's early and later educational success and well-being. The impacts of health and education outcomes of salient programs, policies, and practices are summarized with an emphasis on policy implications.

The chapters present conceptual issues, research findings, and program and policy implications of promoting good health and school readiness in the first five years of life. These chapters were written by leading researchers in the multidisciplinary study of early learning and human capital formation and represent revised and updated versions of present-ations made at a national invitational conference that was held at the Federal Reserve Bank of Minneapolis in late 2010.

The book addresses three important themes. The first is the integration of both early health and education as important building blocks of current and later child well-being. Health practices and behaviors interact with educational and social experiences to affect outcomes for children and families. A variety of determinants of child and adult well-being such as prenatal care, family poverty, and access to high-quality early learning programs express their influence early in life yet are often investigated in isolation from each other. This is due in part to the fragmentation of fields of inquiry and the allocation of resources and funding. A multidisciplinary approach to summarizing knowledge in these areas is important for a more holistic perspective on the common predictors of early childhood outcomes and the importance of early childhood experiences for understanding longer-term differences in well-being.

The roles of early skills and capabilities for promoting future well-being are of central importance in many fields in social science and public health. Economist James Heckman has formulated a formal model of skill development that explicitly demonstrates that "students with greater early capacities (cognitive, noncognitive and health) are more efficient in later learning of both cognitive and noncognitive skills and in acquiring stocks of health capital" (Heckman, 2007, p. 4). This is consistent with ecological and life course models of human development (O'Connell, Boat, and Warner, 2009). Human capital investments are multifaceted, including academic skills, socio-emotional skills or behaviors, and health, and research suggests cross-linkages among them. For example, Cunha and Heckman (2008) show that the accumulation of socio-emotional skills promotes the acquiring of cognitive skills. Greater cognitive and socio-emotional capabilities may promote health and vice versa. Early accumulation of all three types of capabilities makes later investments in them more effective. The discussion in this volume is enhanced by the wide range of disciplinary approaches represented by the authors as they provide examples and summarize the literature on these linkages among education and health. Just as access to early childhood education programs contributes to later health outcomes and the reduction of health disparities, prenatal care and nutrition contribute to school readiness and the reduction of disparities in educational achievement.

The second theme is a focus on the wide set of possibilities for interventions and policies that begin in the earliest years of child development. The etiology of child outcomes begins prenatally and the magnitude and significance of early influences remain important throughout the early years of childhood (O'Connell et al., 2009; Reynolds, Temple, and White, 2011). Not only are the determinants of learning (e.g., school readiness) and socio-emotional skills and health behaviors (e.g., antisocial behavior and obesity) expressed early but the opportunities in the early years to effectively intervene to prevent learning problems and to promote positive behavioral and health outcomes are great. This volume covers a wide spectrum of these early determinants of child outcomes ranging from poverty, prenatal nutrition, and oral health to parenting practices, cognitive development, and social-emotional skills. A comprehensive set of early interventions also are considered including their health and educational impacts in the short and longer term. These include prenatal nutrition programs, home visiting, early learning programs in child care and Head Start centers, income support programs, and intervention to prevent obesity and early conduct problems. Educational and health policy reforms also are covered.

The third theme of the volume is the focus on multiple levels of strategies to promote early development. Interventions to improve well-being vary dramatically in scale including programs offered to individuals and families, to policies intended to affect school and community contexts and to large-scale reforms in education and health care systems. Each of these levels is part of the ecological perspective that is necessary to address health and social issues comprehensively. Prenatal nutrition and home visiting interventions to strengthen parenting skills, for example, directly impact child development outcomes whereas multi-component early childhood interventions enrich the learning environments of young children in a broader way. Social and health policies and reforms (e.g., access to health care or early childhood education) increase resources and access to needed services, which are expected to carry over to child and family outcomes. Consistent with the ecological perspective, this book will include the full continuum of interventions.

These themes provide a unique and comprehensive framework to better understand how early childhood health and education predictors and interventions contribute to well-being at individual, family, community, and societal levels and to policy development. Key child outcomes in the chapters include nutritional status, parenting, cognitive development and school readiness, conduct problems and antisocial behavior, obesity, and well-being in later childhood and adulthood. These outcomes are representative of the targeted goals established by the Centers for Disease Control and Prevention in the US Department of Health and Human Services. To promote a more integrated vision of health promotion, the Centers for Disease Control and Prevention established the Healthy People Initiative. The four comprehensive, national goals of Healthy People 2020 are as follows:

- attain high-quality, longer lives free of preventable disease, disability, injury, and premature death;
- achieve health equity, eliminate disparities, and improve the health of all groups;
- create social and physical environments that promote good health for all;
- promote quality of life, healthy development, and healthy behaviors across all life stages.

Although these overarching goals and the many related health-promoting activities ranging from nutrition and oral health to prevention of violence and mental health problems have their origin in prenatal and early childhood development, the importance and complicated nature of these goals reinforce the importance of interdisciplinary research spanning education, allied health, psychology, economics, and policy fields. Among the topics identified by Healthy People 2020 that are covered in this volume are oral health, nutrition and weight status, social determinants of health, mental health and mental disorders, maternal, infant and child health, injury and violence prevention, disability and health, educational and community-based programs, access to health services, and physical activity.

Many of the health and education topics policies recommended in this volume are or potentially could be recommended to policymakers on the basis of their cost-effectiveness. The impact and cost-effectiveness of health and educational interventions are an increasingly important area of focus. The avoidable annual costs of violence (Cohen, 1998), school dropout (Levin et al., 2007), substance abuse, and mental health problems (O'Connell, Boat, and Warner, 2009; Greenberg et al., 2003) exceed $500 billion.

A summary of current evidence on the economic returns of many interventions affecting young children is shown in Table 1.1. More discussion of the estimates in this table can be found in Reynolds, Temple, and White (2011). Most of the interventions that have had economic analysis of costs and benefits show a return of at least one dollar for every dollar of cost. Several programs, such as preschool interventions primarily for children at risk, show benefits that far exceed costs. Certainly, many effective programs and those programs that are promising in the early stages may be worth implementing even though the return on investment has not been calculated. Scaling up small proven or promising programs to include more families while ensuring effective implementation is a critical need at the forefront of health and educational policy development.

Overview of individual chapters

The volume begins with a set of chapters that provide a broad overview of the determinants of health disparities beginning in childhood. Part I begins with Paula Braveman and her co-authors Susan Egerter and Robin Mockenhaupt discussing the social determinants of health with a focus on the role of education. The social determinants of health include factors outside of medical care that can be influenced by social policies and are likely to have important effects on child and adult well-being. Recent evidence is presented revealing marked disparities in health by income and education as well as by race or ethnic group in the US. Braveman and colleagues present a conceptual framework for considering and addressing how health disparities are created, exacerbated, and perpetuated across the lifetimes of individuals and across generations.

Identifying the relationship between early childhood poverty and adult productivity and health is the objective of the chapter by Greg Duncan,

Table 1.1 *Cost-effectiveness estimates for early childhood programs, birth to third grade.*

Development stage	Source	Focus	Location	2007 dollars[a]			
				Benefits	Costs	B-C	B/C
Birth to age 3							
WIC[b]	Avruch and Cackley (1995)	Targeted	National	1,206	393	813	3.07
NFP, Low SES	Glazner et al. (2004)	Targeted	Elmira, NY	83,850	16,727	67,123	5.01
NFP, Higher SES	Glazner et al. (2004)	Targeted	Elmira, NY	25,317	16,727	8,590	1.51
preschool							
Child–Parent Centers	Reynolds et al. (2002)	Targeted	20 Chicago sites	86,401	8,512	77,889	10.15
Perry Preschool	Schweinhart et al. (2005)	Targeted	1 Ypsilanti site	294,716	18,260	276,456	16.14
Abecedarian[c]	Barnett and Masse (2007)	Targeted	1 NC site	182,422	73,159	109,263	2.49
RAND study of preschool in CA	Karoly et al. (2005)	Universal	State of CA	12,818	4,889	7,929	2.62
National pre-K synthesis for 2050[d]	Lynch (2007)	Targeted	National	20,603	6,479	14,124	3.18
	Lynch (2007)	Universal	National	12,958	6,479	6,479	2.00
Synthesis study	Aos et al. (2004)	Targeted	58 programs	19,826	8,415	11,411	2.36
Kindergarten							
Full-day K synthesis[e,f]	Aos et al. (2007)	Universal	23 programs	0	2,685	-2,685	0
School-age							
Tennessee STAR (class size reduction, K-3)	Krueger (2003)	Universal	79 schools	27,561	9,744	17,817	2.83
Synthesis of reduced class sizes, K-2[e,g]	Aos et al. (2007)	Universal	38 studies	6,847	2,454	4,393	2.79
Synthesis of reduced class sizes, grade 3–6[e,g]	Aos et al. (2007)	Universal	38 studies	3,387	2,454	933	1.38
Child–Parent Centers School-Age Program	Reynolds et al. (2002)	Targeted	20 Chicago sites	8,089	3,792	4,297	2.13
Reading Recovery[g]	Shanahan and Barr (1995)	Targeted	General	1,679	5,596	-3,151	0.30
Skills, Opportunities, and Recognition	Aos et al. (2004)	Universal	Seattle schools	16,256	5,172	11,084	3.14

Table 1.1 (*cont.*)

| Development stage | Source | Focus | Location | 2007 dollars[a] | | |
				Benefits	Costs	B-C	B/C
PK-3 Intervention							
Child–Parent Centers Extended Program	Reynolds et al. (2002)	Targeted	20 Chicago sites	47,161	5,175	41,986	9.11

Note. Findings from the Perry Preschool are at age 40. At age 27, B-C was $141,350 and B/C ratio was $8.74 (Barnett, 1996).

[a] All estimates are converted to 2007 dollars using the Consumer Price Index for All Urban Consumers (CPI-U).

[b] Estimates are based on a meta-analysis of studies investigating the effects of WIC.

[c] The cost for the Abecedarian Program represents the total costs of the intervention.

[d] Estimates for Lynch's (2007) synthesis of targeted and universal preschool represent annual per pupil program costs and associated annual government budget benefits. Total accrued benefits to government, the general public, and program participants and their parents relative to costs are $12.10:1 and $8.20:1 for the targeted and universal programs, respectively.

[e] Estimates are not based on formal cost–benefit analyses.

[f] The cost of full-day kindergarten is relative to the cost of half-day kindergarten in Washington State.

[g] Estimates from syntheses of reduced class sizes assume a reduction from 25 to 15 pupils per class.

Ariel Kalil, and Kathleen Ziol-Guest. Analyses of correlational data show that children from poorer families have lower achievement, exhibit more problem behaviors, and have worse health compared to children from more affluent families. Duncan and co-authors focus on a set of studies that attempt to identify the causal impact of poverty in early childhood on later educational attainment and health. The authors argue that poverty during the prenatal time period as well as in early childhood has substantial negative effects on adult earnings, work hours, and specific health conditions.

Michael Georgieff's chapter on the impact of maternal and child nutrition on cognitive development focuses on the scientific evidence for the role of certain important nutrients in brain development and function. Georgieff argues that deficiencies in some nutrients can cause brain dysfunction not only during the time of deficiency but long after repletion. Awareness of the role of nutrition in brain development and brain functioning is important for developing and supporting policies and programs to improve the nutritional status of pregnant women, newborns, and children.

The first section of this volume concludes with an overview of children and dental care by epidemiologist Cheri Rolnick. She summarizes the literature on oral health in children as well as the relationship between oral health and child outcomes. Children from poorer families have worse oral health than their more advantaged peers, and research suggests a connection between oral health and school performance that appears to operate in part through increased absences of children with dental problems.

Part II of the volume focuses on the effects of health interventions on child development and outcomes throughout the life course. Sai Ma, Kevin Frick, Alyssa Crawford, and Bernard Guyer contribute a chapter on early childhood health promotion and its health consequences over the life course. The authors explore whether health promotion efforts targeted at preschool-age children can improve health over the lifespan and generate higher economic returns to society. They review a large literature on health promotion and provide a comprehensive update of an earlier study for the areas of tobacco exposure, unintentional injury, obesity, and mental health. Given that these four areas are the early antecedents of significant health problems across the lifespan, the authors conclude that the evidence is especially strong that health interventions to reduce tobacco exposure and the prevention of injuries are especially deserving of public attention.

Katina D'Onise, Robyn McDermott, and John Lynch provide an overview of the literature connecting early childhood interventions to improvements in child and adult health. This chapter is based on two earlier reviews by the authors on the effects of preschool on child health outcomes and on adult outcomes. Notably, the findings from the research synthesis indicate that health improvements are more likely to result if the preschool intervention is comprehensive and especially if a parenting component is part of the intervention. Improvements in child and adult health are observed even if the preschool intervention did not explicitly include a health services component. The chapter concludes with an especially detailed discussion of the limitations in the existing studies.

Following the research synthesis by D'Onise et al. on the role of early childhood interventions in promoting health, Karen Bierman, Robert Nix, Celene Domitrovich, Janet Welsh, and Scott Gest focus on a specific intervention offered in Head Start centers. The Head Start REDI (Research Based, Developmentally Informed) project was designed to determine the feasibility and effects of enriching Head Start programs with a comprehensive set of evidence-based curriculum components that target social-emotional as well as emerging literacy skills. One of the important components of the REDI project is professional development for teachers. Analysis of study findings from a randomized control trial suggests that the REDI intervention has effects on important child outcomes that include better self-control, better problem solving skills, and reduced aggression.

Catherine Ayoub, Jessica Dym Bartlett, Rachel Chazen-Cohen, and Helen Raikes discuss the impacts of Early Head Start for families experiencing parental mental health challenges. Head Start programs are believed to positively affect children's development by protecting the family from stress and promoting positive relationships between parents and children despite the presence of stress. Ayoub and her co-authors present findings that Early Head Start protects parenting, child language, and self-regulatory development from the effects of parenting stress and socioeconomic risks. Early Head Start can serve as a buffer between the negative effects of parent mental health conditions including maternal depression and anxiety and isolation. The authors argue that early prevention and intervention programs that support parent mental health, improve socioeconomic status, and improve child–parent interactions are likely to be important tools in promoting positive child well-being.

Michelle Englund, Barry White, Arthur Reynolds, Lawrence Schweinhart, and Frances Campbell contribute an innovative and important chapter integrating findings from three major longitudinal studies of high-quality preschool education targeted toward economically disadvantaged children. Reynolds, Schweinhart, and Campbell are known for their lengthy, significant involvement in studies of the Chicago Child–Parent Centers, the HighScope Perry Preschool

Program, and the Carolina Abecedarian Project, respectively. In order to gain a more thorough understanding of the impact of education on adult health outcomes, this chapter reports on a multi-study analysis examining the influence of not only preschool involvement and educational attainment on health outcomes in adulthood but also the intervening educational factors. The Englund et al. study uses longitudinal data from the three preschool intervention programs conducted at different points in time and in different locations and examines similar factors across interventions and time. Investigated are the effect of participation in a high-quality preschool program, school-age educational factors, and educational attainment at age 21 on health and health compromising behaviors in adulthood. The authors attempt to answer whether involvement in a high-quality preschool program directly affects health and health behaviors in adulthood or whether it sets the stage for a reduction in the probability of engaging in health compromising behaviors with other intervening educational factors directly influencing later health behaviors.

Momoko Hayakawa and Arthur Reynolds examine the long-term impact of a preschool instructional approach on adult well-being using a unique, orthogonal classification of instructional approaches. The impact of preschool instructional approach on educational and social well-being in adulthood was assessed for participants of the Chicago Child–Parent Center program. Hayakawa and Reynolds break away from the traditional perspective of dichotomizing instructional approaches (teacher-directed vs. child-initiated) and update literature by examining the effect of combinations of teacher-directed and child-initiated strategies. Findings show that child-initiated instructional strategies link to lower rates of adult crime.

Part III of this volume contains chapters that focus on the effects of health and education policy on child development. While many of the previous chapters focus closely on the importance of specific health conditions for promoting children's educational success and well-being, a few of the final chapters in this volume focus on broader issues involving health knowledge or literacy and federal health care reform.

Two contributions to this section make connections between broader public policies in the US affecting health and their potential impacts on children by examining the significance of federal legislation called the Patient Protection and Affordable Care Act (ACA, commonly known as Obamacare) signed into law by President Obama in March 2010. First, Samuel Kleiner offers commentary on the provisions of this health care reform that are likely to affect the well-being of children. He refers to the many provisions of the Affordable Care Act as the "most sweeping pieces of health care legislation in decades." Kleiner's short commentary identifies relevant studies in health economics that can help predict the likely effects of the health care law on children's well-being.

Jean Abraham and co-authors Pinar Karaca-Mandic and Sung Choi Yoo expand on Kleiner's commentary by providing a more detailed look at the relevant aspects of the complicated, comprehensive set of provisions in the ACA that are likely to affect what Abraham et al. refer to as the ABCs of child health, where A refers to health care *access*, B refers to the financial *burden*, and C refers to the *consumption* of the health care services. The writers make a valuable contribution in this chapter by explaining the relevant portions of this complex legislation and identifying the relevant economics and health care studies that can help predict how changes in health care policy brought about by the Affordable Care Act are likely to affect the well-being of children.

In the penultimate chapter of the volume, Laurie Martin and Peggy Chen add to the discussion of the importance of child health for school readiness by expanding consideration of health influences beyond socioeconomic status, parental heath, and health behaviors. Martin and Chen suggest that parent health literacy is a critical factor typically unexplored in studies of the socio-economic determinants of health and education outcomes. Their chapter presents a theoretical model and life course perspective of how health and education systems influence parental health literacy, child health, and academic outcomes. They outline implications for policy and future research as they highlight current programs and strategies for improving health literacy and related outcomes in the three contexts of the health system, the education system, and culture and society.

Part III concludes with a chapter by Dianne Stanton Ward and Temitope Erinosho that emphasizes the significant health concerns caused by child obesity. While child obesity is an area of current interest for researchers, health care professionals and policymakers, most attention has been paid to children school aged or older. Few interventions target children under 6. In their chapter on promoting healthy weight in child care centers, Ward and Erinosho argue that given the sizable amount of time that children under the age of 6 spend in various child care settings, it is imperative that interventions to address childhood obesity focus on these settings to ensure the children develop healthy nutrition and physical activity habits early. The authors specifically discuss the intervention called NAP SACC, which stands for Nutrition and Physical Activity Self-Assessment for Child Care. The NAP SACC program encourages child care centers to improve their nutrition and physical activity environments by encouraging self-assessments and goal setting, and through the provision of technical support by local health professionals. Ward and Erinosho report an evaluation of the NAP SACC program that indicates that centers that adopt all or most portions of the intervention demonstrate improved nutrition and physical activity scores. Given that child obesity is a serious public health problem, the development and implementation of successful interventions targeting early childhood can be useful contributions to promoting child health and ultimately later educational success and well-being.

Conclusion

As described and illustrated in the volume, the predictors and processes leading to positive health and well-being can occur very early in life and influence cognitive, social-emotional, nutritional, physical health, parenting, and life-course outcomes. The specificity and level of these influences vary widely (e.g., micronutrients to programs and policies) but are amenable to change through educational and health interventions. The recurring theme of the chapters is that to address the educational and health needs of young children most effectively programs and policies must be comprehensive, appropriately timed and of sufficient duration, and implemented on larger scales.

The close connection between the achievement gap and adult health disparities described in several chapters suggests that efforts to close one will affect the other and vice versa. Bruininks, Susman-Stillman, and Thorp's concluding essay makes this clear. Similar links between many other health and education influences in early childhood covered in the volume are also complex yet can be a focus of improvement efforts. Among these are prenatal nutrition and cognitive development, education and cardiovascular risk of disease, preschool curricula and crime prevention, early education and social-emotional health, physical activity in child care and obesity prevention, and early childhood poverty and adult economic well-being.

Although accumulated wisdom and evidence across disciplines indicate that an "ounce of prevention is worth a pound of cure," the benefits of preventive and human capital interventions cannot completely inoculate children against continuing disadvantages. While James Heckman's work based on the model of skill formation leads to the conclusion that later investments in human capital (i.e., education, health, and training) are more effective when early capabilities are enhanced, additional interventions may still be needed to promote the sustainability of these early benefits among disadvantaged youth. Most realistically, education and health interventions can achieve sizable effects that endure if they are high in quality, duration, and intensity, as well as comprehensive in scope, and if levels of support provided in succeeding years reinforce and extend on earlier levels. While these principles of effectiveness do not receive enough attention in reform efforts, the volume can help address this gap and point the way toward new solutions.

References

Aos, S., Lieb, R., Mayfield, J., Miller, M., and Pennucci, A. (2004). *Benefits and costs of prevention and early intervention programs for youth.* Olympia, WA: Washington State Institute for Public Policy. www.wsipp.wa.gov/rptfiles/04-07-3901.pdf.

Aos, S., Miller, M., and Mayfield, J. (2007). *Benefits and costs of K-12 education policies: evidence-based effects of class size reductions and full-day kindergarten.* Olympia, WA: Washington State Institute of Public Policy.

Avruch, S., and Cackley, A. P. (1995). Savings achieved by giving WIC benefits to women prenatally. *Public Health Reports,* 110, 27–34.

Barnett, W. S. (1996). *Lives in the balance: age 27 benefit–cost analysis of the High/Scope Perry Preschool Program.* Ypsilanti, MI: High/Scope Press.

Barnett, W. S., and Masse, L. (2007). Early childhood program design and economic returns: comparative benefit–cost analysis of the Abecedarian program and policy implications. *Economics of Education Review,* 26, 113–125.

Cohen, Mark A. (1998). The monetary value of saving a high-risk youth. *Journal of Quantitative Criminology,* 14, 5–33.

Cunha, Flavio, and Heckman, James J. (2008). Formulating, identifying and estimating the technology of cognitive and noncognitive skill formation. *Journal of Human Resources,* 43, 738–782.

Glazner, J., Bondy, J., Luckey, D., and Olds, D. (2004). *Effects of the Nurse Family Partnership on government expenditures for vulnerable first-time mothers and their children in Elmira, New York, Memphis, Tennessee, and Denver, Colorado.* Washington, DC: Administration for Children and Families, US Department of Health and Human Services.

Greenberg, Peter E., Kessler, Ronald C., Bimbaum, H. G., et al. (2003). The economic burden of depression in the United States: how did it change between 1990 and 2000? *Journal of Clinical Psychiatry,* 64, 1465–1475.

Heckman, James J. (2007). The technology and neuroscience of capacity formation. *Proceedings of the National Academy of Sciences,* 104(3), 13250–13255.

Karoly, L. A., and Bigelow, J. H. (2005). *The economics of investing in universal preschool education in California.* Santa Monica, CA: RAND.

Krueger, A. B. (2003). Economic considerations and class size. *Economic Journal,* 113, F34–F63.

Levin, Henry L., Belfield, Clive, Muennig, Peter, and Rouse, Cecelia (eds.) (2007). *The price we pay: economic and social consequences of inadequate education.* Washington, DC: Brookings Institution Press.

Lynch, R. G. (2007). *Enriching children, enriching the nation: public investment in high quality prekindergarten.* Washington, DC: Economic Policy Institute.

O'Connell, M. E., Boat, T., and Warner, K. E. (eds.) (2009). *Preventing mental, emotional and behavioral disorders among young people: progress and possibilities.* National Research Council. Washington, DC: National Academy Press.

Reynolds, Arthur J., Temple, Judy A., and White, Barry A. B. (2011). Economic benefits of intervention programs implemented in the first decade of life. In Edward Zigler, Walter S. Gilliam, and W. Steven Barnett (eds.), *The Prek Debates: current controversies and issues* (pp. 173–180). Baltimore, MD: Brookes Publishing.

Reynolds, A. J., Temple, J. A., Roberson, D. L., and Mann, E. A. (2002). Age 21 cost–benefit analysis of the Title I Chicago Child–Parent Centers. *Educational Evaluation and Policy Analysis*, 24(4), 267–303.

Schweinhart, L. J., Montie, J., Xiang, Z., Barnett, W. S., Belfield, C. R., and Nores, M. (2005). *Lifetime effects: the High/Scope Perry Preschool Study through age 40.* Ypsilanti, MI: High/Scope Press.

Shanahan, T., and Barr, R. (1995). Reading recovery: an independent evaluation of the effects of an early intervention for at-risk learners. *Reading Research Quarterly*, 30, 958–997.

Part I

Effects of health disparities on child
development and throughout the life course

2   Health is more than health care

*Paula A. Braveman, Susan Egerter, and
Robin E. Mockenhaupt*

Overview

This chapter provides an overview of current knowledge of the importance of social determinants of health – factors outside of medical care,
such as education, that can be influenced by policies and are likely to have
important effects on health. Recent evidence is presented revealing
marked disparities in health by income and education as well as by race
or ethnic group in the United States. Plausible explanations for the
patterns are discussed in light of current knowledge of how social factors
may influence health. A conceptual framework is presented for considering – and for addressing – how health disparities by race and class are
created, exacerbated, and perpetuated, across the lifetimes of individuals
and across generations. The authors argue that while ensuring that individuals have access to appropriate medical care and information about
health-promoting behaviors is important, effective solutions also will
require taking into account the social and physical contexts that powerfully shape health behaviors and health itself.

Introduction

More spending, less health

Most people recognize the importance of health in human terms. Good
health is essential to well-being and being able to participate fully in
society, and poor health entails suffering, disability, and/or loss of life.
The economic implications of health have become increasingly apparent
as well. In the United States, health care spending has continued to rise
dramatically during a period of time when the overall economy has
markedly contracted (Truffer et al., 2010). In the United States, more is
spent per person on medical care than in any other nation; projections
based on current trends estimate that by 2019 medical care costs in the
United States will reach more than 19 percent of the Gross Domestic

Product. Although the Affordable Care Act of 2010, if fully implemented, should help many Americans obtain and keep coverage, the costs of medical care and insurance will continue to be out of reach for many households. Employers also are impacted by these costs, which are a deterrent to creating jobs. Medical care spending at the local, state, and federal level limits government investments in other crucial areas including infrastructure and education. The rising costs of providing care to an aging population and the growing number of obese Americans will further strain public and private budgets.

What do we have to show for our investments in medical care? Despite spending more by far on medical care than any other nation, the United States has for some time ranked at or near the bottom among industrialized countries on key indicators of the health of populations. For example, while both infant mortality and life expectancy in the US have improved over the last few decades relative to their prior levels, the rankings of the US relative to thirty-three other OECD nations have fallen – from eighteenth in 1980 to thirty-first in 2011 for infant mortality, and from fourteenth in 1980 to twenty-seventh in 2011 for life expectancy (Organization for Economic Co-operation and Development, 2012; Population Reference Bureau, Life Expectancy at Birth, 2011; Population Reference Bureau, Infant Mortality Rate, 2011). These large and unfavorable disparities in average health between the United States and other affluent countries are accompanied by large disparities in health by income, education, and racial/ethnic group within the US (Braveman et al., 2010a). This is not only an issue for the poor or minorities; while middle-class Americans have worse health than their counterparts in the UK and France (Woolf and Aron, 2013).

Large socioeconomic and racial/ethnic disparities in health within the US

In the US, the measures used most frequently to measure socioeconomic status or position (SES) are education and income. Evidence has repeatedly shown that Americans who are poor generally are substantially less healthy than those who are not poor (Centers for Disease Control and Prevention [CDC], 2011; Krieger, 2007; Lynch, Kaplan, and Salonen, 1997; Schiller et al., 2012). Recent evidence, moreover, shows that the disparities in the US are not only between the poor or uneducated and everyone else, or between the poor/uneducated and the wealthiest/most educated. At each step as income or education rises, it appears that health improves (Braveman, et al. 2010a; Minkler, Fuller-Thomson, and Guralnik, 2006; Pamuk, 1999). There are exceptions, but socioeconomic gradients appear to be the rule for non-Latino blacks and whites (Braveman et al., 2010a). Stepwise

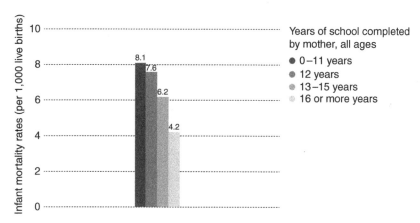

Figure 2.1 Infant mortality by mother's education.

socioeconomic gradients were first observed in the United Kingdom (Marmot et al., 1978; Marmot et al., 1991; Whitehead, 1992) and have been seen in all affluent countries (Mackenbach, 2002) but have not received as much attention in the US until recently. Socioeconomic disparities in health affect Americans of all ages, and apply across a wide range of health outcomes (Braveman et al., 2010a). Figures 2.1–2.5 illustrate examples of those disparities, based on analyses conducted by the authors and other colleagues using nationally representative data from the US Centers for Disease Control and Prevention (CDC). These analyses were conducted for the Robert Wood Johnson Foundation Commission to Build a Healthier America, which was convened by the Foundation during 2008–9 and again in 2013 (Braveman and Egerter, 2008, 2013) to recommend approaches to reduce social disparities in health while improving the health of the nation overall. For most of these health outcomes, the impressions are substantially similar whether examining differences by income or by education (Braveman et al., 2010a).

What do these data reveal? They provide clear evidence that health varies in the US by education and income, from birth on. For example, as shown in Figure 2.1, babies born to mothers who have completed fewer than twelve years of schooling are nearly twice as likely to die before their first birthdays as babies born to mothers who have completed sixteen or more years of schooling, illustrating how social factors in one generation shape the health and survival of the next. Higher educational attainment is also linked with longer life: men and women who have graduated from college can expect to live at least five years longer on average than their same-age counterparts who have not completed high school (see

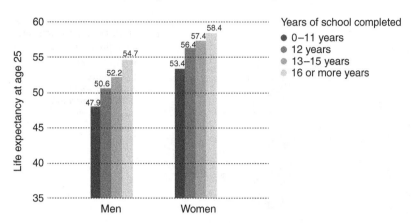

Figure 2.2 Life expectancy at age 25, by education.

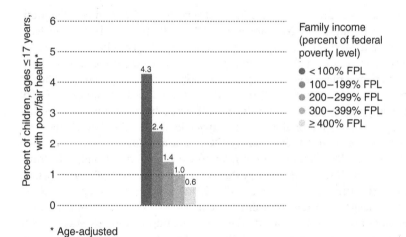

* Age-adjusted

Figure 2.3 Unequal chances of poor or fair health in childhood, by income.

Figure 2.2). A similar pattern in life expectancy is seen by income, with higher-income men and women living longer than people with lower incomes. It is important to note that associations do not prove causation; this issue is discussed later.

Further evidence of intergenerational effects is shown in Figure 2.3, displaying results of our analyses of data from the CDC's National Center for Health Statistics revealing that children's health status (as reported by parents or guardians) varies dramatically by parents' income; the patterns were similar by parents' educational attainment (not shown) (Schiller et al., 2012). Figure 2.3 shows, for example, that children of parents with incomes at or below the federal poverty line are seven times as likely to be in poor or fair (as opposed to good, very good, or excellent) health, when compared with children of parents with incomes four times the federal poverty level. Reports by adults of whether their health is poor, fair, good, very good, or excellent are widely used as indicators of their health status, based on their correlations with objective clinical measures (Burström and Fredlund, 2001; Idler and Benyamini, 1997; Idler and Kasl, 1995; McGee et al., 1999), although some concerns have been raised about potential differences in reporting across different social groups (Dowd and Zajacova, 2007; Salomon et al., 2009).

The percentage of US adults overall who report being in poor or only fair (rather than good or better) health increases as levels of income (Figure 2.4) and education (not shown) decrease (Braveman and Egerter, 2008, 2013). For example, as shown in Figure 2.4, poor adults are nearly five times as likely to report being in poor or only fair health as adults with family incomes above 400 percent of the federal poverty level; the same figure also displays racial/ethnic disparities in adult health, which will be discussed later. Individuals in more disadvantaged groups also are more likely to have a chronic disease that limits their activity. For example, compared with higher-income adults, adults with family incomes below the federal poverty level are more than three times as likely to report activity limitation (inability or limited ability to work, requiring help with personal care, inability to perform activities usual for individuals their age) due to chronic illness, more than twice as likely to have diabetes, and nearly 1.5 times as likely to have coronary heart disease (Braveman and Egerter, 2008).

It is not difficult to understand why poverty might result in ill health. The link can be explained in many ways – e.g., higher risks of poor nutrition, poor-quality housing with exposure to lead, dust, mites, mold; living in unhealthy neighborhoods where there is no safe or pleasant place to exercise; inadequate medical care; chronic stress from facing the constant challenge of coping with inadequate resources; and family conflict generated by chronic financial strain. But it is not so easy to explain the patterns seen here, in Figures 2.4 and 2.5, which mirror patterns seen in other countries (Marmot et al., 1991; Whitehead, 1992). The figures displayed here reveal the largest disparities when comparing the worst-off to the best-off groups; they also show, however, health differences at each step of increased or lower income, including health differences between the next-to-highest income and those with even higher incomes. Similar

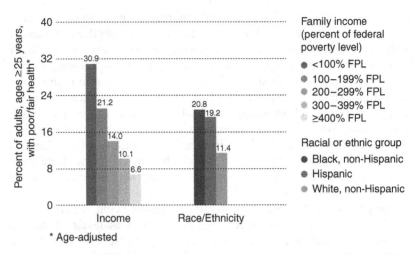

Figure 2.4 Disparities in adults' self-reported poor or fair health by income and race/ethnicity.

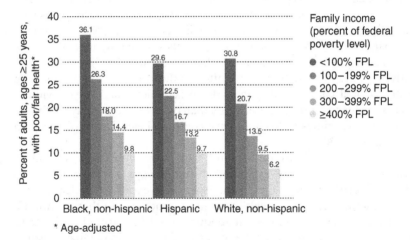

Figure 2.5 Poor/fair health among adults, by income in each racial/ethnic group.

relationships exist between health and varying levels of educational attainment. These examples – and evidence from other studies in the United States and elsewhere – illustrate that the effects of socioeconomic disparities in health are not limited to those in the most disadvantaged groups (Braveman et al., 2010a; Lantz et al., 1998;

Marmot et al., 1991; Pamuk, 1999; Whitehead, 1992). The poorest
health is generally seen in the socioeconomically worst-off (poorest,
least educated) groups; it is not so easy to explain why Americans
who by most standards are considered "middle-class" (those with
incomes from three to four times the federal poverty level, for example), however, are on average less healthy than their counterparts with
higher income or education levels. In the US as well as other affluent
countries where this has been studied, one sees a recurring stepwise
gradient pattern, with incremental increases in social and economic
advantage corresponding to better health. The socioeconomic gradient is not seen for all conditions, which should not be surprising,
given the different etiologies of different health conditions; our
examination of a wide range of indicators among children and adults
revealed, however, that it applies in most cases (Braveman et al.,
2010a). Furthermore, the gradient does not necessarily follow a
straight line (Braveman et al., 2010a; Deaton, 2002); increases in
income for people at the lower end of the income scale tend to
translate into larger increases in health. One might not expect to
see better health associated with higher income when comparing
people all of whose incomes are already very high (Deaton, 2002;
Wagstaff and Van Doorslaer, 2000). Minkler et al. (2006), however,
observed stark gradients in health (reflected by functional status)
among the elderly according to their incomes, across multiple income
groups categorized in increments of the federal poverty level, up to
seven times the federal poverty level; that level is quite high, corresponding to an income of around $161,000 for a family of four.
These findings are particularly notable given that it has been thought
that health differences by income among the elderly underestimate
differences at other life stages, because income is typically lower in
retirement.

These examples of the strong relationships observed repeatedly
between socioeconomic factors and health are noted here as illustrations.
Studies – such as those whose results are presented here – that can only
look at whether income and education are *associated with* each other
cannot establish that income or education is in fact *the cause* of the
observed levels of health, only that they are correlated. These striking
observational findings, however, illustrate conclusions by multiple
experts that rest on a very large and growing body of evidence that
includes research using a range of techniques to diminish the likelihood
of bias. This body of research includes studies of likely pathways and
physiological mechanisms, and suggests likely causal roles in many health
conditions for income, education, and/or factors tightly linked with

income and education (Adler and Stewart, 2010; Berkman, 2009; Chandola et al., 2008; Cubbin and Winkleby, 2005; Kramer et al., 2001; Marmot, Shipley, Hemingway, Head, and Brunner, 2008). The effects of income, wealth, and education on health are indirect, and play out across complex pathways that in many cases encompass decades or generations. Reverse causation – with poor health leading to lower income – undoubtedly occurs and may contribute to income gradients in health; it is, however, unlikely to explain the magnitude of income effect that has been observed widely (e.g., in examples provided in this chapter) and is unlikely to explain the disparities by education, since educational attainment is not reversed, once a given level is reached.

Observing the socioeconomic gradient in health requires explanations that are more complex than the common assumptions about why the poor are likely to have worse health than everyone else. The gradient suggests a dose–response relationship between socioeconomic factors and health, calling for explanations of why health improves incrementally at every step, although it is reasonable to speculate that this incremental improvement may cease at a very high socioeconomic level, beyond which further increases in resources may not confer better health.

How are racial or ethnic disparities in health related to health differences by income or education?

The primary focus of efforts to reduce health disparities in the US has been on disparities in health across different racial or ethnic groups. This is in contrast to efforts in other countries, which have primarily focused on socioeconomic differences (using the term "health inequalities" rather than "health disparities" and often measuring socioeconomic differences according to rank in an occupational hierarchy determined by prestige as well as earnings). Racial or ethnic disparities in health are relatively well documented, in part because routine public health data in the United States generally have been reported by racial or ethnic group but less frequently by socioeconomic factors such as income, education, accumulated wealth, or occupation (Krieger, Chen, and Ebel, 1997; Krieger and Fee, 1996). Much published research as well as routine reports on health includes very little socioeconomic information, and researchers often conclude that an observed racial or ethnic disparity must be due to underlying biological or deeply rooted cultural differences, without considering the potential effects of unmeasured socioeconomic (and other social) factors.

These approaches to research and routine public health reporting fail to recognize a body of scientific knowledge that shows that racial or ethnic differences in health often disappear or are markedly reduced when one controls even partially for socioeconomic differences by adjusting for income or education. Because of the legacy of racial discrimination in the US, there are dramatic racial or ethnic differences in income and in educational attainment; these differences persist because of deeply rooted structural processes – e.g., racial residential segregation and its link to school quality – that track people of different racial or ethnic groups into different opportunities, even when there is no longer any intent to discriminate. Furthermore, income and education alone do not fully capture racial/ethnic differences in socioeconomic resources and experiences; at the same level of current income or education, people in different racial/ethnic groups in the US are likely to differ on levels of accumulated wealth, on socioeconomic characteristics of their neighborhoods, and on their childhood socioeconomic circumstances (Braveman et al., 2005). Without adequate socioeconomic information, however, racial or ethnic differences in health may be – and often are – interpreted implicitly if not explicitly as reflecting genetic or entrenched "cultural" differences that are unlikely to be influenced by policy.

In fact, modifiable social factors shaped by income, education, wealth, and childhood and neighborhood socioeconomic conditions, which vary systematically by race or ethnic group, are likely to be crucial in explaining health differences by race or ethnicity (Braveman et al., 2005; Williams and Jackson, 2005). Because of a long legacy of racial/ethnic discrimination with profound consequences with respect to economic opportunity, blacks, Hispanics, and American Indians, as well as some Pacific Islander and Asian-American groups, are disproportionately represented among the more socioeconomically disadvantaged groups in the United States (US Census Bureau, 2004a–e: The American Community – American Indians and Alaska Natives; Asians; Pacific Islanders; Blacks; Hispanics). Researchers at the US Centers for Disease Control and Prevention (CDC) have estimated that 38 percent of the twofold excess mortality among black adults compared with whites in the United States was related to differences in income (Otten et al., 1990). Differences in current income can grossly underestimate socioeconomic differences, given the large racial/ethnic differences in accumulated wealth at a given income level (Braveman et al., 2005).

The links between socioeconomic and racial or ethnic differences in health underscore a consensus among social scientists and many medical researchers (including the architects of the Human Genome Project (Collins, 2004)) that racial or ethnic groups are primarily social rather than biological constructs. The genetic differences reflected by superficial secondary characteristics such as skin color and hair texture are unlikely to reflect fundamental biological differences that would explain large, widespread health disparities across multiple health indicators. Rather, racial or ethnic differences in health are more likely to reflect profound differences in people's experiences from birth on, based on the relatively advantaged or disadvantaged position in society of the race or ethnic group of the families into which they are born (Braveman et al., 2009).

Socioeconomic factors need to be considered along with racial or ethnic group. This is illustrated by examples in Figures 2.4 and 2.5. As noted earlier, Figure 2.4 shows that both higher-income and white adults are less likely to be in poor or fair (distinguished from good, very good, or excellent) health, as reflected by self-reported health status. Because health in the US is typically reported by race/ethnic group and not by socioeconomic measures, some observers, on seeing the differences by income (or education, not shown) may assume that the income or education differences primarily reflect the racial/ethnic differences. Figure 2.5, however, examines health by both income and race/ethnicity at the same time, by looking at differences in adult health by income, within each racial or ethnic group. Figure 2.5 clearly shows that when income and racial or ethnic group are considered jointly, however, the income gradients in fair or poor health are seen within each racial or ethnic group, at least as strikingly as when examined (in Figure 2.4) for the entire population considered together. Lack of information on racial/ethnic disparities in income or education could lead to erroneously attributing poorer health among blacks and Hispanics to cultural or biological factors (considered not amenable to policy change) rather than to income, education, or a related socioeconomic factor for both observed gradients (Braveman et al., 2005).

It is important to note, however, that race or ethnic group cannot be reduced to socioeconomic status. Information is needed on both, as both can affect health. For example, one also can use Figure 2.5 to examine racial and ethnic differences within each income group (in contrast to examining income differences within each racial or ethnic group, as discussed above). The racial/ethnic differences within income groups are considerably less striking than the socioeconomic differences within racial/ethnic groups in Figure 2.5. The racial/ethnic differences within each income group could reflect unmeasured socioeconomic differences. At the same level of income, black and Hispanic adults have far less wealth, are more likely to have grown up in households with fewer socioeconomic advantages, and are more likely to live in socioeconomically disadvantaged neighborhoods (Braveman et al., 2005; Williams and Jackson, 2005), where conditions such as inadequate housing, crime, noise, pollution, and lack of services may have health impacts that could have health effects that exacerbate those associated with the income or educational attainment of individual residents (Williams and Collins, 2001). These residual racial or ethnic differences also may reflect health effects of experiences of discrimination, including subtle everyday experiences in which discrimination may not have been consciously intended (Williams, 2006). The patterns – displayed here for self-reported health status but seen in the literature across a wide range of health conditions – indicate that *both* socioeconomic advantage or disadvantage *and* other social advantages or disadvantages associated with race, independently and in combination, contribute to health inequalities in the United States.

Social advantage or disadvantage and health vary widely across places within the US

Dramatic geographic differences in health have been seen across the US, particularly in combination with racial differences and differences in income and education. A 1998 study revealed dramatic disparities in life expectancy across US counties overall, particularly when racial or ethnic differences were also considered. For example, black men in the county with the shortest life expectancy for blacks lived only 58 years (well below average life expectancy in many developing nations), while white men in the county with the longest life expectancy for whites could expect to live to age 78 – two decades longer (Murray, 1998). A more recent study showed that whites in Louisiana, where median household income in 2005–6 was $37,472, had a death rate 30 percent higher than that for whites in Minnesota, where the median household income was $56,102. The discrepancy between the two states is even greater for blacks, whose death rate was 37 percent higher in Louisiana (US Census Bureau, 2007; National Center for Health Statistics, 2012). Findings from a recent report (Robert Wood Johnson Foundation and University of Wisconsin Population Health Institute, 2013) that ranked counties both on health indicators and on a set of key social and economic factors found that counties with higher levels of health also were more likely to rank favorably on measures of advantage including rates of high school graduation, employment, and children living in poverty. These geographic differences add to other evidence, including findings from studies adjusting for other potentially relevant factors (De Walque, 2004; Marmot et al., 1997; Winkleby et al., 1992), of the important role in health disparities played by modifiable conditions linked with income, education, and/or occupation.

Explaining these patterns? A different conceptual framework

The need to consider "the causes of the causes" (Rose, 1993)

Above, we have presented examples of how health is patterned within the US, by factors such as income, education, and race or ethnic group. But none of these factors affects health directly; their effects occur only through intermediate factors tightly linked to them. We know that health is influenced by many biologically determined factors, including individual characteristics like age, sex, and genetic makeup. Because individuals have little or no control over these biologically determined risk factors (and, despite high hopes, the yield of gene therapy for improving population health is as yet largely unproven), it makes sense to focus health policies on risk factors that are potentially modifiable, including those that may interact with genetic makeup. When considering strategies for addressing such modifiable factors on a large scale to improve health, medical care is clearly important; in fact, many use the terms "health" and "health care" almost interchangeably. Widespread and substantial socioeconomic and racial or ethnic disparities have been documented in access to and quality of medical care for many serious health conditions, such as heart disease and cancer (US Department of Health and Human Services [DHHS] National Healthcare Disparities Report, 2006; Smedley and Stith, 2003), and reducing these disparities is essential. Such efforts alone, however, will not be sufficient to substantially reduce socioeconomic and racial or ethnic disparities in health. Despite its importance, particularly after disease or injury occurs, we now know that medical care often has little impact on the underlying causes of disease or injury – for example, the array of health-related behaviors, including smoking and physical inactivity, that have been identified as major causes of preventable deaths (Danaei et al., 2009; McGinnis and Foege, 1993), and we need to consider what has been learned about the more fundamental causes of immediate causes of ill health such as health behaviors – "the causes of the causes," in the words of the distinguished epidemiologist Geoffrey Rose (1993).

The general public has become increasingly aware of the strong influences on health exerted by health-related behaviors – whether or not an individual exercises regularly, eats a nutritious diet, abstains from smoking, and limits his or her alcohol intake. Along with efforts to improve medical care access and quality, prevailing strategies for improving health in the United States have often focused on promoting behavior change – beginning by increasing awareness of how individuals' behaviors affect their health, and in some cases providing tools and resources to support individuals' efforts. Although these approaches undoubtedly have contributed to overall improvements in health, as reflected in average national statistics, there has been limited evidence that progress has been made in reducing relative health disparities across social groups (DHHS Healthy People, 2010; Midcourse Review, 2006). Disparities in some key health-related behaviors have persisted and in some cases have widened (De Walque, 2004; Woolf et al., 2011; Brownson, Boehmer, and Luke, 2005; Centers for Disease Control and Prevention [CDC], 2004; Kanjilal et al., 2006). For example, although the prevalence of high cholesterol and smoking – two cardiovascular disease risk factors – decreased overall during the period from 1971 to 2002, the decrease was smallest among adults with lower family incomes (Kanjilal et al., 2006). Income disparities in diabetes, an adverse health outcome in itself and another important risk factor for cardiovascular disease, have widened in the same period, corresponding to greater increases in prevalence among adults in lower-income groups (Kanjilal et al., 2006).

These disappointing trends indicate the need to reassess current strategies for improving health and the assumptions on which they are based, in the light of major scientific advances achieved since 1995. Positive changes in health-related behaviors clearly depend on individuals making choices that promote good health. While such choices typically begin with awareness of the benefits and risks of particular behaviors, they also, however, require opportunities and support in the environments where people live, learn, work, and play. Experience has shown that efforts focused solely on informing or encouraging individuals to modify behaviors, without taking into account their physical and social environments, too often fail to reduce – and may even exacerbate – health inequalities (Glouberman, 2001; Levine et al., 2010; Mechanic, 2002). Making further improvements – and reducing disparities – in health-related behaviors will require adopting a much broader perspective based on a deeper understanding of what shapes behaviors as well as other factors that influence health (Institute of Medicine, 2000).

A large and growing body of research has shown how the contexts in which people live and work – their physical and social environments at home, in neighborhoods, at schools and work, and when traveling in between – can shape many behaviors with strong effects on health (Frieden, 2010; Institute of Medicine, 2000; Leventhal and Brooks-Gunn, 2000; Lynch et al., 1997; Marmot, Friel, Bell, Houweling, and Taylor, 2008; McNeill, Kreuter, and Subramanian, 2006; Villard, Rydén, and Ståhle, 2007; Yen and Syme, 1999). Physical and social environments can be overtly hazardous, exposing people to high levels of pollution or crime, for example. They also can severely limit choices and resources available to individuals. For example, an individual's ability – and motivation – to exercise and avoid smoking and excessive drinking can be limited by living in a neighborhood that lacks safe areas for exercise, where liquor stores abound and intensive tobacco and alcohol advertising target poorer and minority youth, and where healthy role models and hope or optimism are scarce. A neighborhood's socioeconomic conditions can affect whether its residents smoke (Chuang et al., 2005; Datta et al., 2006), drink alcohol (Pickett and Pearl, 2001), have healthy diets (Diez-Roux et al., 1999; Lee and Cubbin, 2002), and pursue protective reproductive health behaviors (Averett, Rees, and Argys, 2002). By the same token, aspects of living and work environments – such as the presence of sidewalks and playgrounds in neighborhoods, after-school physical activity programs for children and youth, nutritious food services in schools and workplaces, and on-site facilities for breast-feeding – can promote health by encouraging healthy behaviors and making it easier to adopt and maintain them. It has been very difficult to study the impact of neighborhood environments independently of the characteristics of the individuals who live in them, because neighborhood environments' effects on health may occur largely by how they affect characteristics of the individuals within them.

But what determines the quality of living and working conditions? People are not randomly distributed into healthy and unhealthy circumstances. Living and working conditions are shaped by many factors, including geography, climate, culture, and individual choices. In addition, living and working conditions (and medical care and behaviors) are also powerfully shaped by factors – such as income or wealth, education and social standing (respect, prestige, or acceptance in society) – that reflect people's *economic and social resources and opportunities* and influence their ability to make healthier choices. Education, for example, can correspond to knowledge about health and healthy choices, and to feeling able to take control of one's life. Education is also tightly linked with income and wealth. Greater educational attainment typically translates into increased opportunities for more rewarding and higher-paying employment, which in turn is associated both with healthier working conditions, better health-related benefits including medical insurance, and greater ability to accumulate wealth and economic security for oneself and one's family. Higher income and accumulated wealth make it easier for people to pay for medical insurance premiums, deductibles, co-payments, and medicines; to purchase more nutritious foods; to obtain quality child care (which can affect a parent's ability to keep a job and can also reduce stress); and to live in a neighborhood with resources to support good schools and recreational facilities. Conversely, limited economic means can make everyday life an all-consuming struggle, leaving little or no time or energy to adopt a healthier lifestyle, and even crushing personal motivation.

This conceptual framework may help explain the stepwise incremental gradient in health that was discussed earlier. As levels of income or wealth and education rise, people have more resources and opportunities that permit them to live, work, learn, play, and raise their families in conditions that promote health. And racial inequality in fundamental opportunities and resources leads to racial inequality in health, by tracking different racial/ethnic groups into more or less healthy conditions.

Stress is likely to be an important piece of the puzzle

The period since 1995 has seen marked increases in scientific knowledge about causal pathways and physiological mechanisms that help explain the links between socioeconomic factors and health. An important example includes physiological damage to multiple vital organ systems caused by chronic stress, through neuroendocrine and immune pathways (Bauer and Boyce, 2004; Cohen et al., 1986; Hertzman and Power, 2003; McEwen, 2006; Sapolsky, 2005; Steptoe and Marmot, 2002; Taylor, Repetti, and Seeman, 1997). Stressful experiences – like those associated with greater socioeconomic disadvantage (Braveman et al., 2010b; Evans and Kim, 2007) or with racial discrimination (Williams and Mohammed, 2009) – can trigger the release of hormones and other substances which, particularly with repeated stresses over time, can damage immune defenses and vital organs (McEwen, 2000). This physiological chain of events can result in more rapid onset and progression of chronic illnesses, including cardiovascular disease (Steptoe and Marmot, 2002), and the bodily wear and tear associated with chronic stress may accelerate aging (McEwen, 2006; Seeman et al., 1998; Seeman et al., 2001). Increasing evidence indicates that the accumulated strain from trying to cope with daily challenges (e.g., noise, crime, and negative influences on children in one's neighborhood; feeling disrespected, intimidated, or powerless at work; or having inadequate financial resources for decent housing, food, child care, transportation, or medical care) may, over time, lead to far more physiological damage than a single stressful event, even if it is dramatic (McEwen, 2006).

Chronic stress due to ongoing struggles to make ends meet in the face of inadequate resources could be important in explaining both the socioeconomic gradient in health and racial or ethnic disparities in health. As income or educational levels rise, so do material and psychosocial

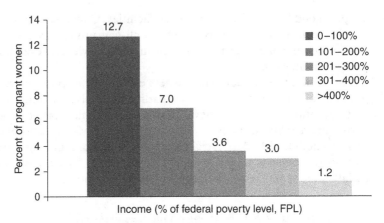

Figure 2.6 Less income, more stressors. Percentage of women experiencing separation or divorce during pregnancy.

resources and opportunities, making it incrementally easier to cope with stressors. In addition, lack of resources is likely to result in experiencing more stressors, as illustrated by Figure 2.6 (rising incidence of divorce/ separation during pregnancy with rising income). Stress may also help explain racial/ethnic disparities in health, in two ways: (1) many blacks and Latinos experience more stress because on average they have fewer economic resources and opportunities, given the strong link between socio-economic factors and race/ethnicity; and (2) experiences of racial discrimination could be an additional, important stressor, including subtle but chronic experiences and a chronically heightened awareness that one may be judged or treated differently because of race, even in the absence of overt incidents (Williams and Mohammed, 2009; Nuru-Jeter et al., 2009).

A life course and intergenerational view of social advantage and health

Figure 2.7 reflects an attempt to schematically illustrate that, at each life stage, social advantage or disadvantage leads to health advantage or disadvantage in that life stage and subsequent periods. In addition, social and economic disadvantage and health disadvantage accumulate over time, creating ever more daunting constraints on a person's ability to be healthy. These obstacles to health are transmitted across generations, as disadvantaged children become adults with limited socioeconomic resources and health who in turn are less able to provide healthy environments for their children, etc. Conversely, social advantages or disadvantages can accumulate across lifetimes and generations, to produce better health.

Figure 2.7 Finding solutions: understanding how health is transmitted across lifetimes and generations.

Socioeconomic conditions – like family income, education, and concentrated neighborhood poverty – affect health at every stage of life. The effects of socioeconomic adversity on young children, however, may be most dramatic, because of vulnerability during stages of rapid physiological, cognitive, and emotional development, and because the consequences may play out across entire lifetimes. A body of research shows that children's nutrition varies with parents' income and education (Bhattacharya, Currie, and Haider, 2004; Bradley and Corwyn, 2002; Variyam et al., 1999), and that nutrition in childhood can have lasting effects on health throughout life (Nishida et al., 2004; Lynch and Smith, 2005; Wadsworth, 1997). Lead poisoning in childhood – commonly due to lead-based paint in substandard housing – can lead to irreversible neurological damage, and unsafe levels of lead have been found more frequently among lower-income children than among their high-income counterparts (CDC, 1997).

Socioeconomic adversity in childhood can shape child health and development in other ways as well. Parents with low educational attainment and/or low income may face greater obstacles – such as lack of knowledge, skills, time, money, or other resources – to creating healthy home environments and modeling healthy behaviors for their children. Recent scientific advances have shed light on other ways in which economic and social conditions during the first few years of life affect brain development in infants and toddlers. It has been repeatedly observed that children in more favorable socioeconomic circumstances often receive more positive stimulation from parents and caregivers (Bradley and Corwyn, 2002; Evans, 2004; Guo and Harris, 2000; Votruba-Drzal, 2004; Yeung, Linver, and Brooks-Gunn, 2002) and high levels of such stimulation are associated with increased brain, cognitive, behavioral, and physical development. Thus, biological changes due to adverse socioeconomic conditions in infancy and the toddler years can become literally embedded in a child's body, limiting developmental capacity (Hertzman, 2006). Early childhood developmental interventions have been shown to greatly ameliorate the effects of social disadvantage on children's physical, mental, and social development; the first three to five years of life appear to be most crucial (Shonkoff and Phillips, 2000; Currie, 2000), although opportunities for intervention appear to continue throughout childhood (Shonkoff and Phillips, 2000) and adolescence (Fergus and Zimmerman, 2005).

A child's health also predicts his or her health in adulthood. For example, a baby born too small (with low birth weight, less than 5½ pounds) or too early (prematurely, before 37 completed weeks of pregnancy) is more likely to be cognitively, behaviorally, and physically handicapped as a child, and to develop high blood pressure, heart disease, and diabetes as an adult (Barker, 2004; Behrman and Butler, 2007). Obese children are more likely to be obese as adults (Power, Lake, and Cole, 1997), increasing their risk of serious chronic diseases including diabetes, heart disease, and stroke. Poor dental health in childhood can lead to painful, disabling, or disfiguring dental problems in adulthood (Thomson et al., 2004; DHHS, 2000). Poor childhood health, furthermore, can limit educational attainment, which in turn can limit adult health in multiple ways (Liu and Hummer, 2008; Mirowski and Ross, 2003; Palloni, 2006; van de Mheen et al., 1998).

That health in childhood shapes health in adulthood has been known for some time. Only since the 1990s, however, has there been a growing awareness of powerful links between socioeconomic circumstances in childhood and health in adulthood. Childhood economic deprivation or trauma has been associated with an array of health outcomes that manifest only later in life, including cardiovascular disease, diabetes, and premature mortality (Barker et al., 2005; Bauer and Boyce, 2004; Hertzman and Power, 2003). In addition to exerting effects on health and well-being over the course of an individual's lifetime, social factors also strongly influence the transmission of health across generations (Barker, 2004; Wadsworth, 1997; Case, Fertig, and Paxson, 2005; Gluckman, Hanson, and Beedle, 2007). Economists have shown how family income in one generation shapes family income in the next (Solon, 1992; Zimmerman, 1992). Socioeconomic disadvantage in childhood has been linked repeatedly with lower educational attainment (Arnold and Doctoroff, 2003; Duncan et al., 1998; Haveman and Smeeding, 2006; Haveman and Wolfe, 1995; Rouse and Barrow, 2006), and poverty in early childhood may be particularly damaging to chances of high educational attainment (Duncan et al., 1998). Lower educational attainment leads to lower chances of good jobs in adulthood, which then means lower income (and potentially poorer nutrition, housing, and schools, and lack of medical insurance) for the next generation. Researchers are beginning to link these bodies of evidence – examining the interplay between economic and social resources (such as income and education) and health, and the influence of those resources on the transmission of health across lifetimes and generations (Currie and Lin, 2007; Johnson and Schoeni, 2007).

Promising directions for seeking solutions

The disparities between America's overall population health and that of people in other affluent (and some resource-poor) countries, as well as the stark disparities in health across different socioeconomic and racial/ethnic groups within the country, reflect America's unmet health potential. Differences in genetic endowment are not plausible reasons for these between- and within-country health disparities. Recognizing that social factors are fundamental causes of these disparities necessarily implies that solutions will not be simple. This may, however, be a particularly timely moment to seek and pursue the solutions to unmet health potential. Widespread concern – on the part of business, government, and the general public – about medical care costs has created a sense of urgency and increased attention to potential solutions beyond the realm of medical care. This is evidenced by the American Recovery and Reinvestment Act's creation of new grants for state policy and community-level prevention and wellness initiatives (DHHS, 2010;

CDC, 2010) and by the community prevention and wellness provisions in the Patient Protection and Affordable Care Act signed early in 2010 (Democratic Policy Committee, 2010). Concerns about global economic competitiveness add to pressures not only to reduce medical care costs but to have a healthier and more economically productive workforce; other potential savings – associated with less crime, reduced welfare dependency, and lower Medicaid expenditures, for example – also should be considered (Braveman and Egerter, 2008). The public and policymakers may be more receptive than ever to recognizing the human and economic costs associated with health disparities between the US and other nations as well as within the US (Schoeni et al., 2011).

While the current economic crisis makes it more difficult to undertake ambitious social policies, it may present new opportunities. For example, increased media coverage of poverty, social class, and economic inequality in recent years are likely to have increased many Americans' – including middle-class Americans' – awareness of their potential vulnerability and of how difficult it can be to overcome obstacles related to social and economic disadvantage. The unequally distributed misery and death in the aftermath of Hurricane Katrina shocked many Americans, providing stark testimony of deep divides by class and race within our society. This memory should be refreshed and updated with the emerging data on the numbers of formerly middle-class but now financially insecure Americans affected by job loss and/or home foreclosures and dependent on public assistance (Goodman, 2010). Furthermore, poverty in America increasingly is not restricted to inner cities and rural areas; by 2005, 1 million more poor Americans lived in suburbs than lived in cities (Berube and Kneebone, 2006), making poverty more visible to the middle class.

While public concern about poverty may create momentum for addressing disparities, middle-class Americans are increasingly concerned about their own economic security as well. Economic inequality has increased in the United States, and the middle class has lost ground. Since the 1990s, the middle class has become increasingly insecure financially (i.e., less able to weather a job loss or serious medical crisis), in part because of rising costs of medical care, housing, and education; many middle-class families have had to work longer hours to maintain their standard of living, leaving parents less time to spend with their children (Weller, 2005). Information from the US Census Bureau shows that since 1981 the wealthiest 20 percent of Americans experienced dramatic increases in their incomes, while the rest of the population experienced little improvement (DeNavas-Walt, Proctor, and Smith,

2009) and this rising inequality has become increasingly recognized by the public and acknowledged by policymakers. From 1970 to 2000, the percentage of middle-income neighborhoods decreased, while the percentage of both very high- and very low-income neighborhoods increased (Galster, Cutsinger, and Booza, 2009). Both current Federal Reserve Chairman Bernanke and former Chairman Greenspan have called rising economic inequality a serious concern for the American economy (Aron-Dine, 2007).

In the face of these concerns about the nation's economic security, existing knowledge can – and must – be applied to reduce health disparities and improve health for all Americans. As health policy continues to be an important issue for both policymakers and the public, this is a particularly timely moment to ensure that the powerful health influences of social factors – such as child care, education, and housing – receive attention. Along with the growing body of scientific knowledge about how social and economic advantage, particularly in early childhood, can affect health throughout lifetimes and across generations, practical experiences in the United States (Almond, Chay, and Greenstone, 2001) and other countries (Mackenbach, 2002; Marmot, Friel et al., 2008; National Association of City and County Health Officials, 2010; Whitehead, Judge, and Benzeval, 1995; Irwin and Scali, 2005) offer guidance for effective action. Reducing health disparities in the United States and other affluent countries will require expanding our focus beyond medical care and personal behaviors to the broader social and economic contexts that influence health, in part by enabling or constraining healthy behaviors. In the private sector and at every level of government, effective policies will need to address the differences in underlying resources and opportunities that are the root causes of health inequalities across social groups.

The Robert Wood Johnson Foundation Commission to Build a Healthier America (2009; 2013) has explored a wide range of promising, knowledge-based directions for action, including: programs to improve development in early childhood, which should improve adult health through effects both on child health and on educational attainment; economic development initiatives targeting and engaging disadvantaged communities; and community-focused initiatives that can lead to healthier communities by attracting additional resources and by building on and developing community strengths. Recognizing the strength of evidence both about the importance of early childhood experiences and about known, effective interventions, the Commission's first recommendation was:

Ensure that all children have high-quality early developmental support (child care, education, and other services). This will require committing substantial resources to meet the early developmental needs particularly of children in low-income families. (Robert Wood Johnson, 2009)

Other important strategies not addressed by the Commission include programs to improve the quality of K-12 education, picking up where early childhood programs leave off; youth development programs targeting youth in disadvantaged communities; and efforts to strengthen community colleges and increase financial access to college for low-income and middle-class students.

Most smaller-scale community-level interventions have not been rigorously evaluated, yet many appear to have improved diverse aspects of health and/or health risks in disadvantaged communities. Careful review of the evidence from such local efforts and consideration of costs could provide a rationale for scaling up some of the most promising models; the final report of the Robert Wood Johnson Foundation Commission to Build a Healthier America provides a compendium of many promising examples from recent experiences in the US (Robert Wood Johnson, 2009). Successful initiatives illustrate principles with wide generalizability, including the need to simultaneously address risks to health from multiple causes, rather than looking for a single magic bullet; the need for mutually reinforcing efforts in different domains, such as providing high-quality child care for toddlers along with support to strengthen their parents' abilities as effective parents; and a focus on capacity-building. The White House's Social Innovations Fund (Corporation for National and Community Service, 2010) is an effort to identify and scale-up promising initiatives led by nonprofit organizations, particularly at the community level; while not its primary focus, improvements in health are likely to be achieved if efforts to improve social conditions in communities prove successful.

Every nation is unique in many ways, and there often is particular resistance in the US to adopting strategies proved successful elsewhere. This resistance needs to be overcome, given the valuable experience accumulated in Europe and elsewhere since at least the 1990s with interventions (both successful and unsuccessful) aiming to narrow socioeconomic inequalities in health in relatively affluent countries (Mackenbach, 2002). The US needs to study and adapt international experience to its unique circumstances, rather than reject it. The 1998 report from the World Health Organization's European Office, titled *Social Determinants of Health: The Solid Facts* (and a more technical reference document supporting that document), reviewed evidence both of the social causes of ill health and, when available, of interventions to reduce social inequalities in health, in nine areas: stress, early life, social exclusion, work, unemployment, social support, addiction, food, and transportation. Over a decade ago, the authors concluded that, in a number of these areas, the evidence was sufficient to act (Wilkinson and Marmot, 2003). For example, to promote health in early childhood (and ultimately throughout life) policies should aim to "reduce parents' smoking; increase parents' knowledge of health and understanding of children's emotional needs; introduce preschool programs not only to improve reading and stimulate cognitive development but also to reduce behavior problems in childhood and promote educational attainment, occupational chances, and healthy behavior in adulthood" (Wilkinson and Marmot, 2003). Although general recommendations like these do not provide a blueprint for designing specific programs, they add to evidence from the United States and should increase the confidence of US policymakers in pursuing health strategies focusing on social factors. The work of the World Health Organization's (WHO) recently concluded Commission on the Social Determinants of Health supports those conclusions on a global level and provides an array of resources with relevance for efforts in countries of all levels of economic development, including the United States. On the basis of the large bodies of international evidence amassed by its Knowledge Networks about what does and does not work, the WHO Commission concluded that "the knowledge exists to make a huge difference to people's life chances and hence to provide marked improvements in health equity" (Executive Summary, p. 1) (Marmot, Friel et al., 2008).

Policymakers also should look to past successes in reducing health and medical care inequalities within this country. Although there is evidence of the importance of intervening throughout children's lives (O'Connell, Boat, and Warner, 2009) the strongest scientific case at present probably can be made for intervening early in life (Shonkoff and Phillips, 2000; Currie, 2000) to interrupt the vicious cycle of social disadvantage and poor health. Scientists agree that the mental and behavioral development of children in less favorable socioeconomic circumstances can be markedly improved through high-quality early child care (Currie, 2000; Hertzman and Wiens, 1996; Karoly, Kilburn, and Cannon, 2005; Levin et al., 2007; Shonkoff and Phillips, 2000). The evidence for the effectiveness of early childhood development programs is so strong that national business groups – including the Committee for Economic Development (CED), PNC Financial Services Group, and the Business Roundtable (PNC Financial Services Group, 2010; Committee for Economic

Development, 2006; The Business Roundtable, 2003) – and economists, including Nobel laureate Heckman as well as Rolnick and Grunewald of the Federal Reserve Bank of Minneapolis (Heckman and Masterov, 2007; Rolnick and Grunewald, 2003), have called for universal early childhood development programs as a wise financial investment in the future US workforce. The strength of this consensus is reflected in the RWJF Commission's first recommendation (Robert Wood Johnson, 2009; 2013).

Many questions remain, and support for high-quality research to identify, develop, and implement the most effective and efficient approaches will be crucial, but we know enough to act now in a number of important areas. Particularly with greater attention to the health impacts of current policies, societal resources could be directed to higher-yielding investments. In weighing whether to act now, policymakers must also weigh the enormous human and economic costs society incurs every day because of lost opportunities to help everyone in the United States achieve her or his full health potential (Schoeni et al., 2011).

References

Adler, N. E., and Stewart, J. (2010). Preface to the biology of disadvantage: socioeconomic status and health. *Annals of the New York Academy of Sciences*, 1186(1), 1–4.

Almond, D. V., Chay, K. Y., and Greenstone, M. (2001). *Civil rights, the war on poverty, and black–white convergence in infant mortality in Mississippi*. Berkeley: Center for Labor Economics, University of California.

Arnold, D. H., and Doctoroff, G. L. (2003). The early education of socioeconomically disadvantaged children. *Annual Review of Psychology*, 54(1), 517–545.

Aron-Dine, A. (2007). *New data show income concentration jumped again in 2005*. Washington, DC: Center on Budget and Policy Priorities.

Averett, S. L., Rees, D. I., and Argys, L. M. (2002). The impact of government policies and neighborhood characteristics on teenage sexual activity and contraceptive use. *American Journal of Public Health*, 92(11), 1773.

Barker, D. J. P. (2004). The developmental origins of adult disease. *Journal of the American College of Nutrition*, 23 (suppl. 6), 588S–595S.

Barker, D. J., Osmond, C., Forsén, T. J., Kajantie, E., and Eriksson, J. G. (2005). Trajectories of growth among children who have coronary events as adults. *New England Journal of Medicine*, 353(17), 1802–1809.

Bauer, A. M., and Boyce, W. T. (2004). Prophecies of childhood: how children's social environments and biological propensities affect the health of populations. *International Journal of Behavioral Medicine*, 11(3), 164–175.

Behrman, R. E., and Butler, A. S. (2007). *Preterm birth: causes, consequences, and prevention*. Washington, DC: National Academy Press.

Berkman, L. F. (2009). Social epidemiology: social determinants of health in the United States: are we losing ground? *Annual Review of Public Health*, 30, 27–41.

Berube, A., and Kneebone, E. (2006). *Two steps back: city and suburban poverty trends*. Living cities census series. Washington, DC: The Brookings Institution.

Bhattacharya, J., Currie, J., and Haider, S. (2004). Poverty, food insecurity, and nutritional outcomes in children and adults. *Journal of Health Economics*, 23(4), 839–862.

Bradley, R. H., and Corwyn, R. F. (2002). Socioeconomic status and child development. *Annual Review of Psychology*, 53(1), 371–399.

Braveman, P., et al. for the Robert Wood Johnson Foundation (2009). *Issue Brief 5: Race and socioeconomic factors: Report from the Robert Wood Johnson Foundation to the Commission to Build a Healthier America*. Princeton, NJ: Robert Wood Johnson Foundation.

Braveman, P. A., Cubbin, C., Egerter, S., Chideya, S., Marchi, K. S., Metzler, M., and Posner, S. (2005). Socioeconomic status in health research. *Journal of the American Medical Association*, 294(22), 2879–2888.

Braveman, P. A., Cubbin, C., Egerter, S., Williams, D. R., and Pamuk, E. (2010a). Socioeconomic disparities in health in the United States: what the patterns tell us. *American Journal of Public Health*, 100(1), 186–196.

Braveman, P., and Egerter, S. (2008). *Overcoming obstacles to health*. Princeton, NJ: Robert Wood Johnson.

Braveman, P. and Egerter, S. (2013). *Overcoming Obstacles to Health in 2013 and Beyond*. Princeton, NJ: Robert Wood Johnson Foundation.

Braveman, P., Marchi, K., Egerter, S., Kim, S., Metzler, M., Stancil, T., and Libet, M. (2010b). Poverty, near-poverty, and hardship around the time of pregnancy. *Maternal and Child Health Journal*, 14(1), 20–35.

Brownson, R. C., Boehmer, T. K., and Luke, D. A. (2005). Declining rates of physical activity in the United States: what are the contributors? *Annual Review of Public Health*, 26, 421–443.

Burström, B., and Fredlund, P. (2001). Self rated health: is it as good a predictor of subsequent mortality among adults in lower as well as in higher social classes? *Journal of Epidemiology and Community Health*, 55(11), 836–840.

The Business Roundtable and Corporate Voices for Working Families (2003). *Early Childhood Education: A Call to Action from the Business Community*; available at www.businessroundtable.org/sites/default/files/20030505_early-childhood_education_a_call_to_action_from_the_business_community.pdf (accessed February 13, 2014).

Case, A., Fertig, A., and Paxson, C. (2005). The lasting impact of childhood health and circumstance. *Journal of Health Economics*, 24(2), 365–389.

Centers for Disease Control and Prevention (1997). Update: blood lead levels – United States, 1991–1994. *Morbidity and Mortality Weekly Report*, 46(7), 141–146.

(2004). Cigarette smoking among adults – United States, 2002. *Morbidity and Mortality Weekly Report*, 53(20), 427–431.

(2010). *The American Recovery and Reinvestment Act: communities putting prevention to work* (CPPW); available at www.cdc.gov/CommunitiesPutting PreventiontoWork/program/index.htm (accessed April 14, 2010).

(2011). *Health, United States, 2011: Poverty*. Available from www.cdc.gov/nchs/hus/poverty.htm (accessed August 13, 2012).

Chandola, T., Britton, A., Brunner, E., Hemingway, H., Malik, M., Kumari, M., ... and Marmot, M. (2008). Work stress and coronary heart disease: what are the mechanisms? *European Heart Journal*, 29(5), 640–648.

Chuang, Y. C., Cubbin, C., Ahn, D., and Winkleby, M. A. (2005). Effects of neighbourhood socioeconomic status and convenience store concentration on individual level smoking. *Journal of Epidemiology and Community Health*, 59(7), 568–573.

Cohen, S., Evans, G. W., Stokols, D., and Krantz, D. S. (1986). *Behavior, health, and environmental stress*. New York: Plenum Press.

Collins, F. S. (2004). What we do and don't know about "race", "ethnicity", genetics and health at the dawn of the genome era. *Nature Genetics*, 36, S13–S15.

Committee for Economic Development (2006). *The Economic Promise of Investing in High-Quality Preschool: Using Early Education to Improve Economic Growth and the Fiscal Sustainability of States and the Nation*, June; available at http://ced.issuelab.org/research (accessed February 19, 2014).

Corporation for National and Community Service (2010). Social Innovation Fund. Retrieved from www.nationalservice.gov/programs/social-innovation-fund (accessed February 19, 2014).

Cubbin, C., and Winkleby, M. A. (2005). Protective and harmful effects of neighborhood-level deprivation on individual-level health knowledge, behavior changes, and risk of coronary heart disease. *American Journal of Epidemiology*, 162(6), 559–568.

Currie, J. (2000). *Early childhood intervention programs: what do we know?* Los Angeles, CA: UCLA, NBER.

Currie, J., and Lin, W. (2007). Chipping away at health: more on the relationship between income and child health. *Health Affairs*, 26(2), 331–344.

Danaei, G., Ding, E. L., Mozaffarian, D., Taylor, B., Rehm, J., Murray, C. J., and Ezzati, M. (2009). The preventable causes of death in the United States: comparative risk assessment of dietary, lifestyle, and metabolic risk factors. *PLOS Medicine*, 6(4), e1000058.

Datta, G. D., Colditz, G. A., Kawachi, I., Subramanian, S. V., Palmer, J. R., and Rosenberg, L. (2006). Individual-, neighborhood-, and state-level socioeconomic predictors of cervical carcinoma screening among US black women. *Cancer*, 106(3), 664–669.

De Walque, D. (2004). Education, information, and smoking decisions: evidence from smoking histories, 1940–2000. *World Bank Policy Research Working Paper*, 3362.

Deaton, A. (2002). Policy implications of the gradient of health and wealth. *Health Affairs*, 21(2), 13–30.

Democratic Policy Committee (2010). The Patient Protection and Affordable Care Act: promoting prevention and improving public health. Available at http://dpc.senate.gov/healthreformbill/healthbill75.pdf (accessed April 14, 2010).

DeNavas-Walt, C., Proctor, B. D., and Smith, J. (2009). *Income, poverty, and health insurance coverage in the United States: 2006*. Washington, DC: US Census Bureau; 2007. *Current Population Reports*, P60, 233.

Diez-Roux, A. V., Nieto, F. J., Caulfield, L., Tyroler, H. A., Watson, R. L., and Szklo, M. (1999). Neighbourhood differences in diet: the Atherosclerosis

Risk in Communities (ARIC) Study. *Journal of Epidemiology and Community Health*, 53(1), 55–63.

Dowd, J. B., and Zajacova, A. (2007). Does the predictive power of self-rated health for subsequent mortality risk vary by socioeconomic status in the US? *International Journal of Epidemiology*, 36(6), 1214–1221.

Duncan, G. J., Yeung, W. J., Brooks-Gunn, J., and Smith, J. R. (1998). How much does childhood poverty affect the life chances of children? *American Sociological Review*, 63(3), 406–423.

Evans, G. W. (2004). The environment of childhood poverty. *American Psychologist*, 59(2), 77–92.

Evans, G. W., and Kim, P. (2007). Childhood poverty and health cumulative risk exposure and stress dysregulation. *Psychological Science*, 18(11), 953–957.

Fergus, S., and Zimmerman, M. A. (2005). Adolescent resilience: a framework for understanding healthy development in the face of risk. *Annual Review of Public Health*, 26, 399–419.

Frieden, T. R. (2010). A framework for public health action: the health impact pyramid. *Journal Information*, 100(4), 590–5.

Galster, G., Cutsinger, J., and Booza, J. C. (2009). Where did they go? The decline of middle-income neighborhoods in metropolitan America. In *Living Cities Census Series* 2006. Washington, DC: Brookings Institution.

Glouberman, S. (2001). *Towards a new perspective on health policy*. Canadian Policy Research Networks.

Gluckman, P. D., Hanson, M. A., and Beedle, A. S. (2007). Non-genomic transgenerational inheritance of disease risk. *Bioessays*, 29(2), 145–154.

Goodman, P. S. (2010). The new poor: despite signs of recovery, chronic joblessness rises. *The New York Times*, February 20, A1.

Guo, G., and Harris, K. M. (2000). The mechanisms mediating the effects of poverty on children's intellectual development. *Demography*, 37(4), 431–447.

Haveman, R. H., and Smeeding, T. M. (2006). The role of higher education in social mobility. *The Future of Children*, 16(2), 125–150.

Haveman, R., and Wolfe, B. (1995). The determinants of children's attainments: a review of methods and findings. *Journal of Economic Literature*, 33(4), 1829–1878.

Heckman, J. J., and Masterov, D. V. (2007). The productivity argument for investing in young children. *Applied Economic Perspectives and Policy*, 29(3), 446–493.

Hertzman, C. (2006). The biological embedding of early experience and its effects on health in adulthood. *Annals of the New York Academy of Sciences*, 896(1), 85–95.

Hertzman, C., and Power, C. (2003). Health and human development: understandings from life-course research. *Developmental Neuropsychology*, 24(2–3), 719–744.

Hertzman, C., and Wiens, M. (1996). Child development and long-term outcomes: a population health perspective and summary of successful interventions. *Social Science and Medicine*, 43(7), 1083–1095.

Idler, E. L., and Benyamini, Y. (1997). Self-rated health and mortality: a review of twenty-seven community studies. *Journal of Health and Social Behavior*, 38(1), 21–37.

Idler, E. L., and Kasl, S. V. (1995). Self-ratings of health: do they also predict change in functional ability? *Journals of Gerontology Series B: Psychological Sciences and Social Sciences*, 50(6), S344.

Institute of Medicine, Committee on Capitalizing on Social Science and Behavioral Research to Improve the Public's Health, and Division of Health Promotion and Disease Prevention (2000). *Promoting health: intervention strategies from social and behavioral research*, ed. B. D. Smedley and S. L. Syme. Washington, DC: National Academies Press.

Irwin, A., and Scali, E. (2005). *Action on the social determinants of health: learning from previous experiences: a background paper*. World Health Organization, Secretariat of the Commission on Social Determinants of Health.

Johnson, R. C., and Schoeni, R. F. (2007). *The influence of early-life events on human capital, health status, and labor market outcomes over the life course*. Institute for Research on Labor and Employment Working Paper Series. Berkeley, CA.

Kanjilal, S., Gregg, E. W., Cheng, Y. J., Zhang, P., Nelson, D. E., Mensah, G., and Beckles, G. L. (2006). Socioeconomic status and trends in disparities in 4 major risk factors for cardiovascular disease among US adults, 1971–2002. *Archives of Internal Medicine*, 166(21), 2348.

Karoly, L. A., Kilburn, M. R., and Cannon, J. S. (2005). *Early childhood interventions: proven results, future promise* (vol. 341). Santa Monica, CA: RAND Corporation.

Kramer, M. S., Goulet, L., Lydon, J., Séguin, L., McNamara, H., Dassa, C., … and Koren, G. (2001). Socio-economic disparities in preterm birth: causal pathways and mechanisms. *Paediatric and Perinatal Epidemiology*, 15(s2), 104–123.

Krieger, N. (2007). Why epidemiologists cannot afford to ignore poverty. *Epidemiology*, 18(6), 658–663.

Krieger, N., Chen, J. T., and Ebel, G. (1997). Can we monitor socioeconomic inequalities in health? A survey of US health departments' data collection and reporting practices. *Public Health Reports*, 112(6), 481.

Krieger, N., and Fee, E. (1996). Measuring social inequalities in health in the United States: a historical review, 1900–1950. *International Journal of Health Services*, 26(3), 391–418.

Lantz, P. M., House, J. S., Lepkowski, J. M., Williams, D. R., Mero, R. P., and Chen, J. (1998). Socioeconomic factors, health behaviors, and mortality. *Journal of the American Medical Association*, 279(21), 1703–1708.

Lee, R. E., and Cubbin, C. (2002). Neighborhood context and youth cardiovascular health behaviors. *Journal Information*, 92(3), 428–436.

Leventhal, T., and Brooks-Gunn, J. (2000). The neighborhoods they live in: the effects of neighborhood residence on child and adolescent outcomes. *Psychological Bulletin*, 126(2), 309.

Levin, H., Belfield, C., Muennig, P., and Rouse, C. (2007). *The costs and benefits of an excellent education for all of America's children*. New York: Teachers College, Columbia University.

Levine, R. S., Rust, G. S., Pisu, M., Agboto, V., Baltrus, P. A., Briggs, N. C., … and Hennekens, C. H. (2010). Increased black–white disparities in mortality after the introduction of lifesaving innovations: a possible consequence of US federal laws. *American Journal of Public Health*, 100(11), 2176.

Liu, H., and Hummer, R. A. (2008). Are educational differences in US self-rated health increasing? An examination by gender and race. *Social Science & Medicine*, 67(11), 1898–1906.

Lynch, J., and Smith, G. D. (2005). A life course approach to chronic disease epidemiology. *Annual Review of Public Health*, 26, 1–35.

Lynch, J. W., Kaplan, G. A., and Salonen, J. T. (1997). Why do poor people behave poorly? Variation in adult health behaviours and psychosocial characteristics by stages of the socioeconomic lifecourse. *Social Science and Medicine*, 44(6), 809–819.

Mackenbach, J. (2002). *Reducing inequalities in health: a European perspective.* London: Routledge.

Marmot, M. G., Bosma, H., Hemingway, H., Brunner, E., and Stansfeld, S. (1997). Contribution of job control and other risk factors to social variations in coronary heart disease incidence. *The Lancet*, 350(9073), 235–239.

Marmot, M., Friel, S., Bell, R., Houweling, T. A., and Taylor, S. (2008). Closing the gap in a generation: health equity through action on the social determinants of health. *The Lancet*, 372(9650), 1661–1669.

Marmot, M. G., Rose, G., Shipley, M., and Hamilton, P. J. (1978). Employment grade and coronary heart disease in British civil servants. *Journal of Epidemiology and Community Health*, 32(4), 244–249.

Marmot, M. G., Shipley, M. J., Hemingway, H., Head, J., and Brunner, E. J. (2008). Biological and behavioural explanations of social inequalities in coronary heart disease: the Whitehall II study. *Diabetologia*, 51(11), 1980–1988.

Marmot, M. G., Stansfeld, S., Patel, C., North, F., Head, J., White, I., ... and Smith, G. D. (1991). Health inequalities among British civil servants: the Whitehall II study. *The Lancet*, 337(8754), 1387–1393.

McEwen, B. S. (2000). The neurobiology of stress: from serendipity to clinical relevance. *Brain Research*, 886(1), 172–189.

(2006). Protective and damaging effects of stress mediators: central role of the brain. *Dialogues in Clinical Neuroscience*, 8(4), 367–381.

(1998). Stress, adaptation, and disease: allostasis and allostatic load. *Annals of the New York Academy of Sciences*, 840(1), 33–44.

McGee, D. L., Liao, Y., Cao, G., and Cooper, R. S. (1999). Self-reported health status and mortality in a multiethnic US cohort. *American Journal of Epidemiology*, 149(1), 41–46.

McGinnis, J. M., and Foege, W. H. (1993). Actual causes of death in the United States. *Journal of the American Medical Association*, 270(18), 2207–2212.

McNeill, L. H., Kreuter, M. W., and Subramanian, S. V. (2006). Social environment and physical activity: a review of concepts and evidence. *Social Science & Medicine*, 63(4), 1011–1022.

Mechanic, D. (2002). Disadvantage, inequality, and social policy. *Health Affairs*, 21(2), 48–59.

Minkler, M., Fuller-Thomson, E., and Guralnik, J. M. (2006). Gradient of disability across the socioeconomic spectrum in the United States. *New England Journal of Medicine*, 355(7), 695–703.

Mirowsky, J., and Ross, C. E. (2003). *Education, social status, and health*. New York: Aldine de Gruyter.

Murray, C. J., Harvard Center for Population and Development Studies. Burden of Disease Unit, and National Center for Chronic Disease Prevention and Health Promotion (US) (1998). *US patterns of mortality by county and race: 1965–1994*. Cambridge, MA: Harvard Burden of Disease Unit, Harvard Center for Population and Development Studies.

National Association of City and County Health Officials (2010). *Tackling Health Inequities through Public Health Practice: Theory to Action*, ed. R. Hofrichter and R. Bhatia, 2nd edn. New York: Oxford University Press.

National Center for Health Statistics (2012). *Health, United States, 2011: with special feature on socioeconomic status and health*. Hyattsville, MD.

Nishida, C., Uauy, R., Kumanyika, S., and Shetty, P. (2004). The joint WHO/FAO expert consultation on diet, nutrition and the prevention of chronic diseases: process, product and policy implications. *Public Health Nutrition*, 7 (1A; SPI), 245–250.

Nuru-Jeter, A., Dominguez, T. P., Hammond, W. P., Leu, J., Skaff, M., Egerter, S., ... and Braveman, P. (2009). "It's the skin you're in": African-American women talk about their experiences of racism. An exploratory study to develop measures of racism for birth outcome studies. *Maternal and Child Health Journal*, 13(1), 29–39.

O'Connell, M. E., Boat, T. F., and Warner, K. E. (eds.) (2009). *Preventing mental, emotional, and behavioral disorders among young people: progress and possibilities*. Washington, DC: National Academy Press.

Organization for Economic Co-operation and Development, Directorate for Employment, Labour and Social Affairs (2012). *OECD health data 2012 – frequently requested data*. Available at www.oecd.org/document/16/0,3343, en_2649_34631_2085200_1_1_1_1,00.html.

Otten, M. W., Jr., et al. (1990). The effect of known risk factors on the excess mortality of black adults in the United States. *Journal of the American Medical Association*, 263(6), 845–850.

Palloni, A. (2006). Reproducing inequalities: luck, wallets, and the enduring effects of childhood health. *Demography*, 43(4), 587–615.

Pamuk, E. (ed.) (1999). *Health, United States, 1998: with socioeconomic status and health chartbook*. Darby, PA: DIANE Publishing.

Pickett, K. E., and Pearl, M. (2001). Multilevel analyses of neighbourhood socio-economic context and health outcomes: a critical review. *Journal of Epidemiology and Community Health*, 55(2), 111–122.

PNC Financial Services Group (2010). *About PNC grow up great*. Retrieved from www.pncgrowupgreat.com/about/index.html (accessed March 2, 2010).

Population Reference Bureau, Infant Mortality Rate (2011) (infant deaths per 1,000 live births) – limited to OECD countries. World Population Data Sheet 2011. Available from www.prb.org/DataFinder/Topic/Rankings.aspx?ind=5 (accessed August 13, 2012).

Population Reference Bureau, *Life expectancy at birth (2011), by gender (limited to OECD countries)*. World Population Data Sheet 2011. Available from www. prb.org/DataFinder/Topic/Rankings.aspx?ind=6 (accessed August 13, 2012).

Power, C., Lake, J. K., and Cole, T. J. (1997). Measurement and long-term health risks of child and adolescent fatness. *International Journal of Obesity and Related Metabolic Disorders: Journal of the International Association for the Study of Obesity*, 21(7), 507–526.

Robert Wood Johnson Foundation (2009). *Beyond health care: new directions to a healthier America*. Washington, DC: Robert Wood Johnson Foundation.

(2013). *Time to act: investing in the health of our children and communities*. Washington, DC: Robert Wood Johnson Foundation.

Robert Wood Johnson Foundation and University of Wisconsin Population Health Institute (2013). *Country Health Rankings and Roadmaps, 2013*; available at www.countyhealthrankings.org/apptt/home (accessed February 19, 2014).

Rolnick, A., and Grunewald, R. (2003). Early childhood development: economic development with a high public return. *Fedgazette*, March 2003; available at https://www.minneapolisfed.org/publications_papers/pub_display.cfm?id=3832 (accessed February 13, 2014)

Rose, G. (1993). *Rose's strategy of preventive medicine*. Oxford University Press.

Rouse, C. E., and Barrow, L. (2006). US elementary and secondary schools: equalizing opportunity or replicating the status quo? *The Future of Children*, 16(2), 99–123.

Salomon, J. A., Nordhagen, S., Oza, S., and Murray, C. J. (2009). Are Americans feeling less healthy? The puzzle of trends in self-rated health. *American Journal of Epidemiology*, 170(3), 343–351.

Sapolsky, R. M. (2005). The influence of social hierarchy on primate health. *Science*, 308(5722), 648–652.

Schiller, J., Lucas, J. W., Ward, B. W., and Peregoy, J. A. (2012). Summary health statistics for U.S. adults: National Health Interview Survey. *Vital Health Statistics 10*, 252, 1–207.

Schoeni, R. F., Dow, W. H., Miller, W. D., and Pamuk, E. R. (2011). The economic value of improving the health of disadvantaged Americans. *American Journal of Preventive Medicine*, 40(1), S67–S72.

Seeman, T. E., McEwen, B. S., Rowe, J. W., and Singer, B. H. (2001). Allostatic load as a marker of cumulative biological risk. MacArthur studies of successful aging. *Proceedings of the National Academy of Sciences*, 98(8), 4770–4775.

Seeman, T. E., Singer, B. H., Rowe, J. W., Horwitz, R. I., and McEwen, B. S. (1997). Price of adaptation – allostatic load and its health consequences. MacArthur studies of successful aging. *Archives of Internal Medicine*, 157(19), 2259–2268.

Shonkoff, J. P., and Phillips, D. (2000). *From neurons to neighborhoods: the science of early childhood development*. Washington, DC: National Academies Press.

Smedley, B. D., and Stith, A. Y. (2003). *Unequal treatment: confronting racial and ethnic disparities in health care* (vol. 1). Washington, DC: National Academies Press.

Solon, G. (1992). Intergenerational income mobility in the United States. *American Economic Review*, 82, 393–408.

Steptoe, A., and Marmot, M. (2002). The role of psychobiological pathways in socioeconomic inequalities in cardiovascular disease risk. *European Heart Journal*, 23(1), 13–25.

Taylor, S. E., Repetti, R. L., and Seeman, T. (1997). Health psychology: what is an unhealthy environment and how does it get under the skin? *Annual Review of Psychology*, 48(1), 411–447.

Thomson, W. M., Poulton, R., Milne, B. J., Caspi, A., Broughton, J. R., and Ayers, K. M. S. (2004). Socioeconomic inequalities in oral health in childhood and adulthood in a birth cohort. *Community Dentistry and Oral Epidemiology*, 32(5), 345–353.

Truffer, C. J., Keehan, S., Smith, S., Cylus, J., Sisko, A., Poisal, J. A., ... and Clemens, M. K. (2010) Health spending projections through 2019: the recession's impact continues. *Health Affairs*, 29(3), 522–529.

US Census Bureau (2004a). *The American community – American Indians and Alaska Natives: 2004. American Community Survey Reports.* Retrieved December 11, 2009 from www.census.gov/prod/2007pubs/acs-07.pdf.

(2004b). *The American community – Asians: 2004. American Community Survey Reports.* Retrieved December 11, 2009 from www.census.gov/prod/2007pubs/acs-05.pdf.

(2004c). *The American community – Blacks: 2004. American Community Survey Reports.* Retrieved December 11, 2009 from www.census.gov/prod/2007pubs/acs-04.pdf.

(2004d). *The American Community – Hispanics: 2004. American Community Survey Reports.* Retrieved December 11, 2009 from www.census.gov/prod/2007pubs/acs-03.pdf.

(2004e). *The American Community – Pacific Islanders: 2004. American Community Survey Reports.* Retrieved December 11, 2009 from www.census.gov/prod/2007pubs/acs-06.pdf.

(2007). *Housing and Household Economic Statistics Division. Current Population Survey, 2005 to 2007 Annual Social and Economic Supplements.* Retrieved March 2, 2010 from www.census.gov/hhes/www/poverty/publications/pubs-cps.html.

US Department of Health and Human Services, Agency for Healthcare Research and Quality (2006). *National Healthcare Disparities Report, 2006.* Retrieved from http://archive.ahrq.gov/qual/nhdr06/nhdr06.htm.

US Department of Health and Human Services, *Healthy people 2010 Midcourse Review* (2006). Accessed at www.healthypeople.gov/2010/redirect.aspx?url=/2010/.

US Department of Health and Human Services, National Institute of Dental and Craniofacial Research, National Institutes of Health (2000). *Oral health in America: a report of the Surgeon General.* Retrieved from www.nidcr.nih.gov/datastatistics/surgeongeneral/report/executivesummary.htm.

US Department of Health and Human Services (2010). *Summary of the Prevention and Wellness Initiative.* Available at www.hhs.gov/recovery/programs/cdc/chronicdisease.html (accessed April 14, 2010).

van de Mheen, H., Stronks, K., Looman, C. W., and Mackenbach, J. P. (1998). Role of childhood health in the explanation of socioeconomic inequalities in early adult health. *Journal of Epidemiology and Community Health*, 52(1), 15–19.

Variyam, J. N., Blaylock, J., Lin, B. H., Ralston, K., and Smallwood, D. (1999). Mother's nutrition knowledge and children's dietary intakes. *American Journal of Agricultural Economics*, 81(2), 373–384.

Villard, L. C., Rydén, L., and Ståhle, A. (2007). Predictors of healthy behaviours in Swedish school children. *European Journal of Cardiovascular Prevention & Rehabilitation*, 14(3), 366–372.

Votruba-Drzal, E. (2004). Income changes and cognitive stimulation in young children's home learning environments. *Journal of Marriage and Family*, 65 (2), 341–355.

Wadsworth, M. E. J. (1997). Health inequalities in the life course perspective. *Social Science and Medicine*, 44(6), 859–870.

Wagstaff, A., and Van Doorslaer, E. (2000). Income inequality and health: what does the literature tell us?. *Annual Review of Public Health*, 21(1), 543–567.

Weller, C. E. (2005). *Middle-class progress: families work longer to pay for middle-class living than a quarter-century ago*. Washington, DC: Center for American Progress.

Whitehead, M. (1992). The health divide. In *Inequalities in Health: The Black Report and the Health Divide*, 2nd edn. London: Penguin Books.

Whitehead, M., Judge, K., and Benzeval, M. (eds.) (1995). *Tackling inequalities in health: an agenda for action*. London: King's Fund Centre.

Wilkinson, R. G., and Marmot, M. G. (eds.) (2003). *Social determinants of health: the solid facts*. Geneva: World Health Organization.

Williams, D. R. (2006). Race, socioeconomic status, and health: the added effects of racism and discrimination. *Annals of the New York Academy of Sciences*, 896 (1), 173–188.

Williams, D. R., and Collins, C. (2001). Racial residential segregation: a fundamental cause of racial disparities in health. *Public Health Reports*, 116(5), 404.

Williams, D. R., and Jackson, P. B. (2005). Social sources of racial disparities in health. *Health Affairs*, 24(2), 325–334.

Williams, D. R., and Mohammed, S. A. (2009). Discrimination and racial disparities in health: evidence and needed research. *Journal of Behavioral Medicine*, 32(1), 20–47.

Winkleby, M. A., Jatulis, D. E., Frank, E., and Fortmann, S. P. (1992). Socioeconomic status and health: how education, income, and occupation contribute to risk factors for cardiovascular disease. *American Journal of Public Health*, 82(6), 816–820.

Woolf, S. and Aron, L. (2013). *U.S. Health in International Perspective: Shorter Lives, Poorer Health*. National Research Council and Institute of Medicine. Washington, DC: National Academies Press.

Woolf, S. H., Dekker, M. M., Byrne, F. R., and Miller, W. D. (2011). Citizen-centered health promotion: building collaborations to facilitate healthy living. *American Journal of Preventive Medicine*, 40(1), S38–S47.

Yen, I. H., and Syme, S. L. (1999). The social environment and health: a discussion of the epidemiologic literature. *Annual Review of Public Health*, 20(1), 287–308.

Yeung, W. J., Linver, M. R., and Brooks-Gunn, J. (2002). How money matters for young children's development: parental investment and family processes. *Child Development*, 73(6), 1861–1879.

Zimmerman, D. J. (1992). Regression toward mediocrity in economic stature. *American Economic Review*, 82, 409–429.

3 Early childhood poverty and adult productivity and health

Greg J. Duncan, Ariel Kalil, and Kathleen M. Ziol-Guest

Introduction

Using a poverty line of about $23,000 for a family of four, the Census Bureau counted more than 16 million US children living in poor families in 2011. Poor children begin school well behind their more affluent age mates and, if anything, lose ground during the school years. On average, poor US kindergarten children have lower levels of reading and math skills and are rated by their teachers as less well behaved than their more affluent peers. As we document below, children from poor families also go on to complete less schooling, work and earn less, and are less healthy. Understanding the origins and persistence of these differences in fortune is a vital step toward ensuring the prosperity of future generations.

Our focus is on what low income in childhood, particularly early child-hood, means for health and a successful labor market career later in life. Identifying causal impacts is tricky, since poverty is associated with a cluster of disadvantages that may be detrimental to children, such as low levels of parental education and living with a single parent. To determine how children would be affected by a policy that increased family incomes but did nothing else, we focus on distinguishing the effects of family income from those of other sources of disadvantage. In policy terms, this approach will enable us to address the following question: to what extent are successes in adulthood affected by a policy such as the US Earned Income Tax Credit that boosts the family incomes of low-income parents with children, but does not directly change any other character-istic of their family environments?

Almost universally neglected in the poverty scholarship is the *timing* of economic hardship across childhood and adolescence. Emerging research in neuroscience, social epidemiology, and developmental psychology suggests that poverty early in a child's life may be particularly harmful. Not only does the astonishingly rapid development of young children's brains leave them sensitive (and vulnerable) to environmental conditions, but the family context (as opposed to schools or peers) dominates children's everyday lives.

After a brief review of the scope of childhood poverty in the United States, possible mechanisms linking early poverty to adult outcomes, and some of the experimental and nonexperimental empirical literature, we highlight emerging research based on newly available data linking poverty measured as early as the prenatal year to adult health and labor market outcomes measured in the fourth decade of life. We conclude with thoughts about how policy attention might focus on deep and persistent poverty occurring early in childhood.

Poverty in the United States and elsewhere

The official US definition of poverty is based on a comparison of a household's total income with a threshold level of income that varies with family size and inflation. The 2011 poverty line was drawn at $18,123 for a single parent living with two children and at $22,811 for a four-person family with two children. Since the 1990s, the fraction of young children classified as poor has ranged from about 18 percent to 25 percent; the recent recession has pushed the number of poor young children to their highest levels since these data have been gathered (Figure 3.1).

Based on a poverty line defined as 50 percent of a country's median income, nearly one-quarter of US children are classified as poor (Figure 3.2) (Gornick and Jantti, 2009). While higher than that of any other developed country, the US rate is only a few points above rates in the UK, Canada, and Poland. More striking are the cross-country differences when the poverty threshold is set at a more austere 40 percent of median

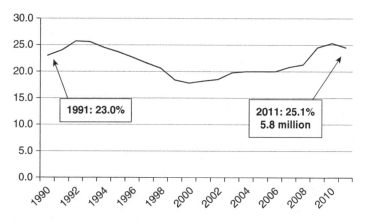

Figure 3.1 Poverty rate for children <6 years old. *Source:* US Bureau of the Census.

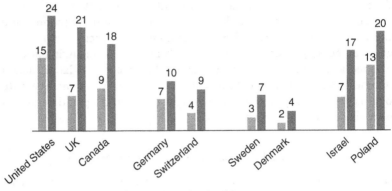

40% of median – $23,000 for a family of 3
50% of median – $29,000 for a family of 3

Figure 3.2 Poverty rates for young children.

disposable income (about $23,000). The 15 percent US poverty rate is more than half again as high as that of any country other than Poland. Thus deep poverty among children is considerably more pervasive in the US than in most Western industrialized countries.

Why poverty may hinder development

What are the consequences of growing up in a poor household? Economists, sociologists, developmental psychologists, neuroscientists, and social epidemiologists emphasize different pathways by which poverty may influence children's development. Economic models of child development focus on what money can buy (Becker, 1981). They view families with greater economic resources as being better able to purchase or produce important "inputs" into their young children's development (e.g., nutritious meals; enriched home learning environments and child care settings outside the home; safe and stimulating neighborhood environments), and, with older children, higher-quality schools and post-secondary education.

Psychologists and sociologists point to the quality of family relationships to explain poverty's detrimental effects on children. Their theoretical models emphasize the role of higher incomes in improving parents' psychological well-being and family processes, in particular the quality of parents' interactions with their children (Chase-Lansdale and Pittman, 2002; McLoyd, 1990; McLoyd et al., 1994). A long line of research has found that low-income parents, as compared with middle-class parents, are more likely to employ an authoritarian and punitive parenting style and less likely to provide their children with stimulating learning experiences in the home. Poverty and economic insecurity take a toll on a parent's mental health, which may be an important cause of low-income parents' non-supportive parenting (McLoyd, 1990). Depression and other forms of psychological distress can profoundly affect parents' interactions with their children (Zahn-Waxler, Duggal, and Gruber, 2002).

Emerging evidence from neuroscience and social epidemiology suggests that the *timing* of child poverty matters, and that for some outcomes later in life, particularly those related to attainment and health, poverty *early* in a child's life may be particularly harmful. Both human and animal studies highlight the critical importance of early childhood for brain development and for establishing the neural functions and structures that will shape future cognitive, social, emotional, and health outcomes (Sapolsky, 2004; Knudsen et al., 2006). Essential properties of most of the brain's architecture are established very early in life by genes and, importantly, early experience. Children's brains are "programmed" to be wired efficiently based on everyday interactions with sights, sounds, and supportive caregivers. The brains of children in deprived or traumatic environments often develop differently (Nelson et al., 2007). Traumatic stress that arises from child maltreatment, for example, produces measurable changes in brain structures and is likely to impart long-lasting disadvantages for adult mental and physical health and labor market functioning.

Using insights from this emerging neuroscience literature, Cunha, Heckman and their colleagues propose an economic model of development in which preschool cognitive and social-emotional capacities are key ingredients for human capital acquisition during the school years (Cunha et al., 2005). In their model, "skill begets skill" and early capacities can affect the likelihood that later school-age human capital investments will be successful and productive. This model predicts that economic deprivation in early childhood creates disparities in school readiness and early academic success that widen over the course of childhood.

Complementary studies in psychology and social epidemiology illustrate that both *in utero* environments and early childhood experiences can have long-run impacts on adult physical and mental health (Barker et al., 2002; Danese et al., 2007; Poulton and Caspi, 2005). The "fetal origins hypothesis" posits a programming process whereby stimulants and insults during the prenatal period have long-lasting implications for physiology and disease risk (Strauss, 1997). Chronic stress from growing up poor could also play a role in dysregulation across multiple physiological systems whose effects persist (or possibly compound) into adulthood. For example, Evans and Schamberg (2009) showed that childhood poverty increases allostatic load, a biological index of the cumulative wear and tear on the body, during the teenage years. Moreover, the longer the children had lived in poverty, the higher their allostatic load.

Allostatic load is caused by the mobilization of multiple physiological systems in response to chronic stresses in the environment. Thus childhood poverty may actually "reset" the immune system so that inflammation processes become dysregulated, resulting in higher levels and prolonged production of proinflammatory cytokines (i.e., chemical signals that can cause blood vessels to leak, leading to the swelling and redness that is associated with inflammation) (Miller et al., 2009).

Methods for assessing causal impacts of poverty

Regardless of the timing of low income, isolating its causal impact on children's well-being is very difficult. Since poverty is associated with other experiences of disadvantage, it is difficult to determine whether it is poverty per se that really matters or, instead, other related experiences, for example a low level of maternal education or being raised in a single-parent family. The best way to identify how much money itself really matters is to conduct an experiment that compares families that receive some additional money with families that are otherwise similar, but do not receive such money. The only large-scale randomized interventions to alter family income directly were the US Negative Income Tax Experiments, which were conducted between 1968 and 1982 with the primary goal of identifying the influence of guaranteed income on parents' labor force participation. Researchers found that elementary school children in the experimental group (whose families enjoyed a 50 percent boost in their income) exhibited higher levels of early academic achievement and school attendance than the control group (Maynard and Murnane, 1979). No test score differences were found for adolescents, although youth in the experimental group did have higher rates of high school completion and educational attainment (Salkind and Haskins, 1982). This suggests that higher income may indeed cause higher achievement, although even in this case it is impossible to distinguish the effects of income from the possible benefits to children from the reductions in parental work time that accompanied the income increases.

Providing income support to working poor parents through wage supplements has been been shown to improve children's achievement, according to data from experimental welfare reform evaluation studies undertaken during the 1990s. One study analyzed data from seven random-assignment welfare and antipoverty programs, all of which increased parental employment, while only some increased family income (Morris et al., 2001). Preschool and elementary school children's academic achievement was improved by programs that boosted both income and parental employment, but not by programs that only increased employment. The school achievement of adolescents did not appear to benefit from either kind of program.[1] A separate analysis of the data on younger children suggests that a $3,000 increase in annual income is associated with a gain of about one-fifth of a standard deviation in achievement test scores (Duncan, Morris, and Rodrigues, 2011).

Convincing evidence can sometimes be derived from nonexperimental studies that are careful to compare families that differ in terms of income, but are otherwise similar. One such study took advantage of the fact that, between 1993 and 1997, the maximum US Earned Income Tax Credit for working poor families increased by more than $2,000 for a family with two children (Dahl and Lochner, 2012). The authors compared the school achievement of children before and after this generous increase. They found improvements in low-income children's achievement in middle childhood that coincided with the policy change. A second study, based in Canada, found similar results when it took advantage of variation across Canadian provinces in the generosity of the National Child Benefit program to estimate income impacts on child achievement (Milligan and Stabile, 2008).

Linking early poverty to adult outcomes

None of this past income literature has been able to relate family income early in a child's life to adult attainments, largely because no single study had collected data on both early childhood income and later adult outcomes. However, recent research has made this link using data from the Panel Study of Income Dynamics, which has followed a nationally representative sample of US families and their children since 1968 (Duncan, Ziol-Guest, and Kalil, 2010). The study is based on children born between 1968 and 1975 and collected information on their economic fortunes between ages 25 and 37. Health conditions were assessed in 2006, when these individuals were between the ages of 30 and 37.

The study measured income in every year of a child's life from the prenatal period through age 15. This enabled Duncan and colleagues (2010) to measure poverty across several distinct periods of childhood,

---

[1] Though leveraging experimental data, the analysis itself is not an experiment as families were not randomly assigned across types of treatments.

Table 3.1 *Adult outcomes by poverty status between the prenatal year and age 5.*

	Early childhood income below the official US poverty line	Early childhood income between one and two times the poverty line	Early childhood income more than twice the poverty line
	Mean or %	*Mean or %*	*Mean or %*
Completed schooling (years)	11.8	12.7	14.0
Adult earnings between ages 25 and 37 (in $10,000)	$17.9	$26.8	$39.7
Annual work hours between ages 25 and 37	1,512	1,839	1,963
Food stamps between ages 25 and 37	$896	$337	$70
Ever arrested (men only)	26%	21%	13%
Nonmarital birth (women only)	50%	28%	9%
Poor health in 2005	13%	13%	5%
Obese in 2005 (BMI > 30)	45%	32%	26%
Hypertension in 2005	25%	10%	9%
Arthritis in 2005	7%	7%	3%
Diabetes in 2005	4%	6%	2%
Work-limiting hypertension in 2005	4%	2%	2%

Note: The sample consists of individuals born between 1968 and 1975 in the PSID. Earnings and food stamp values are in 2005 dollars.

distinguishing income early in life (prenatal through 5th year) from income in middle childhood and adolescence. The simple associations between income early in life and adult outcomes are striking (Table 3.1).[2] Compared with children whose families had incomes of at least twice the poverty line during their early childhood, poor children completed two

[2] Data on all but the last four health conditions appear in Duncan et al. (2010). Data on health conditions come from additional calculations using the same PSID-based sample.

fewer years of schooling, earned less than half as much, worked 451 fewer hours per year, and received $826 per year more in food stamps as adults. Poor males were twice as likely to be arrested. For females, poverty was associated with a more than fivefold increase in the likelihood of bearing a child out of wedlock prior to age 21. As for health, poor children were nearly three times as likely to report poor overall health as adults and more than twice as likely to report various activity-limiting health conditions, and members of this group were 19 percentage points more likely to be overweight.

Looking beyond these simple correlations, Duncan and colleagues regressed the adult outcomes listed in Table 3.1 on three childhood stage-specific measures of family income – average income between the prenatal year and age 5, average income between ages 6 and 10, and average income between ages 11 and 15 – plus an extensive list of background controls.[3] To account for the possibility that income effects are nonlinear, two coefficients were estimated for each childhood stage, the first reflecting the estimated effect of an additional $3,000 of annual income[4] in the given stage for children whose income during that stage averaged less than $25,000 and the second reflecting comparable effects for higher-income children (all three sets of income variables, plus other controls, are included in all regressions).

Turning first to their central measure of labor market productivity – average annual earnings between ages 25 and 37 – Duncan and colleagues found that for children growing up in families with average early childhood incomes below $25,000, a $3,000 annual boost to family income between the prenatal year and age 5 was associated with a 17 percent increase in adult earnings (Figure 3.3). For children growing up in higher-income households (more than $25,000 per year), a $3,000 boost to

---

[3] "Background controls" consist of birth year, race, sex, whether the child's parents were married and living together at the time of the birth, mother's age at birth, region, number of siblings, parent schooling, parent test score, cleanliness of the house, parent's expectations for child, parent achievement motivation, parent locus of control, and parent risk avoidance. The regression, then, e.g., for earnings regressed average earnings between ages 25 and 37, averaged over as many of these years as possible, on average annual income between the prenatal year and age 5, between ages 6 and 10, and between age 11 and 15, plus these background variables. Each of the three income measures were expressed as two-piece linear splines, with knots at $25,000. Considerable experimentation showed that $25,000 was the income that best balanced different slopes and the precision with which the slopes were estimated.

[4] The $3,000 amount was chosen for the interpretation of coefficients because it is well within the range of an actual US policy – the Earned Income Tax Credit. Given that a linear function was fit to the entire income range up to $25,000, estimated impacts of income increments smaller or larger than $3,000 can be obtained with proportionate reductions or increases in the impacts shown in the figures.

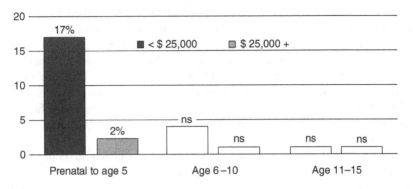

"ns" means not statistically significant at $p<.10$

Figure 3.3 Percentage increase in adult earnings associated with a $3,000 annual increase in childhood income.

family income was statistically significant but was estimated to increase adult earnings by only about 2 percent. None of the income increments later in childhood was estimated to have statistically significant effects on later earnings.

Results for work hours are broadly similar to those for earnings, showing a highly significant estimated impact of early, but not later, childhood income. In this case, a $3,000 annual increase in the prenatal to age 5 average income of low-income families is associated with 152 additional work hours per year after age 25. This is shown as the first bar in Figure 3.4. Other results presented in Figure 3.4 show that the boost in adult productivity associated with additional income in early childhood also led to significantly less food stamp receipt.

Earnings are the product of work hours and the hourly wage rate. There is clearly a strong relationship between early income and work hours, but it is also important to determine how important early income is for the hourly wage rate. In results not shown, Duncan and colleagues (2010) found no connection between early income and hourly earnings – virtually all of the earnings effect was carried by increases in labor supply rather than the wage rate. Accordingly, it is perhaps not surprising that early income was not significantly related to completed schooling, the most potent determinant of hourly wage rates.[5] Nor were there significant impacts of early poverty on problem behavior – being arrested or

---

[5] The completed schooling picture is a bit more complicated. Although early income did not matter for eventual completed schooling, it did have a significant effect on completed

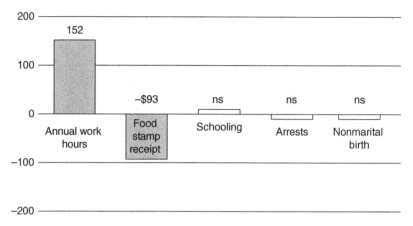

Figure 3.4 Impacts on various adult outcomes associated with a $3,000 annual increase in prenatal to age 5 income, for incomes < $25,000.

incarcerated (for males) or having a nonmarital birth (for females); family income during adolescence seemed to matter more for these outcomes.

So if neither the human capital (schooling and wage rates) nor the behavioral outcomes (lack of arrests or nonmarital births) account for links between early income and adult labor market productivity, what does? Consistent with the "early origins" work in social epidemiology and neuroscience, it appears that early income has long-term effects on work-limiting health conditions.

Regression results are shown in Figure 3.5. As with earnings and work hours, each of the health conditions was regressed on stage-specific childhood income, demographic control variables. As before, the income associations are allowed to be nonlinear, with one linear segment fit across average annual incomes within a given childhood stage up to $25,000 and another fit to incomes above $25,000. Only the coefficients on the low-income segment for early childhood are shown in Figure 3.5.[6] Given the dichotomous nature of the health outcomes, we estimated these models with logistic regression. The bars in Figure 3.5 represent the percentage reductions in the odds of a given condition associated with a $3,000 increase in annual income between the prenatal year and age 5.

schooling by age 21. So it appears that early income may matter more for the "on time" completion of schooling by the end of adolescence than for the sporadic increases in schooling that often occur later.

[6] These regression results do not appear in Duncan et al. (2010) but use the same sample. In only one case – for incomes above $25,000 for ages 11 to 15 in the diabetes regression – was the coefficient more than twice its standard error.

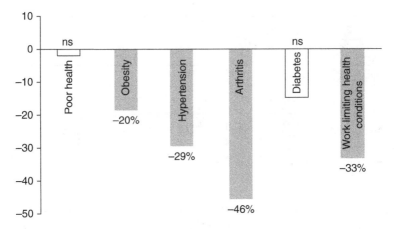

Figure 3.5 Percentage reductions in odds of various health conditions in 2006 associated with a $3,000 annual increase in prenatal to age 5 income, for family incomes < $25,000.

Figure 3.5 shows a remarkable pattern of effects on the emerging (mid to late 30s) adult health problems. Although increments to early income do not appear to affect self-rated overall adult health or diabetes, $3,000 increments to low income early in life are associated with a 20 percent reduction in the odds of obesity, a 29 percent reduction in the odds of reporting hypertension, a 46 percent reduction in the odds of reporting arthritis, and a 33 percent reduction in the odds of reporting a health-related work limitation. Although more research is obviously needed, these health pathways involving stress and inflammation appear to be very promising linkages between poverty early in life and adult labor market productivity.

Some policy implications

Our review concludes that early childhood is a particularly sensitive period in which economic deprivation may compromise children's health and employment opportunities. This research suggests that greater policy attention should be given to remediating situations involving deep and persistent poverty *in utero* and occurring early in childhood. In terms of indicators, it is crucial to track rates of poverty among children – especially deep poverty occurring early in childhood – to inform policy discussions regarding children's well-being.

In the case of welfare policies, sanctions and other regulations denying benefits to families with very young children would appear particularly harmful. Not only do young children appear to be most vulnerable to the consequences of deep poverty, but mothers with very young children are also least able to support themselves through employment in the labor market.

More effective would be income transfer policies that provided more income to families with young children. In the case of work support programs like the Earned Income Tax Credit, this might mean extending more generous credits to families with young children. In the case of child tax credits, this could mean making the credit refundable and also providing larger credits to families with young children. Interestingly, several European countries gear the time-limited benefits provided by their assistance programs to the age of children. In Germany, a modest parental allowance is available to a mother working fewer than 20 hours per week until her child is 18 months old. France guarantees a minimum income to most of its citizens, including families with children of all ages. Supplementing this basic support is the Allocation de Parent Isolé (API) program for lone parents with children under age 3. In effect, the API program acknowledges a special need for income support during this period, especially if a parent wishes to care for very young children and forgo income from employment. The state-funded child care system in France beginning at age 3 alleviates the problems associated with a parent's transition into the labor force.

In emphasizing the potential importance of policies to boost income in early childhood, we do not mean to suggest that this is the only policy path worth pursuing. Obviously investments later in life and those that provide direct services to children and families may also be well advised. Economic logic requires a comparison of the costs and benefits of the various programs that seek to promote the development of disadvantaged children throughout the life course. In this context, expenditures on income-transfer and service-delivery programs should be placed side by side and judged by their benefits and society's willingness to pay for the outcomes they produce, relative to their costs.

References

Barker, D., Forsén, T., Eriksson, J., and Osmond, C. (2002). Growth and living conditions in childhood and hypertension in adult life: a longitudinal study. *Journal of Hypertension*, 20(10), 1951–1956.

Becker, G. (1981). *A treatise on the family*. Cambridge, MA: Harvard University Press.

Chase-Lansdale, P.L., and Pittman, L. (2002). Welfare reform and parenting: reasonable expectations. *Future of Children*, 12, 167–185.

Cunha, F., Heckman, J. J., Lochner, L., and Masterov, D. (2005). Interpreting the evidence on life cycle skill formation. In E. Hanushek and F. Welch (eds.), *Handbook of the economics of education* (pp. 697–812). Amsterdam: North Holland.

Dahl, G., and Lochner, L. (2012). The impact of family income on child achievement: evidence from the earned income tax credit. *American Economic Review* 102, 1927–1956.

Danese, A., Pariante, C., Caspi, A., Taylor, A., and Poulton, R. (2007). Childhood maltreatment predicts adult inflammation in a life-course study. *Proceedings of the National Academy of Sciences*, 104(4), 1319–1324.

Duncan, G., Morris, P., and Rodrigues, C. (2011). Does money matter? Estimating impacts of family income on young children's achievement with data from random-assignment experiments. *Developmental Psychology*, 47(5), 1263–1279.

Duncan, G., Ziol-Guest, K., and Kalil, A. (2010). Early childhood poverty and adult attainment, behavior and health. *Child Development*, 81(1), 306–325.

Evans, G., and Schamberg, M. (2009). Childhood poverty, chronic stress, and adult working memory. *Proceedings of the National Academy of Sciences*, 106, 6545–6549.

Gornick, J., and Jantti, M. (2009). Child poverty in upper-income countries: lessons from the Luxembourg Income Study. In Sheila B. Kamerman, Shelley Phipps, and Asher Ben-Arieh (eds.), *From child welfare to child well-being: an international perspective on knowledge in the service of making policy*. A special volume in honor of Alfred J. Kahn. New York: Springer Publishing Company.

Knudsen, E., Heckman, J., Cameron, J., and Shonkoff, J. (2006). Economic, neurobiological, and behavioral perspectives on building America's future workforce. *Proceedings of the National Academy of Sciences*, 103, 10155–10162.

Maynard, R., and Murnane, R. (1979). The effects of a negative income tax on school performance: results of an experiment. *Journal of Human Resources*, 14(4), 463–476.

McLoyd, V. (1990). The impact of economic hardship on black families and children: psychological distress, parenting and socioeconomic development. *Child Development*, 61, 311–346.

McLoyd, V. C., Jayaratne, T. E., Ceballo, R., and Borquez, J. (1994). Unemployment and work interruption among African American single mothers: effects on parenting and adolescent socioemotional functioning. *Child Development*, 65, 562–589.

Miller, G. E., Chen, E., Fok, A. K., Walker, H., Lim, A., Nicholls, E. F. et al. (2009). Low early-life social class leaves a biological residue manifested by decreased glucocorticoid and increased proinflammatory signaling. *Proceedings of the National Academy of Sciences*, 106, 14716–14721.

Milligan, K., and Stabile, M. (2008). *Do child tax benefits affect the well-being of children? Evidence from Canadian child benefit expansions*. Cambridge, MA: NBER Working Paper No. 14264.

Morris, P., Huston, A., Duncan, G., Crosby, D., and Bos, H. (2001). *How welfare and work policies affect children: a synthesis of research*. New York: MDRC.

Nelson, C. A., Zeanah, C. H., Fox, N. A., Marshall, P. J., Smyke, A. T., and Guthrie, D. (2007). Cognitive recovery in socially deprived young children: the Bucharest Early Intervention Project. *Science*, 318(5858), 1937–1940.

Poulton, R., and Caspi, A. (2005). Commentary: how does socioeconomic disadvantage during childhood damage health in adulthood? Testing psychosocial pathways. *International Journal of Epidemiology*, 34(2), 344–345.

Salkind, N., and Haskins, R. (1982). Negative income tax: the impact on children from low-income families. *Journal of Family Issues*, 3, 165–180.

Sapolsky, R. (2004). Mothering style and methylation. *Nature Neuroscience*, 7, 791–792.

Strauss, R. (1997). Effects of the intrauterine environment on childhood growth. *British Medical Bulletin*, 53(1), 81–95.

Zahn-Waxler, C., Duggal, S., and Gruber, R. (2002). Parental psychopathology. In M. H. Bornstein (ed.), *Handbook of parenting* (2nd edn, vol.4, pp. 95–328). Mahwah, NJ: Lawrence Erlbaum Associates.

4 The impact of maternal/child nutrition on cognitive development: prevention implications

Michael K. Georgieff

History

The research that supports the concept that maternal and child nutrition status has a significant impact on childhood cognitive development has a long and compelling history. Ancient texts as well as manuscripts published during the age of enlightenment and the industrial revolution highlight the importance of maternal health and well-being in producing a healthy vigorous offspring. Moreover, maternal post-partum nutritional status and health have direct effects on the adequacy of the infant's primary nutritional source, breast milk. The adequacy of the infant's postnatal diet has a large impact on concurrent and subsequent cognitive development. These effects were so apparent historically that human milk substitutes were present in ancient times in order to nurture infants whose mothers were unable to provide adequate nutrition for their offspring.

The modern research context for the effect of fetal and neonatal nutrition status on cognitive development can be traced to the seminal work of Myron Winick and colleagues in the early 1960s (Winick and Rosso, 1969). His work demonstrated that intrauterine growth restriction (IUGR) due to malnutrition results in reduction in brain size, neuronal number, and neuronal complexity. Maternal malnutrition during pregnancy, a potentially preventable condition, is a primary cause of IUGR world-wide. Societies in which mothers are chronically malnourished are likely to have malnourished children as well. Given that a major portion of brain development in humans occurs between the last trimester in fetal life and 3 years postnatally (Dobbing and Sands, 1979; Thompson and Nelson, 2001) it is not surprising that a malnourished maternal–fetus/infant dyad poses a significant risk to cognitive development. It has been estimated that correction of nutrient deficits could shift the world's intelligence quotient (IQ) by 10 points to the positive (Morris, Cogill, and Uauy, 2008).

There is also a rich research history to support the hypothesis that nutritional interventions for the mother, the infant, or both have a significant positive impact on cognitive development. Early work by Ernesto Pollitt was seminal in establishing the importance of providing supplemental nutrients to populations (Pollitt and Gorman, 1994). Interventional studies have ranged from supplementation of specific single nutrients to comprehensive nutrition support programs at the population level. Research on the former indicates that, while the developing brain needs all nutrients, certain nutrients are particularly important during this critical period of early brain development (reviewed in Fuglestad, Rao, and Georgieff, 2008). Research on the latter tends to be on the population level and the nutritional intervention is often part of a more general program of health promotion (e.g., WIC) or education (e.g., Head Start; school lunch).

The emphasis on optimizing nutritional status in fetuses, infants, and young children is embedded in the philosophy that "nutrition is something one can do something about." While this is theoretically the case, the causes of malnutrition vary in populations around the world. Lack of access to food is a major concern in certain areas and results in a shortage of all nutrients important for brain development. Other populations in the world are plagued by deficiencies of specific nutrients (e.g., iron, selenium) as a function either of a diet that is customary to the population (e.g., vegetarian; diets that inhibit iron absorption) or of the lack of nutrient in the soil (e.g., selenium, iodine) that results in low food value. Programs that seek to optimize nutrition in these populations are present and have met with variable success dependent on the nutrient in question, the ability to place that nutrient in a palatable and widely distributable form, and distribution pathways. Nevertheless, the history of nutrient supplementation has been one of success in providing better substrate for neurodevelopment and enhancing cognitive function.

Overview of current "research state of the art"

Several overarching principles govern the relationship between early nutrition and brain development. These principles must be taken into account when assessing literature that purports to demonstrate a relationship between maternal or child nutrition and later child cognitive function. In turn, adherence to these principles allows researchers to identify nutrients of particular importance to early brain development, thereby promoting sound public policy regarding maternal and infant nutrition.

The positive or negative effect of any given nutrient (or its deficiency) on brain development is governed by the timing, dose, and duration of the exposure (Kretchmer, Beard, and Carlson, 1996). This principle is driven by the understanding that the brain is not a homogeneous organ even though it is frequently referred to in that manner. On the contrary, the brain has diverse cell populations that coalesce into "mini-organs" or nuclei that work together in circuits or systems that underlie different behavioral functions. Each brain region has a different developmental trajectory. Some, such as the hippocampus which subserves recognition learning and memory, develop late in fetal life, while others, such as the frontal lobes, develop after birth (Nelson, 1995). Thus, the neonate is capable of recognition memory behavior (e.g., recognizing its mother's voice) but does not exhibit the ability to multi-task until later in life. Brain-wide processes exist and also exhibit a developmental trajectory. In the case of myelination, this trajectory proceeds in a rostral-caudal direction and takes years to reach adult levels (Thompson and Nelson, 2001).

The vulnerability of a brain region to a particular nutrient deficit is dependent on when the nutrient deficit is likely to occur within childhood intersecting with the brain region's requirement for that nutrient at those times (Kretchmer et al., 1996). For example, iron deficiency has three peak incidence time periods; during the third trimester of fetal life, between 9 and 24 months of age, and during the teenage years particularly in females (Lozoff et al., 2006). The stressors that result in imbalances of iron supply and demand are quite different in the three time periods, but in each case regional brain iron deficiency results when supply does not meet regional demand. The regions and processes of the brain that require iron during these three times periods are quite different (Lozoff et al., 2006; Thompson and Nelson, 2001). Not surprisingly, behavioral symptomatology varies among the three groups based on the region or process at risk. In the late fetal period, the hippocampus is one region of the brain that is rapidly developing. Iron demand is high because it is a required nutrient for brain energy generation (see below). The behavioral sequelae of fetal iron deficiency are particularly centered on learning and memory (Siddappa et al., 2004), the very behavior that the hippocampus subserves (Nelson, 1995). On the other hand, other brain regions are not nearly as rapidly growing during that time period and have much lower iron demands. Abnormal behaviors noted later in childhood are based on circuitry found in those slow-growing structures and thus should not be attributed to fetal iron deficiency. This leads to the axiom that behavioral changes that are ascribed to an earlier period of malnutrition should make mechanistic sense in that they should map onto those brain structures altered earlier by the nutrient deficit.

The "biological proof" of a nutrient effect on the brain is not easy to obtain. Fundamentally, the questions being asked of nutritional neuroscientists are: (1) Do nutritionally induced alterations in brain development

Table 4.1 *An interdisciplinary research approach to assess nutrient effects on human brain development.*

Domain	Human assessment	Model assessment
Behavior	Of primary interest	Fit to human
Brain structure (neuroanatomy)	Magnetic Resonance Imaging (MRI)	MRI; microscopy
Neuronal performance (electrophysiology)	Electroencephalogram; Event Related Potentials; Evoked Potentials	Direct *in vivo* recording *Ex vivo* recording in culture
Neuronal biochemistry (neurochemistry; neurometabolism)	Magnetic Resonance Spectroscopy (MRS)	MRS Direct biochemical assessment
Cellular/molecular regulation	Genome-wide association studies and targeted assessment of risk alleles	Genetic models; gene expression analysis

alter the behavioral output of the brain? (2) If so, how close is the linkage for each nutrient and for each time period of development? (3) Finally, is the effect transiently present only during the period of deficiency, or does the nutrient deficiency result in behavioral deficits that last beyond the period of deficiency? Answering such questions in humans is particularly difficult since tissue level analysis is rarely available. Instead, biological proofs of nutrient effects on human brain development rely on integration of evidence at multiple levels (Table 4.1) from human behavior to cellular processes in animal models.

These proofs can be driven top-down (i.e., based originally on behavioral findings in humans) or bottom-up (e.g., based on findings in the wet laboratory). Certain rules must be adhered to in establishing such biological proofs. Approaches must be complementary between the models and the human condition by tapping into similar neurobehavioral processes that obey the laws of timing, dose, and duration of insult. The models must be developmentally appropriate and reflect regional nutrient–brain effects. Finally, deficiencies induced in animal models must coincide developmentally with the time of deficiency in the human. In some cases, this may result in a fetal condition in the human being studied after birth in the model. For example, the human hippocampus in the third trimester of the fetus is similar in maturity to the postnatal rat hippocampus between postnatal days 3 and 10 (Nelson et al., 2002).

Nutrients affect all brain cell types. While much is (rightfully) made of nutrient deficiency effects on the neurons, it is important to also consider potential effects on the supporting cells of the brain: oligodendrocytes, astrocytes, and microglia. Similarly, while neuroanatomical changes are most frequently examined, consideration must also be given to nutritionally induced neurochemical and neurophysiologic effects. Negative nutrient effects on neurons include reduced cell division and cell differentiation. The former results in fewer neurons and is most often seen with early fetal effects when proliferation is at its greatest, while the latter results in less complex neurons and is a result of late fetal and postnatal malnutrition. Poorer complexity is anatomically manifested by less neuronal dendrite arborization and smaller dendrite spines. The functionality of the brain is closely related to its neuronal complexity (Spruston, 2008). Nutrients that have particularly prominent effects on these developing processes include protein energy, iron, zinc, iodine, and long-chain polyunsaturated fatty acids (LC-PUFAs, also known as "fish oils"). Neurochemical alterations driven by the deficiency of nutrients such as protein, iron, zinc, and choline include lower neurotransmitter concentrations, and alterations in receptor numbers and neurotransmitter re-uptake mechanisms (Beard and Connor, 2003). Ultimately, anatomic and neurochemical changes must manifest themselves as alterations in the neurophysiology (i.e., electrical activity) of the brain to result in behavioral changes. Nutrients that alter the neurophysiology of the developing brain include glucose, protein, iron, zinc, iodine, and choline.

Major impacts

It is beyond the scope of this chapter to catalogue the effect of every nutrient during pregnancy, lactation, and early childhood on the developing brain. While all nutrients are important for brain development, certain ones are more critical during the period of most rapid brain development in the human from the beginning of the third trimester to 3 years of age (Table 4.2).

Table 4.2 *Nutrients that have a particularly large impact on early brain development.*

Macronutrients	Micronutrients	Vitamins/cofactors
Protein (especially branch chain amino acids)	Iron	B vitamins (e.g., B6, B12)
Fats (especially LC-PUFA)	Zinc	Vitamin A
Glucose	Copper	Folate
	Iodine	Choline

These nutrients appear to be particularly salient during this developmental epoch because they support fundamental neuronal metabolic processes and thus dictate neuronal cell proliferation and survival and ultimately differentiation. Their importance derives chiefly from the fact that the rapidly growing brain during this time period is metabolically more active and thus has its highest demand for nutritional substrates that support that metabolism (Institute of Medicine, 2000). Of these, some are more likely than others to be deficient in the diets of maternal and child populations. Protein, LC-PUFAs, zinc, iron, iodine, vitamin A, and folate fall into this category. An in-depth review of the biological effects of these nutrients on the developing brain is also beyond the scope of this chapter, but the reader can access more in-depth information in a study by Fuglestad and colleagues (2008). These nutrients tend to be the subjects of more intensive nutritional neuroscience investigation and the focus of public policy initiatives. The remainder of this section focuses on the young brain's requirements for these nutrients, the populations at risk for their deficiencies, and the multi-tiered scientific evidence that supports the assertion that they are important for fetal and childhood brain development. Extensive, specific dietary intake recommendations for each of these nutrients for pregnant women, lactating mothers, and children, and the rationales for these recommendations, have been published by the Institute of Medicine (2000). Specific recommendations for children of all ages can be found in the Pediatric Nutrition Handbook published by the American Academy of Pediatrics (2009).

The assimilation of nutrients by the fetus and neonate is frequently a facilitated process so that the recipient fetus or neonate will preferentially accrete them at the expense of the donor (e.g., the mother). Similar active and regulated transport systems at the cellular levels of the placental syncytiotrophoblast and the mammary gland epithelial cell attempt to ensure sufficient nutrient supply to the developing offspring. These types of transport systems protect the young offspring, who has limited nutrient reserves, from the hourly, daily, and perhaps longer cycles of nutrient availability for the mother. Nevertheless, prolonged periods of malnutrition will ultimately reduce maternal reserves to levels that active transport systems cannot overcome and the fetus will then suffer the effects of reduced nutrient supply. In this condition, prioritization of nutrients within the offspring's body occurs such that certain organs are preferentially provided the nutrient while others are short changed. This is especially evident for nutrients such as glucose, amino acids, oxygen, and iron that support fundamental metabolism of the organs. In this sense, the brain appears as one of the "most-favored" organs, demonstrating significant sparing of its growth during periods of protein-energy malnutrition, oxygenation during fetal hypoxia, and iron content during periods of iron deficiency (Georgieff et al., 1992). Similarly, intra-organ prioritization occurs, with certain brain regions or processes spared or sacrificed at the expense of others. In this context, the hippocampus appears particularly vulnerable to early protein or iron deficiency manifested by greater loss of nutrient content and function compared to other regions (deUngria et al., 2000; Lee et al., 1997).

Protein

While the brain's functional fuel is glucose, protein is responsible for its proper structural development and maintenance. Dietary protein is broken down in the intestinal lumen and the liver to amino acids that subsequently form the building blocks for new protein synthesis. The brain requires amino acids for DNA and RNA synthesis and maintenance that in turn determine cell number and cell size and complexity, respectively. Amino acids are the backbone for small functional proteins such as neurotransmitters and growth factors as well as large structural proteins involved in neuron cell integrity. The latter are necessary for the neuron to send out extensions to other neurons (i.e., axons) and to establish the receptive fields (i.e., dendrites) to receive information from other neurons. The complexity of the dendrite arbor is an important factor in the functional capability of the neuron (Spruston, 2008). Protein assembly occurs not only in the cell body, but in these peripheral extensions at the point of synapses between neurons. Thus, protein malnutrition can negatively affect the ultrastructure and functionality of the connections between neurons.

Several clinical conditions early in life lead to protein malnutrition that affects the developing brain, including intrauterine growth restriction (IUGR), starvation during childhood, and chronic illnesses that prohibit adequate feeding. The latter include prematurity and chronic kidney, liver, heart, lung, and infectious diseases. None of these clinical conditions is pure protein malnutrition. Unlike what can be induced experimentally in laboratory models, protein malnutrition in human populations is usually associated with multiple other nutrient deficiencies (that also affect brain development) since the most common cause of protein malnutrition in childhood is a general lack of access to adequate amounts of food. Patients who are protein malnourished due to restricted food supply are also frequently zinc deficient and iron deficient.

Protein malnutrition due to lack of adequate maternal or childhood dietary protein places the developing brain at risk throughout gestation and early childhood. One peak period of malnutrition occurs during the last trimester, when fetal protein requirements are high because of the rate of fetal brain growth coupled with a higher probability of maternal hypertension that restricts maternal–placental–fetal blood flow. A second peak occurs after 6 months of age when mother's milk protein content declines precipitously, children are weaned from their mother's milk, and they become dependent on other dietary sources of protein that may be low in the community. Indeed, a major nutritional tipping point in both developed and developing countries occurs when infants stop receiving feedings from a highly regulated, full-nutrient source (human milk or formula) and are expected to thrive on whatever diverse diet caregivers choose to or are able to provide for them. In developed countries, such diets may be low in nutrient value, favoring high fat and salt content. In developing countries, diets may be low in all nutrients.

Some brain processes that are affected by fetal protein malnutrition in contrast to childhood protein malnutrition after 1 year of age are different by virtue of the timing of the development of these processes. Fetal protein restriction tends to affect the hippocampus, the cerebellum, and the auditory cortex, while childhood protein malnutrition is more likely to affect higher cognitive functions such as language, attention, and working memory. The development of other brain regions and processes such as myelination and experience dependent synaptogenesis extends through both time periods and is affected by either condition.

IUGR is defined as an abnormally low birth weight for gestational age due to a pathologic process that slowed fetal growth. Maternal protein and energy malnutrition is the most common etiology in the developing world while gestational hypertension is the most common cause in the developed world. Extensive clinical studies have demonstrated a detrimental effect on neurodevelopment particularly when the head circumference, which indexes brain size, is also affected (Strauss and Dietz, 1998). Children assessed following IUGR demonstrate poorer verbal outcome and visual recognition memory and a higher incidence of mild neurodevelopmental abnormalities (reviewed in Fuglestad et al., 2008). Their intelligence quotient at 7 years of age is on average 6.8 points lower than infants born with normal birth weights (Strauss and Dietz, 1998). Postnatal growth failure compounds the losses in a dose dependent manner based on its duration (Pylipow et al., 2009).

Animal models confirm and extend the findings of the effect of IUGR and protein restriction on brain anatomy and biochemistry as initially described by Winick (Lee et al., 1997; Winick and Rosso, 1969). These include reduced cell DNA, cell RNA, total and regional brain size, growth factor concentrations, and neurotransmitter production, as well as ultrastructural changes in synapses and altered myelin structural protein profiles. IUGR also induces changes in regional brain gene expression with particular effects on genes regulating synaptic plasticity and growth factors. Of particular concern are epigenetic modifications that not only may affect the offspring long after resolution of IUGR but may be heritable to the next generation (Ke et al., 2005).

Prevention of IUGR due to maternal malnutrition is, not surprisingly, closely linked to eradication of poverty and overall improvement of nutrient delivery. In areas of the world where calories are abundant but the protein is of poor quality, efforts could center on improvement of the latter through supplementation of key amino acids that could be limiting fetal growth and development. In developed countries, better maternal prenatal care characterized by earlier and more assiduous blood pressure monitoring could significantly reduce the incidence of maternal hypertension and IUGR. It should be recognized that increasing protein in the diets of hypertensive mothers who are protein sufficient will not alter maternal–fetal protein transport and may be dangerous. Thus, a "nonnutritional" approach (i.e., treating or preventing hypertension during pregnancy) is the best solution for a nutritional problem in this case.

In general, the American diet already contains sufficient if not excessive protein and thus protein deficiency is rare in the general population. Vegetarian diets are not typically protein deficient and are easily adaptable for toddlers and children to provide adequate, quality protein (AAP Handbook). The effects of postnatal protein malnutrition occurring in populations where childhood starvation is common have been studied between 6 months of age and adulthood. The studies of Ernesto Pollitt's group are particularly instructive (Pollitt and Gorman, 1994). His group established an early supplemental feeding program between birth and 7 years in four Guatemalan villages with endemic protein malnutrition. The mothers, infants, and children in two villages received protein supplements that gave them 25 percent more protein and additional calories than in the two other villages. The group followed outcomes for up to 26 years and noted improved test scores of the children on general knowledge, numeracy, reading, processing time, and vocabulary. Interestingly, there was also an improvement in socioeconomic status as adults, whereas there had been no difference in socioeconomic status between the groups in childhood. Notably, the behavioral outcomes were predictable from brain development events during the period of nutrient intervention.

Micronutrients

The impact of micronutrient deficiencies on cognitive development is staggering and has been underestimated when compared to the effect of protein malnutrition (Benton, 2008; Black, 2003). Elimination of micronutrient deficiencies has been estimated to have the capacity to raise the world's IQ by 10 points with an attendant shift in education and working capacity (Morris et al., 2008). WHO statistics indicate that iron deficiency is the most common nutrient deficiency in the world, affecting 2 billion people (a third of the world's population). Some 30 to 50 percent of pregnant women are iron deficient, placing their fetuses and newborns at risk for the condition. Zinc deficiency affects 1.8 billion people and is usually found in the context of protein deficiency. Two billion people world-wide are iodine deficient with 30 percent during school age. Iodine is a necessary nutrient for thyroid hormone synthesis, which is critical for normal brain development. The hypothyroid state induces the global neurodevelopmental delays termed cretinism.

Moreover, micronutrient deficiencies have the capacity to interact, thus compounding the neurodevelopmental risk. For example, copper deficiency, while relatively rare compared to the others, causes brain iron deficiency because transport of iron across the blood–brain barrier occurs by a copper dependent mechanism (Xu et al., 2004). Iron (or copper) deficiency in turn causes thyroid deficiency (Bastian et al., 2010), which places the brain at risk independent from the direct effects of iron deficiency (Benton, 2008). Iron deficiency increases uptake of lead from the environment because of a common intestinal transporter mechanism (Shah et al., 2010). If dietary iron is not available, the transporter is upregulated in order to capture and transport every possible iron molecule available. However, if iron is not available, other divalent metals will be transported. Among these, lead has the highest affinity for the transporter, although it will also increase potentially toxic manganese or cadmium. Lead toxicity remains a major cause of neurodevelopmental handicap in industrialized societies (Shah et al., 2010). As with studies demonstrating the positive benefits of macronutrient supplementation, there are multiple studies that suggest specific micronutrient supplementation improves acute and long-term cognitive function (reviewed in Benton, 2008; Black, 2003; Morris et al., 2008).

Iron

The developing brain requires iron for enzymes and hemo-proteins that are involved in important cellular processes, including fatty acid production, dopamine neurotransmitter synthesis, and neuronal energy production (Lozoff et al., 2006). The effect on fatty acids results in altered myelin synthesis leading to reduced neuronal processing speed. Iron deficient infants have slower electrical conduction in the central nervous system (Roncagliolo et al., 1998) and this finding persists after iron repletion (Algarin, Peirano, Garrido, Pizarro, and Lozoff, 2003), suggesting that disruption of myelin production during a critical period of its development early in postnatal life results potentially in long-term if not permanent changes in processing speed.

Disruption of monoamine neurotransmitter synthesis was suspected over thirty-five years ago, since tyrosine hydroxylase, a critical enzyme in the synthesis of dopamine, is iron dependent (Youdim et al., 1980). Alterations in dopaminergic neural activity are postulated to lead to the common iron deficiency symptoms of altered mood, paucity of movement, and reduced motivational drive (Lozoff et al., 2006). Newborn infants born to iron deficient mothers show poorer attachment and altered temperament. Combined with the mothers' own iron deficiency symptoms, the maternal–infant dyad can be disrupted from the time of birth (Wachs, 2005). Extensive research in iron deficient rodents and monkeys confirms long-term changes in dopaminergic activity with persistence of behavioral abnormalities (reviewed in Beard and Connor, 2003; Lozoff et al., 2006).

Iron-containing cytochromes located in the mitochondria are responsible for electron transport and adenosine tri-phosphate (ATP) generation to maintain cellular energy status (Dallman, 1986). Energy production and availability is critical for rapidly differentiating neurons that are in the active phase of dendrite and axon formation. Iron deficiency appears to result in reduced ATP generation, essentially creating a metabolic "brown-out" accompanied by sub-par neuronal performance, particularly in brain areas that are highly metabolic (deUngria et al., 2000; Jorgenson et al., 2005). The perinatal hippocampus is one such region and it is not surprising that maternal–fetal iron deficiency negatively impacts hippocampal development and cognitive behaviors by altering dendritic structural development (Carlson et al., 2009).

Children are at particularly greater risk for iron deficiency during three time periods: the fetal/neonatal period, toddlerhood, and adolescence. All of these epochs represent times when the balance between iron supply and iron demand are more likely to be perturbed. Iron deficiency during adolescence is a particular problem for females because of the increased loss of iron rich blood through the onset of menses. Of note, the two earlier time periods are characterized by an extensive literature that suggests the brain does not fully recover from iron deficiency in spite of prompt diagnosis and treatment (Lozoff et al., 2006). The findings are consistent with the concept that prevention of conditions that cause iron deficiency during pregnancy and during the toddler years is the most effective public health method to eradicate long-term neurodevelopmental effects. In contrast, while iron deficiency during the teenage years will alter brain function acutely, long-term effects do not appear to occur. Overall, these findings are consistent with the hypothesis that iron is important for early developmental processes that have finite "critical periods" and that early iron deficiency permanently and irreversibly changes the brain and its function. Later-onset iron deficiency may change the neurochemistry, but not the neuroanatomy and thus allow for more complete recovery with iron treatment.

Fetal/neonatal iron deficiency is a result of maternal gestational conditions that lead to an imbalance of maternal iron supply and/or fetal iron demand (Siddappa et al., 2007). The most common cause world-wide is maternal iron deficiency anemia where the fetus appears to be significantly compromised when the maternal hemoglobin concentration is less than 85 g/L. Maternal anemia of this degree is relatively less common in the developed world due to routine supplementation of mothers during pregnancy and diets that promote iron sufficiency in the pre-pregnancy state. Nevertheless, in low-income populations, the problem continues to exist (Iannotti et al., 2005) and is an opportunity for intervention policy. More common causes of fetal/neonatal iron deficiency in developed countries include maternal cigarette smoking, hypertension, and diabetes mellitus (Siddappa et al., 2007). Gestational hypertension resulting in intrauterine growth restriction complicates up to 5 percent of pregnancies and causes reduced newborn iron stores in 50 percent of the offspring (Chockalingam et al., 1987). The iron deficiency is likely caused by restricted placental flow due to the effects of hypertension on placental structure. Glucose intolerance during pregnancy (gestational diabetes) causes increased fetal demand for iron because of fetal hypoxemia (Georgieff et al., 1990). The increased demand for iron outstrips the placenta's ability to transport maternal iron to the fetus, thus causing a state of iron deficiency. Between 5 and 10 percent of pregnancies are complicated by gestational glucose intolerance and 65 percent of poorly controlled infants born to diabetic mothers have low iron stores (Georgieff et al., 1990). Infants of diabetic mothers and intrauterine growth-restricted infants have a 30–40 percent reduction in brain iron (Petry et al., 1992). Fetal–neonatal iron deficiency results in abnormal recognition memory processing at birth (Siddappa et al., 2004), changes in infant temperament (Wachs et al., 2005), slower neuronal conduction (Amin et al., 2010), poorer learning and memory at 3.5 years (Riggins et al., 2009), and poorer school-age performance (Tamura et al., 2002).

Iron deficiency during toddlerhood is classically due to inadequate dietary iron during a period of relatively rapid growth (Lozoff et al., 2006). Growth puts a great deal of pressure on iron balance because the red blood cell mass must expand rapidly at the same time as the remainder of the body. The red cells are the main repository for body iron and receive prioritization for iron compared to the brain (Georgieff et al., 1992). This prioritization means that once iron deficiency has resulted in anemia, the brain has already lost substantial amounts of iron. Gastrointestinal blood loss contributes to the imbalance of iron supply and iron demand by increasing the demand. Intestinal parasites are the most common cause of intestinal blood loss in developing countries while cow milk allergy is a contributor in developed countries. In the United States, all infant formulas are fortified with sufficient iron to maintain iron homeostasis in the non-stressed, average infant. However, "low-iron" formulas have a smaller margin of error when iron homeostasis is perturbed. Postnatal iron deficiency during toddlerhood affects all three neurologic domains: myelination, dopamine metabolism, and energy production (Lozoff et al., 2006). There are over fifty studies demonstrating that these protean effects of early postnatal iron deficiency on the developing nervous system culminate in overall poorer school performance (Lozoff et al., 2000), slower nerve conduction velocity (Algarin et al., 2003; Roncagliolo et al., 1998), motor abnormalities (Angulo-Kinzler et al., 2002), and cognitive delays and executive functioning abnormalities decades following iron repletion (Lukowski et al., 2010). Iron deficiency in the teenage and early childbearing years has been linked to poorer memory formation; however, treatment reverses these abnormalities, suggesting that the effects are acute neurotransmitter (e.g., dopamine) and energy metabolism effects (Murray-Kolb and Beard, 2007).

Animal models support the findings in humans. Rodents that were iron deficient during gestation and lactation demonstrate abnormal fatty acid profiles during the period of deficiency and well into adulthood following treatment (Connor and Menzies, 1996). These studies support the findings of slower conduction velocity in iron deficient humans (Algarin et al., 2003; Roncagliolo et al., 1998). The extensive alterations in dopaminergic mesocorticolimbic, nigrostriatal, and tuberohypophyseal include alterations in dopamine concentrations as well as in the regional content pathways of dopamine receptors and re-uptake proteins. In the rodent model, these changes are regional with particularly large effects in the striatum. The alteration of striatal dopamine D2 receptors is not rescued by supplementation after weaning and is associated with persistent behavioral abnormalities (reviewed in Beard and Connor, 2003). Finally, iron deficiency induces reduced energy status (deUngria et al., 2000), short- and long-term gene changes (Carlson et al., 2007), abnormal dendrite morphology (Carlson et al., 2009), long-term suppression of brain derived neurotrophic factor (Tran et al., 2009), and reduced electrophysiologic capacity (Jorgenson et al., 2005) in the hippocampus, resulting in poorer short- and long-term learning and memory behavior (Felt and Lozoff, 1996). Iron transport into the hippocampus is required for learning (Carlson et al., 2009), and exclusive disruption of hippocampal iron metabolism through genetic models leads to abnormal recognition memory.

The prevention of maternal iron deficiency anemia is quite straightforward through better identification during prenatal visits and routine iron supplementation. Ironically, the best treatment for iron deficiency due to gestational hypertension or diabetes is not nutritionally based, but through control of those disease processes by screening for glucose intolerance at 28 weeks gestation and through routine blood pressure monitoring during pregnancy. Mothers with pre-pregnancy diabetes mellitus or hypertension deserve closer surveillance. At birth, routine screening of iron status in not warranted except potentially in known risk populations where a serum ferritin concentration and whole blood hemoglobin concentration should be assessed. Current dietary iron recommendations for neonates are published by the American Academy of Pediatrics in their Pediatric Nutrition Handbook (American Academy of Pediatrics, 2009), and by the Institute of Medicine (Institute of Medicine, 2000). Additional iron beyond baseline should be considered for babies who are preterm or small for gestational age, but currently not for infants of diabetic mothers. The AAP and the CDC recommend routine screening for iron deficiency anemia at 9 months of age. The spirit of screening is laudable and important for public health even though the currently used metrics are limited (Beard et al., 2007). Screening for iron deficiency in toddlerhood through the assessment of the presence of anemia makes little sense as public health policy, particularly since there is incomplete behavioral recovery following early brain iron deficiency. However, the diagnosis of pre-anemic iron deficiency is difficult. While serum ferritin concentrations index iron stores, this biomarker is not uniformly available and has the potential for false negatives when the child is infected (Beard et al., 2007). Recently, the CDC has been piloting potentially more sensitive and specific markers of iron status to be applied population-wide. Meat-derived iron is the most bio-available source for toddlers since plant sources frequently contain phytates that bind iron in the intestine and prevent its absorption.

Zinc

The brain requires zinc to be incorporated into enzymes mediating protein and nucleic acid biochemistry. Zinc interacts with DNA and its regulation through zinc fingers (Duncan and Hurley, 1978). It stimulates chloride influx into neurons and is released from presynaptic boutons, thus affecting neurophysiologic efficacy in the central nervous system (Li, Rosenberg, and Chiu, 1994). This appears to be particularly prominent in the developing autonomic nervous system that will ultimately regulate stress responses. Zinc regulates brain growth since it is an important co-factor in the expression of insulin-like growth factor-I (IGF-I) (McNall, Etherton, and Fosmire, 1995), a finding that seems particularly salient to the developing hippocampus in the young child (Fredrickson and Danscher, 1990).

Humans are at risk for zinc deficiency in the fetal period due to maternal zinc deficiency and in the postnatal period, often coupled with protein malnutrition since protein is a major source of dietary zinc. While not particularly common in the United States, zinc deficiency is very common world-wide because of poor dietary zinc intake (particularly in societies that do not consume meat routinely) and the fact that recurrent and chronic infections reduce zinc availability (Black, 2003; Golub et al., 1994). Fetuses of zinc deficient mothers demonstrate reduced fetal movement and decreased heart rate variability, both signs of altered autonomic nervous system stability. After birth, these infants demonstrate reduced preferential looking behavior indicative of disordered hippocampal development and a harbinger of longer-term cognitive dysfunction. The effects are subtle, however, with no apparent cognitive reduction on the Bayley Scales of Infant Development. Postnatal zinc deficiency occurs after 6 months of age and can extend throughout childhood. Infants with postnatal acquired dietary zinc deficiency exhibit abnormal medial temporal lobe, frontal lobe, and cerebellar-based behaviors, including reduced performance on delayed match and non-match to sample, short-term visual memory, spatial orientation memory, and abstract reasoning and concept formation (reviewed in Black, 2003; Duggan et al., 2005).

Animal models confirm these regional and global effects on cognitive and non-cognitive systems. The effects of fetal zinc deficiency due to maternal causes indicate that the autonomic nervous system, the cerebellum, and the hippocampus are at risk (Fredrickson and Danscher, 1990; Sandstead et al., 2000). Zinc deficiency results in decreased fetal brain DNA, RNA, and protein content (Duncan and Hurley, 1978), and reduced IGF-I and growth hormone receptor gene expression (McNall et al., 1995). Two-year-old zinc deficient rhesus monkeys demonstrate reduced spontaneous motor activity and poorer short-term memory (Golub et al., 1994), consistent with the cerebellar and hippocampal effects suggested by the human studies (Black, 2003; Duggan et al., 2005).

Fetal zinc deficiency is preventable by maintaining dietary zinc adequacy in the mother and treating gastrointestinal infections that might impair zinc metabolism. The breastfed or formula-fed infant is relatively protected from zinc deficiency. However, the risk of postnatal zinc deficiency increases after 6 months of age because the concentrations of divalent cations (e.g., iron, zinc, copper) decrease in breast milk irrespective of maternal diet. Introduction of complementary foods after this age to supply these cations is necessary (Krebs and Hambidge, 2007). In older children, zinc sufficiency can be maintained either by providing an adequate source of zinc in the natural diet (e.g., meat) or by supplementation (e.g., a multivitamin that also contains minerals). Irrespective, control of chronic or recurrent infections is key to assuring that the dietary zinc is appropriately assimilated.

Iodine

The brain's requirement for iodine stems from its primary role in thyroid hormone synthesis. Iodine is incorporated into thyroxine (T4) and tri-iodothyronine (T3). Thyroid hormone regulates neuronal metabolic rate, neuronal cell replication, and neuronal differentiation. Thyroid hormone also regulates fatty acid synthesis and thus is crucial in myelination. Absence of thyroid hormone results in cretinism, which is a major cause of cognitive disability world-wide (reviewed in Anderson, Schoonover, and Jones, 2003; Black, 2003; Morris et al., 2008).

Fetuses and children are at risk for iodine deficiency throughout their entire developmental period if they live in a region of the world that is endemically low in iodine such as Africa, Central and Southeast Asia, India and China (www.worldmapper.org/display). Cassava root is a major and cheap source of staple food (and a cash crop) in many parts of the world. While an excellent source of calories, it contains a compound, thiocyanate, which inhibits iodine absorption. The effects are exacerbated in populations where mild to moderate iodine deficiency already exists (Zimmermann et al., 2000). Timing of the deficiency is critical, since the effects on the fetus are much more profound than during later childhood. The greatest effects of iodine deficiency are during the first 12 weeks of fetal life, a time period where a large number of women will not have confirmed that they are pregnant. Iodine deficiency during fetal life results in reduced head size and irreversible global mental deficits that may reduce the total IQ by 15 points or more. Cretinism is the most profound preventable cause of IQ deficit in the world. Iodine deficiency during childhood reduces verbal IQ and decreases reaction time on motor tasks (Lomborg, 2009). The effects on older children appear to be more reversible, suggesting that hypothyroidism causes a reduction in metabolic processing of the brain as opposed to an anatomic defect as might be expected in the younger child or fetus. In this timing sense, iodine deficiency is similar to iron deficiency.

Animal models of early iodine deficiency support the global and region-specific effects noted in humans. These include lower total brain weight and DNA, reduced dendritic arborization, less myelination, and reduced synaptic counts (reviewed in Anderson et al., 2003). As with the human studies, timing appears to be critical with earlier iodine deficiency causing more global and irreversible effects.

Prevention of iodine deficiency must begin in the preconceptional time period in order to protect the offspring's brain health, since the most major effects occur in the first 12 weeks of pregnancy. As cassava becomes a more and more attractive cash crop, particularly in iodine deficient areas of Africa, efforts to detoxify cassava during its processing will be an important part of the intervention. Newborn iodine deficiency may well present as congenital hypothyroidism that will be picked up on newborn screening in countries that practice it. In the United States, all states have newborn screening of thyroid status. Postnatal iodine deficiency is rare in the United States because of the use of iodized salt, but is far more common in other countries that do not iodize their salt, do not consume marine life, or consume goitrogenic foods such as cassava root.

Vitamins

Parents in the United States appear to be fixated on vitamins for their children as a nutritional panacea. Nothing could be further from the truth in the US where the general population is sufficient with respect to vitamins. While certain vitamins (e.g., A, B6, B12, C) have an important role in brain development and brain function, their deficiencies are exceedingly rare. The only exception may be vitamin D, where there is a growing concern about deficiency in children. Vitamin D deficiency stems primarily from a lack of adequate sunlight exposure, although the condition can be treated with dietary vitamin D. Vitamin D may play a role in brain development through its regulation of large numbers of genes (Levenson and Figueiroa, 2008), but studies on regional or global effects of vitamin D deficiency as a function of timing, dose, and duration have not been performed. In developing countries, the picture is quite different. Vitamin A deficiency continues to be a problem in Africa. Vitamin A is necessary for normal visual development. B12 deficiency has also been documented as a cause of abnormal neurodevelopment (Dror and Allen, 2008).

The routine supplementation of pregnant women with vitamins is becoming standard practice in the United States and many women continue these preparations post-partum into the lactation period. Breastfed infants should receive a source of vitamin D (American Academy of Pediatrics, 2009) because human milk is low in vitamin D and mothers are not encouraged to expose their babies to sunlight. Formula-fed infants receive sufficient vitamin D. Routine vitamin supplementation of older children is discouraged by the AAP (American Academy of Pediatrics, 2009), unless there are extenuating circumstances that put the child at risk for deficiency such as malabsorption syndromes or a particularly unbalanced diet.

Can nutrients enhance brain development?

There has always been interest in potential "brain foods" that would sustainably enhance brain development. Unfortunately, it has been difficult to truly establish where the point of repletion of a deficiency ends and supplementation begins within a population or a model system. The danger of the "if some is good, more must be better" thinking is that it ignores the risks associated with nutrient excess. Most nutrients demonstrate a U-shaped risk curve (Figure 4.1).

While the increased risks of undernutrition are well recognized because as a species we have primarily been concerned with having an adequate amount to eat throughout our history, the risks of overnutrition have only recently risen to the surface. Nevertheless, the hunt for "brain enhancers" continues and a number of candidates are on the horizon, including choline, oligosaccharides, neurotrophic factors, and supplemental fish oils. Many of the investigations are driven by the finding that breastfed infants have superior neurodevelopment in a manner dose-dependent to the duration of human milk feeding (Mortensen et al., 2002). Human milk has many candidate molecules that support optimal brain development including those listed above. However, it must be noted that the matrix in which nutrients are delivered is an important determinant of efficacy and, conversely, isolating a single factor and placing it in a

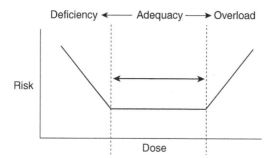

Figure 4.1 The U-shaped nutrition risk curve.

different matrix (e.g., formula or a supplement) may reduce or abolish its efficacy.

The scientific literatures on dietary choline and docosohexaenoic acid (DHA) are the most extensive. DHA is a long-chain polyunsaturated fatty acid (LC-PUFA) found in breast milk and in multiple food sources but in highest concentration in cold-water fatty fish. It is transported by the placenta to the fetus and has effects on myelin production, neuronal membrane fatty acid composition, and synaptogenesis. It may be involved in cell signaling. Severe deficiency leads to altered fatty acid profiles and abnormal behavior including visual speed of processing (reviewed in Georgieff and Innis, 2005; Heird and Lapillonne, 2005). Premature birth disrupts transplacental delivery and places the preterm infant at risk for deficiency since the ability to synthesize these compounds *de novo* is limited in the preterm infant. Consumption of fish in the United States is quite low in comparison to other regions of the world, resulting in lower maternal serum and breast milk levels.

Human studies on DHA are quite variable in their impact on brain development. Long-term outcome trials of DHA supplementation of pregnant women, preterm infants, term infants, and children are ongoing. Most do not make a distinction between supplementation of populations that are deficient (or at risk for deficiency) versus those that are sufficient. The effects of supplementation on cognitive development are somewhat persuasive in preterm infants (Heird and Lapillonne, 2005), but not in term infants (Simmer, Patole, and Rao, 2008). Whether any improvements are consistently sustained into later childhood has not been determined. It is possible that, like many early neural enhancements, effects will wash out over time, particularly if the dietary supplement is not maintained. Pregnant women are now supplemented with DHA because it is effective in reducing the rate of preterm birth (Carlson, 2009). Whether the offspring of those women demonstrate superior cognitive development remains to be shown.

The research on dietary choline supplementation has quite different roots from DHA. Choline is quite ubiquitous in the human diet (e.g., eggs are a good source). Studies in pregnant rodents previously established that offspring of choline deficient mothers perform poorly on memory tasks. More importantly, supplementation of choline beyond sufficient amounts in the pregnant dam enhanced hippocampal development and learning and memory performance in the offspring. The findings include more complex neuronal structure, improved synaptogeneis, improved electrophysiology, and modification of genes that influence neuronal cell cycle, differentiation learning, and memory (Wong-Goodrich et al., 2008; Zeisel, 2009). Rodents with significant and quite varied risk factors to neurodevelopment, including those exposed to fetal alcohol (Thomas et al., 2010) and those with a Rett's Syndrome or Down's Syndrome phenotype, showed behavioral improvement when the mothers were treated with choline during specific time points in pregnancy (Ward et al., 2009; Moon et al., 2010). This has led to a number of ongoing human trials of choline supplementation, mostly in risk populations. Whether the enhancement of learning and memory in normal rats will be translated into human studies and ultimately into human dietary recommendations remains to be seen.

Nutrient delivery and nutrient assimilation: the roles of stress and poverty in nutrition

There is growing concern that simply considering nutrient supply is not wholly adequate to address the issues of the brain effects of malnutrition. Nutrient absorption, trafficking within the body, and assimilation into tissue growth are complex processes mediated only in part by the availability of the nutrient to the fetus or child. Most nutrients are not 100 percent absorbed by the intestine. The uptake of some nutrients (e.g., iron) is regulated by body stores and perceived demand, in order to meet supply without resulting in overload. These regulatory processes may be immature in young infants and result in less than precise regulation of uptake. Moreover, non-nutritional conditions such as generalized or local gastrointestinal infection can reduce nutrient absorption, particularly iron and zinc. Thus, measuring intake may not give an accurate assessment of nutrient availability for tissue growth. Once absorbed, nutrients are trafficked to various organs, including the brain, and priorities are made within the organ on how and where the nutrients are utilized. For example, iron is preferentially trafficked to the fetal and neonatal red cells over the brain and thus brain iron sufficiency cannot be ensured in the face of insufficient iron for red cell production (Georgieff et al., 1992). In perhaps a rather unique example, body iron is sequestered in the reticulo-endothelial system during infections to limit its availability for bacterial growth and replication. The resultant lack of availability of iron for erythropoiesis results in the anemia of inflammation (Ganz and Nemeth, 2009) and also likely brain iron deficiency.

Finally, nutrients do not act alone. Their metabolic effects in the cell are mediated by signaling cascades like mammalian target of rapamycin (mTOR) that regulate rates of protein translation (e.g., tissue generation), incidence of autophagy, and actin polymerization (Wullschleger, Loewith, and Hall, 2006). The effect on actin polymerization is particularly important for optimizing neuronal dendrite complexity. The signaling cascade is controlled by the availability of favorable nutrient conditions combined with the presence of growth factors, which are small-sized proteins (e.g., IGF-I, growth hormone, BDNF, Nerve Growth Factor). Some growth factors are general and are synthesized both in the liver and in the target organ, while others are more organ specific. Without growth factors, cells will not differentiate in spite of adequate nutrients, and conversely, without nutrients, growth factors cannot mediate growth. Growth factors are regulated by nutrient availability, especially protein and zinc, and their synthesis is suppressed by infection as well as malnutrition (Srinivasan, 2010). The role of infection in nutritional physiology thus cannot be ignored. Chronically infected children grow poorly, are anemic, and, not surprisingly, perform poorly on developmental tests and in the classroom. Non-infectious stress activates similar pathways that induce insulin resistance and activates cortisol and pro-inflammatory cytokine production (Jones et al., 2006). These, in turn, divert amino acids from protein synthesis, sending them through gluconeogenic pathways to maintain acute energy sufficiency.

Poverty plays an important role in the stress–nutrition interaction. A state of poverty frequently dictates making food choices driven by financial rather than nutritional concerns. In addition, recent evidence suggests that anxiety and stress increase food consumption. When this is combined with foods of poor nutritional value, it should not be surprising to find that obesity is a sign of poverty. Recent investigations suggest that certain populations of rapidly growing newborns (Pylipow et al., 2009) and obese children demonstrate aberrant cognitive functioning (Lokken et al., 2005). Although the mechanisms are likely to be multi-factorial, the role of stress and its interaction with nutrition probably reside in the equation. Future research should consider in greater depth whether the success of nutritional intervention programs is being compromised by non-nutritional factors.

Implications for policy

The need to provide optimal nutrition to its population has been a mainstay of American domestic policy and world-wide relief efforts for decades. The key goal of policies should be to rectify chronic deficiencies of nutrients in mothers and in young children that have an impact on children's brain development and cognitive functioning. Generally, these deficiencies are well documented in populations and their rectification involves better delivery systems and education of the population. Relieving this chronic burden world-wide will have potential far-reaching educational and employment consequences (Morris et al., 2008; Pollitt and Gorman, 1994). The fundamental impediments to adequate nutrition are two: poverty and ignorance. The former tends to be the issue in developing countries, although there is concern about malnutrition (particularly iron deficiency) in low-income populations in the US (Iannotti et al., 2005). Poverty impedes adequate nutrition in both cases due to a reliance on diets that are dominant in carbohydrates and fat (and in the US, salt), and inadequate in protein, zinc, and iron. In developing countries, diets are often based on foods that are only locally available. When these foods are inadequate in a given macro- or micronutrient or inhibit the absorption of important micronutrients, supplementation programs are likely the best policy option.

In the US, where diverse food is relatively available, changes in nutritional quality should be encouraged to occur through consumption of food products rather than supplements. Poor food choices are made on an economic basis (e.g., poor-quality food is generally less expensive) or because of ignorance. The former is solved through programs that ensure good-quality foods for mothers, newborns, and young children, of which WIC is a good example. School lunch programs are effective, particularly for children who would not otherwise receive lunch. School breakfast programs would provide another excellent opportunity to ensure children are not starting the school day hungry (Hoyland, Dye, and Lawton, 2009). To further improve nutrition through this mechanism, it is important for children to make informed choices about the foods provided in these programs. Unfortunately, nutrient-poor food options (along with the good choices) continue to exist in subsidized school lunch programs and, not surprisingly, children will tend to choose the poor-quality foods that are high in salt and fat because they are more flavorful.

Willful or non-willful ignorance of good nutrition is problematic to deal with at the policy level. There are many influences on family food choices, including parental influence (e.g., family custom), peer pressure, and taste (e.g., salty and fatty foods) and, perhaps, health care professionals. The role of family custom and peer pressure is evident in the choice a new mother makes whether to breastfeed or not (Gartner et al., 2005). In school lunch programs, there would have to be virtual elimination of poor-quality food options in order to ensure adequate nutrition – something the government has not been willing to enforce in its contracts with schools and food suppliers. Nutrition education of the consumer and the health care professional would seem to play an important part as well. Sadly, very little nutritional training currently takes place in medical schools, and health care providers, particularly physicians, seem reluctant to inquire about and counsel families on adequate nutrition.

Thus, from a population-based standpoint, prevention of nutrient deficiencies that affect offspring cognitive development begin with the mother prior to her pregnancy to ensure that she is entering the pregnancy in optimal nutritional condition. During pregnancy, mothers should be routinely supplemented with prenatal vitamins that contain iron and likely DHA. Moreover, non-nutritional factors that affect maternal–fetal nutritional status such as diabetes mellitus, hypertension, and infections must be screened for and treated and monitored if present. Thus, adequate prenatal care is a non-nutritional intervention that can have a powerful impact. Finally, mothers must be counseled during their pregnancy about the benefits of breastfeeding their newborn since the decision to breast-feed is rarely made after the infant is born (Gartner et al., 2005). All mothers should be encouraged to breastfeed their infants, unless there is a medical contraindication, in order to optimize their infants' brain health (Gartner et al., 2005). In the US, campaigns that demonstrate breastfeeding as normative and incentivize it are critical to change public perception and behavior (Gartner et al., 2005). Infants should be breastfed for one year, following which balanced nutrient diet becomes the responsibility of the family. While social programs (e.g., WIC) are helpful, full implementation of balanced nutrient diets will likely rely on behavioral changes including limitation of potentially nutrient poor foods. In a free market society, this is quite difficult to achieve, particularly if it relies on universal screening, dietary change, and supplementation. Instead, the medical community must have the knowledge base and resources to perform targeted screening for at-risk nutrients in their community and to act upon that information – a relatively inefficient solution. Internationally, it is critical to sustain and expand programs that deliver nutrients that are known to be endemically deficient (e.g., iron, iodine, zinc, protein).

While this chapter has dealt predominantly with prevention of long-standing nutrient deficits that affect brain development (e.g., protein and iron deficiencies), it is important to note that nutrients also acutely affect brain performance. Hungry children do not perform well in school (Hoyland et al., 2009) even if they are otherwise total body nutrient sufficient. Thus, school breakfast and lunch programs serve the dual purpose of preventing long-term deficits as well as providing adequate fuel to the functioning brain.

References

Algarin, C., Peirano, P., Garrido, M., Pizarro, F., and Lozoff, B. (2003). Iron deficiency anemia in infancy: long-lasting effects on auditory and visual system functioning. *Pediatric Research*, 53, 217–223.

American Academy of Pediatrics (2009). *Pediatric nutrition handbook* (6th edn). Elk Grove Village, IL: AAP Press.

Amin, S. B., Orlando, M., Eddins, A., MacDonald, M., Monczynski, C., and Wang, H. (2010). In utero iron status and auditory neural maturation in premature infants as evaluated by auditory brainstem response. *Journal of Pediatrics*, 156(3), 377–381.

Anderson, G. W., Schoonover, C. M., and Jones, S. A. (2003). Control of thyroid hormone action in the developing rat brain. *Thyroid*, 13, 1039–1056.

Angulo-Kinzler, R. M., Peirano, P., Lin, E., Garrido, M., and Lozoff, B. (2002). Spontaneous motor activity in human infants with iron-deficiency anemia. *Early Human Development*, 66, 67–79.

Bastian, T. W., Prohaska, J. R., Georgieff, M. K., and Anderson, G. W. (2010). Perinatal iron and copper deficiencies alter neonatal rat circulating and brain thyroid hormone levels. *Endocrinology*, 151, 4055–65.

Beard, J. L., and Connor, J. R. (2003). Iron status and neural functioning. *Annual Review of Nutrition*, 23, 41–58.

Beard, J. L., de-Regnier, R. A., Shaw, M., Rao, R., and Georgieff, M. K. (2007). Diagnosis of iron deficiency in infants. *Laboratory Medicine*, 38, 103–108.

Benton, D. (2008). Micronutrient status, cognition and behavioral problems in childhood. *European Journal of Nutrition*, 47(3), 38–50.

Black, M. M. (2003). Micronutrient deficiencies and cognitive functioning. *Journal of Nutrition*, 133, 3927S–3931S.

Carlson, E. S., Stead, J. D. H., Neal, C. R., Petryk, A., and Georgieff, M. K. (2007). Perinatal iron deficiency results in altered developmental expression of genes mediating energy metabolism and neuronal morphogenesis in hippocampus. *Hippocampus*, 17, 679–691.

Carlson, E. S., Tkac, I., Magid, R., O'Connor, M. B., Andrew, N. C., Schallert, T., ... and Petryk, A. (2009). Iron is essential for neuron development and memory function in mouse hippocampus. *Journal of Nutrition*, 139, 672–679.

Carlson, S. E. (2009). Docosahexaenoic acid supplementation in pregnancy and lactation. *American Journal of Clinical Nutrition*, 89, 678S–684S.

Chockalingam, U. M., Murphy, E., Ophoven, J. C., Weisdorf, S. A., and Georgieff, M. K. (1987). Cord transferrin and ferritin values in newborn infants at risk for prenatal uteroplacental insufficiency and chronic hypoxia. *Journal of Pediatrics*, 111, 283–286.

Connor, J. R., and Menzies, S. L. (1996). Relationship of iron to oligodendrocytes and myelination. *Glia*, 17, 83–93.

Dallman, P. R. (1986). Biochemical basis for the manifestations of iron deficiency. *Annual Review of Nutrition*, 6, 13–40.

deUngria, M., Rao, R., Wobken, J. D., Luciana, M., Nelson, C. A., and Georgieff, M. K. (2000). Perinatal iron deficiency decreases cytochrome c oxidase activity in selective regions of neonatal rat brain. *Pediatric Research*, 48, 169–176.

Dobbing, J., and Sands, J. (1979). Comparative aspects of the brain growth spurt. *Early Human Development*, 3, 79–83.

Dror, D. K., and Allen, L. H. (2008). Effect of vitamin B12 deficiency on neuro-development in infants: current knowledge and possible mechanisms. *Nutrition Review*, 66, 250–255.

Duggan, C., MacLeod, W. B., Krebs, N. F., Westcott, J. L., Fawzi, W. W., Zul, G. P., ... and Zinc Against Plasmodium Study Group (2005). Plasma zinc concentrations are depressed during the acute phase response in children with falciparum malaria. *Journal of Nutrition*, 1325, 802–807.

Duncan, J., and Hurley, L. (1978). Thymidine kinase and DNA polymerase activity in normal and zinc deficient developing rat embryos. *Proceedings of the Society of Experimental Biology Medicine*, 159, 39–43.

Felt, B. T., and Lozoff, B. (1996). Brain iron and behavior of rats are not normal-ized by treatment of iron deficiency anemia during early development. *Journal of Nutrition*, 126, 693–701.

Fredrickson, C., and Danscher, G. (1990). Zinc-containing neurons in hippo-campus and related CNS structures. *Progress in Brain Research*, 83, 71–84.

Fuglestad, A. J., Rao, R., and Georgieff, M. K. (2008). The role of nutrition in cognitive development. In C. A. Nelson and M. Luciana (eds.), *Handbook of developmental cognitive neuroscience* (2nd edn, pp. 623–637). Cambridge, MA: The MIT Press.

Ganz, T., and Nemeth, E. (2009). Iron sequestration and anemia of inflamma-tion. *Seminars in Hematology*, 46, 387–93.

Gartner, L. M., Morton, J., Lawrence, R. A., Naylor, A. J., O'Hare, D., Schanler, R. J., and Eidelman, A. I. (2005). Breastfeeding and the use of human milk. *Pediatrics*, 115, 496–506.

Georgieff, M. K., and Innis, S. (2005). Controversial nutrients in the perinatal period that potentially affect neurodevelopment: essential fatty acids and iron. *Pediatric Research*, 57, 99R–103R.

Georgieff, M. K., Landon, M. B., Mills, M. M., Hedlund, B. E., Faassen, A. E., Schmidt, R. L., ... and Widness, J. A. (1990). Abnormal iron distribution in infants of diabetic mothers: spectrum and maternal antecedents. *Journal of Pediatrics*, 117, 455–461.

Georgieff, M. K., Schmidt, R. L., Mills, M. M., Radmer, W. J., and Widness, J. A. (1992). Fetal iron and cytochrome c status after intrauterine hypoxemia and erythropoietin administration. *American Journal of Physiology*, 262, R485–R491.

Golub, M. S., Takeuchi, P. T., Keen, C. L., Gershwin, M. E., Hendrickx, A. G., and Lonnerdal, B. (1994). Modulation of behavioral performance of prepu-bertal monkeys by moderate dietary zinc deprivation. *American Journal of Clinical Nutrition*, 60, 238–243.

Heird, W. C., and Lapillonne, A. (2005). The role of essential fatty acids in development. *Annual Review of Nutrition*, 25, 549–571.

Hoyland, A., Dye, L., and Lawton, C. L. (2009). A systematic review of the effect of breakfast on the cognitive performance of children and adolescents. *Nutrition Research Reviews*, 22, 220–243.

Iannotti, L. L., O'Brien, K. O., Chang, S. C., Mancini, J., Schulman-Nathanson, M., Liu, S., ... and Witter, F. R. (2005). Iron deficiency anemia and depleted body iron reserves are prevalent among pregnant African-American adoles-cents. *Journal of Nutrition*, 135(11), 2572–2577.

Institute of Medicine (2000). *DRI: Dietary reference intakes.* Washington, DC: National Academy Press.

Jones, A., Godfrey, K. M., Wood, P., Osmond, C., Goulden, P., and Phillips, D. I. (2006). Fetal growth and the adrenocortical response to psychological stress. *Journal of Clinical Endocrinology*, 91(5), 1868–1871.

Jorgenson, L. A., Sun, M., O'Connor, M., and Georgieff, M. K. (2005). Fetal iron deficiency disrupts the maturation of synaptic function and efficacy in area CAI of the developing rat hippocampus. *Hippocampus*, 15, 1094–1102.

Ke, X., Lei, Q., James, S. J., Kelleher, S. L., Melnyk, S., Jernigan, S., ... and Lane, R. H. (2005). Uteroplacental insufficiency affects epigenetic determinants of chromatin structure in brains of neonatal and juvenile IUGR rats. *Physiological Genomics*, 25, 16–28.

Krebs, N. F., and Hambidge, K. M. (2007). Complementary feeding: clinically relevant factors affecting timing and composition. *American Journal of Clinical Nutrition*, 85, 639S–645S.

Kretchmer, N., Beard, J. L., and Carlson, S. (1996). The role of nutrition in the development of normal cognition. *American Journal of Clinical Nutrition*, 63, 997S–1001S.

Lee, K-H., Kalikoglu, A., Ye, P., and D'Ercole, A. J. (1997). Insulin-like growth factor-I (IGF-I) ameliorates and IGF binding protein-1 (IGFBP-1) exacerbates the effects of undernutrition on brain growth during early postnatal life: studies of IGF-I and IGFBP-1 transgenic mice. *Pediatric Research*, 45, 331–336.

Levenson, C. W., and Figueiroa, S. M. (2008). Gestational vitamin D deficiency: long-term effects on the brain. *Nutrition Review*, 66, 726–729.

Li, M., Rosenberg, H., and Chiu, T. (1994). Zinc inhibition of GABA-stimulated Cl-flux in rat brain regions is unaffected by acute or chronic benzodiazepine. *Pharmacology Biochemistry and Behavior*, 49, 477–482.

Lokken, K. L., Boeka, A. G., Austin, H. M., Gunstad, J., and Harmon, C. M. (2005). Evidence of executive dysfunction in extremely obese adolescents: a pilot study. *Surgery for Obesity and Related Diseases*, 5, 547–572.

Lomborg, B. (2009). *Global crises, global solutions* (2nd edn). Cambridge University Press.

Lozoff, B., Beard, J., Connor, J., Felt, B., Georgieff, M., and Schallert, T. (2006). Long-lasting neural and behavioral effects of early iron deficiency in infancy. *Nutrition Review*, 64, S34-S43.

Lozoff, B., Jimenez, F., Hagen, J., Mollen, E., and Wolf, A. W. (2000). Poorer behavioral and developmental outcome more than 10 years after treatment for iron deficiency in infancy. *Pediatrics*, 105, E51.

Lukowski, A. F., Koss, M., Burden, M. J., Jonides, J., Nelson, C. A., Kaciroti, N., ... and Lozoff, B. (2010). Iron deficiency in infancy and neurocognitive functioning at 19 years: evidence of long-term deficits in executive function and recognition memory. *Nutritional Neuroscience*, 13(2), 54–70.

McNall, A., Etherton, T., and Fosmire, G. (1995). The impaired growth induced by zinc deficiency in rats is associated with decreased expression of hepatic insulin-like growth factor 1 and growth hormone receptor genes. *Journal of Nutrition*, 124, 874–879.

Moon, J., Chen, M., Gandhy, S. U., Strawderman, M., Levitsky, D. A., Maclean, K. N., and Stupp, B. J. (2010). Perinatal choline supplementation improves cognitive functioning and emotion regulation in the Ts65Dn moue model of Down syndrome. *Behavioral Neuroscience*, 124, 346–361.

Morris, S. S., Cogill, B., and Uauy, R. (2008). Maternal and child undernutrition study group. Effective international action against undernutrition: why has it proven so difficult and what can be done to accelerate progress? *The Lancet*, 16, 371(9612), 608–621.

Mortensen, E. L., Michaelsen, K. F., Sanders, S. A., and Reinisch, J. M. (2002). The association between duration of breastfeeding and adult intelligence. *Journal of the American Medical Association*, 287, 2365–71.

Murray-Kolb, L. E., and Beard, J. L. (2007). Iron treatment normalizes cognitive functioning in young women. *American Journal of Clinical Nutrition*, 85, 778–787.

Nelson, C. A. (1995). The ontogeny of human memory: a cognitive neuroscience perspective. *Developmental Psychopathology*, 31, 723–738.

Nelson, C. A., Bloom, F. E., Cameron, J. L., Amaral, D., Dahl, R. E., and Pine, D. (2002). An integrative, multidisciplinary approach to the study of brain–behavior relations in the context of typical and atypical development. *Developmental Psychopathology*, 14, 499–520.

Petry, C. D., Eaton, M. A., Wobken, J. D., Mills, M. M., Johnson, D. E., and Georgieff, M. K. (1992). Iron deficiency of liver, heart, and brain in newborn infants of diabetic mothers. *Journal of Pediatrics*, 121, 109–114.

Pollitt, E., and Gorman, K. S. (1994). Nutritional deficiencies as developmental risk factors. In C. A. Nelson (ed.), *Threats to optimal development. The Minnesota Symposia on Child Psychology* (vol. 27, pp. 121–144). Hillsdale, NJ: Erlbaum Associates.

Pylipow, M., Spector, L. G., Puumala, S. E., Boys, C., Cohen, J., and Georgieff, M. K. (2009). Early postnatal weight gain, intellectual performance, and body mass index (BMI) at seven years of age in term infants with intrauterine growth-restriction (IUGR). *Journal of Pediatrics*, 154, 201–206.

Riggins, T., Miller, N. C., Bauer, P. J., Georgieff, M. K., and Nelson, C. A. (2009). Electrophysiological indices of memory for temporal order in early childhood: implications for the development of recollection. *Developmental Science*, 12, 209–219.

Roncagliolo, M., Garrido, M., Walter, T., Peirano, P., and Lozoff, B. (1998). Evidence of altered central nervous system development in infants with iron deficiency anemia at 6 mo: delayed maturation of auditory brainstem responses. *American Journal of Clinical Nutrition*, 68, 683–690.

Sandstead, H. H., Fredrickson, C. J., and Penland, J. G. (2000). History of zinc as related to brain function. *Journal of Nutrition*, 130, 496S–502S.

Shah, F., Kazi, T. G., Afridi, H. I., Baig, J. A., Khan, S., Kolachi, N. F., ... and Shah, A. Q. (2010). Environmental exposure of lead and iron deficient anemia in children age ranged 1–5 years: a cross sectional study. *Science of the Total Environment*, 408, 5325–5330.

Siddappa, A. M., Georgieff, M. K., Wewerka, S., Worwa, C., Nelson, C. A., and Deregnier, R. A. (2004). Iron deficiency alters auditory recognition memory in newborn infants of diabetic mothers. *Pediatric Research*, 55, 1034–1041.

Siddappa, A. M., Rao, R., Long, J. D., Widness, J. A., and Georgieff, M. K. (2007). The assessment of newborn iron stores at birth: a review of the literature and standards for ferritin concentrations. *Neonatology*, 92, 73–82.

Simmer, K., Patole, S. K., and Rao, S. C. (2008). Longchain polyunsaturated fatty acid supplementation in infants born at term. *Cochrane Database System Review*, 23(1), CD000376.

Spruston, N. (2008). Pyramidal neurons: dendritic structure and synaptic integration. *Nature Reviews Neuroscience*, 9, 206–221.

Srinivasan, B. (2010). Somatotropic axis dysfunction in pediatric sepsis-induced multiple organ dysfunction syndrome ... a matter of "growing" importance! *Pediatric Critical Care Medicine*, 11, 145–146.

Strauss, R. S., and Dietz, W. H. (1998). Growth and development of term children born with low birth weight: effects of genetic and environmental factors. *Journal of Pediatrics*, 133, 67–72.

Tamura, T., Goldenberg, R. L., Hou, J. R., Johnston, K. E., Cliver, S. P., Ramey, S. L., and Nelson, K. G. (2002). Cord serum ferritin concentrations and mental and psychomotor development of children at five years of age. *Journal of Pediatrics*, 140, 165–170.

Thomas, J. D., Idrus, N. M., Monk, B. R., and Dominguez, H. D. (2010). Prenatal choline supplementation mitigates behavioral alterations associated with prenatal alcohol exposure in rats. *Birth Defects Research A Clinical and Molecular Teratology*, Aug.12 [Epub.].

Thompson, R. A., and Nelson, C. A. (2001). Developmental science and the media: early brain development. *American Psychologist*, 56(1), 5–15.

Tran, P. V., Fretham, S. J. B., Carlson, E. S., and Georgieff, M. K. (2009). Long term reduction of hippocampal brain derived neurotrophic factor activity after fetal neonatal iron deficiency in adult rats. *Pediatric Research*, 65, 493–498.

Wachs, T. D., Pollitt, E., Cueto, S., and Jacoby, E. (2005). Relation of neonatal iron status to individual variability in neonatal temperament. *Developmental Psychobiology*, 46, 141–153.

Ward, B. C., Kolodny, N. H., Nag, N., and Berger-Sweeney, J. E. (2009). Neurochemical changes in a mouse model of Rett syndrome: changes over time and in reponse to perinatal choline nutritional supplementation. *Journal of Neurochemistry*, 108, 361–371.

Winick, M., and Rosso, P. (1969). The effect of severe early malnutrition on cellular growth of the human brain. *Pediatric Research*, 3, 181–184.

Wong-Goodrich, S. J. E., Glenn, M. J., Mellott, T. J., Blusztajn, J. K., Meck, W. H., and Williams, C. L. (2008). Spatial memory and hippocampal plasticity are differentially sensitive to the availability of choline in adulthood as a function of choline supply in utero. *Brain Research*, 1237, 153–166.

Wullschleger, S., Loewith, R., and Hall, M. N. (2006). TOR signaling in growth and metabolism. *Cell*, 124, 471–484.

Xu, X., Pin, S., Gathinji, M., Fuchs, R., and Harris, Z. L. (2004). Aceruloplasminemia: an inherited neurodegenerative disease with impairment of iron homeostasis. *Annals of the New York Academy of Science*, 1012, 299–305.

Youdim, M. B. H., Green, A. R., Bloomfield, M. R., Mitchell, B. D., Heal, D. J., and Grahamesmith, D. G. (1980). The effects of iron deficiency on brain biogenic monoamine biochemistry and function in rats. *Neuropharmacology*, 19, 259–267.

Zeisel, S. H. (2009). Epigenetic mechanisms for nutrition determinants of later health outcomes. *American Journal of Clinical Nutrition*, 89, S1488–S1493.

Zimmermann, M., Adou, P., Torresani, T., Zeder, C., and Hurrell, R. (2000). Persistence of goiter despite oral iodine supplementation in goitrous children with iron deficiency anemia in Côte d'Ivoire. *American Journal of Clinical Nutrition*, 71, 88–93.

5   Dental health in at-risk children

Sharon Rolnick

Background

Oral health in children is often overlooked, yet tooth decay is the most common disease in children (Edelstein, 2002; Edelstein and Douglass, 1995; Silk, 2010; Yost and Li, 2008). Oral health problems affect a significant number of children and those from low-income families are at greatest risk. Some studies have reported that poor oral health is associated with failure to thrive in infants (Berg and Coniglio, 2006; Mouradian, Berg, and Somerman, 2003), but the most compelling evidence is on the connection between poor dental health and school absences (Berg and Coniglio, 2006; Jackson et al., 2011; Pourat and Nicholson, 2009).

One study assessed school days missed due to dental issues for children age 5–17 in the Los Angeles school system in 2007. Of 7,240,000 children, an estimated 504,000 missed at least one day of school, with those who were unable to afford care more likely to miss more school days (Pourat and Nicholson, 2009). Silk (2010) reported 51,000,000 school hours are missed annually in the United States due to oral-health related illness.

Tooth decay (also called caries) impacts 40 percent of all children age 2–11 (Edelstein and Chinn, 2009) with disparities well documented. Literature has reported that 80 percent of the decay of teeth in a pediatric population is experienced by 25 percent of children (Kaste et al., 1996; Wysen et al., 2004), with poor children three to five times more likely to experience decay that goes untreated (Lewis et al., 2000; Newacheck et al., 2000). This is especially concerning given the numbers affected. In Medicaid Head Start programs, nearly 30 percent of preschoolers were reported living at <100 percent of the federal poverty level (FPL) and another 25 percent living at 101–200 percent FPL (Schneider, Rossetti, and Crall, 2007). Further, caries has been documented to be a progressive disease, becoming a growing problem as children age. Both state-wide and national data have reported on disease progression. In Head Start populations in Maryland, caries were found in 46 percent of 3-year-old enrollees rising to 64 percent of 4 year olds (Edelstein and Douglass,

1995). Wisconsin data reported 22 percent decay in those under 3, and 35 percent in 3 to 4 year olds, rising to 51 percent in those 4 and older (Edelstein and Chinn, 2009). National rates of early onset, decay progression, and cumulative disease found 11 percent of 2 year olds, 21 percent in 3 year olds, 34 percent in 4 year olds and 55 percent in 5 year olds (Kaste et al., 1996; Edelstein and Chinn, 2009).

National reports reiterate the especially poor condition of oral health in young, minority, and low-income children (age 5 and under). The Report of Surgeon General in 2000 on oral health reports disparities (Berg and Coniglio, 2006; Edelstein and Chinn, 2009). The National Health and Nutrition Examination Survey (NHANES) data indicate that 60 percent of children evidence caries in primary teeth by age 5, with poorer children at higher risk (US Department of Health and Human Services, 2000). The NHANES survey broke out data by race and by income in children aged 2 to 11. Whereas 76 percent of white parents reported their children's teeth were in "good to excellent" condition, this percentage fell to 61 percent for black parents and 47 percent of Hispanic parents. When examining the data by income, 83 percent of high-income and 75 percent of middle-income parents reported their children's teeth to be in good to excellent condition compared to 60 percent of low-income parents and 49 percent of poor parents (Edelstein and Chinn, 2009). Children with special needs due to chronic diseases and disabilities, while few in number, also represent a segment that is unlikely to receive adequate oral health care (Crall, 2005).

There have been some attempts to expand dental care through programs such as the State Children's Health Insurance Program (SCHIP) and they have had positive results in increasing the number of young children seen for dental exams, prevention, and treatment. But much more is needed to impact the oral health of the population. This chapter will present a brief overview of what we have learned to date from research on children and oral health, examine the current guidelines that have resulted from what has been learned, cite barriers to care, and provide both policy and research suggestions to improve our understanding and provision of oral health for children, particularly for those at highest risk.

Research overview

There is currently a limited literature on studies related to oral health in young children. Randomized trials are difficult to conduct in those under age 18 and the awareness of the need to include an oral health component to overall health in young children, while now being touted, is relatively recent (DHHS, 2000). Articles from PubMed searches on oral health in infants and young children and oral health in children at risk were found to be primarily a review of the need to do more, with some research focused on program evaluation, health outcomes, financial outcomes, and perceptions on oral health gleaned from surveys. Methodologies were not always robust (Schroth, Harrison, and Moffatt, 2009) and findings not always consistent. What follows is a sampling from each category. Generally, the data reiterate the prevalence of the problem, particularly for minority and poor children, and indicate that where resources are provided both education and care can be delivered and that early preventive care appears to have both health and financial benefit.

Program evaluation

Several reports in the literature provide information on programs that have made a difference either in the number of children screened, the number who are treated when decay is found, or the number who receive fluoride as a preventive measure. While results from these reports are impressive, most are reporting on program delivery rather than documenting a reduction in decay. With longer-term follow-up, such reductions would be expected.

In a Seattle program "Kids Get Care," aimed at low-income children (birth to 5 years), a team received a grant to provide a multifaceted intervention which included case management, provider training, and community outreach. The goal was to increase the number of children who received fluoride. The intervention was successful in doubling screening rates, but ongoing funding was needed to offset costs of care for families that are uninsured. While this is beneficial, sustaining the gain is a challenge (Wysen et al., 2004).

Another program, "Mouths of Babes," reimbursed providers through Medicaid to provide dental care. Using non-dentists and providing education to parents, the program is currently underway to increase the use of fluoride varnish in high-risk children. The goal is to promote dental care in primary care visits, as children are seen by physicians with far greater frequency than by dentists (Rozier et al., 2003).

In 2003, Capital Region Family Health Center in Concord, New Hampshire set up a caries prevention program using primary care providers (Wawrzyniak et al., 2006). Grant dollars were received to develop methods to deliver care to high-risk children. The providers were trained in oral health issues and how to apply varnish. They documented the content of their well-visits from a child's 6 month visit through 2 years of age. At baseline, none of the providers was deemed competent with oral health screening, but after two years this changed dramatically. The percentage of providers competent with screening and varnish application went from 0 to 69 percent; the percentage providing oral health service delivery rose from 0 to 80 percent. Training changed primary practice.

Head Start has had success with oral health initiatives to improve access to care and oral health awareness. The program invested $2 million in grant dollars to fifty-two Head Start, Early Head Start, and Migrant/Seasonal Head Start programs to design and implement oral health programs for the communities they served. While the programs were independently created, they all incorporated similar elements partnering and collaborating with their communities. The programs provided education to parents, children, and pregnant women on the importance of oral health and dental hygiene. Preventive services included on-site care in order to reach as many people as possible. Community referral networks were also expanded to ensure follow-up treatment where needed. Staff members assisted with appointments and transportation, and provided translators where necessary. Finally oral hygiene supplies were provided to enable families to put education into action. Early reports indicate increased utilization of care. Whereas 34 percent received at least one service during 2006–7, the percentage rose to 63 percent for 2007–8. Most visits were for preventive care and screening rather than for fillings or extractions (Administration for Children and Families, 2008).

In one of the few comparative studies designed to assess the benefit of early oral health intervention in those age 2 to 3, significant outcomes related to decreased decay were found. In this study, all 2 year olds (n = 880) born in Malmo, Sweden between the years 1998 and 2000 were invited to participate in an oral health intervention. Of these, 804 accepted the invitation and comprised the intervention group. The program included educating parents on oral health with a focus on tooth-brushing and using fluoride supplements. Parents were invited to education sessions. Those in the intervention group attended at least four sessions, and thus were considered actively engaged. Participants were also called every three months to document how they were doing with their child's oral health. Most participants were immigrants.

At the end of the year, 651 (81 percent) were reached for follow-up. Their results were compared to a historical non-intervention group of 238 children born between July and December 1997, of whom 201 could be reached at follow-up. Comparing the two groups, the researchers found fewer caries in the intervention group, 5.4 versus 6.9 (p < 0.001). Self-reported tooth-brushing was better in those who received the intervention, as were diet and use of fluoride tablets (Wennhall et al., 2008).

Research related to health outcomes

Several studies have examined health outcomes for children ages 5 and under with oral health problems. Yost reported that pain can impact eating (thus growth) and talking. There was some evidence that speech may be affected by decay (Koroluk and Riekman, 1991; Riekman and el Badrawy, 1985; Yost and Li, 2008). In these studies decay was associated with speech distortion. Improvement was found with treatment in both sleep (Shantinath et al., 1996) and behavior (Koroluk and Riekman, 1991; Thomas and Primosch, 2002; White, Lee, and Vann, 2003), and pain was decreased. Studies reporting on height and weight outcomes for those with and without oral health problems have found mixed results. In one study examining height in children age 3 to 5, with and without caries, those that were cavity-free were significantly taller than those with decay ($p < 0.05$) (Ayhan, Suskan, and Yildirim, 1996). A study of Chinese children also found an association with caries and lower height for age (Li, Navia, and Bian, 1996). However, these results were not supported in studies within the United Kingdom, nor in the US NHANES data where no association was found in height based on caries status (Dye et al., 2004; Williams, Kwan, and Parsons, 2000).

Weight was another area with mixed results. While there is conjecture that dental decay could impair eating and lead to lower weight, findings have been quite inconsistent.

Studies have reported that those young children with decay weigh significantly less than their caries-free counterparts (Acs, Lodolini, Kaminsky, and Cisneros, 1992; Oliveira, Sheiham, and Bonecker, 2008). Other studies have found no association (Chen et al., 1998; Dye et al., 2004). A recent report of a convenience sample of children in Brazil (a group readily accessible, neither representative nor random) found those 12–35 month olds with higher caries had significantly higher body mass indexes than those who were caries-free (Reifsnider, Mobley, and Menendez, 2004). This finding may be due to high carbohydrate diets that have been associated with both tooth decay and weight gain. There have also been studies examining the link between dental decay and middle ear infection, where results are again mixed. One study reported an association (Alaki, Burt, and Garetz, 2008), while another found none (Nelson et al., 2005).

Research related to financial benefit of early care

In one of the more comprehensive studies assessing cost and care conducted by Savage and colleagues, early care was found to have financial benefit.

Table 5.1 *Dental visits by age of child and associated cost.*

Number seen by age	Age at first	Cost per child
23	Less than 1 year	$226
249	Age 1–2	$339
465	Age 2–3	$449
915	Age 3–4	$492
823	Age 4–5	$546
Total 2,475		

In this study, over 9,000 children in North Carolina who were Medicaid eligible were followed longitudinally for five years. The researchers examined the number who accessed dental care, age of first dental visit, and cost. There were several interesting findings. Of the 9,000 children, 2,475 or 27.5 percent were seen for dental care. The breakdown of when children had their first dental visit found that the majority seen were 4 or 5 years old. Twenty-three were seen before age 1, 249 between age 1 and 2, 465 between 2 and 3, 915 between 3 and 4, and 823 between 4 and 5. Of those examined, 2 percent of the cohort had decay by 23 months and 19 percent had at least one tooth with decay between ages 2 and 5. Decay was associated with lower weight, failure to thrive in infants, missed school for the child, and missed work for the parent. In addition, the authors found cost differences based on when children received dental care. The cost for those who had an oral health visit by 12 months was $262 compared to those who were seen between ages 4 and 5 where the cost was $556. Table 5.1 lists the number of children seen at each age interval and the associated costs (Savage et al., 2004).

Survey data

Some surveys have been conducted to assess provider willingness to provide care and parent health concerns. Dental care was not a high priority in either group generally, so needs were likely to go unmet.

Involving primary care providers in oral health care

In a national survey 1,600 pediatric physicians were randomly selected from an American Medical Association roster. Of these, 1,386 were eligible and 862 responded. The pediatricians reported they would be willing to include dental care but would need to receive training in oral health. They see their role not as replacing the dentist but rather in doing a screening assessment. This extra responsibility, however, would require additional resources (Lewis et al., 2000). While the majority seemed supportive of adding to their role, many did not agree with the American Association of Pediatric Dentistry guideline encouraging children to be seen for a dental assessment by age 1.

Survey of health coverage

In the National Survey of Children's Health 2003–4 a random sample of parents and guardians of 102,353 children were asked about insurance. Coverage rates were found to differ by race. In addition, health concerns varied by race. African Americans were more likely to report problems with asthma, behavior, and speech. Dental needs were not mentioned. Native Americans reported problems with hearing and vision. Their overall lack of coverage left them with no source for care, so they were more likely to use emergency room services for all care. The majority of Asian Americans reported not seeing a doctor in the past year, making them highly unlikely to see a dentist (Flores and Tomany-Korman, 2008). Knowing that the majority of decay is found in minority populations, it is evident that there is limited awareness in the eyes of the public about the importance of oral health. Dental needs are not receiving adequate attention.

Current recommendations

While the published data are limited as to the exact optimal time to begin dental care, the few reports with comparative data have shown that having early intervention (by age 1 or 2) is beneficial. As a result, several organizations have published guidelines to promote improved oral health. The United States Preventive Services Task Force, American Academy of Family Physicians, American Academy of Pediatric Dentistry, and American Dental Association now call for the first dental appointment to occur within six months of the first tooth eruption or to occur not later than 1 year of age (American Academy of Pediatric Dentistry, 1999; Berg and Coniglio, 2006; The Nation's Health – The Official Newspaper of the American Public Health Association, 1999). The recommendations have been in place since the 1990s.

In addition to the timing of initial assessment, there have been articles recommending the promotion of education to parents on limiting sugar intake in infants. Some have also called for including oral health in primary care well-visits and giving parents samples of dental care products to encourage use with their children. The focus on primary care is tied to the fact that children are likely to see their primary care provider more often than a dental provider, and if an oral assessment could become embedded in a well-visit far fewer children would develop serious dental problems.

Several articles offer suggestions for primary care involvement. Silk in an article on making oral health a priority in pediatric visits includes a table of topics to include in well-visits that are age-relevant and doable in limited time (Silk, 2010).

Despite the good intentions, the guidelines have had limited impact on practice (Herman, 2001; Waldman and Perlman, 1999). Herman reports that visits to the dentist are "rarely part of a young child's routine before age 3." Slayton cites that only 2 percent of children had a visit by age 1, 11 percent by age 2, and 26 percent by age 3 (Slayton et al., 2002).

Educating parents is an important step in oral health promotion. Poor oral hygiene in parents is a risk factor for children (Edelstein, 2000). Mothers whose teeth are high in decay are likely to have children with similar problems. Additionally and sometimes overlooked is the communicable nature of decay-promoting bacteria (specifically Strep mutans). Siblings or primary caregivers with active decay (i.e., untreated cavities) may transmit these bacteria through close contact and shared items (e.g., bottles, toys, cups, utensils). Infants exposed to highly active Strep mutans will be at higher risk themselves (Berkowitz, 2006; Caufield, Cutter, and Dasanayake, 1993; Kohler, Bratthall, and Krasse, 1983; Li and Caufield, 1995). Therefore, preventing and treating tooth decay in pregnant women, family members, and caregivers may help prevent or delay decay in young children. While disease transmission and even genetics can play a role, poor hygiene (i.e., brushing and flossing) and diet (e.g., between-meal consumption of sugary foods and beverages) are also primary contributors. Following the advice regarding diet and habits shown in Table 5.2 has the ability to decrease dental problems. Yet there are numerous barriers to optimal oral health.

Barriers to care

The barriers to providing optimal oral health care to young children relate to both patient and system issues. Factors affecting parents include missing work, transportation costs of getting a child to care, and child care needs (Edelstein et al., 2006). One-parent households cannot provide the same resources as those with two parents and 54 percent of black children live in female-headed households. This compares to 26 percent Hispanic and 15 percent white female-headed households (Edelstein, 2002; Waldman and Perlman, 1999). Inadequate funding for dental services is another concern, even if a parent could potentially get their child to care, such care is not always covered. In addition to issues of access, parent

Table 5.2 *Hugh Silk's dental topics for well-child visits.*

Age at visit	Advice for parents
0–2 months	Diet: no bottle propping; only water in bottle Habits: pacifier use OK; may help prevent SIDS
4 months	Diet: no bottle propping; only water or formula in bottle; no bottle in bed Caries risk assessment: family history, preterm infant, socioeconomic status, special health care needs, dental insurance Fluoride: assess need for supplementation
6–9 months	Diet: introduce cup; no bottle by age 1; limit ad lib feedings, drinks Oral hygiene: brush as teeth erupt; use a smear of fluoridated toothpaste Dental screening: assess eruption pattern, hygiene, defects, caries Fluoride: prescribe fluoride supplement if needed; counsel on fluorosis Habits: create bedtime rituals: "bath, bottle/cup, brush, book, bed"
12 months to 3 yrs	Diet: promote planned sugar-free snacks and drinks; remove bottle Oral hygiene: brush teeth twice daily; use a smear of fluoridated toothpaste; parental supervision Dental screening: assess hygiene and caries Fluoride: prescribe fluoride supplement if needed Habits: end pacifier use Dental referral: ideally at age 1; or high-risk at age 1, all other by age 3
More than 3 years	Diet: promote planned sugar-free snacks and drinks Oral hygiene: brush teeth twice daily with fluoridated toothpaste; parental supervision until age 7; floss permanent teeth; avoid smoking, alcohol use Dental screening: assess hygiene and caries Fluoride: prescribe fluoride supplement if needed until age 16 Habits: end thumb sucking Oral safety: mouth guards for sports; avoid oral piercings (remove for sports)

comfort level with dentists varies. Currently there is a paucity of dentists from minority cultures (Edelstein, 2002).

The problems parents face are exacerbated by system-related issues. There are currently too few dentists to serve the overall population (Administration for Children and Families, 2008; Berg and Coniglio, 2006) and their geographic distribution does not allow for easy access to all. Further, the dental student population is declining (Edelstein, 2000). While many call for appropriate training for non-dentists as first-line conduits for screening, building in time for primary care providers to do this in their already overburdened schedules is not easy. More screening adds not only to the care responsibilities of that provider but also to the administrative burden (Edelstein, 2000). Even within the dental community more awareness is needed to improve oral population health. For most dentists, their skills and experience with the young is deficient (Waldman and Perlman, 1999) and not all embrace the value of providing care to the very young. In a survey of Washington dentists fewer than one in three felt it definitely important to provide care to babies and toddlers (Milgrom, 1998).

Lessons learned and future directions

Having reviewed the literature to date, it is evident that more carefully designed studies are needed. While some data exist, populations were not always representative and often sample sizes have been small. It is unclear exactly when intervention is most optimal, although some time in infancy appears essential especially for children at elevated risk. It is also not known if different populations should be targeted differently and/or what interventions might be most useful for various groups. More robust studies would provide a greater clarity on health outcomes and the cost-effectiveness of early intervention. It would be beneficial to continue research on the etiology of caries as well as optimal fluoride application strategies. Studies investigating patient compliance and cultural receptivity to oral health recommendations are also important.

Despite the limited literature, guidance for policy in certain areas is clear. Oral health incorporated into a comprehensive health focus for all children and early intervention accepted as a key strategy to improving the current state of oral health would be beneficial. While the problems are more pronounced in minority populations and disparities have been clearly identified, the needs for improved oral health for infants and young children must be for the full population, making certain that resources are available to ensure access and coverage to the most vulnerable.

Based on what we currently know, three primary focuses are apparent:
1. making prevention a priority
2. employing multiple avenues to provide education to parents, children, and pregnant women
3. educating and encouraging a range of providers to deliver oral health care for infants and young children.

Making prevention a priority

Recognizing that dental decay is the most prevalent childhood disease, impacting 40 percent of children between ages 2 and 11, it is clear that preventive action is needed (DHHS, 2000; Flores and Tomany-Korman, 2008). Promotion of current guidelines must continue to ensure that all children receive screening in infancy (Lee et al., 2006). Further, additional efforts are needed to reach the most at-risk communities. Policies need to be crafted that promote timely, affordable dental care with a focus on the most vulnerable. Currently, poor children come to care because of pain and disease, not for prevention. We need to change this pattern. There is much that can be done to avoid dental decay and its sequelae. We need to ensure accessibility. To date, only one in five Medicare-eligible children receives care (Mouradian, Wehr, and Crall, 2000).

Employing multiple avenues to provide education to parents, children, and pregnant women

To make primary prevention a reality, we need to increase awareness of its importance. The impact of oral health and activities that promote optimal oral health must be conveyed to pregnant women to improve their own oral hygiene and prepare them to care for the oral health of their children (Edelstein, 2002). This information needs to be targeted to parents or caregivers and to children directly through whatever avenues are available. Mentors, home health nurses, preschool programs, elementary schools, doctors, nurses, dentists can all be prepared to deliver the message that this is an important component of overall health. The numerous program evaluations have shown this can be done successfully (Administration for Children and Families, 2008; Peterson-Sweeney and Stevens, 2010; Wawrzyniak et al., 2006; Wennhall et al., 2008).

Educating and encouraging a range of providers to deliver oral health care for infants and young children

While guidelines exist to promote dental screening early in a child's life, they have not yet been fully embraced (Herman, 2001; Lee et al., 2006; Slayton et al., 2002; Waldman and Perlman, 1999). This is due in part to a shortage of dentists as well as a lack of awareness on the part of parents and a lack of training on the part of professionals. Several articles indicated that when providers are trained in screening, assessment, and fluoride application, they are able to deliver the needed care (Rozier et al., 2003; Wysen et al., 2004; Wawrzyniak et al., 2006). Wawrzyniak and colleagues (2006) wrote of a family medicine program that incorporated caries prevention into the well-child visit. It was successfully done and could be readily replicated to other sites. If such visits could be covered, providers are able and willing to do this. Nurses could also provide screening and fluoride application services (Peterson-Sweeney and Stevens, 2010).

Rather than working in competition with dentists, these providers would provide first-line screening and then could refer patients for follow-up.

In a study conducted in a large Midwestern integrated health system examining the uptake, sustainability, and response of primary care providers to an initiative for primary care providers to apply fluoride varnish in young, at-risk children, the results were quite positive. Of the over 12,000 children age 1–5 eligible for fluoride application, over 80 percent received the treatment.

Further, the project appears to be sustaining in all clinics within the health system (Rolnick et al., 2013). Moreover, when providers were surveyed about the initiative, 72 percent claimed it was important and served as a positive catalyst to discussion of oral health issues with parents. The three challenges to the policy most noted were: initial fear or resistance to the application by the child or parent (30 percent), time to apply the varnish (26 percent), and time to provide counseling to parents (18 percent). Even with these comments, however, nearly half of the providers surveyed stated there were no challenges faced in supporting the initiative and 86 percent claimed the application took three minutes or less. In open-ended comments, 10 percent suggested it would be valuable to provide this to all children, not just those considered to be at risk (Rolnick, Jackson, and DeFor, 2013). So, while not challenge-free, such efforts are possible to implement.

The new affordable health care act, or Obamacare, has taken some steps in needed directions, particularly for children at risk. The legislation is providing millions of dollars for a Health and Dentistry headquarters whose mission it is to provide primary and preventive health care to all, including vulnerable populations. Health and Dentistry offers a sliding fee scale for qualifying uninsured patients. There are nominal fees for uninsured patients whose total household incomes are at or below the federal poverty level. Money has also been allocated to expand community health centers to provide overall primary and preventive care in multiple areas.[1]

Policy considerations will need to include reimbursement issues and greater promotion of current guidelines for all children, with a special emphasis for those at highest risk. Perhaps policies should be developed for pregnant women as well, to ensure oral health becomes part of their awareness. Including a dental childhood component in all dentistry residencies and pediatrics would provide the needed training to deliver comprehensive dental care to all children. Knowing that a comprehensive oral health program starting in infancy significantly reduces caries is a

---

[1] In administering many aspects of the Affordable Health Care Act, there is concern that some states may cut dental benefits.

worthy investment. It will lead to reduced pain for children and improve school success by reducing days missed, as dental problems are the number one reason for missing school. Assuring training for professionals is important in preparing an adequate workforce to deliver the needed care. We have the knowledge and the tools to eradicate poor dental health in all our children. Through collaborative efforts involving many facets of the community, we have the ability to make this eradication a reality.

References

Acs, G., Lodolini, G., Kaminsky, S., and Cisneros, G. J. (1992). Effect of nursing caries on body weight in a pediatric population. *Pediatric Dentistry*, 14(5), 302–305.

Administration for Children and Families (2008). *Strategies for promoting prevention and improving oral health care delivery in Head Start: findings from the Oral Health Initiative Evaluation.* Washington, DC: Office of Planning, Research and Evaluation.

Alaki, S. M., Burt, B. A., and Garetz, S. L. (2008). Middle ear and respiratory infections in early childhood and their association with early childhood caries. *Pediatric Dentistry*, 30(2), 105–110.

American Academy of Pediatric Dentistry (1999–2000). Infant oral health care policy statement. *Journal of Pediatric Dentistry Special Issue Reference Manual*, 21(5).

Ayhan, H., Suskan, E., and Yildirim, S. (1996). The effect of nursing or rampant caries on height, body weight and head circumference. *Journal of Clinical Pediatric Dentistry*, 20(3), 209–212.

Berg, P., and Coniglio, D. (2006). Oral health in children overlooked and under-treated. *Journal of the American Academy of Physician Assistants*, 19(4), 40, 42, 44.

Berkowitz, R. J. (2006). Mutans streptococci: acquisition and transmission. *Pediatric Dentistry*, 28(2), 106–109, 192–208.

Caufield, P. W., Cutter, G. R., and Dasanayake, A. P. (1993). Initial acquisition of mutans streptococci by infants: evidence for a discrete window of infectivity. *Journal of Dental Research*, 72(1), 37–45.

Chen, W., Chen, P., Chen, S. C., Shih, W. T., and Hu, H. C. (1998). Lack of association between obesity and dental caries in three-year-old children. *Zhonghua Min Guo Xiao Er Ke Yi Xue Hui Za Zhi*, 39(2), 109–111.

Crall, J. J. (2005). Development and integration of oral health services for preschool-age children. *Pediatric Dentistry*, 27(4), 323–330.

Dye, B. A., Shenkin, J. D., Ogden, C. L., Marshall, T. A., Levy, S. M., and Kanellis, M. J. (2004). The relationship between healthful eating practices and dental caries in children aged 2–5 years in the United States, 1988–1994. *Journal of the American Dentistry Association*, 135(1), 55–66.

Edelstein, B. L. (2000). Access to dental care for Head Start enrollees. *Journal of Public Health Dentistry*, 60(3), 221–229, discussion 230–232.

    (2002). Dental care considerations for young children. *Special Care Dentistry*, 22(3), 11S–25S.

Edelstein, B. L., and Chinn, C. H. (2009). Update on disparities in oral health and access to dental care for America's children. *Academic Pediatric Journal*, 9(6), 415–419.

Edelstein, B. L., and Douglass, C. W. (1995). Dispelling the myth that 50 percent of US schoolchildren have never had a cavity. *Public Health Reports*, 110(5), 522–530.

Edelstein, B., Vargas, C. M., Candelaria, D., and Vemuri, M. (2006). Experience and policy implications of children presenting with dental emergencies to US pediatric dentistry training programs. *Pediatric Dentistry*, 28(5), 431–437.

Flores, G., and Tomany-Korman, S. C. (2008). Racial and ethnic disparities in medical and dental health, access to care, and use of services in US children. *Pediatrics*, 121(2), e286–298.

Herman, N. G. (2001). Ten oral health strategies to keep kids pain-free and problem-free throughout childhood. *New York State Dental Journal*, 67(7), 20–25.

Jackson, S. L., Vann Jr., W. F., Kotch, J. B., Pahel, B. T., and Lee, J. Y. (2011). Impact of poor oral health on children's school attendance and school performance. *American Journal of Public Health*, 101(10), 1900–1906.

Kaste, L. M., Selwitz, R. H., Oldakowski, R. J., Brunelle, J. A., Winn, D. M., and Brown, L. J. (1996). Coronal caries in the primary and permanent dentition of children and adolescents 1–17 years of age: United States, 1988–1991. *Journal of Dental Research*, 75, 631–641.

Kohler, B., Bratthall, D., and Krasse, B. (1983). Preventive measures in mothers influence the establishment of the bacterium Streptococcus mutans in their infants. *Archives of Oral Biology*, 28(3), 225–231.

Koroluk, L. D., and Riekman, G. A. (1991). Parental perceptions of the effects of maxillary incisor extractions in children with nursing caries. *ASDC Journal of Dentistry for Children*, 58(3), 233–236.

Lee, J. Y., Bouwens, T. J., Savage, M. F., and Vann Jr., W. F. (2006). Examining the cost-effectiveness of early dental visits. *Pediatric Dentistry*, 28(2), 102–105.

Lewis, C. W., Grossman, D. C., Domoto, P. K., and Deyo, R. A. (2000). The role of the pediatrician in the oral health of children: a national survey. *Pediatrics*, 106(6), E84.

Li, Y., and Caufield, P. W. (1995). The fidelity of initial acquisition of mutans streptococci by infants from their mothers. *Journal of Dental Research*, 74(2), 681–685.

Li, Y., Navia, J. M., and Bian, J. Y. (1996). Caries experience in deciduous dentition of rural Chinese children 3–5 years old in relation to the presence or absence of enamel hypoplasia. *Caries Research*, 30(1), 8–15.

Marino, R. V., Bomze, K., Scholl, T. O., and Anhalt, H. (1989). Nursing bottle caries: characteristics of children at risk. *Clinical Pediatrics (Philadelphia)*, 28(3), 129–131.

Milgrom, P. (1998). Response to Reisine and Douglass: psychosocial and behavioral issues in early childhood caries. *Community Dentistry and Oral Epidemiology*, 26(1), 45–48.

Mouradian, W. E., Berg, J. H., and Somerman, M. J. (2003). Addressing disparities through dental–medical collaborations, part 1. The role of cultural competency in health disparities: training of primary care medical practitioners in children's oral health. *Journal of Dental Education*, 67(8), 860–868.

Mouradian, W. E., Wehr, E., and Crall, J. J. (2000). Disparities in children's oral health and access to dental care. *Journal of the American Medical Association*, 284(20), 2625–2631.

Nelson, S., Nechvatal, N., Weber, J., and Canion, S. (2005). Dental caries and ear infections in preschool-aged children. *Oral Health Preventive Dentistry*, 3(3), 165–171.

Newacheck, P. W., Hughes, D. C., Hung, Y. Y., Wong, S., and Stoddard, J. J. (2000). The unmet health needs of America's children. *Pediatrics*, 105, 989–997.

Oliveira, L. B., Sheiham, A., and Bonecker, M. (2008). Exploring the association of dental caries with social factors and nutritional status in Brazilian preschool children. *European Journal of Oral Sciences*, 116(1), 37–43.

Peterson-Sweeney, K., and Stevens, J. (2010). Optimizing the health of infants and children: their oral health counts! *Journal of Pediatric Nursing*, 25(4), 244–249.

Pourat, N., and Nicholson, G. (2009). Unaffordable dental care is linked to frequent school absences. *Policy Brief UCLA Center for Health Policy Research*, Nov. 2009(PB2009–10), 1–6.

Reifsnider, E., Mobley, C., and Menendez, D. B. (2004). Childhood obesity and early childhood caries in a WIC population. *Journal of Multicultural Nursing and Health*, 10, 24–31.

Riekman, G. A., and el Badrawy, H. E. (1985). Effect of premature loss of primary maxillary incisors on speech. *Pediatric Dentistry*, 7(2), 119–122.

Rolnick, S. J., Jackson, J. M., and DeFor, T. A. (2013). *Primary care providers' perspectives on fluoride varnish application for at-risk children*. Under review.

Rolnick, S. J., Jackson, J. M., DeFor, T. A., and Flottemesch, T. J. (2013). *Providing fluoride varnish application in the primary care setting*. Under review.

Rozier, R. G., Sutton, B. K., Bawden, J. W., Haupt, K., Slade, G. D., and King, R. S. (2003). Prevention of early childhood caries in North Carolina medical practices: implications for research and practice. *Journal of Dental Education*, 67(8), 876–885.

Savage, M. F., Lee, J. Y., Kotch, J. B., and Vann Jr., W. F. (2004). Early preventive dental visits: effects on subsequent utilization and costs. *Pediatrics*, 114(4), e418–423.

Schneider, D., Rossetti, J., and Crall, J. J. (2007). *Assuring comprehensive dental services in medicaid and head start programs: planning and implementation considerations*. Los Angeles, CA: National Oral Health Policy Center.

Schroth, R. J., Harrison, R. L., and Moffatt, M. E. (2009). Oral health of indigenous children and the influence of early childhood caries on childhood health and well-being. *Pediatric Clinics of North America*, 56(6), 1481–1499.

Shantinath, S. D., Breiger, D., Williams, B. J., and Hasazi, J. E. (1996). The relationship of sleep problems and sleep-associated feeding to nursing caries. *Pediatric Dentistry*, 18(5), 375–378.

Silk, H. (2010). Making oral health a priority in your preventive pediatric visits. *Clinical Pediatrics (Philadelphia)*, 49(2), 103–109.

Slayton, R. L., Warren, J. J., Levy, S. M., Kanellis, M. J., and Islam, M. (2002). Frequency of reported dental visits and professional fluoride applications in a cohort of children followed from birth to age 3 years. *Pediatric Dentistry*, 24(1), 64–68.

Thomas, C. W., and Primosch, R. E. (2002). Changes in incremental weight and well-being of children with rampant caries following complete dental rehabilitation. *Pediatric Dentistry*, 24(2), 109–113.

US Department of Health and Human Services (DHHS) (2000). *Oral health in America: a report of the Surgeon General*. Rockville, MD: US Department of Health and Human Services, National Institute of Dental and Craniofacial Research, National Institutes of Health.

Waldman, H. B., and Perlman, S. P. (1999). Are we reaching very young children with needed dental services? *ASDC Journal of Dentistry for Children*, 66(6), 390–394.

Wawrzyniak, M. N., Boulter, S., Giotopoulos, C., and Zivitski, J. (2006). Incorporating caries prevention into the well-child visit in a family medicine residency. *Family Medicine*, 38(2), 90–92.

Wennhall, I., Matsson, L., Schroder, U., and Twetman, S. (2008). Outcome of an oral health outreach programme for preschool children in a low socioeconomic multicultural area. *International Journal of Paediatric Dentistry*, 18(2), 84–90.

White, H., Lee, J. Y., and Vann Jr., W. F. (2003). Parental evaluation of quality of life measures following pediatric dental treatment using general anesthesia. *Anesthesia Progress*, 50(3), 105–110.

Williams, S. A., Kwan, S. Y., and Parsons, S. (2000). Parental smoking practices and caries experience in pre-school children. *Caries Research*, 34(2), 117–122.

Wysen, K. H., Hennessy, P. M., Lieberman, M. I., Garland, T. E., and Johnson, S. M. (2004). Kids get care: integrating preventive dental and medical care using a public health case management model. *Journal of Dental Education*, 68(5), 522–530.

Yost, J., and Li, Y. (2008). Promoting oral health from birth through childhood: prevention of early childhood caries. *American Journal of Masternal/Child Nursing*, 33(1), 17–23.

Part II

Effects of health interventions on child
development and throughout the life course

6   Early childhood health promotion and its life course health consequences

Sai Ma, Kevin D. Frick, Alyssa Crawford, and Bernard Guyer

Introduction

Previous publications and research conferences from the Human Capital Research Collaborative have built support for the argument that early childhood programs strengthen health outcomes and school readiness (University of Minnesota and the Federal Reserve Bank of Minneapolis, 2010). The case for promoting investments in early childhood health, however, must be based on strong evidence that such investments will result in specific health benefits to young children, health improvements across the lifespan, and economic returns to society. Recent research shows that the earliest period of life forms the foundation for a healthier life course, and interventions are now available to address the important health problems of early life.

Background

Children are recognized as the most vulnerable and dependent members of society (Jameson and Wehr, 1993), and measures of infant and child well-being are often used to measure the overall health of a society. Disparities in health and social gradients in health indicators are shaped early in life and sustained across the lifespan (Conley, Strully, and Bennett, 2003). Health is important for many reasons, including the fact that it is a critical determinant of economic productivity across the lifespan; the ability of adults to be productive workers is influenced by their health status.

Barker and his supporters have made a convincing case that fetal and child health and development have implications for adult health five and six decades later (Barker, 1998; Gluckman, Hanson, and Beedle, 2007). Intrauterine conditions – including nutrition, inflammation, and infection – interact with the genetic make-up of the fetus, influencing organ development and creating vulnerability to later environment–gene

113

interactions. Such early influences and subsequent environmental exposures across the lifespan increase the risk of heart disease, stroke, and cancer.

Health is shaped by a broad set of determinants, including socioeconomic status, physical and social-emotional environments, genetic endowment and biological influences, and access to preventive and curative medical technologies. In the case of young children, these forces act upon them both directly and through the circumstances confronted by their families. The case for child health as an outcome with multiple fiduciary and other payoffs to society as a whole is one that can now be put forward.

Goal of this chapter

The overall goal of this chapter is to extend and update an earlier literature review[1] that explored whether health promotion efforts targeted at preschool age children can improve health across the lifespan and yield future economic returns to society. Specifically, we examined the magnitude of four health problems – exposure to tobacco, unintentional injury, obesity, and mental health problems – including their prevalence during this age period, their cost implications across the lifespan, the availability of preventive interventions in this period of life, and the evidence that preventing these problems in early life will "pay off" or save costs (such as medical care, other effects of morbidity, and early mortality) in the future.

Methodology

Selection of topics

This project set out to review the availability of evidence to support policies of societal investments in early child health by selecting health

[1] This chapter is primarily based on our publications: Bernard Guyer, Sai Ma, Holly Grason, Kevin D. Frick, Deborah Perry, Alyssa Sharkey, and Jennifer McIntosh, "Early childhood health promotion and its life-course health consequences," *Academic Pediatrics*, 2009, 9(3), 142–149.e1–71; Kevin D. Frick and Sai Ma, "Overcoming challenges for the economic evaluation of investments in children's health," *Academic Pediatrics*, 2009, 9(3), 136–137. We have updated the literature review to April 2010 for this chapter, using the same search strategies and review process as described in the methods. Our updated search resulted in an additional twenty-six studies that we add to this review.

This study is funded by both the Partnership for America's Economic Success and the Zanvyl and Isabelle Krieger Fund. The authors appreciate the thoughtful review from Susan Bales and Beth Hare, and support from Sara Watson, Elaine Weiss, and Lauren Zerbe. We also appreciate the contributions from co-authors of the earlier article: Holly Grason, Deborah Perry, Alyssa Sharkey, and Jennifer McIntosh.

topics that would be meaningful to a policy audience. In order to limit the scope of the study, four health problems (tobacco exposure, unintentional injury, obesity, and mental health) were chosen based on the following rationale: the topics comprise priorities set in *The Year 2020 Objectives for the Nation* by including both physical and mental health issues. Each of the four health problems is prevalent among young children at a level that indicates a true public health problem, thereby assuring their relevance to population health. Finally, the selected topics demonstrate the need to combine a wide range of clinical, public health, and public policy approaches to address their social and environmental determinants effectively.

Review of the literature: search strategies and inclusion criteria

To be able to identify relevant literature comprehensively and systematically, and to minimize selection bias, we established search strategies in advance, including using combined keywords searches, setting inclusion/exclusion criteria, and manual checking.

We initially searched early childhood interventions in five databases: PubMed, PscyINFO, National Health Service Economic Evaluation Database, National Bureau of Economic Research's working paper database, and EconLit. A set of keywords such as intervention, program, prevention, or evaluation were selected to combine with specific keywords for each topic. The search was restricted to studies that satisfy each of the following inclusion criteria: young-child-focused, English language, publication dates January 1996 to June 2007, experimental or quasi-experimental design, and measuring outcome changes (such as overweight rate) or behavioral changes (such as installation of smoke detectors). For completeness, we manually checked publications of key authors in each field and bibliographies of key review articles. Because most of the relevant studies for the original review were located using PubMed, our updated search focused on PubMed through April 2010, using the same search strategies and inclusion/exclusion criteria.

Presentation of findings

Synopses of the findings

This chapter contains synopses of the findings from each of the four literature reviews. We present the effectiveness of interventions according to levels of the intervention. Before reporting financial results, we used the Consumer Price Index (CPI) to translate dollar amounts presented to the value of the US dollar in 2010.

A lifespan conceptual framework

In order to conceptualize the interactions between the nature and the effect of interventions, we developed a lifespan impact framework. In this chapter, we have presented review results for each health topic in a unique lifespan figure (as shown in Tables 6.1 to 6.4). Interventions are placed in the row corresponding to the level of the intervention: individual, family, community, and national. These levels are defined by the identity of the primary target of the interventions, rather than by the settings where the interventions took place. While this distinction was at times difficult to make, our rule of thumb was to examine the far periphery of an intervention first. For example, if an intervention involved national-level campaigns or law enforcement, then we classified this intervention as national-level, even if it incorporated family-level components.

The columns represent four lifespan stages: preconception/pregnancy, infant/childhood, adolescence, and adulthood. For each intervention, we used dark grey shading to indicate when an intervention took place, and lighter shading to designate the evidence of extended impact for that intervention. For example, a car safety-seat adoption campaign targets parents with very young children (age 0–3), but a long-term evaluation may find positive spillover effects in the use of booster seats and seatbelts when those children grow up. In this case, we would depict this intervention in dark grey in the infant/childhood column (when it takes place) and in light grey in adolescence and adulthood columns (extended impact). Since the present study focuses on the interventions targeting young children, we did not search for or include interventions that exclusively target other age groups. A blank cell in the adolescent or adult periods should not be interpreted as indicating an absence of interventions; rather this age range is beyond the search scope of the present study.

Evidence table[2]

Each of the four synopses is supported by an evidence table that includes extensive details of the reviewed interventions, including first author's name and publication year, study question, study design (e.g., randomized controlled trial, quasi-experimental design), nature of the intervention (e.g., components, length, intensity), targeted population, the intervention settings, sample size and attrition rate, measure of outcomes, and results.

---

[2] The most updated evidence tables and complete bibliographies are available upon request from the authors; and the previous evidence tables and bibliographies are available through the journal *Academic Pediatrics*.

Table 6.1 *Lifespan impact of tobacco treatment and prevention efforts.*

LEVEL OF INTERVENTION	LIFESPAN STAGE INTERVENTION AND IMPACT			
	Preconception/ pregnancy	Infant/childhood	Adolescence	Adulthood
Individual	Smoking cessation therapy for pregnant women[a]		Smoking cessation therapy[b]	
	Smoking cessation therapy with partner support[c]			
	Smoking cessation therapy targeting relapse[d]			
Family		Smoking cessation for adults living with children[e]		
Local/ community/ workplace/ school			Media campaigns[f]	
	Bans/restrictions in workplaces and public[g]			
			Community mobilization[h]	
National/state			Price increases[i]	
			Enforcement of age ban on sales[j]	

[a] Albrecht et al., 2006; Lumley et al., 2004; Johnson et al., 2005; DiClemente et al., 2000; Fiore et al., 2000; USDHHS, 2001; NIH, 1994; Melvin et al., 2000; Walsh et al., 1997; Windsor et al., 1985; 1993; Ershoff et al., 1989; Samet et al., 1994.

[b] Lantz et al., 2000; Thomas and Perera, 2006; Levy et al., 2004; Ranney et al., 2006; McDonald et al., 2003; Albrecht et al., 2006; Colby et al., 2005; Sussman, 2002.

[c] Donatelle et al., 2000; Stanton et al., 2004.

[d] Fang et al., 2004.

[e] Emmons et al., 2001; Hovell et al., 2000; 1994; Hovell et al., 2002; Wahlgren et al., 1997; Zhang and Qiu, 1993; Abdullah et al., 2005.

[f] Lantz et al., 2000; Sowden and Arblaster, 2000; Task Force on Community Preventive Services, 2003; Hersey et al., 2005, Hyland et al., 2006.

[g] Hopkins et al., 2001; Levy et al., 2004; USDHHS, 2001.

[h] Lantz et al., 2000; Slater et al., 2006.

[i] CDC, 2000; Levy et al., 2004; Task Force on Community Preventive Services, 2000; Ranney et al., 2006.

[j] Pbert et al., 2003; Task Force on Community Preventive Services, 2000; DiFranza et al., 2001.

▢ Age period when interventions take place

▢ Age period with continuing positive impacts of intervention

Table 6.2 *Lifespan impact of obesity interventions.*

	LIFESPAN STAGE INTERVENTION AND IMPACT			
LEVEL OF INTERVENTION	Preconception/ pregnancy	Infant/childhood	Adolescence	Adulthood
Individual	Observational studies[a]			
		Observational studies[b]		
Family		Preschool education[c]		
		Parent education[d]		
		Restricting use of technology[e]		
Local/ community/ workplace/ school		Teacher curriculum[f]		
National/state				

[a] Eriksson et al., 2001; Nader et al., 2006.
[b] Field et al., 2005.
[c] Fitzgibbon et al., 2005.
[d] Golan et al., 2006.
[e] Epstein et al., 2008.
[f] Summerbell et al., 2003.
▭ Age period when interventions take place
▭ Age period with continuing positive impacts of intervention

Results: synopses of the literature reviews

Tobacco exposure

While tobacco use has long been recognized as a major public health concern, there is increasing evidence about the harmful effects of tobacco on children, namely through prenatal exposure and environmental tobacco smoke (ETS). Prenatal exposure to cigarette smoking is associated with many risks, including negative birth outcomes (e.g., preterm delivery, premature rupture of membranes, placenta previa, low birth weight, spontaneous abortion (US Department of Health and Human Services, 2001)), and Sudden Infant Death Syndrome (SIDS) (Hunt and Hauck, 2006) as well as later-life effects (e.g., attention deficit hyperactivity disorder (ADHD) (Braun et al., 2006)). Additionally, children exposed to ETS are more likely to suffer from respiratory issues and infections, such as more frequent and/or severe asthma attacks, allergies, and ear infections (Cook and Strachan, 1999). This is no small problem; almost half a million US babies each year are born to mothers who

Table 6.3 *Lifespan impact of injury prevention efforts.*

	LIFESPAN STAGE INTERVENTION AND IMPACT			
LEVEL OF INTERVENTION	Preconception/ pregnancy	Infant/childhood	Adolescence	Adulthood
Individual		Gun safety education[a]		
Family		Home visits[b]		
	Prenatal home visitation[c]			
	Education against the use of baby walkers[d]			
		Tailored parent and provider education[e]		
Local/ community/ workplace/ school		Community education combined with incentives distribution for road safety[f]		
		Smoke detector distribution		
National/state		Changes in baby walker safety standards[g]		
		Child passenger safety laws[h]		

[a] Hardy, 2002.
[b] Johnston, 2000; Posner, 2004; Mallonee, 2000; Sznajder, 2003.
[c] Kitzman, 1997.
[d] Kendrick et al., 2005.
[e] Nansel et al., 2008.
[f] Greenberg-Seth et al., 2004.
[g] Rodgers and Leland, 2005.
[h] Segui-Gomez et al., 2001.
▨ Age period when interventions take place
▢ Age period with continuing positive impacts of intervention

smoked during pregnancy and recent estimates suggest that one in four children are exposed to ETS at home (Soliman, Pollack, and Warner, 2004).

Society stands to reap significant benefits from prevention of tobacco exposure, and cessation of smoking at home and in public can improve the health of children and throughout the lifespan. Fortunately, even simple interventions targeting pregnant women can be effective both at promoting smoking cessation and in improving birth outcomes. While a review of eighteen household ETS exposure reduction interventions reported wide variation in impact, three randomized control studies reported self-reported

Table 6.4 *Lifespan impact of interventions for mental health disorders.*

	LIFESPAN STAGE INTERVENTION AND IMPACT			
LEVEL OF INTERVENTION	Preconception/ pregnancy	Infant/childhood	Adolescence	Adulthood
Individual		Child-focused training[a]		
	Parent-focused programs[b]			
		Child-focused training[c]; parent-focused training programs[d]		
Family		Parent- and child-focused programs[e]; collaborative problem solving[f]		
Local/ community/ workplace/ school		School-based: Fast Track[g]		
		Primary Care Practice Training[h]		
National/State		New Hope[i]		

[a] Abecedarian Project. McLaughlin et al., 2007; Chicago Child–Parent Center program (CPC). Reynolds et al., 2007.
[b] Healthy Steps. Johnston et al., 2006; Minkovitz et al., 2003; Early Head Start. Administration for Children and Families, 2006.
[c] Incredible Years' Dinosaur Curriculum. Webster-Stratton, Reid, and Hammond, 2001; Webster-Stratton, Reid, and Stoolmiller, 2008.
[d] Triple P. Bor, Sanders, and Markie-Dadds, 2002; Connell, Sanders, and Markie-Dadds, 1997; Leung et al., 2003; Sanders et al., 2000; Zubrick et al., 2005; Sanders, Bor, and Morawska, 2007.
[e] Infant Health and Development Program (IHDP); Berlin et al.,1998; Blair et al., 2003; Webster-Stratton and Hammond, 1997.
[f] Greene et al., 2004.
[g] Conduct Problems Prevention Research Group, 2004; Beirman et al., 2004.
[h] Wissow et al., 2008.
[i] Huston et al., 2005.
▭ Age period when interventions take place
▭ Age period with continuing positive impacts of intervention

parental smoking at home and household nicotine levels were significantly reduced by 25–30 percent, which is twice the reduction seen in the control group (Roseby et al., 2008). Another controlled trial found similar impact of home-based parenting smoking cessation (Hovell et al., 2009). In addition, mass media campaigns combined with youth and policy level interventions (e.g., increasing the price of tobacco products and enforcing age bans) can potentially reduce smoking prevalence by 7 percent (Levy, Chaloupka, and Gitchell, 2004).

The negative child health impacts of tobacco exposure translate into substantial monetary burdens for society. The CDC estimated that maternal smoking is responsible for $161 million (in 2010 dollars) of neonatal medical care annually (Centers for Disease Control, 2008), and an economic evaluation concluded that $8.6 billion a year of pediatric care in the United States was attributable to treating childhood illnesses caused by parental smoking.[3] As such, a 15 percent reduction in parental smoking could save society up to $1.3 billion of direct medical care during pregnancy, infancy, and childhood. Assuming conservatively that only 50 percent of these costs could be avoided by interventions targeting children under the age of 5, the United States could still save $650 million (in 2010 dollars) in medical expenses. In summary, there is considerable evidence that many anti-tobacco interventions, particularly those that are multifaceted, are effective at improving child health and producing a new savings of health care dollars (Fiore, Bailey, and Cohen, 2000).

Obesity

Consistent trends toward increased childhood obesity[4] pose a significant problem. Since 1980, the obesity rate nearly tripled among preschool children, from 5 to 14 percent, with even higher prevalence among certain ethnic and racial minority populations (IOM, 2005; Desjardins and Schwartz, 2007). This increase cannot be blamed on genetic predisposition, but instead is the result of a collection of societal changes that encourage a higher caloric intake and a decrease in physical activity: the heavy reliance on and pervasiveness of fast food chains, persistent commercial marketing of food with low nutritional value, suburbanization/urban sprawl and dependence on automobiles, lack of safe outdoor places, and the excessive recreational use of computers, televisions, and other electronic devices.

Without successful interventions, many overweight children will continue to be overweight throughout their lives. Children who are overweight by the time they are in preschool are five times more likely to be overweight at the age of 12 than preschool children with normal weights (Nader et al., 2006).

---

[3] Extrapolation to 2006 dollars is based on calculations in Aligne and Stoddart, 1997.

[4] Although measures and cutoff points of defining childhood obesity have changed over time, the US Centers for Disease Control and Prevention (2000), which uses the term "overweight" rather than "obesity," uses a cutoff of body mass index (weight [kg] / height [m^2]) at or above the 95th percentile for age and sex based on the reference population of the CDC 2000 growth charts. The CDC designates children "at risk for overweight" if they have a BMI between the 85th and 95th percentiles.

Obesity also persists into adulthood for approximately 50–80 percent of overweight children (Whitlock et al., 2005), and obese adolescents are up to twenty times more likely to become obese adults than their normal weight peers (Field, Cook, and Gillman, 2005; Whitaker, Wright, Pepe, Seidel, and Deitz, 1997).

Being overweight as a child can lead to numerous impacts on physical health, including orthopedic complications, metabolic disturbances, type 2 diabetes, disrupted sleep patterns, poor immune function, endocrine problems, impaired mobility, increased blood pressure and hypertension, and increased risk of coronary heart disease in adulthood (Daniels, 2006; Baker, Olsen, and Sørensen, 2007). In addition, childhood obesity can lead to increased risk of psychosocial consequences such as low self-esteem (Doak et al., 2006; Loke, 2002), social alienation (Doak et al., 2006; Daniels, 2006), discrimination (Dietz, 1998; Loke, 2002), lower self-reported quality of life (Daniels, 2006), and depression (Erickson et al., 2000; Loke, 2002). Furthermore, obese children and adolescents who become obese as adults are likely to suffer additional health problems. It is projected that pediatric obesity might shorten life expectancy in the United States by 2 to 5 years by the middle of the twenty-first century (Ludwig, 2007; Olshansky et al., 2005). Obesity is also associated with higher morbidity and mortality among pregnant women, placing them at increased risk for pregnancy, labor, and delivery complications, as well as needing a cesarean section, regardless of their health prior to pregnancy (Must et al., 1998; Weiss et al., 2004).

Although in some cases obesity can shorten one's life so substantially that it may actually result in less lifetime medical cost (van Baal et al., 2008), studies have shown that pediatric obesity can lead to excess medical expenditures over one's lifetime for most people. Some research based on mathematic modeling has shown that early investment in preventing and intervening on obesity among young children could be financially justified if there were long-term effective interventions (Trasande, 2010; Ma and Frick, 2011). However, the overall effectiveness of interventions to prevent or treat overweight in childhood based on reports in the available literature is still unclear: a 2005 Cochrane Review concluded that studies to prevent childhood overweight were "heterogeneous in terms of study design, quality, target population, theoretical underpinning, and outcome measures, making it impossible to combine study findings using statistical methods" (Summerbell et al., 2005). While few studies have specifically targeted young children, there are some promising findings. One example of a preschool-focused intervention, the "Hip-Hop to Health Jr." program, was successful when implemented among a group of African American children (Fitzgibbon et al., 2006), and a small-scale study of clinic-based motivational interviewing for parents showed promising changes in unhealthy eating behaviors of 3- to 7-year-old children (Schwartz et al., 2007). Furthermore, systematic reduction of television and computer screen time has been found to statistically improve BMI and eating behaviors in at-risk children ages 4 to 7 (Epstein et al., 2008). Because of the limited evidence to date, the most likely strategy for effectively reducing childhood obesity requires multi-faceted educational, environmental, and structural components rather than simpler and solitary behavioral interventions (Müller and Danielzik, 2007; Lawlor and Chaturvdei, 2006).

Despite the lack of clarity on the most effective methods of reducing childhood obesity, society stands to gain significant economic benefit if successful in ameliorating this public health issue. The annual cost of obesity in the US is estimated to reach $199 billion (in 2010 dollars), almost 60 percent of which is devoted to direct costs.[5] Prenatal care for women who are overweight is estimated to cost 5 to 16 times more than for women at healthy weights, with the most overweight patients requiring the greatest expenditures (Galtier-Dereure et al., 1995). Childhood obesity also has significant economic consequences: obesity-related hospital costs for children aged 6–17 rose from $48 million to $174 million (in 2010 dollars) between 1979 and 1999, an almost fourfold increase.[6] Every obese child aged 8–19 was estimated to incur an average of $220 more on medical expenditures every year than a normal weight child of the same age (Finkelstein and Trogdon, 2008).

Unintentional injury prevention

Injuries are the leading causes of death, disability, and health care utilization for US children and teenagers between the ages of 1 and 19. For instance, approximately 150,000 children and adolescents became permanently disabled due to unintentional injury in 1996 (Miller, Romano, and Spicer, 2000). In addition, over 73,000 children and adolescents died from injuries between 2000 and 2006, and 20 percent of these deaths were among children younger than 4 years old (Borse and Sleet, 2009). While injuries can happen to anyone, they are associated with environmental hazards and poor quality of housing, in addition to other issues such as poverty, poor parenting, single parenting, alcohol and substance abuse, and neglect (Cummins and Jackson, 2001; Deal et al., 2000).

Historical trends show that the occurrence of injuries can be reduced. For example, the injury incidence rate decreased from

---

[5] Extrapolation to 2006 dollars is based on calculations in Colditz, 1999.
[6] Extrapolation to 2006 dollars is based on calculations in Wang and Dietz, 2002.

2,259 to 1,740 per 10,000 among children 0–4 years old between 1985 and 2000 (Corso et al., 2006). In addition, many studies show that preventive interventions can effectively reduce the incidence of injuries in such areas as gun, road, home, and community safety. A majority of interventions aimed at improving road and home safety found statistically significant changes in safety-related behaviors. For example, one program that provided bilingual education materials and rewards for positive behaviors to families in a low-income Hispanic community significantly increased the practice of child rear seating from 33 to 49 percent (Greenberg-Seth et al., 2004). In another study, persuasive communication and activities designed to promote the purchase and use of bicycle helmets for elementary school children in Quebec were found to significantly increase the practice of wearing helmets from 1.3 to 33 percent within the study community (Farley, Haddad, and Brown, 1996). Similarly, a multifaceted community campaign in Washington State involving education, training, and discount coupons considerably increased booster seat use (Ebel et al., 2003). In another instance, providing tailored educational materials to both primary care physicians and parents was more effective at changing safety behaviors than only educating parents (Nansel, Weaver, and Jacobson, 2008). Finally, among eight home safety intervention studies, seven (Clamp and Kendrick, 1998; Johnston et al., 2000; Johnston et al., 2006; King et al., 2001; Posner et al., 2004; Sznajder et al., 2003; Odendaal et al., 2009) found significant improvements in at least one safety measure, such as lowering tap water temperature.

Studies assessing the monetary burdens of child injuries often use a societal perspective to reflect costs to victims, families, governments, insurers, and taxpayers, estimating both immediate medical expenses and longer-term costs related to losses in productivity. One study (Corso et al., 2006) concluded that fatal and nonfatal injuries among children aged 0–4 resulted in $5.1 billion (in 2010 dollars) for lifelong medical costs and $15 billion (in 2010 dollars) for present and future productivity losses. In 1996, about three in every ten children suffered unintentional injuries serious enough to require medical treatment or restrict activity for at least half a day, resulting in estimated average costs of $5,020 (in 2010 dollars) per victim (Miller et al., 2000).

In sum, unintentional injury prevention is a public health area where a majority of preventive interventions, especially those addressing engineering or environmental aspects, improve parental and child knowledge, perception, and safety behaviors. The few studies that have investigated changes in the injury rate as outcomes have found positive impacts in this population-level measure as well.

Mental health

Mental health is a major concern for children of all ages. An estimated 20 percent of children aged 9–17 suffer from at least mild functional impairments due to a mental of behavioral disorder (US Department of Health and Human Services, 1999), and a significant number of infants, toddlers, and preschoolers exhibit some form of problematic behavior. For instance, 3.4–6.6 percent of children between the ages of 1 and 6 display externalizing behaviors, often referred to as "acting out," while 3.0–6.6 percent exhibit internalizing behaviors, such as withdrawal, depression, or anxiety (McCarty et al., 2005; Silverstein et al., 2006). Many of these children require treatment for their emotional and behavioral disorders; 5.1 percent of children are prescribed medication and 5.3 percent received at least one alternative form of treatment (Simpson et al., 2008).

Early childhood mental and behavioral health problems are linked to a multitude of genetic, dispositional, and environmental factors. For instance, the incidence of early childhood behavior problems has been associated with poverty, maternal depression, insecure attachment to caregivers, and harsh or inconsistent discipline. For instance, a systematic review identified that young children living in poverty are more likely to exhibit behavioral problems during early childhood than the general population (Qi and Kaiser, 2003), and maternal depression has consistently been shown to increase the risk for child behavioral and emotional problems (Birmaher et al., 1996; Cicchetti and Toth, 1998; Cicchetti, Toth, and Rogosch, 1999; Kovacs, 1996). Other studies support the impact of insecure attachment to caregivers and harsh or inconsistent discipline on childhood mental health (Berlin and Cassidy, 1999; Patterson, 1988).

While many believe that preschoolers exhibiting emotional and behavioral problems are "normal" or will eventually "outgrow" their problems (Bryant et al., 1999; Nikkel, 2007), extensive research shows that early disruptive and aggressive behaviors often persist and develop into chronic and severe forms of antisocial behavior (Aguilar et al., 2000; Moffitt et al., 2002; Shaw et al., 2006; Campbell, 1995; Lavigne et al., 1998). In other instances, behavior problems within one domain can spread into others; serious externalizing problems in early childhood have been demonstrated to lower academic competency and promote the emergence of internalizing problems in young adulthood (Masten et al., 2005). As such, early childhood mental health problems can negatively impact other outcomes, including educational attainment (Currie and Stabile, 2004), unemployment (Rutter, Giller, and Hagell, 1998), and perpetration of violent crimes (Offord, Boyle, and Racine, 1991).

A variety of early intervention strategies with different targets and theoretical underpinnings have emerged since 2000. The majority (48 of 74) of the studies examined here used parent-focused training, where parents study effective behavior management skills with the assistance of psychologists/educators or video tapes, and some of the more intensive interventions have demonstrated promising results (Gardner, Burton, and Klimes, 2006; Linares et al., 2006; Kennedy, Rapee, and Edwards, 2009; van den Hoofdakker et al., 2007). While few studies have measured the long-term impact of these trainings, short-term studies have illustrated small to moderate effect sizes (Reyno and McGrath, 2006).

Other programs have combined instruction on disruptive behavior management with efforts designed to improve the quality of the parent–child relationship, and most have improved either infant/toddler–parent interaction (Nixon et al., 2003; Niccols, 2009; Walker et al., 2008; Cheng et al., 2007), children's security or behaviors (Gianni et al., 2006; Phillips et al., 2008), or/and maternal depressive symptoms (Cicchetti et al., 1999; van Doesum et al., 2008). Again, meta-analyses of these types of interventions have reported small effect sizes in the short term but limited long-term follow-up data (Barlow, Parsons, and Stewart-Brown, 2005). In addition, many studies, such as Webster-Stratton and Hammond (1997), targeted various risk factors while training both parents and children, often in group settings. Both parental and child-focused components contribute uniquely to improving child mental health, although characteristics of the children, parents, and family context appear to moderate the effectiveness of such interventions (Lundahl, Risser, and Lovejoy, 2006).

While there have been great improvements to mental health systems of care for children in the United States (Stroul and Blau, 2008), few efforts have focused on young children with emotional or behavioral problems (Perry et al., 2008). To date, the only randomized system-level study of relevance was *New Hope*, an employment-based antipoverty program that used child care assistance and health care subsidies to support working parents. The authors reported improvements in children's social behaviors after providing social services to children with teacher-reported behavioral problems and relocating families to neighborhoods with lower concentrations of poverty (Huston et al., 2005).

One of the few research efforts to examine the long-term impacts of early interventions on mental health is the Carolina Abecedarian Project, a comprehensive early education program for at-risk preschoolers. At age 21, recipients of this full-time, high-quality educational intervention reported fewer depressive symptoms (26 percent) than those in the control group (37 percent) (McLaughlin et al., 2007). While these data suggest a good return on investment of high-quality early childhood programs, their generalizability is limited by a small sample size of high-risk children. Another study examining the long-term impact of early intervention is the Chicago Longitudinal Study that followed young children who enrolled in the Child–Parent Center (CPC) program till they were 24 years old. It reported that, relative to the comparison group, the CPC participants had higher rates of school completion and attendance in college, and lower rates of felony arrests (Reynolds et al., 2007).

Although economic evaluations are growing more frequent in many fields, they are still rare in the area of child mental health prevention and intervention. In one of the few such evaluations, Scott and colleagues (Scott, 2001; Scott et al., 2001) determined that a 13–16-week Webster-Stratton basic videotape program administered to parents of children of 3–8 years old with antisocial behavior was more cost-effective than routine clinic treatment. In particular, they found that the program cost £571 ($1,190 in 2010 US dollars) per child and produced an effect size of 1.06 for the primary outcome measure, giving a cost of £540 ($1,125 in 2010 US dollars) per standard deviation improvement in antisocial behavior, but this number is difficult to interpret unless other interventions report results in similar units. Similarly, Muntz et al. (2004) suggested that treatment using video-taped recording of parent–child interactions may be more cost-effective than standard parent-training programs. Jensen et al. (2005), in the only cost-effectiveness analysis of major ADHD treatments conducted to date, reported that for 14 months of treatment, medical management costs ($1,499 in 2010 dollars per group) and routine community care ($1,361 in 2010 dollars) were relatively low cost, while intensive behavior treatment ($8,879 in 2010 dollars) and combined medical management and behavior treatment ($9,945 in 2010 dollars) were much more expensive. They concluded that while medical management treatment was not as effective as medical management and behavior treatment combined, it was likely a more cost-effective treatment for children with ADHD, especially those without comorbid disorders. On the other hand, Home Start, a UK program that offered volunteer support to families under stress with at least one child under the age of 5, was not a cost-effective alternative to standard health visitor based services, and in fact cost £8,831 ($18,661 in 2010 US dollars) more per family on average after including volunteer time (McAuley et al., 2004).

The United States and other countries stand to gain significant economic benefit by preventing or treating mental and behavioral disorders in young children. Specifically, the annual cost of treating these disorders nationwide in children between the ages of 1 and 5 was estimated at $1.02

billion in 2010 dollars (Sturm et al., 2001). Busch and Barry (2007) have demonstrated, from a family perspective and using a US national data set, that caring for a child with mental health needs affects financial well-being significantly, often more so than caring for a child with other special health care needs. These higher expenses persist when examining costs from a societal perspective; a UK study assessing six domains (foster and residential care in childhood, special educational provision, state benefits received in adulthood, breakdown of relationship, health, and crime) estimated that a child 10 years of age with persistent antisocial behavior would cost society £70,019 ($153,207 in 2010 US dollar) by the time he/she was 28 years old – ten times higher than for those without such problems (Scott et al., 2001; Knapp et al., 2002).

In summary, interventions that focus on multiple risk factors are more effective. In addition, many studies explicitly target externalizing behavior problems in children, especially ODD/CD or ADHD, but few intentionally target internalizing behavior problems, and there is a lack of strong economic evaluations.

Discussion, inferences, and conclusions

This chapter both encompasses the presentation made at the Human Capital Research Collaborative (HCRC) Conference on "Health and Early Child Development" in Minneapolis in October 2010, and updates a previous publication by the authors reviewing the evidence for a policy argument to increase societal investment in early child health as a way to improve children's health, improve health across the lifespan, and yield economic benefits to societal savings in health care and related costs. We argue that the foundations of a healthy life course are formed during the earliest period of life – preconceptionally, prenatally, and in the first five years; that interventions exist to prevent or treat early health problems effectively; and that these early interventions will reduce costs later in life, sometimes enough to create a new savings.

The topics selected for review reflect national priorities, have significant prevalence, involve both physical and mental health issues, and have strong social and environmental determinants. Thus, the argument presented here complements the presentations at the HCRC conference made by Braveman and Duncan. We assessed three components of the argument: the magnitude of each of the problems, the cost implications of the problems both in childhood and later in adult life, and the availability of effective interventions that have monetary benefits. The updated literature review (papers published in July 2007 to April 2010) identified twenty-six additional interventions that target young children that provide supplementary evidence, but none of the new studies added substantially to the evidence for the argument or contradicted it. Therefore, we have not substantially changed the conclusions drawn from that earlier review.

Overall magnitude of children's health burden

We estimated the overall magnitude of the burden of the following four conditions on the health of America's children. The compiled findings showed, first, that 25% of children are exposed to environmental tobacco smoke by household members, and 10% of women giving birth in 2004 smoked during pregnancy. Second, the prevalence of childhood obesity has reached 14 percent. Third, three in ten children suffer an unintentional injury serious enough to require medical treatment or restrict activity. Finally, for children between the ages of 1 and 6, approximately 3 to 7% are estimated to have externalizing or internalizing mental health problems. There is no simple way, however, to arrive at a single estimate of the overall burden of these conditions on preschool children in the US. Adding up the prevalence would overestimate the total burden because these conditions can overlap in the population. It would not be unreasonable to estimate, however, that nearly all low-income/disadvantaged preschoolers are affected by one or more of these problems, and that the total prevalence declines among more affluent children. Although, we expect some overlap between the four health issues among children, the correlations are unlikely to be 0 percent or 100 percent. As a result, we estimate approximately one-third to one-half of each US birth cohort children are affected by one or more of the four health issues.

Economic burden of children's health conditions

The evidence for the economic costs and long-term consequences of these four health problems among preschool children is compelling. Since the economic data come from a wide variety of sources and types of studies, it is not possible to create an exact estimate for their total economic cost. However, it is likely that the *lifetime societal* burden of these problems, if untreated, runs into hundreds of billions of dollars for each birth cohort. Assuming that the four health problems combined affect approximately one-third to half of each US birth cohort – about 1.3 to 2 million children each year – we calculate that as little as a total lifetime societal cost (including health care, special education, productivity loss, civil justice, etc.) of $50,000 per child will translate to between $65 billion and $100 billion for the whole birth cohort.

Availability of effective and cost-effective interventions

The four children's health topics we selected demonstrate that the policy solutions needed to address them go well beyond the medical model of a doctor treating a sick child. As Braveman et al. argue in Chapter 2 of this volume, health is more than health care. The causes of those health problems have deep socioeconomic roots, and therefore effectiveness of interventions will be limited without addressing bigger issues in social environment. Meeting the underlying health needs of American children will require decision-makers and practitioners to understand complex multiple determinants of health and diseases as well as public health approaches that involve family, community, and national interventions.

The review found the evidence from intervention studies across the four child health areas to be uneven; the strategies behind the interventions are different, and the effectiveness of programs is mixed. The best evidence for effective interventions is available for tobacco control and injury prevention; model programs are available for implementation at clinical and community levels and both net and gross cost savings from their implementation would be considerable. To date, unfortunately, few interventions have targeted obesity prevention among preschoolers. Within early childhood mental health, there are many interventions that have focused on symptom reduction and building parents' skills to manage problem behaviors, but no rigorous studies of effective population-based approaches to promoting social-emotional health in children under the age of 5. Furthermore, some effective interventions may affect multiple domains of child health (i.e., reducing maternal depression might lead to declines in both unintended injuries and children's behavioral problems).

The evidence for the cost-effectiveness of interventions is also mixed. The best evidence, again, is available for tobacco control and injury prevention. This unevenness reflects the paucity of research on effective interventions that have long-term consequences. Data are absent at all points along the continuum – including cost data, effectiveness data, and clear links to long-term consequences. The absence of economic evaluations of interventions to prevent early child obesity is particularly obvious.

The review identified significant limitations in the intervention literature. Among them is the lack of studies that followed populations long enough to demonstrate their full life-course impact. This limitation reflects the logistical difficulties of conducting long-term follow-ups in experimental intervention studies and the related failure of public and private research funders to support longitudinal research. The cost of such research must be compared with the expected costs of doing nothing, and the expected improvement in societal outcomes and cost savings.

Conclusion

This chapter is an updated review of the literature that was presented at the Human Capital Research Collaborative Conference on "Health and Early Child Development" in October 2010. The review found convincing evidence that in early life the four issues – tobacco exposure, unintentional injury, obesity, and mental health – constitute significant burdens on the health of children and are the early antecedents of health problems across the lifespan. The evidence for the cost consequences of these problems is strong, although more uneven than the epidemiological evidence.

In contrast, the review of the preventive intervention research and economic evaluation literature in the prenatal and preschool period found considerable gaps in the evidence, making us more cautious about drawing policy implications. There is an urgent need for carefully targeted, specific, rigorous research to examine the longitudinal causal relationships between early childhood preventive interventions and health outcomes across the life course. Specifically, such new research must include preconceptional and prenatal interventions, testing hypotheses that arise from life course epidemiological studies. The research should be carried out in a broad range of socioeconomic, racial, and ethnic groups to assess its impact on health disparities. Finally, the most rigorous implementation studies and economic study designs are needed to convince policymakers to bring such research into the policymaking process. Such intervention research must address the complex clinical, environmental, familial, and public health dimensions of these problems.

One economic study estimated that the federal government's total "investment" spending for children of all ages in 2006 was 1.6% of GDP, and the share of the budget was projected to decline by 14 to 29% between 2006 and 2017 (Steuerle, Reynolds, and Carasso, 2008). Now may be the time to reverse this trend of disinvestment, if the nation is to improve the health of children and avert future health and cost consequences. The failure to strengthen prevention research and practice in this young age group brings with it the risk that future researchers will find an even greater magnitude of the poor health burden attributable to missed opportunities for early prevention. While waiting for new longitudinal research which measures and catalogs outcomes of specific early child health interventions, we conclude that the available research justifies targeted investments in early childhood health promotion.

References

Abdullah, A. S., Mak, Y. W., Loke, A. Y., and Lam, T. H. (2005). Smoking cessation intervention in parents of young children: a randomised controlled trial. *Addiction* (Abingdon, UK), 100(11), 1731–1740.

Administration for Children and Families, US Department of Health and Human Services (2006). *Research to practice: Early Head Start benefits: Children and families: Early Head Start research and evaluation project.* Washington, DC.

Aguilar, B., Sroufe, L. A., Egeland, B., and Carlson, E. (2000). Distinguishing the life-course-persistent and adolescent-limited antisocial behavior types: from birth to 16 years. *Development and Psychopathology*, 12, 109–132.

Albrecht, S. A., Caruthers, D., Patrick, T., Reynolds, M., Salamie, D., Higgins, L. W., ... and Mlynarchek, S. (2006). A randomized controlled trial of a smoking cessation intervention for pregnant adolescents. *Nursing Research*, 55(6), 402–410.

Aligne, C. A., and Stoddard, J. J. (1997). Tobacco and children: an economic evaluation of the medical effects of parental smoking. *Archives of Pediatric and Adolescent Medicine*, 151, 648–653.

Baker, J. L., Olsen, L. W., and Sørensen, T. I. (2007). Childhood body-mass index and the risk of coronary heart disease in adulthood. *New England Journal of Medicine*, 357(23), 2329–2337.

Barker, D. J. P. (1998). *Mothers, babies, and health in later life.* Edinburgh: Churchill Livingstone.

Barlow, J., Parsons, J., and Stewart-Brown, S. (2005). Preventing emotional and behavioural problems: the effectiveness of parenting programmes with children less than 3 years of age. *Child: Care, Health and Development*, 31, 33–42.

Berlin, L. J., and Cassidy, J. (1999). Relations among relationships: contributions from attachment theory and research. In J. Cassidy and P. R. Shaver (eds.), *Handbook of attachment: theory, research, and clinical applications* (pp. 688–712). New York: Guilford Press.

Berlin, L. J., Brooks-Gunn, J., McCarton, C., and McCormick, M. C. (1998). The effectiveness of early intervention: examining risk factors and pathways to enhanced development. *Preventive Medicine*, 27(2), 238–245.

Birmaher, B., Ryan, N. D., Williamson, D. E., Brent, D. A., Kaufman, J., Dahl, R. E., Perel, J., and Nelson, B. (1996). Childhood and adolescent depression: a review of the past 10 years. Part I. *Journal of the American Academy of Child and Adolescent Psychiatry*, 35(11), 1427–1439.

Bierman, K. L., Coie, J. D., Dodge, K. A., Foster, E. M., Greenberg, M. T., Lochman, J. E., ... and Conduct Problems Prevention Research Group (2004). The effects of the fast track program on serious problem outcomes at the end of elementary school. *Journal of Clinical Child and Adolescent Psychology*, 33(4), 650–661.

Blair, C., Peters, R., and Lawrence, F. (2003). Family dynamics and child outcomes in early intervention: the role of developmental theory in the specification of effects. *Early Childhood Research Quarterly*, 18(4), 446–467.

Bor, W., Sanders, M. R., and Markie-Dadds, C. (2002). The effects of the triple P-positive parenting program on preschool children with co-occurring disruptive behavior and attentional/hyperactive difficulties. *Journal of Abnormal Child Psychology*, 30(6), 571–587.

Borse, N., and Sleet, D. A. (2009). CDC childhood injury report: patterns of unintentional injuries among 0- to 19-year olds in the United States, 2000–2006. *Family & Community Health*, 32(2), 189.

Braun, J. M., Kahn, R. S., Froehlich, T., Auinger, P., and Lanphear, B. P. (2006). Exposures to environmental toxicants and attention deficit hyperactivity disorder in US children. *Environmental Health Perspectives*, 114, 1904–1909.

Bryant, D., Vizzard, L. H., Willoughby, M., and Kupersmidt, J. (1999). A review of intervention for preschoolers with aggressive and disruptive behavior. *Early Education & Development*, 10(1), 47–68.

Busch, S. H., and Barry, C. L. (2007). Mental health disorders in childhood: assessing the burden on families. *Health Affairs*, 26(4), 1088–1095.

Centers for Disease Control and Prevention (2000). *Reducing tobacco use: a report of the surgeon general*. Washington, DC: Government Printing Office.

Campbell, S. B. (1995). Behavior problems in preschool children: a review of recent research. *Journal of Child Psychology Psychiatry*, 36(1), 113–149.

Centers for Disease Control and Prevention (2008). Smoking-attributable mortality, morbidity, and economic costs (SAMMEC). Online Application. Available at http://apps.nccd.cdc.gov/sammec/index.asp (accessed December, 2008).

Cheng, S., Kondo, N., Aoki, Y., Kitamura, Y., Takeda, Y., and Yamagata, Z. (2007). The effectiveness of early intervention and the factors related to child behavioural problems at age 2: a randomized controlled trial. *Early Human Development*, 83(10), 683–691.

Cicchetti, D., and Toth, S. L. (1998). The development of depression in children and adolescents. *American Psychologist*, 53(2), 221–241.

Cicchetti, D., Toth, S. L., and Rogosch, F. A. (1999). The efficacy of toddler–parent psychotherapy to increase attachment security in offspring of depressed mothers. *Attachment and Human Development*, 1, 34–66.

Clamp, M., and Kendrick, D. A. (1998). Randomised controlled trial of general practitioner safety advice for families with children under 5 years. *British Medical Journal*, 316(7144), 1576–1579.

Conley, D., Strully, K. W., and Bennett, N. G. (2003). *The starting gate: birth weight and life chances*. Berkeley, CA: University of California Press.

Colditz, G. A. (1999). Economic costs of obesity and inactivity. *Medicine and Science in Sports and Exercise*, 31(11), S663–667.

Connell, S., Sanders, M. R., and Markie-Dadds, C. (1997). Self-directed behavioral family intervention for parents of oppositional children in rural and remote areas. *Behavior Modification*, 21(4), 379–408.

Colby, S. M., Monti, P. M., O'Leary Tevyaw, T., Barnett, N. P., Spirito, A., Rohsenow, D. J., ... and Lewander, W. (2005). Brief motivational intervention for adolescent smokers in medical settings. *Addictive Behaviors*, 30(5), 865–874.

Cook, D. G., and Strachan, D. P. (1999). Summary of effects of parental smoking on the respiratory health of children and implications for research. *Thorax*, 54, 357–366.

Corso, P., Finkelstein, E., Miller, T., Fiebelkorn, I., and Zaloshnja, E. (2006). Incidence and lifetime costs of injuries in the United States. *Injury Prevention*, 12(4), 212–218.

Cummins, S. K., and Jackson, R. J. (2001). The built environment and children's health. *Pediatric Clinics of North America*, 48(5), 1241–1252.

Currie, J., and Stabile, M. (2004). *Child mental health and human capital accumulation: the case of ADHD*. NBER Working Paper Series w10435. Available at SSRN http://ssrn.com/abstract=532994.

Daniels, S. R. (2006). The consequences of childhood overweight and obesity. *Future of Children*, 16(1), 47–67.

Deal, L. W., Gomby, D. S., Zippiroli, L., and Behrman, R. E. (2000). Unintentional injuries in childhood: analysis and recommendations. *Future of Children*, 10(1), 4–22.

Desjardins, E., and Schwartz, A. (2007). Collaborating to combat childhood obesity. *Health Affairs*, 26(2), 567–571.

Dietz, W. H. (1998). Health consequences of obesity in youth: childhood predictors of adult disease. *Pediatrics*, 101(3), s518–525.

DiClemente, C. C., Dolan-Mullen, P., and Windsor, R. A. (2000). The process of pregnancy smoking cessation: implications for interventions. *Tobacco Control*, 9(3), iii16–iii21.

DiFranza, J. R., Peck, R. M., Radecki, T. E., and Savageau, J. A. (2001). What is the potential cost-effectiveness of enforcing a prohibition on the sale of tobacco to minors? *Preventive Medicine*, 32(2), 168–174.

Doak, C. M., Visscher, T. L. S., Renders, C. M., and Seidell, J. C. (2006). The prevention of overweight and obesity in children and adolescents: a review of interventions and programmes. *Obesity Reviews*, 7, 111–136.

Donatelle, R. J., Prows, S. L., Champeau, D., and Hudson, D. (2000). Randomised controlled trial using social support and financial incentives for high risk pregnant smokers: significant other supporter (SOS) program. *Tobacco Control*, 9 Suppl 3, III67–9.

Ebel, B. E., Koepsell, T. D., Bennett, E. E., and Rivara, F. P. (2003). Use of child booster seats in motor vehicles following a community campaign: a controlled trial. *Journal of the American Medical Association*, 289(7), 879–884.

Emmons, K. M., Hammond, S. K., Fava, J. L., Velicer, W. F., Evans, J. L., and Monroe, A. D. (2001). A randomized trial to reduce passive smoke exposure in low-income households with young children. *Pediatrics*, 108(1), 18–24.

Epstein, L. H., Roemmich, J. N., Robinson, J. L., Palunch, R. A., Winiewicz, D. D., Fuerch, J. H., and Robinson, T. N. (2008). A randomized trial of the effects of reducing television viewing and computer use on body mass index in young children. *Archives of Pediatrics and Adolesent Medicine*, 162(3), 239–245.

Eriksson, J., Forsen, T., Tuomilehto, J., Osmond, C., and Barker, D. (2001). Size at birth, childhood growth and obesity in adult life. *International Journal of Obesity and Related Metabolic Disorders: Journal of the International Association for the Study of Obesity*, 25(5), 735–740.

Erickson, S. J., Robinson, T. N., Haydel, K. F., and Killen, J. D. (2000). Are overweight children unhappy? Body mass index, depressive symptoms, and overweight concerns in elementary school children. *Archives of Pediatrics and Adolesent Medicine*, 154, 931–935.

Ershoff, D. H., Mullen, P. D., and Quinn, V. P. (1989). A randomized trial of a serialized self-help smoking cessation program for pregnant women in an HMO. *American Journal of Public Health*, 79(2), 182–187.

Fang, W. L., Goldstein, A. O., Butzen, A. Y., Hartsock, S. A., Hartmann, K. E., Helton, M., and Lohr, J. A. (2004). Smoking cessation in pregnancy: a review of postpartum relapse prevention strategies. *Journal of the American Board of Family*, 17(4), 264–275.

Farley, C., Haddad, S., and Brown, B. (1996). The effects of a 4-year program promoting bicycle helmet use among children in Quebec. *American Journal of Public Health*, 86(1), 46–51.

Field, A. E., Cook, N. R., and Gillman, M. W. (2005). Weight status in childhood as a predictor of becoming overweight or hypertensive in early adulthood. *Obesity Research*, 13, 163–169.

Finkelstein, E. A., and Trogdon, J. G. (2008). Public health interventions for addressing childhood overweight: analysis of the business case. *American Journal of Public Health*, 98(3), 411–415.

Fiore, M. C., Bailey, W. C., and Cohen, S. J. (2000). *Treating tobacco use and dependence*. Rockville, MD: US Department of Health and Human Services.

Fitzgibbon, M. L., Stolley, M. R., Schiffer, L., Van Horn, L., Kaufer Christoffel, K., and Dyer, A. (2006). Hip-hop to health jr. for latino preschool children. *Obesity*, 14(9), 1616–1625.

Fitzgibbon, M. L., Stolley, M. R., Schiffer, L., Van Horn, L., Kaufer Christoffel, K., and Dyer, A. (2005). Two-year follow-up results for hip-hop to health jr.: a randomized controlled trial for overweight prevention in preschool minority children. *Journal of Pediatrics*, 146(5), 618–625.

Galtier-Dereure, F., Montpeyroux, F., Boulot, P., Bringer, J., and Jaffiol, C. (1995). Weight excess before pregnancy: complications and cost. *International Journal of Obesity Related Metabolic Disorders*, 19, 443–448.

Gardner, F., Burton, J., and Klimes, I. (2006). Randomised controlled trial of a parenting intervention in the voluntary sector for reducing child conduct problems: outcomes and mechanisms of change. *Journal of Child Psychology and Psychiatry*, 47(11), 1123–1132.

Gianni, M. L., Picciolini, O., Ravasi, M., Gardon, L., Vegni, C., Fumagalli, M., and Mosca, F. (2006). The effects of an early developmental mother–child intervention program on neurodevelopment outcome in very low birth weight infants: a pilot study. *Early Human Development*, 82, 691–695.

Gluckman, P. D., Hanson, M. A., and Beedle, A. S. (2007). Early life events and their consequences for later disease: a life history and evolutionary perspective. *American Journal of Human Biology*, 19(1), 1–19.

Golan, M., Kaufman, V., and Shahar, D. R. (2006). Childhood obesity treatment: targeting parents exclusively v. parents and children. *British Journal of Nutrition*, 95(5), 1008–1015.

Greenberg-Seth, J., Hemenway, D., Gallagher, S. S., Ross, J. B., and Lissy, K. S. (2004). Evaluation of a community-based intervention to promote rear seating for children. *American Journal of Public Health*, 94(6), 1009–1013.

Greene, R. W., Ablon, J. S., Goring, J. C., Raezer-Blakely, L., Markey, J., Monuteaux, M. C., ... and Rabbitt, S. (2004). Effectiveness of collaborative problem solving in affectively dysregulated children with oppositional-defiant disorder: initial findings. *Journal of Consulting and Clinical Psychology*, 72(6), 1157–1164.

Hardy, M. S. (2002). Teaching firearm safety to children: failure of a program. *Journal of Developmental and Behavioral Pediatrics*, 23(2), 71–76.

Hersey, J. C., Niederdeppe, J., Ng, S. W., Mowery, P., Farrelly, M., and Messeri, P. (2005). How state counter-industry campaigns help prime perceptions of tobacco industry practices to promote reductions in youth smoking. *Tobacco Control*, 14(6), 377–383.

Hopkins, D. P., Husten, C. G., Fielding, J. E., Rosenquist, J. N., and Westphal, L. L. (2001). Evidence reviews and recommendations on interventions to reduce tobacco use and exposure to environmental tobacco smoke: a summary of selected guidelines. *American Journal of Preventive Medicine*, 20(2 Suppl.), 67–87.

Hovell, M. F., Zakarianm, J. M., Matt, G. E., Hofstetter, C. R., Bernert, J. T., and Pirkle, J. (2009). Counseling to reduce children's secondhand smoke exposure and help parents quit smoking: a controlled trial. *Nicotine and Tobacco Research*, 11(12), 1383–1394. Epub Oct. 29, 2009.

Hovell, M. F., Meltzer, S. B., Wahlgren, D. R., Matt, G. E., Hofstetter, C. R., Jones, J. A., ... and Pirkle, J. L. (2002). Asthma management and environmental tobacco smoke exposure reduction in Latino children: a controlled trial. *Pediatrics*, 110(5), 946–956.

Hovell, M. F., Meltzer, S. B., Zakarian, J. M., Wahlgren, D. R., Emerson, J. A., Hofstetter, C. R., ... and O'Connor, R. D. (1994). Reduction of environmental tobacco smoke exposure among asthmatic children: a controlled trial. *Chest*, 106(2), 440–446.

Hovell, M. F., Zakarian, J. M., Matt, G. E., Hofstetter, C. R., Bernert, J. T., and Pirkle, J. (2000). Effect of counselling mothers on their children's exposure to environmental tobacco smoke: randomised controlled trial. *BMJ* (Clinical Research Edition), 321(7257), 337–342.

Hunt, D. E., and Hauck, F. R. (2006). Sudden infant death syndrome. *Canadian Medical Association Journal*, 174, 1861–1869.

Huston, A. C., Duncan, G. J., McLoyd, V. C., Crosby, D. A., Ripke, M. N., Weisner, T. S., and Eldred, C. A. (2005). Impacts on children of a policy to promote employment and reduce poverty for low-income: new hope after five years. *Developmental Psychology*, 41, 902–918.

Hyland, A., Wakefield, M., Higbee, C., Szczypka, G., and Cummings, K. M. (2006). Anti-tobacco television advertising and indicators of smoking cessation in adults: a cohort study. *Health Education Research*, 21(2), 296–302.

IOM (2005). *Preventing childhood obesity: health in the balance*. Washington, DC: National Academies Press.

Jameson, E. J., and Wehr, E. (1993). Drafting national health care reform legislation to protect the health interests of children. *Stanford Law and Policy Review*, 51, 152–155.

Jensen, P. S., Garcia, J. A., Glied, S., Crowe, M., Foster, M., Schlander, M., ... and Wells, K. (2005). Cost-effectiveness of ADHD treatments: findings from the multimodal treatment study of children with ADHD. *American Journal of Psychiatry*, 162(9), 1628–1636.

Johnston, B. D., Britt, J., D'Ambrosio, L., Mueller, B. A., and Rivara, F. P. (2000). A preschool program for safety and injury prevention delivered by home visitors. *Injury Prevention*, 6(4), 305–309.

Johnston, B. D., Huebner, C. E., Anderson, M. L., Tyll, L. T., and Thompson, R. S. (2006). Healthy steps in an integrated delivery system: child and parent outcomes at 30 months. *Archives of Pediatric and Adolescent Medicine*, 160(8), 793–800.

Johnson, S., Ring, W., Anderson, P., and Marlow, N. (2005). Randomised trial of parental support for families with very preterm children: outcome at 5 years. *Archives of Disease in Childhood*, 90(9), 909–915.

Johnston, B. D., Britt, J., D'Ambrosio, L., Mueller, B. A., and Rivara, F. P. (2000). A preschool program for safety and injury prevention delivered by home visitors. *Injury Prevention: Journal of the International Society for Child and Adolescent Injury Prevention*, 6(4), 305–309.

Johnston, B. D., Huebner, C. E., Anderson, M. L., Tyll, L. T., and Thompson, R. S. (2006). Healthy steps in an integrated delivery system: child and parent outcomes at 30 months. *Archives of Pediatric and Adolescent Medicine*, 160(8), 793–800.

Kendrick, D., Illingworth, R., Woods, A., Watts, K., Collier, J., Dewey, M., ... and Chen, C. M. (2005). Promoting child safety in primary care: a cluster randomised controlled trial to reduce baby walker use. *British Journal of General Practice: The Journal of the Royal College of General Practitioners*, 55 (517), 582–588.

Kennedy, S. J., Rapee, R. M., and Edwards, S. E. (2009). A selective intervention program for inhibited preschool-aged children of parents with an anxiety disorder: effects on current anxiety disorders and temperament. *Journal of the American Academy of Child and Adolescent Psychiatry*, 48, 602–609.

King, W. J., Klassen, T. P., LeBlanc, J., Bernard-Bonnin, A-C., Robitaille, Y., Pham, P., ... and Pless, I. B. (2001). The effectiveness of a home visit to prevent childhood injury. *Pediatrics*, 108(2), 382–388.

Kitzman, H., Olds, D. L., Henderson, C. R., Jr., Hanks, C., Cole, R., Tatelbaum, R., ... and Barnard, K. (1997). Effect of prenatal and infancy home visitation by nurses on pregnancy outcomes, childhood injuries, and repeated childbearing: a randomized controlled trial. *Journal of the American Medical Association*, 278(8), 644–652.

Knapp, M., McCrone, P., Fombonne, E., Beecham, J., and Wostear, G. (2002). The Maudsley long-term follow-up of child and adolescent depression: 3. Impact of comorbid conduct disorder on service use and costs in adulthood. *British Journal of Psychiatry*, 180, 19–23.

Kovacs, M. (1996). Presentation and course of major depressive disorder during childhood and later years of the life span. *Journal of the American Academy of Child and Adolescent Psychiatry*, 35(6), 705–715.

Lantz, P. M., Jacobson, P. D., Warner, K. E., Wasserman, J., Pollack, H. A., Berson, J., and Ahlstrom, A. (2000). Investing in youth tobacco control: a review of smoking prevention and control strategies. *Tobacco Control*, 9(1), 47–63.

Lavigne, J. V., Arend, R., Rosenbaum, D., Binns, H. J., Christoffel, K. K., and Gibbons, R. D. (1998). Psychiatric disorders with onset in the preschool years: II. Correlates and predictors of stable case status. *Journal of the American Academy of Child and Adolescent Psychiatry*, 37(12), 1255–1261.

Lawlor, D. A., and Chaturvdei, N. (2006). Treatment and prevention of obesity – are there critical periods for intervention? *International Journal of Epidemiology*, 35, 3–9.

Leung, C., Sanders, M. R., Leung, S., Mak, R., and Lau, J. (2003). An outcome evaluation of the implementation of the triple P-positive parenting program in Hong Kong. *Family Process*, 42(4), 531–544.

Levy, D. T., Chaloupka, F., and Gitchell, J. (2004). The effects of tobacco control policies on smoking rates: a tobacco control scorecard. *Journal of Public Health Management and Practice*, 10, 338–353.

Linares, L. O., Montalto, D., Li, M., and Oza, V. S. (2006). A promising parenting intervention in foster care. *Journal of Consulting and Clinical Psychology*, 74 (1), 32–41.

Loke, K. Y. (2002). Consequences of childhood and adolescent obesity. *Asia Pacific Journal of Clinical Nutrition*, 11(3), s702–704.

Ludwig, D. S. (2007). Childhood obesity – the shape of things to come. *New England Journal of Medicine*, 357(23), 2325–2327.

Lumley, J., Oliver, S. S., Chamberlain, C., and Oakley, L. (2004). Interventions for promoting smoking cessation during pregnancy. *Cochrane Database of Systematic Reviews*, 4(4), CD001055.

Lundahl, B., Risser, H. J., and Lovejoy, M. C. (2006). A meta-analysis of parent training: moderators and follow-up effects. *Clinical Psychology Review*, 26, 86–104.

Ma, S. and Frick, K. (2011). A simulation of affordability and effectiveness of childhood obesity interventions. *Academic Pediatrics*, 11(4), 342–350.

Mallonee, S. (2000). Evaluating injury prevention programs: the Oklahoma city smoke alarm project. *The Future of Children / Center for the Future of Children, the David and Lucile Packard Foundation*, 10(1), 164–174.

Masten, A. S., Roisman, G. I., Long, J. D., Burt, K. B., Obradović, J., ... and Tellegen, A. (2005). Developmental cascades: linking academic achievement and externalizing and internalizing symptoms over 20 years. *Developmental Psychology*, 41(5), 733–746.

McAuley, C., Knapp, M., Beecham, J., McCurry, N., and Sleed, M. (2004). *Young families under stress: outcomes and costs of Home-Start support*. York: Joseph Rowntree Foundation. http://eprints.soton.ac.uk/41029/.

McCarty, C. A., Zimmerman, F. J., Digiuseppe, D. L., and Christakis, D. A. (2005). Parental emotional support and subsequent internalizing and externalizing problems among children. *Journal of Developmental and Behavioral Pediatrics*, 26(4), 267–275.

McDonald, P., Colwell, B., Backinger, C. L., Husten, C., and Maule, C. O. (2003). Better practices for youth tobacco cessation: evidence of review panel. *American Journal of Health Behavior*, 27 Suppl. 2, S144–58.

McLaughlin, A. E., Campbell, F. A., Pungello, E. P., and Skinner, M. (2007). Depressive symptoms in young adults: the influences of the early home environment and early educational child care. *Child Development*, 78, 746–756.

McLaughlin, A. E., Campbell, F. A., Pungello, E. P., and Skinner, M. (2007). Depressive symptoms in young adults: the influences of the early home environment and early educational child care. *Child Development*, 78(3), 746–756.

Melvin, C. L., Dolan-Mullen, P., Windsor, R. A., Whiteside, H. P., Jr, and Goldenberg, R. L. (2000). Recommended cessation counselling for pregnant women who smoke: a review of the evidence. *Tobacco Control*, 9 Suppl. 3, III80–4.

Miller, T. R., Romano, E. O., and Spicer, R. S. (2000). The cost of childhood unintentional injuries and the value of prevention. *Future of Children*, 10(1), 137–163.

Minkovitz, C. S., Hughart, N., Strobino, D., Scharfstein, D., Grason, H., Hou, W., ... and Guyer, B. (2003). A practice-based intervention to enhance quality of care in the first 3 years of life: the healthy steps for young children program. *Journal of the American Medical Association*, 290(23), 3081–3091.

Moffitt, T. E., Caspi, A., Harrington, H., and Milne, B. J. (2002). Males on the life-course-persistent and adolescence-limited antisocial pathways: follow-up at age 26 years. *Development and Psychopathology*, 14, 179–207.

Müller, M. J., and Danielzik, S. (2007). Childhood overweight: is there a need for a new societal approach to the obesity epidemic? *Obesity Reviews*, 8, 87–90.

Muntz, R., Hutchings, J., Edwards, R. T., Hounsome, B., and O'Ceilleachair, A. (2004). Economic evaluation of treatments for children with severe behavioural problems. *Journal of Mental Health Policy and Economics*, 7(4), 177–189.

Must, A., Spadano, J., Coakley, E. H., Field, A. E., Colditz, G., and Dietz, W. H. (1998). The disease burden associated with overweight and obesity. *Journal of the American Medical Association*, 282, 1523–1529.

Nader, P. R., O'Brien, M., Houts, R., Bradley, R., Belsky, J., Crosnoe, R., ... and Susman, E. J. (2006). Identifying risk for obesity in early childhood. *Pediatrics*, 118(3), e594–601.

Nansel, T. R., Weaver, N. L., Jacobsen, H. A., Glasheen, C., and Kreuter, M. W. (2008). Preventing unintentional pediatric injuries: a tailored intervention for parents and providers. *Health Education Research*, 23(4), 656–669. Epub Sept. 28, 2007.

National Institutes of Health, US Department of Health and Human Services. (1994). *Tobacco and the clinician: interventions for medical and dental practice.* Smoking and Tobacco Control Monograph 5. Bethesda, MD:

Niccols, A. (2009). Immediate and short-term outcomes of the "COPEing with Toddler Behaviour" parent group. *Journal of Child Psychology and Psychiatry*, 50(5), 617–626.

Nikkel, P. (2007). Building partnerships with families. In Deborah F. Perry, Roxane K. Kaufmann, and J. Knitzer (eds.), *Social and emotional health in early childhood: building bridges between services and systems* (pp. 147–167). Baltimore, MD: Paul H. Brookes Publishing.

Nixon, R. D. V., Sweeney, L., Erickson, D. B., and Touyz, S. W. (2003). Parent–child interaction therapy: a comparison of standard and abbreviated treatments for oppositional defiant preschoolers. *Journal of Consulting and Clinical Psychology*, 71, 251–60.

Odendaal, W., van Niekerk, A., Jordaan, E., and Seedat, M. (2009). The impact of a home visitation programme on household hazards associated with unintentional childhood injuries: a randomised controlled trial. *Accident Analysis and Prevention*, 41(1), 183–190. Epub Nov. 14, 2008.

Offord, D. R., Boyle, M. H., and Racine, Y. A. (1991). The epidemiology of antisocial behavior in childhood and adolescence. In D. J. Pepler and K. H. Rubin (eds.), *The development and treatment of childhood aggression* (pp. 31–54). Hillsdale, NJ: Erlbaum.

Olshansky, S. J., Passaro, D. J., Hershow, R. C., Layden, J., Carnes, B. A., Brody, J., Hayflick, L., ... and Ludwig, D. S. (2005). A potential decline in life expectancy in the United States in the 21st century. *New England Journal of Medicine*, 352(11), 1138–1145.

Patterson, J. M. (1988). Families experiencing stress: I. The family adjustment and adaptation response model II. Applying the FAAR model to health related issues for intervention and research. *Family Systems Medicine*, 6, 202–237.

Pbert, L., Moolchan, E. T., Muramoto, M., Winickoff, J. P., Curry, S., Lando, H., ... and Tobacco Consortium, Center for Child Health Research of the American Academy of Pediatrics (2003). The state of office-based interventions for youth tobacco use. *Pediatrics*, 111(6 Pt. 1), e650–660.

Perry, D. F., Kaufmann, R. K., Hoover, S., et al. (2008). Services for young children and their families in systems of care. In B. Stroul and G. Blau (eds.), *The system of care handbook* (pp. 419–516). Baltimore, MD: Brookes Publishing.

Phillips, J., Morgan, S., Cawthorne, K., and Barnett, B. (2008). Pilot evaluation of parent–child interaction therapy delivered in an Australian community early childhood clinic setting. *Australian and New Zealand Journal of Psychiatry*, 42 (8), 712–719.

Posner, J. C., Hawkins, L. A., Garcia-Espana, F., and Derbin, D. R. (2004). A randomized, clinical trial of a home safety intervention based in an emergency department setting. *Pediatrics*, 113(6), 1603–1608.

Roseby, R., Waters, E., Polnay, A., Campbell, R., Spencer, N., ... and Ferguson-Thorne, G. (2008). Family and carer smoking control programmes for reducing children's exposure to environmental tobacco smoke. *Cochrane Database of Systematic Reviews*, 8(4), 10.

Qi, C. H., and Kaiser, A. P. (2003). Behavior problems of preschool children from low-income families: review of the literature. *Topics in Early Childhood Special Education*, 23(4), 188–216.

Ranney, L., Melvin, C., Lux, L., McClain, E., Morgan, L., and Lohr, K. N. (2006). Tobacco use: prevention, cessation, and control. *Evidence Report/Technology Assessment*, 140, 1–120.

Reynolds, A. J., Temple, J. A., Ou, S. R., Robertson, D. L., Mersky, J. P., Topitzes, J. W., and Niles, M. D. (2007). Effects of a school-based, early childhood intervention on adult health and well-being: a 19-year follow-up of low-income families. *Archives of Pediatrics and Adolescent Medicine*, 161(8), 730–739.

Reyno, S. M., and McGrath, P. J. (2006). Predictors of parent training efficacy for child externalizing behavior problem – a meta-analytic review. *Journal of Child Psychology and Psychiatry*, 47, 99–111.

Rodgers, G. B., and Leland, E. W. (2005). An evaluation of the effectiveness of a baby walker safety standard to prevent stair-fall injuries. *Journal of Safety Research*, 36(4), 327–332.

Rutter, M., Giller, H., and Hagell, A. (1998). *Antisocial behavior by young people.* Cambridge University Press.

Samet, J. M., Lewit, E. M., and Warner, K. E. (1994). Involuntary smoking and children's health. *The Future of Children / Center for the Future of Children, the David and Lucile Packard Foundation*, 4(3), 94–114.

Sanders, M. R., Bor, W., and Morawska, A. (2007). Maintenance of treatment gains: a comparison of enhanced, standard, and self-directed triple P-positive parenting program. *Journal of Abnormal Child Psychology*, 35(6), 983–998.

Sanders, M. R., Markie-Dadds, C., Tully, L. A., and Bor, W. (2000). The triple P-positive parenting program: a comparison of enhanced, standard, and self-directed behavioral family intervention for parents of children with early onset conduct problems. *Journal of Consulting and Clinical Psychology*, 68(4), 624–640.

Schwartz, R. P., Hamre, R., Dietz, W. H., Wasserman, R. C., Slora, E. J., Myers, E. F., Sullivan, S., ... and Resnicow, K. A. (2007). Office-based motivational interviewing to prevent childhood obesity: a feasibility study. *Archives of Pediatrics and Adolescent Medicine*, 161(5), 495–501.

Scott, S. (2001). Deciding whether interventions for antisocial behaviour work: principles of outcome assessment and practice in a multicentre trial. *European Child and Adolescent Psychiatry*, 10(1), 159–170.

Scott, S., Knapp, M., Henderson, J., and Maughan, B. (2001). Financial cost of social exclusion: follow up study of antisocial children into adulthood. *British Medical Journal*, 323(7306), 191.

Segui-Gomez, M., Wittenberg, E., Glass, R., Levenson, S., Hingson, R., and Graham, J. D. (2001). Where children sit in cars: the impact of Rhode Island's new legislation. *American Journal of Public Health*, 91(2), 311–313.

Shaw, D. S., Dishion, T. J., Supplee, L., Gardner, F., and Arnds, K. (2006). Randomized trial of a family-centered approach to the prevention of early conduct problems: 2-year effects of the family check-up in early childhood. *Journal of Consulting and Clinical Psychology*, 74(1), 1–9.

Silverstein, M., Augustyn, M., Cabral, H., and Zuckerman, B. (2006). Maternal depression and violence exposure: double jeopardy for child school functioning. *Pediatrics*, 118(3), e792–800.

Simpson, G. A., Cohen, R. A., Pastor, P. N., and Reuben, C. A. (2008). Use of mental health services in the past 12 months by children aged 4–17 years: United States, 2005–2006. *NCHS Data Brief*, 8, 1–8.

Slater, M. D., Kelly, K. J., Edwards, R. W., Thurman, P. J., Plested, B. A., Keefe, T. J., ... and Henry, K. L. (2006). Combining in-school and community-based media efforts: reducing marijuana and alcohol uptake among younger adolescents. *Health Education Research*, 21(1), 157–167.

Soliman, S., Pollack, H. A., and Warner, K. E. (2004). Decrease in the prevalence of environmental tobacco smoke exposure in the home during the 1990s in families with children. *American Journal of Public Health*, 94, 314–320. www.ncbi.nlm.nih.gov/entrez/utils/fref.fcgi?PrId=3051&itool=AbstractPlus-def&uid=14759948&db=pubmed&url=http://www.ajph.org/cgi/pmidlookup?view=long&pmid=14759948.

Stanton, W. R., Lowe, J. B., Moffatt, J., and Del Mar, C. B. (2004). Randomised control trial of a smoking cessation intervention directed at men whose partners are pregnant. *Preventive Medicine*, 38(1), 6–9.

Steuerle, C. E., Reynolds, G., and Carasso, A. (2008). Investing in children. Partnership for America's economic success report. Available at www.partnershipforsuccess.org/index.php?id=07 (accessed December 2008).

Stroul, B., and Blau, G. (eds.) (2008). *The system of care handbook*. Baltimore, MD: Brookes Publishing.

Sturm, R., Ringel, J. S., Bao, C., Stein, B., Kapur, K., Zhang, W., and Zeng, F. (2001). National estimates of mental health utilization and expenditures for children in 1998. In *Blueprint for change: research on child and adolescent mental health* (vol. VI, pp. 91–117), Appendices. National Advisory Mental Health Council Workgroup on Child and Adolescent Mental Health Intervention, Development, and Deployment, Washington, DC.

Summerbell, C. D., Ashton, V., Campbell, K. J., Edmunds, L., Kelly, S., and Waters, E. (2003). Interventions for treating obesity in children. *Cochrane Database of Systematic Reviews*, 3, CD001872.

Summerbell, C. D. et al. (2005). Interventions for preventing obesity in children. *Cochrane Database System Review*, 3, CD001871: 3.

Sussman, S. (2002). Effects of sixty-six adolescent tobacco use cessation trials and seventeen prospective studies of self-initiated quitting. *Tobacco Induced Diseases*, 1(1), 35–81.

Sowden, A. J., and Arblaster, L. (2000). Mass media interventions for preventing smoking in young people. *Cochrane Database of Systematic Reviews*, 2, CD001006.

Sznajder, M., Leduc, S., Janvrin, M. P., Bonnin, M. H., Aegerter, P., Baudier, F., and Chevallier, B. (2003). Home delivery of an injury prevention kit for children in four french cities: a controlled randomized trial. *Injury Prevention*, 9(3), 261–265.

Task Force on Community Preventive Services (2000). Strategies for reducing exposure to environmental tobacco smoke, increasing tobacco-use cessation, and reducing initiation in communities and health-care systems. A report on recommendations of the task force on community preventive services. *Morbidity and Mortality Weekly Report. Recommendations and Reports / Centers for Disease Control*, 49(RR-12), 1–11.

Task Force on Community Preventive Services (2003). *The guide to community preventive services: effectiveness of mass media campaigns to reduce initiation of tobacco use and increase cessation.*

Thomas, R., and Perera, R. (2006). School-based programmes for preventing smoking. *Cochrane Database of Systematic Reviews*, 3, CD001293.

Trasande, L. (2010). How much should we invest in preventing childhood obesity? *Health Affairs*, 29(3), 372–378.

University of Minnesota and the Federal Reserve Bank of Minneapolis (2010). Health and early childhood development: the impact of health on school readiness and other education outcomes. National Invitational Conference of the Human Capital Research Collaborative, Minneapolis, MN. October 14–15, 2010.

US Department of Health and Human Services (1999). *Mental health: a report of the surgeon general – executive summary*. Rockville, MD: Substance Abuse and Mental Health Services Administration, Center for Mental Health Services, National Institutes of Health, National Institute of Mental Health. Cambridge University Press.

US Department of Health and Human Services (2001). *Women and smoking: a report of the Surgeon General*. Washington, DC: Government Printing Office.

van Baal, P. H., Polder, J. J., de Wit, G. A., Hoogenveen, R. T., Feenstra, T. L., Boshuizen, H. C., Engelfriet, P. M., and Brouwer, W. B. (2008). Lifetime medical costs of obesity: prevention no cure for increasing health expenditure. *PLOS Medicine*, 5(2), e29.

van den Hoofdakker, B. J., van der Veen-Mulders, L., Sytema, S., Emmelkamp, P. M. G., Minderaa, R. B., and Nauta, M. H. (2007). Effectiveness of behavioral parent training for children with ADHD in routine clinical practice: a randomized controlled study. *Journal of the American Academy of Child and Adolescent Psychiatry*, 46(10), 1263–1271.

van Doesum, K. T., Riksen-Walraven, J. M., Hosman, C. M., and Hoefnagels, C. (2008). A randomized controlled trial of a home-visiting intervention aimed at preventing relationship problems in depressed mothers and their infants. *Child Development*, 79(3), 547–561.

Wahlgren, D. R., Hovell, M. F., Meltzer, S. B., Hofstetter, C. R., and Zakarian, J. M. (1997). Reduction of environmental tobacco smoke exposure in asthmatic children. A 2-year follow-up. *Chest*, 111(1), 81–88.

Walsh, R. A., Redman, S., Brinsmead, M. W., Byrne, J. M., and Melmeth, A. (1997). A smoking cessation program at a public antenatal clinic. *American Journal of Public Health*, 87(7), 1201–1204.

Walker, A. M., Johnson, R., Banner, C., Delaney, J., Farley, R., Ford, M., . . . and Douglas, H. (2008). Targeted home visiting intervention: the impact on mother–infant relationships. *Community Practice*, 81(3), 31–34.

Wang, G., and Dietz, W. H. (2002). Economic burden of obesity in youths aged 6–17 years: 1979–1999. *Pediatrics*, 4109(5), E81–87.

Webster-Stratton, C., and Hammond, M. (1997). Treating children with early-onset conduct problems: a comparison of child and parent training interventions. *Journal of Consulting and Clinical Psychology*, 65, 93–109.

Weiss, J., Malone, F. D., Emig, D., Ball, R. H., Nyberg, D. A., Comstock, C. H., . . . and D'Alton, M. E. (2004). Obesity, obstetric complications and cesarean delivery rate – a population-based screening study. *American Journal of Obstetrics and Gynecology*, 190, 1091–1097.

Webster-Stratton, C., Jamila Reid, M., and Stoolmiller, M. (2008). Preventing conduct problems and improving school readiness: evaluation of the incredible years teacher and child training programs in high-risk schools. *Journal of Child Psychology and Psychiatry, and Allied Disciplines*, 49(5), 471–488.

Webster-Stratton, C., Reid, J., and Hammond, M. (2001). Social skills and problem solving training for children with early-onset conduct problems: who benefits? *Journal of Child Psychology and Psychiatry, and Allied Disciplines*, 42(7), 943–952.

Whitaker, R. C., Wright, J. A., Pepe, M. S., Seidel, K. D., and Dietz, W. H. (1997). Predicting obesity in young adulthood from childhood and parental obesity. *New England Journal of Medicine*, 337(13), 869–873.

Whitlock, E. P., Williams, S. B., Gold, R., Smith, P. R., and Shipman, S. A. (2005). Screening and interventions for childhood overweight: a summary of evidence for the US Preventive Services Task Force. *Pediatrics*, 116(1), e125–144.

Windsor, R. A., Cutter, G., Morris, J., Reese, Y., Manzella, B., Bartlett, E. E., ... and Spanos, D. (1985). The effectiveness of smoking cessation methods for smokers in public health maternity clinics: a randomized trial. *American Journal of Public Health*, 75(12), 1389–1392.

Windsor, R. A., Lowe, J. B., Perkins, L. L., Smith-Yoder, D., Artz, L., Crawford, M., ... Boyd, N. R., Jr. (1993). Health education for pregnant smokers: its behavioral impact and cost benefit. *American Journal of Public Health*, 83(2), 201–206.

Wissow, L. S., Gadomski, A., Roter, D., Larson, S., Brown, J., Zachary, C., ... and Wang, M. C. (2008). Improving child and parent mental health in primary care: a cluster-randomized trial of communication skills training. *Pediatrics*, 121(2), 266–275.

Zhang, D., and Qui, X. (1993). School-based tobacco-use prevention – People's Republic of China, May 1989–January 1990. *Morbidity and Mortality Weekly Report*, 42(19), 370–371, 377.

Zubrick, S. R., Ward, K. A., Silburn, S. R., Lawrence, D., Williams, A. A., Blair, E., ... and Sanders, M. R. (2005). Prevention of child behavior problems through universal implementation of a group behavioral family intervention. *Prevention Science: The Official Journal of the Society for Prevention Research*, 6(4), 287–304.

7 Center-based preschool programs: systematic review of child and adult health outcomes

Katina D'Onise, Robyn A. McDermott, and John W. Lynch

While early childhood development interventions (ECDIs) have the potential to bring about wide-ranging societal benefits in both the short and the long term (Bennett and Tayler, 2006; Engle et al., 2007; Heckman and Masterov, 2004), less is known about the potential for center based ECDIs to improve the health of children and adults. Many governments have invested in nutrition and health services as part of a range of comprehensive services in ECDIs (Currie and Thomas, 1995; Goodson et al., 2000; Kropp et al., 2001), with an expectation that they will improve child health outcomes. The focus of most of the evidence of health effects of ECDIs is on the short-term increased risk of infectious diseases and injury (Ball et al., 2002; Lu et al., 2004; Rivara et al., 1989) from center-based children's services, or a small range of health outcomes examined in infant home visiting programs (Elkan et al., 2000; Gomby, 1999). The health benefits associated with ECDIs are potentially broader in scope than infectious diseases and injury and may extend beyond the preschool years. In addition to the provision of health services, ECDIs that improve educational and social outcomes, lessening the impacts of social disadvantage, may reduce the shorter- and longer-term health differences known to be associated with growing up in poorer social conditions (Galobardes, Lynch, and Davey Smith, 2004).

There are a number of possible pathways through which ECDIs may lead to improved health outcomes. First, many ECDIs include direct health and social services either on site or on a referral basis, which may lead to facilitation of early identification and management of developmental and health problems among young children (Zigler, Piotrkowski, and Collins,

---

This chapter is based on the previously published work: K. D'Onise, J. Lynch, M. Sawyer, and R. McDermott (2010). Can preschool improve child health outcomes? A systematic review. *Social Science and Medicine*, 70, 1423–1440; K. D'Onise, R. McDermott, and J. Lynch (2010). Does attendance at preschool affect adult health? A systematic review. *Public Health*, 124(9), 500–511.

1994). This is particularly important for children living in families who make only limited use of traditional health services. Second, ECDIs that do not include health services may still enhance future health through the provision of parenting programs which can indirectly improve child health outcomes by supporting a healthier home environment, for example improved nutrition and safety (Kendrick et al., 2000). These services might be expected to bring about positive health outcomes initially in early childhood, with benefits of healthy childhood development extending into adulthood.

Third, there may be a cognitive-social pathway from the direct educational component of the intervention. For example, in the Perry Preschool program, cognitive gains were thought to improve school success, with direct benefits on self-esteem, behavior, and motivation (Schweinhart, Barnes, and Weikart, 1993) which may lead to positive effects on health. Benefits on internalizing and externalizing behavior, and social competence may be apparent from early childhood, with a positive developmental trajectory leading to further benefits in adolescence (for example reduced tobacco uptake and less risk-taking behavior) (Fergusson et al., 2007). Enhanced cognitive development may also, through complex pathways (including socioeconomic), lead to improved health. Better cognitive performance in early life has been consistently associated with reduced chronic diseases, some cancers, and mortality (Batty and Dreary, 2004; Calvin et al., 2011). Such benefits may be first apparent in early childhood with enhanced behavioural and social development, leading to reduced involvement in health-risk behaviours and a more health promoting lifestyle in adolescence and into adulthood.

A fourth mechanism for ECDIs leading to improved child and later adult health is through the potential for ECDIs to improve the adult socioeconomic position (SEP), possibly independently of long-term cognitive gain (Shonkoff, Boyce, and McEwen, 2009). For example, a handful of high-quality ECDIs have been shown to enhance educational attainment, increase future adult income, and reduce adult crime (Karoly, Kilburn, and Cannon, 2005), all of which can lead to improved adult health outcomes ranging from a reduced risk of lifestyle related chronic disease (e.g., cardiovascular disease, diabetes mellitus), injury, and drug and alcohol use. While some of these health outcomes might be expected to be evident in adolescence (for example in dietary choices, participation in physical activity, and social/behavioral competency), they may become more apparent in adulthood when many diseases are more prevalent and health decisions are more likely to be made independently of direct parental influence.

Center-based interventions for 3–4 year olds, frequently known as pre-school programs, were chosen as the focus of this review as they are a dominant policy model in the USA, the UK, Canada, and Australia (2008; "Office of Head Start," 2008; "Ontario Early Years Centres," 2007; "Sure Start," 2008). Thus, the aim of this review is to examine the evidence for health effects of center-based preschool programs on children beyond the preschool years through to adulthood.

Scope of the review

This review focused on studies that included center-based preschool for healthy 4 year olds and reported on a health related outcome in the year following the intervention or beyond. This included a wide range of studies that in some cases involved more intervention components than just center-based preschool, for example parenting services, nutrition services, or home visiting services. The studies may also have targeted a wider age range than 4 year olds (from birth through to 8 years old). Health was defined broadly to encompass the presence or absence of disease, disease risk factors, health behaviors, and indicators of well-being.

Both published journal articles and grey literature (non-peer reviewed reports) were included, but conference abstracts were excluded on the basis of inadequate information to assess the study and its outcomes. All studies were required to involve comparison of the intervention with some type of control group (i.e., experimental, quasi-experimental, and cohort study designs, but not solely descriptive papers). While review articles and editorials were retrieved to assist in the search process (by checking the reference lists for any studies missed by the electronic search), only primary research publications were included in the review. Details of the search strategy are shown in Figure 7.1.

Searched databases: Medline, Embase, the Educational Resources Information Center (ERIC), Psych Info, Sociological Abstracts, Head Start research database
Search terms: 'early childhood intervention' (key word), 'early intervention (education)' (MeSH term, limited to preschool age), 'preschool education' (key word and subject term), 'child development' + 'education' (MeSH, limited to preschool age) were used. For ERIC and Psych Info: 'health' was added as a limiter for all the searches, Head Start database: 'health'.
Search limits: articles published in English from 1980 to December 2011.
Reference lists of all included and review articles were searched
Child Development (journal) hand searched from 1980 to 2011.

Figure 7.1 Search strategy.

Quality appraisal

Each paper was critically appraised using the Effective Public Health Practice Project (EPHPP) critical appraisal tool (2008) to ensure a systematic, methodological appraisal of the included studies. This tool is recommended by the Cochrane Collaboration for Health Promotion and Public Health Interventions (Armstrong et al., 2007). The EPHPP tool provides an overall methodological rating based on assessment of potential selection bias, study design, potential for residual confounding, blinding of researchers and participants, data collection methods, and withdrawals/drop outs. Studies were classified overall as of high potential risk of bias ("high risk") if two or more of the above categories were assessed as high risk of bias, moderate potential risk of study bias (less than four low-risk ratings and one high-risk rating, "moderate risk"), or low potential risk of study bias (four low-risk ratings, no high-risk ratings, "low risk"). The quality rating for each study is presented in Table 7.1. Where more information was required beyond that available in the publication, the corresponding author of the study was contacted for further information.

Guide to the presentation of results

While many health outcomes may be influenced by a combination of parenting and direct educational and health/social service access, the results have been presented as being primarily influenced by one of the intervention components to facilitate interpretation. It is possible to conceptualize health effects in childhood as being particularly related to one component of the intervention over another, given the short time between the intervention and when the outcomes are being measured. For example, nutrition related outcomes and health promoting behaviors (including safety behaviors) can be considered to be more likely to be associated with intervention components directed toward enhancing health promoting aspects of the home environment through parenting programs or home visiting (e.g., obesity, injury, growth, preventive health behaviors, diet) evident from early childhood. Enhanced access to health services, either through greater direct provision of health services or through promotion of the importance of health service access to parents, can be considered to primarily influence physical health outcomes (including illness and mortality) and health service use (including immunizations) from early childhood through to adolescence. Direct educational services to children have more influence on the cognitive-social pathway, encompassing social competence, mental health, and risk-taking behaviors in adolescence.

Table 7.1 *Reviewed studies: intervention, population studied, methodological appraisal, and outcomes.*

Study	Intervention	Intervention age	Intervention follow-up age	Sample size	Sample size at final study (% follow up)	Health outcomes	Methodology appraisal, potential risk of bias
Perry Preschool (Meunnig et al., 2009; Schweinhart et al., 1993; Schweinhart et al., 2005; Schweinhart and Weikart, 1980; Weikart et al., 1978) USA	PS, HV	3–4 years	15, 27, and 40 years	123, E = 58, = 65	40 years: 112 E = 54 C = 58 (91%)	Social competence; Smoking, drugs, and alcohol; Chronic disease; Overweight/obesity; Health service use; General health; Preventive health	**Randomized Controlled Trial** Low risk
Carolina Abecedarian (Campbell et al., 2008; Campbell et al., 2002; McLaughlin et al., 2007) USA	Educational child care, HS, SS, school program including PP	6 weeks to 4 years; school 5–8 years	21 years	111, E = 57, C = 54	Preschool group:104, E = 53, C = 51 (94%)	Smoking, drugs, and alcohol; Preventive health; Exercise Depression	**Randomized Controlled Trial** Low risk
Project CARE (Campbell et al., 2008) USA	Educational child care, HV, PP, HS, SS, school program including PP	6 weeks to 4 years; school 5–8 years	21 years	64, E = 16, HV = 25, C = 23	Center-based comparison: E = 14, C = 21 (90%)	Smoking, drugs, and alcohol; Preventive health; Exercise	**Randomized Controlled Trial** Low risk
Chicago Child–Parent Centres (Reynolds, 1994; 1998; Reynolds, Chan, and Temple, 1998;	PS, KG, primary school program, HV, HS, SS	3–9 years	Grade 3–10, 20 years, 22–24 years, 28 years	1539, E = 989, C = 550	1233, E = 808, C = 425 (80%)	Social competence; Delinquency; Depression; Smoking, drugs, and alcohol	**Quasi-experimental cohort** Low risk

Table 7.1 *(cont.)*

Study	Intervention	Intervention age	Intervention follow-up age	Sample size	Sample size at final study (% follow up)	Health outcomes	Methodology appraisal, potential risk of bias
Reynolds et al., 2011; Reynolds et al., 2001; Reynolds et al., 2007) USA	PS, HS, SS, PP, nutrition	4 years	Grade 3 & grade 5	22 782	G3 80% G5 85%	Obesity, Social competence	**Cohort** Moderate risk
Head Start (Zhai, 2008) USA	PS, HS, SS, PP, nutrition	3–4 years	18–35 years	Details not provided	2397, Head Start = 325, Preschool = 572, C = 1542	Smoking, hypertension, Overweight/obesity, General health, Exercise	**Cohort** High risk
Head Start (Anderson et al., 2004) USA							
Brookline Early Education Project (Palfrey et al., 2005) USA	Educational child care, PS (3–4 year olds), HS, SS, HV, PP	0–4 years	Mean 25.4 years	169, E = 169	240, E = 120, C = 120 Suburban E = 95 C = 95 Urban E = 25 C = 25 (71% for E)	Depression, Health service use, Health behaviors, General health	**Quasi-Experimental Cohort** Moderate risk
Comprehensive Child Development Program (Goodson et al., 2000; St. Pierre et al., 1997) USA	PS (half of 4–5 year olds), HV, PP, HS, SS (case management framework)	0–4 years	5 years	4410, E = 2213, C = 2197	E = 74%, C = 78%	Mortality, Injury, Health service use, Behavior	**Randomized Controlled Trial** Moderate risk Note: only half of the children aged 4–5 years had centre-based preschool exposure

Study	Program	Age at intervention	Age at outcome	Sample	Follow-up sample	Outcomes	Design / Risk
Head Start (Ludwig and Miller, 2006) USA	PS, HS, SS, PP, nutrition	3–4 years	5–9 years	43 counties	NA	Mortality	**Regression discontinuity design** High risk
Better Beginnings Better Futures (Peters et al., 2003) Canada	Mix of models: Preschool and primary school education, community development, SS, PP, HV, nutrition	Sub-section 4–8 years	8 years	759, E = 362, C = 397 Cornwall = 530 Highfield = 517 Sudbury = 503	981, E = 328 + 281 additional recruited, C = 372 (92%)	Health service use Immunization Growth, asthma, injury, general health Social competence Mental health	**Quasi-experimental** Low risk
Head Start (Roy, 2003) USA	PS, HS SS, PP	3–4 years	≥ 5 years	Information not provided	1986–2117	Health service use Behavior	**Cohort** High risk
North Carolina Smart Start (Kropp et al., 2001) USA	Mix of program models, educational child care, HS, SS	0–4 years	5 years	2126, E = 711, C = 1415	1661, E = 528, C = 1133 (78%)	General health Immunization Health service use	**Quasi-experimental cohort** Moderate risk
Head Start (Currie & Thomas, 1995) USA	PS, HS, SS, PP, nutrition	3–4 years	Variable, mean 8–9 years	Information not provided	4787, E = 927, Sibling preschool = 1525, Sibling no preschool = 2335	Growth Immunization	**Cohort** High risk
Head Start (Gietzen & Vermeersch, 1980) USA	PS, HS, SS, PP, nutrition	3–4 years	6, 10, 14 years	332, E = 100, Free Lunch = 113, Title1 = 55, Private preschool = 64	NA	Growth General health Fitness	**Retrospective cohort** High risk
Georgia Early Childhood Study (Henry et al., 2004) USA	PS (Pre-K), Head Start, private PS, home care	4 year olds	Grade 1	855, Pre-K = 353, Head Start = 134, private PS = 143, control = 225	670, Georgia pre-K = 272, Head Start = 97, private preschool = 97, control = 204 (78%)	General health Behavior	**Quasi-experimental cohort** Moderate risk

Table 7.1 (*cont.*)

Study	Intervention	Intervention age	Intervention follow-up age	Sample size	Sample size at final study (% follow up)	Health outcomes	Methodology appraisal, potential risk of bias
Head Start Project Star (Kaminski et al., 2002) USA	Head Start (enhanced curriculum) + PP, HV	4 years	5–6 years	146 families, E = 98, C = 48	97 families, E = 63, C = 36 (66%)	Social competence	**Randomized Controlled Trial** High risk
Milwaukee project (Garber, 1988) USA	Center-based educational program, HS, SS, PP, HV	6 months – 5 years	Grade 4 and 8	55, E = 28, C = 27	35, E = 17, C = 18 (64%)	Social competence	**Quasi-experimental cohort** Moderate risk
Early Training Project (Gray et al., 1983) USA	Preschool, HV	3.5–4.5 to 6 years	Grade 11	63, E = 42, C = 21	62, E = 41, C = 21 (98%)	Social competence	**Randomized Controlled Trial** (non-random C2 omitted) Moderate risk
Head Start (Lee et al., 1990) USA	PS, HS, SS, PP, nutrition	3–4 years	5–6 years	696	646, E = 333, C1 other preschool = 109, C2 no preschool = 204 (93%)	Social competence	**Quasi-experimental cohort** High risk
Four preschool comparison study (Miller & Bizzell, 1984) USA	Bereiter-Engelmann PS, DARCEE PS (half had HV), Montessori PS, Head Start PS	4 years	Grade 9–10	248, BE = 64, DARCEE = 64, M = 33 HS = 53, C = 34	164, BE = 37 DARCEE = 32 M = 25 HS = 30 C = 38 (66%)	Social competence	**Quasi-experimental cohort** High risk
Philadelphia study (Beller, 1983) USA	PS, KG, HS, SS, HV	3–4 years	Grade 10	165, E = 60, C1 (KG) = 53, C2 (G 1) = 52	115, E = 41, C1 = 36, C2 = 38 (72%)	Social competence Behavior	**Quasi-experimental cohort** Moderate risk

Study	Type of care	Age range	Sample size	Follow-up age	N (%)	Outcome	Design / Risk
Swedish Day Care study (Andersson, 1992) Sweden	Day care centres (multiple types)	Birth-	128	8 and 13 years	114 (89%)	Social competence	**Cohort** Moderate risk
Child Health and Education Study (Osborn & Milbank, 1987) UK	Government PS, private PS, C-no preschool	0–4 years	15052, GP = 3068, PP = 7466, C = 4283	5 and 10 years	5 year 13135 10 year 14906 Used 6871 sub-group (81%)	Social competence Behavior	**Cohort** Moderate risk
Early Childhood Longitudinal Study – Kindergarten 98/99 (Hickman, 2006) USA	Center-based care, mix of different types	4 year olds	Uncertain, sub-group of 21260	5 years	11007, E = 7645, C = 3362	Social competence	**Cohort** High risk
NICHD Early Child Care Research Network (Belsky et al., 2007; Vandell et al., 2010) USA	Center-based care, mix of different types	3 months–4 years	1364	11–12 and 15 years	958 (70%)	Smoking, drugs, and alcohol Social competence Behavior	**Cohort** Moderate risk
Syracuse Family Development Research Program (Lally, Mangione, & Honig, 1988) USA	Educational day care and preschool, HV, PP, nutrition, HS, SS	6 months–5 years	E = 108, at 60 months 156, E = 82, C = 74	13–16 years	119, E = 65, C = 54 (65%)	Behavior	**Quasi-experimental cohort** Moderate risk
Turkish Early Enrichment Project (Kagitcibasi, Sunar, & Bekman 2001) Turkey	PS +/- HV and PP	3 and 5 years	280	6 and 8 years	255 (91%)	Behavior	**Quasi-experimental cohort** High risk
Effective Provision of Preschool Education Project	Nursery class (NC), playgroup (PG), private	3–4 years	3172, NC = 588, PG = 609, PN = 516	11 years	2664, NC = 470, PG = 523, PN = 456 DN = 358,	Behavior	**Cohort** Moderate risk

Table 7.1 (cont.)

Study	Intervention	Intervention age	Intervention follow-up age	Sample size	Sample size at final study (% follow up)	Health outcomes	Methodology appraisal, potential risk of bias
(Sammons et al., 2007) UK	day nursery (PN), local authority day nursery (DN), nursery school (NS), combined centres (CC), home (H)			DN = 433, NS = 519, CC = 192, H = 315	NS = 448, CC = 154, H = 255 (84%)		
Early Childhood Longitudinal Study – Kindergarten 98/99 (Magnuson et al., 2007) USA	Comparison of E = pre-kindergarten, C1 = PS, C2 = Head Start, C3 = non-parental care, C4 = parental care	4 years	Kindergarten – grade 1	? 21260	10224, E = 1722, C1 = 4649 C2 = 914 C3 = 1216 C4 = 1621	Social competence	**Cohort** Moderate risk
Early Childhood Longitudinal Study – Kindergarten 98/99 (Loeb et al., 2005) USA	E1 = Head Start (PS, HS, SS, PP, nutrition), E2 = mix of center-based care	0–5 years	5 years	21260	14162, E1 = 1093, E2 = 9015, other non-parent = 1691, C = 2363 (67%)	Behavior	**Cohort** Moderate risk
Day Care (Bates et al., 1994) USA	Comparison of day care with parental care	0–5 years	Kindergarten	589	588 (99%)	Behavior	**Cohort** High risk

Study	Components	Age at intervention	Age at follow-up	N	E/C	Outcome	Design	Risk
Head Start (Aughinbaugh, 2001) USA	PS, HS, SS, PP, nutrition	3–4 years	12–17 years	8984	7787 E = 1553, C = 6234 (87%)	Delinquency	Retrospective cohort	High risk
North Carolina (Bryant et al., 1993) USA	PS	3–4 years	5–6 years	536, E = 220, C = 316 (Head Start = 97, other PS = 99, no PS = 120)	494, E = 206, C = 288 (Head Start = 90, other PS = 87, no PS = 111) (92%)	Social competence	Cohort	Moderate risk
Head Start (Caputo, 2004) USA	PS, HS, SS, PP, nutrition	3–4 years	14–21 years	2424	1251, Head Start: mother and child E = 97, mother only E = 114, child only E = 193, control = 847 (52%)	Depression Mastery, self-esteem	Cohort	High risk
Head Start (Caputo, 2003) USA	PS, HS, SS, PP, nutrition	3–4 years	34–41 years	8491	5621, Head Start = 735, other preschool = 928, no preschool = 3958 (66%)	Self-Esteem Mastery Scale	Cohort	High risk
Head Start (Frisvold, 2007) USA	PS, HS, SS, PP, nutrition	3–4 years	5–19 years	3563	2907, 1332 sub-group E = 346, C = 986 (82%)	Overweight/obesity	Cohort	Moderate risk
Educational day care – Learning Games (Haskins, 1985) USA	Educational day care, nutrition	3 months–5 years	6–7 years	87	Year 2: 59, E = 27, C = 32 Year 3: 36, E = 18, C = 18 (41%)	Behavior	Randomized Controlled Trial	High risk
Mauritius study (Raine et al., 2003) Mauritius	PS, HS, nutrition, physical activity	3–5 years	17 and 23–26 years	455, E = 100	438, E = 83, C = 355 (96%)	Mental health	Quasi-Experimental Cohort	Low risk

Table 7.1 (*cont.*)

Study	Intervention	Intervention age	Intervention follow-up age	Sample size	Sample size at final study (% follow up)	Health outcomes	Methodology appraisal, potential risk of bias
Kindergarten Union (D'Onise et al., 2010; D'Onise et al., 2011) Australia	PS, HS, SS, PP, nutrition	3–4 years	34–67 years	1395	1040, E = 466, C = 574 (75%)	Smoking, alcohol, Physical activity, diet	**Retrospective Cohort** High risk
Tulsa Pre-K and Head Start (Gormley et al., 2011) USA	PS, HS, SS, PP, nutrition	4 years	5 years	3166, E = 1463, HS = 366, C = 1463	2832, E = 1318, HS = 363, C = 1151 (89%)	Behavior	**Retrospective cohort** Low risk
Head Start (Zhai et al., 2011) USA	PS, HS, SS, PP, nutrition	3–4 years	5 years	4242	2803, E = 386, C = 2417 (66%)	Behavior Social competence	**Cohort** Low risk
Head Start (Hyman, 2011a) USA	PS, HS, SS, PP, nutrition	3–4 years	5–14 years, 14–17 years	Information not provided	4493	Behavior Self-esteem Depression Mastery scale Drug and alcohol use	**Cohort** Moderate risk

Key: PS – preschool, HS – health services, SS – social services, PP – parenting programs, HV – home visiting, KG – kindergarten program, E – exposed group, C – comparison group

It is more difficult, however, to attribute the effects of individual intervention components on health outcomes in adulthood. The diagnosis of diseases such as diabetes in adulthood follows a highly complex causal pathway from *in utero* through to middle/late adulthood when the diagnosis is generally made. Health behaviors that contribute to the development of diabetes are learnt in part from the childhood home environment but are strongly influenced by the individual's adult income, educational attainment, and occupation, which collectively determine the individual's socioeconomic position (SEP). These socioeconomic factors in adulthood could conceivably stem from an improved home environment from parenting programs, and an improved social and cognitive trajectory from direct educational services to children. Attending a health professional while well (as is generally the case with diabetes in the early stages) in order to have a diagnosis of diabetes is a health behavior that is influenced by SEP but also possibly an acceptance of the value of health services from promotion of health service use in childhood. Given this complexity, for ease of interpretation of the results, adult health outcomes that are an extension of child outcomes were considered to have primarily arisen from that component of the intervention. For example, where nutrition and anthropometry results in childhood were attributed primarily to parenting programs, the adult equivalent of obesity was also presented under the intervention component of parenting programs.

In order to facilitate interpretation of the results, where proportions were presented the outcome measures were converted to relative risk (RR) and absolute risk difference (ARD) with confidence intervals (CI). Outcomes presented as a mean with a measure of variance were converted to Cohen's d effect size estimates. Where this information was not available, the results were presented as reported in the original study. Results regarding preschool program components of interventions were selected where possible for studies that separated the effects of preschool from other components of the intervention. Meta-analysis was not possible due to the heterogeneity of the interventions, study designs, and in many cases outcome measurements (Egger, Davey Smith, and Altman, 2001), and so a narrative synthesis of the results is presented.

Finally, readers should recognize that the majority of the studies undertook a large number of statistical tests given the wide array of social and health outcomes they examined. In any *a posteriori* multiple comparison of outcomes, some of these would be expected to be "significant" by chance alone (Sterne, Smith, and Cox, 2001).

Results

The electronic search identified 4,704 articles. Screening of titles, abstracts, and reference lists identified 217 potentially eligible articles. These articles were retrieved and reviewed in full, leading to fifty-six eligible articles. Four of the fifty-six were excluded because of inadequate reporting, limiting the ability to assess the methods (Borger et al., 1994; Geesaman, 1970; Kotchabhakdi, 1999; Sammons et al., 2007), no control for confounding (Borger et al., 1994; Kotchabhakdi, 1999; Sammons et al., 2007), and publication pre-1980 (Geesaman, 1970). An article from the author's library (Sammons et al., 2007), which did not appear in the electronic search, was also included in the review along with four articles from the hand search of *Child Development*, leading to a total of fifty-seven articles that formed the basis of the review. This represented studies of forty-two different interventions, of which thirty-one only reported child outcomes, six reported adult outcomes, and the remaining five reported both child and adult outcomes. Details of the search results are presented in Figure 7.2 and of the included studies in Table 7.1.

The studies examined a range of program models, including the effects of large government funded programs (such as Head Start and the Chicago Child–Parent Centers), experimental projects (e.g., Perry Preschool study), two of which examined large government funded demonstration projects (Better Beginnings Better Futures (BBBF)) (Peters, Petrunka, and Arnold, 2003), and the Comprehensive Child Development Program (CCDP) (Goodson et al., 2000). The remaining studies evaluated a spectrum of usually available center-based children's services in the community, including day care programs and preschool and government-based programs, generally through comparison with large nationally representative cohort studies.

It is important to understand the heterogeneity of what was offered under the rubric of the ECDIs examined here. There was a wide range of services offered at differing levels of intensity and in different combinations across the different programs. The Head Start studies, which made up the largest group, involved education services (with a focus on age appropriate literacy, numeracy, reasoning, and problem solving), parenting programs (e.g., involvement in Head Start programs, health education, access to social services), health programs (e.g., health screening and early intervention, dental examinations, exercise, motor development), and nutrition programs (screening of height, weight, and hemoglobin, provision of meals, nutrition education). Other programs included various aspects of parenting support (parenting education, volunteering in the classroom, attending school events and field trips, furthering parental

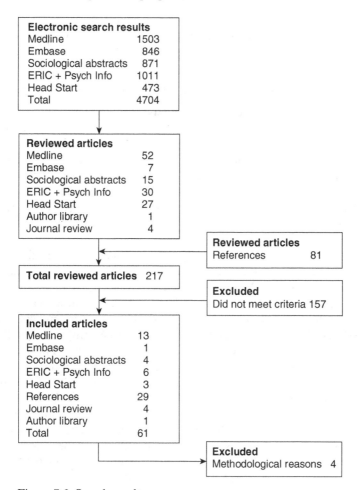

Figure 7.2 Search results.

educational attainment, and home visiting), a community development approach (e.g., BBBF: Peters et al., 2003), or a case management model (e.g., CCDP: Goodson et al., 2000).

The interventions were undertaken for children aged 0–9 years and follow-up ages ranged from 5 to 41 years. The most common follow-up age range included 5–6 year olds (48 percent), immediately following completion of preschool. The majority of the intervention groups were sampled from variously defined populations at risk of school failure, using indicators such as low family income, income below the poverty line, or low maternal IQ. The majority of the studies were conducted in the USA

(83 percent), with two conducted in the UK, one in Canada, one in Sweden, one in Turkey, one in Australia, and one in Mauritius.

Direct educational services to children (cognitive-social pathway)

Smoking, alcohol, and drug use

The only studies to examine drug and alcohol use in children were the low risk of bias Perry Preschool study and a moderate risk of bias Head Start study (Table 7.2) (Hyman, 2011b). Both studies found no difference in the risk of ever using marijuana or drinking alcohol without parental permission, but the Perry Preschool study found a small but statistically insignificant increased risk of ever taking other drugs by age 15 years (ARD 5 percent, 95 percent CI −3.4 to 13.4 percent) (Schweinhart and Weikart, 1980).

Other substance use in adulthood was examined in five studies (Campbell et al., 2002; Campbell et al., 2008; Meunnig et al., 2009; Reynolds et al., 2007; Schweinhart et al., 2005). There was consistent evidence for a reduction in the absolute risk of marijuana use in the methodologically rigorous Perry Preschool, Abecedarian, and Project CARE studies (ARD ranging from −7 to −21 percent) (Campbell et al., 2002; Campbell et al., 2008; Schweinhart et al., 2005). There was however a moderate increase in the absolute risk of binge alcohol drinking in the past month in the Perry Preschool and Abecedarian studies (10 and 13 percent) (Campbell et al., 2002; Schweinhart et al., 2005), but no difference in reports of driving after "probably drinking too much" in the Perry Preschool study (Schweinhart et al., 2005). There was an overall beneficial effect of preschool programs on cocaine or other illicit drug use; however, the absolute numbers of participants who reported heroin or LSD use were small (Schweinhart et al., 2005).

Seven studies examined smoking outcomes in adulthood, six of which found a reduction in the risk of smoking (Table 7.2). For the two high-quality randomized studies, there was an absolute reduction in risk ranging from 13 to 16 percent (Campbell et al., 2008; Schweinhart et al., 2005). The two studies that assessed effects of attendance at a community-based program implemented across multiple sites found a reduced risk of smoking (ARD around 4.0 percent) (D'Onise, Lynch, and McDermott, 2010; Reynolds et al., 2007). One study, with lower methodological quality, found a reduction in the risk of ever and current smoking but not of quitting smoking, suggesting effects on smoking in early but not later adult life when quitting generally occurs (D'Onise et al., 2010). The one negative finding came from the Project Care study that

Table 7.2 *Physical and behavioral health outcomes associated with center-based preschool interventions.*

Health measure	Study	Outcome measurement	Age	Results (95% confidence interval)	Overall direction of association
Mortality	Head Start (Ludwig & Miller, 2006)	Vital statistics	C	RR = 0.59, ARD = −0.0013% (−0.08 to 0.08%)	=
	Comprehensive Child Development Program (St. Pierre et al., 1997)	Parental report	C	RR = 0.77, ARD = −0.25% (−0.95 to 0.45%)	
	Perry Preschool (Meunnig et al., 2009)	Documented	A	ARD = −8.0% p = 0.06	+
Obesity	Head Start (Zhai, 2008)	Measured height and weight	C	Grade 3 Overweight: parental care OR = 1.27 p > 0.1 relative to Head Start Obese: parental care OR = 1.19 p > 0.1 relative to Head Start Grade 5 Overweight: parental care OR = 2.01 p < 0.05 relative to Head Start Obese: parental care OR = 1.14 p > 0.1 relative to Head Start	+
	Head Start (Frisvold, 2007)	Measured height and weight	C	BMI > 85th centile entire cohort ARD = −21% (−73.9 to 32.3%) BMI > 85th centile African Americans ARD = −50% (−90.0 to −9.1%) BMI > 95th centile entire cohort ARD = −42% (−55.7 to −27.8%) BMI > 95th centile African Americans ARD = −44% (−56.0 to −30.3%) BMI > 95th centile African American > 10 years old, ARD = −35% (−104.3 to 34.5%)	

Table 7.2 (cont.)

Health measure	Study	Outcome measurement	Age	Results (95% confidence interval)	Overall direction of association
	Perry Preschool (Meunnig et al., 2009; Schweinhart et al., 2005)	Self report	A	BMI ≥ 25 ARD = 11% p = 0.30 BMI ≥ 30 ARD = −1.0% p = 0.94	−
	Head Start (Anderson et al., 2004)	Self report	A	BMI ≥ 25 ARD = −4.5 (−20.8 to 11.8%) BMI ≥ 25 Head Start > 2 years ARD = 32.7% (−2.8 to 68.2%)	
Hypertension	Perry Preschool (Meunnig et al., 2009; Schweinhart et al., 2005)	Self report	A	ARD = 15% p = 0.12	−
	Head Start (Anderson et al., 2004)	Self report	A	ARD = 6.2% (−4.0 to 16.4%) Head Start > 2 years ARD = 2.2% (−20.3 to 24.7%)	
Diabetes	Perry Preschool (Meunnig et al., 2009; Schweinhart et al., 2005)	Self report	A	ARD = 4% p = 0.41	=
Asthma	Better Beginnings Better Futures (Peters et al., 2003)	Canadian Institute for Health Information	C	Diagnosis and hospitalizations, no difference	=
	Perry Preschool (Meunnig et al., 2009; Schweinhart et al., 2005)	Self report	A	ARD = 5% p = 0.50	=
Arthritis	Perry Preschool (Meunnig et al., 2009; Schweinhart et al., 2005)	Self report	A	ARD = 3% p = 0.72	−
Physical illness	Comprehensive Child Development Program (Goodson et al., 2000)	Parental report	C	Diagnosed physical illness, no difference	=
	Smart Start (Kropp et al., 2001)	Health provider report	C	Illness or developmental problems smart start, no difference	
	Better Beginnings Better Futures (Peters et al., 2003)	Parental report	C	Limitations to activities of daily living, no difference	

	Study (reference)	Measure	A/C	Results	Direction
	Brookline Early Education Project (Palfrey et al., 2005)	Health Behaviors Scale	A	Untreated condition (suburban) RR = 1.9 AD = 15% (3.1 to 26.9%), (urban) RR = 0.7 AD = −12% (−38.4 to 14.4%)	mixed
	Perry Preschool (Schweinhart et al., 1993)	Self report	A	Health problem treated last 5 years RR = 0.95 AD = −2% (−19.5 to 15.5%) Hospitalised in last 12 months RR = 2.0 AD = 15% (0.02 to 30.0%)	
	Perry Preschool (Meunnig et al., 2009; Schweinhart et al., 2005)	Self report	A	Hospitalised in last 12 months ARD = −23% p = 0.36 ≥ 1 scheduled visit treatment or surgery last 12 months RR = 1.57 AD = 8% (−6.2 to 22.2%)	
Growth	Head Start (Gietzen & Vermeersch, 1980)	School records	C	Height for age < 25th centile: Head Start vs. Free Lunch: RR = 0.4 ARD = −24% (−35.5 to −12.5%)	+
	Head Start (Currie & Thomas, 1995)	Parental report	C	Height for age Head Start (white) ARD = 8.4% (−69.8 to 86.6%) Head Start (African American) ARD = 54.9% (−50.9 to 160.7%) Preschool (white) ARD = 58.2% (−4.1 to 120.5%) Preschool (African American) ARD = 18.2% (−81.6 to 118.0%)	
	Better Beginnings Better Futures (Peters et al., 2003)	Measured height and weight	C	Height for age and weight for height, no difference	
General health	Georgia Pre-K (Henry et al., 2004)	Parental/teacher report	C	Teacher assessed health and well-being Pre-K coefficient = −0.05 p > 0.05	mixed
	Head Start (Gietzen & Vermeersch, 1980)	School records	C	Sickness days: Head Start vs. Free Lunch: ES = −0.7 (−2.0 to 1.7) Preschool vs. Free Lunch: ES = −1.3 (−2.0 to 1.1)	
	Better Beginnings Better Futures (Peters et al., 2003)	Scales of Independent Behavior Parental report	C	Scales of Independent Behavior (normal development), no consistent pattern of effects, details not reported General health rating, improvement in rating over time ES = 0.37 p < 0.05	

Table 7.2 (cont.)

Health measure	Study	Outcome measurement	Age	Results (95% confidence interval)	Overall direction of association
	Head Start (Caputo, 2004)	Self report	A	Health status (mean,1 = poor 5 = excellent) Mother and child in Head Start = 3.92, child only in Head Start = 3.83, control = 3.97, F = 1.40 p > 0.05	
	Perry Preschool (Meunnig et al., 2009; Schweinhart et al., 2005)	Self report	A	Good/fair or poor health: ARD = -9% p = 0.39 1+ weeks lost from work in last 15 years due to health RR = 0.78 ARD = -12% (-30.4 to 6.4%)	=
	Brookline Early Education Project (Palfrey et al., 2005)	Health Behaviors Scale	A	Suburban RR = 0.99 ARD = -1% (-11.8 to 9.8%) Urban RR = 1.5 ARD = 22% (-5.0 to 49%)	
	Head Start (Anderson et al., 2004)	Self report	A	Fair or poor: ARD = -0.3% (-8.7 to 8.1%) Head Start > 2 years ARD = -6.7% (-25.3 to 11.9%)	
Tobacco smoking	Perry Preschool (Meunnig et al., 2009; Schweinhart et al., 1993; Schweinhart et al., 2005)	Self report	A	Current smoker RR = 0.80 AD = -11% (-29.0 to 7.0%) Current smoker ARD = -14% p = 0.18	+
	Abecedarian (Campbell et al., 2002)	Self report	A	Ever regular smoker RR = 0.71 AD = -16% (-34.9 to 2.9%)	
	Chicago Child–Parent Centres study (Reynolds et al., 2007)	Self report	A	Current smoker RR = 0.81 AD = -4.2% (-9.7 to 1.2%)	
	Head Start (Anderson et al., 2004)	Self report	A	Current smoker AD = -12.4% (-27.1 to 2.3%)	

Domain	Study	Measure	Rating	Results	
				Current smoker (Head Start exposure 2 years) AD = −33.3% (−65.6 to −1%) Ever smoker AD = −9.6% (−26.3 to 7.1%)	
				Ever smoker (Head Start exposure 2 years) AD = −52.2% (−88.9 to −15.5%)	
	Project CARE (Campbell et al., 2008)	Self report	A	Ever regular smoker RR = 1.4 AD = 19% (−13.9 to 51.9%)	
	Kindergarten Union (D'Onise et al., 2010)	Self report	A	Ever regular smoker RR = 0.87 (0.77–0.98) AD = −7.7% Current smoker RR = 0.77 (0.59–1.0) AD = −4.3% Quit smoking RR = 1.05 (0.92–1.20) AD = 3.2% Age at smoking uptake coefficient −0.29 (−1.05–0.46) AD −0.3 years	
Alcohol	Perry Preschool (Schweinhart & Weikart, 1980)	Self report	C	Drinking (alcohol) without permission (ever) RR = 1.0 ARD = 1% (−16.0 to 18.0%)	mixed
	Abecedarian (Campbell et al., 2002)	Self report	A	5+ alcohol drinks in a row in last month RR = 1.37 AD = 10% (−7.8 to 27.8%)	mixed
	Perry Preschool (Schweinhart et al., 1993; Schweinhart et al., 2005; Meunnig et al., 2009)	Self report	A	Alcohol several times a week/daily (27 years) RR = 0.62 AD = −10% (−24.6 to 4.6%) 5+ alcohol drinks in a row in last month (40 years) RR = 2.08 AD = 13% (−1.3 to 27.3%) Driving when had too much to drink ≥ 1 time past month RR = 1.08 AD = 1% (−11.4 to 13.4%) Daily alcohol use ARD = −13% p = 0.10	

Table 7.2 (*cont.*)

Health measure	Study	Outcome measurement	Age	Results (95% confidence interval)	Overall direction of association
	Kindergarten Union (D'Onise et al., 2011)	Self report	A	High risk alcohol drinker RRR = 1.01 (0.58–1.77)	
	Chicago Child Parent Centres (Reynolds et al., 2011)	Self report	A	Drug and alcohol abuse AD −6.5% p = 0.004	
	Head Start (Hyman, 2011b)		C	Drug and alcohol abuse (child) ES = 0.11 (se 0.06) Drug and alcohol abuse (adolescent) ES = 0.16 (se 0.08)	=
Drug use	Perry preschool (Schweinhart & Weikart, 1980)	Pupil behavior inventory Self report	C	Marijuana (ever) RR = 1.2 ARD = 3% (−11.0 to 17.0%) Other drugs (ever) RR = 3.5 ARD = 5% (−3.4 to 13.4%)	+
	Perry preschool (Meunnig et al., 2009; Schweinhart et al., 1993; Schweinhart et al., 2005)	Self report	A	Heroin last 15 years RR = indeterminate AD = −9% (−16.4 to −1.6%) LSD ARD = −4% p = 0.41 Negative effect in those who used drugs/alcohol RR = 0.82 AD = −9% (−29.9 to 11.9%) Marijuana last 15 years ARD = −10% p = 0.32 Cocaine ARD = −6% p = 0.51 Sedatives ARD = −10% p = 0.30	+
	Chicago Child Parent Centres (Reynolds et al., 2007; Reynolds et al., 2011)	Self report	A	Any substance use age ≥ 16 years RR = 0.91 AD = −2.5% (−8.6 to 3.6%) Frequent substance use RR = 0.82 AD = −3% (−7.2 to 1.1%) Substance abuse AD −5.2% (p = 0.01)	

Category	Study	Measurement	Quality	Outcome	
	Abecedarian (Campbell et al., 2002)	Self report	A	Marijuana in last month RR = 0.46 AD = −21% (−37.9 to −4.1%); Cocaine or other drug ever RR = 1.67 AD = 4% (−6.4 to 14.4%)	
	Project CARE (Campbell et al., 2008)	Self report	A	Marijuana in last month RR = 0.84 AD = −7% (−39.9 to 25.9%)	
Physical activity	Head Start (Gietzen & Vermeersch, 1980)	School records	C	Head Start vs. Free Lunch (boys): ES = 0.6 (−7.1 to 11.3); Head Start vs. Free Lunch (girls): ES = 0.1 (−9.0 to 9.3)	+
	Head Start (Anderson et al., 2004)	Self report	A	Light exercise AD = −3.9% (−23.1 to 15.3%); Light exercise (Head Start > 2 years) AD = 18.4% (−24.7 to 61.5%); Heavy exercise AD = 6.8% (−11.0 to 24.6%); Heavy exercise (Head Start > 2 years) AD = 9.8% (−30.0 to 49.6%)	+
	Project CARE (Campbell et al., 2008)	Self report	A	Active lifestyle RR = 3.7 AD = 52% (−22.9 to 81%)	
	Abecedarian (Campbell et al., 2002)	Self report	A	Active lifestyle RR = 1.3 AD = 10% (−8.7 to 28.7%)	
	Kindergarten Union (D'Onise et al., 2011)	Self report	A	High physical activity RR = 1.99 (1.19–3.35)	
Diet	Better Beginnings Better Futures (Peters et al., 2003)	24 hour child and parent dietary recall	C	24 hour dietary recall, no difference	=
	Kindergarten Union (D'Onise et al., 2011)	Self report	A	Fruit ≥ 2 serves a day RR = 0.85 (0.73–0.99); Vegetable ≥ 5 serves a day RR = 1.41 (0.90–2.19)	=
	Abecedarian (Campbell et al., 2008)	Self report	A	Good dietary habits: no treatment effects	
	Project CARE (Campbell et al., 2008)	Self report	A	Good dietary habits: no treatment effects	

Table 7.2 (cont.)

Health measure	Study	Outcome measurement	Age	Results (95% confidence interval)	Overall direction of association
Preventive behaviors	Better Beginnings Better Futures (Peters et al., 2003)	Parental report Self report	C	Child: Use of bicycle helmets, no consistent differences Traffic safety, no consistent differences	=
	Comprehensive Child Development Program (Goodson et al., 2000)	Parental report	C	Number of injuries requiring hospitalization, no difference Severity of injuries, no difference	
	Brookline Early Education Project (Palfrey et al., 2005)	Self report	A	Health behaviors: suburban Effect size = 0.1 (−1.6 to 1.7), urban Effect size = 0.5 (−3.3 to 4.0) Condom use: suburban RR = 0.92 AD = −2.6% (−15.7 to 10.5%), urban RR = 1.5 AD = 13% (−12.7 to 38.8%)	=
	Perry Preschool (Meunnig et al., 2009)	Self report	A	No seatbelt use (27 years) ARD = −25% p = 0.02 No seatbelt use (40 years) ARD = −3% p = 0.68	
	Abecedarian (Campbell et al., 2008)	Self report	A	Wear a seatbelt usually or always: RR = 0.69 AD = −16% (−50.0 to 17.0%)	
	Project CARE (Campbell et al., 2008)	Self report	A	Wear a seatbelt usually or always: RR = 1.15 AD = 8% (−11.2 to 27.2%)	
Risk taking	NICHD Early Child Care Research Network (Vandell et al., 2010)	Self report	C	Composite of drug and alcohol use, safety and delinquent behaviors: Effect size = 0.09 p > 0.05	=

Key: + beneficial direction of outcome for intervention group, − adverse direction of outcome for intervention group, mixed uncertain, either beneficial or adverse outcome, = no difference between intervention and control.
RR relative risk, ARD absolute risk difference, OR odds ratio, ES Cohen's d, se standard error

based the smoking results on small numbers (nine people in each of the intervention and control groups; Campbell et al., 2008).

In summary, there is good evidence that attendance at a preschool program reduces the risk of tobacco and marijuana smoking as an adult, but has uncertain effects on alcohol drinking and other illicit drug use.

Mental health results: a guide to interpretation

Many of the studies that examined health outcomes looked at factors relating to social competence, including self-esteem and social skills, through to signs of a mental illness. In childhood, mental health was generally measured using behavioral scales that examined child behaviors. These behaviors are measured on scales from normal through to indicative of a clinical diagnosis of mental illness. In childhood these were generally separated into internalizing (e.g., anxiety, depression) or externalizing (disturbed or antisocial behavior) behaviors (Tonge, 1998). Studies that evaluated mental health outcomes in adulthood focused on mental health diagnoses such as anxiety and depression using a range of validated survey instruments.

Social skills and competence

There was consistent evidence that attendance at center-based preschool did not have an effect on self-concept measured in adolescence (Table 7.3). There was also no evidence for an effect on self-esteem from childhood through to adulthood (at age 14–17 and 21 years). The studies examining these outcomes had a number of limitations, however, including two studies establishing exposure to preschool using recall in adulthood, and all studies having a moderate to high risk of bias, suggesting that these outcomes have not been adequately assessed (Beller, 1983; Caputo, 2003; 2004; Garber, 1988; Gray, Ramsey, and Klaus, 1983; 2004; Hyman, 2011b).

Thirteen studies examined overall social competence in childhood, with six of these using the same validated Social Skills Rating Scale measure (Andersson, 1992; Belsky et al., 2007; Bryant, Peisner-Feinberg, and Clifford, 1993; Gray et al., 1983; Hickman, 2006; Kaminski et al., 2002; Lee et al., 1990; Magnuson, Ruhm, and Waldfogel, 2007; Peters et al., 2003; Reynolds, 1994; Weikart, Bond, and McNeil, 1978; Zhai, 2008; Zhai, Brooks-Gunn, and Waldfogel, 2011). Eight studies, including two low and two moderate potential risk of bias studies found beneficial effects of the intervention on social competence (Andersson, 1992; Gray et al., 1983; Kaminski et al., 2002; Lee et al., 1990; Peters et al., 2003; Vandell et al., 2010; Weikart et al., 1978; Zhai et al., 2011) from grade 1 through to grade 11. Four of the six studies that found no effect on social competence (Belsky et al., 2007; Hickman, 2006; Magnuson et al., 2007; Zhai, 2008)

Table 7.3 *Social outcomes associated with center-based preschool.*

Study name	Data source	Social outcome measure	Age group	Results (95% confidence interval)	Overall direction of association
Self concept					
Head Start (Caputo, 2004)	National Longitudinal Survey of Youth (NLSY79) and the National Longitudinal Survey's Child–Mother study	Pearlin Mastery Scale (score 7–28)	C	Head Start exposure (unadjusted mean): mother and child = 21.82, child only = 21.65, control = 22.10 F = 1.80 $p > 0.05$	=
Milwaukee project (Garber, 1988)	Longitudinal follow-up of quasi-experimental cohort	Self concept	C	Self concept, no difference	
Early Training project (Gray et al., 1983)	Longitudinal follow-up of experimental study	Piers–Harris self concept scale	C	Age 7–8 years: self concept, no difference	
Philadelphia study (Beller, 1983)	Longitudinal follow-up of experimental study	Piers–Harris self concept scale, by child age (mean)	C	Preschool = 64.0 Kindergarten = 62.9 Grade1 = 59.4, F = 2.52 $p \leq 0.1$	
Self-esteem					
Early Training project (Gray et al., 1983)	Longitudinal follow-up of experimental study	Rosenberg Self-Esteem Scale	C	Self esteem, no difference	=
Child Health and Education study (Osborn & Milbank, 1987)	Child Health and Education Study	Lawrence Self-esteem Questionnaire	C	No difference, details not reported	
Four preschool program study (Miller & Bizzell, 1984)	Longitudinal follow-up of experimental study	Coopersmith Self-esteem inventory (males)	C	BE ES = 0.01 (−6.9 to 7.6) DARCEE ES = −0.4 (−7.4 to 7.2)	

Study	Source	Measure		Results
		Coopersmith Self-esteem inventory (females)	C	Montessori ES = −0.01 (−11.1 to 7.6) Traditional ES = 0.2 (−8.9 to 7.8) BE ES = 0.1 (−5.8 to 7.2) DARCEE ES = −0.2 (−10.9 to 6.9) Montessori ES = 0.3 (−6.2 to 7.3) Traditional ES = −0.22 (−7.6 to 6.8)
Head Start (Caputo, 2004)	National Longitudinal Survey of Youth (NLSY79) and the National Longitudinal Survey's Child–Mother study	Rosenberg Self Esteem Scale (score 10–40)	C	Adjusted coefficient: Head Start exposure: mother and child = −0.1 (se 0.1), child only = 0.1 (se 0.5), control = 0.7 (se 0.5) $p > 0.05$
Head Start (Caputo, 2003)	National Longitudinal Survey of Youth (NLSY79) and the National Longitudinal Survey's Child–Mother study	Rosenberg Self Esteem Scale (score 10–40) Pearlin Mastery Scale (score 7–28)	C	Head Start = 33.11, other preschool = 34.03, no preschool = 33.55 $p < 0.05$ Head Start = 22.17, other preschool = 22.42, no preschool = 22.14 $p > 0.05$
Head Start (Caputo, 2004)	National Longitudinal Survey of Youth (NLSY79) and the National Longitudinal Survey's Child–Mother study	Pearlin Mastery Scale (score 7–28)	C	Head Start exposure (unadjusted mean): mother and child = 21.82, child only = 21.65, control = 22.10 F = 1.80 $p > 0.05$
Head Start (Hyman, 2011b)	National Longitudinal Survey of Youth (NLSY) Child–Mother study.	Self-Perception Profile for Children Rosenberg Self Esteem Scale (score 10–40) Locus of control	C	ES = 0.05 (se 0.06) ES = 0.07 (se 0.07) ES = 0.08 (se 0.07)

Table 7.3 (cont.)

Study name	Data source	Social outcome measure	Age group	Results (95% confidence interval)	Overall direction of association
Social competence					
Usual services (Belsky et al., 2007)	National Institute of Child Health and Human Development Study	Social Skills Rating Scale (teacher rated) by child care quality	C	ES = 0.02 p > 0.05	=
		Social Skills Rating Scale by intensity of exposure	C	ES = −0.02 p > 0.05	
		Social Skills Rating Scale by center-based care	C	ES = 0.02 p > 0.05	
Usual services (Hickman, 2006)	Early Childhood Longitudinal Study – Kindergarten 98/99	? Social Skills Rating Scale (teacher rated)	C	Self-control: coefficient = −0.052 (se 0.013) p < 0.001	
		? Interpersonal skills measure		Interpersonal skills: coefficient = −0.050 (se 0.013) p < 0.001	
				Externalizing behaviors: coefficient = 0.062 (se 0.012) p < 0.001	
				Internalizing problem behaviors: coefficient = 0.013 (se 0.011) p > 0.05	
Head Start (Zhai, 2008)	Early Childhood Longitudinal Study, Kindergarten Class 1998/1999.	Social Skills Rating Scale (teacher rated, reference category Head Start)	C	Grade 3: Self-control – parental care ES = −0.04 p > 0.1, center-based care ES = −0.15 p < 0.05	
				Externalizing behaviors – parental care ES = 0.06 p > 0.1, center-based care ES = 0.14 p < 0.05	
				Internalizing behaviors – parental care ES = 0.06 p > 0.1, center-based care ES = 0.11 p < 0.1	

Study	Description	Measure		Results
				Grade 5: Self-control – parental care ES = 0.05 $p > 0.1$, center-based care ES = −0.02 $p > 0.1$ Externalizing behaviors – parental care ES = 0.03 $p > 0.1$, center-based care ES = 0.15 $p < 0.05$ Internalizing behaviors – parental care ES = 0.07 $p > 0.1$, center-based care ES = 0.18 $p < 0.01$
Better Beginnings Better Futures Study (Peters et al., 2003)	Longitudinal follow-up of quasi-experimental cohort	Social Skills Rating Scale (teacher rated)	C	Self-control ES = 0.46 $p < 0.01$
North Carolina (Bryant et al., 1993)	Longitudinal follow-up of cohort	Social Skills Rating Scale (teacher rated)	C	Problem behaviors: Public PS ES = 0.09 (−0.9 to 1.4) Head Start ES = 0.15 (−1.2 to 1.4) Community PS ES = −0.09 (−1.5 to 1.2) Social skills: Public PS ES = 0.03 (−1.5 to 2.2) Head Start ES = 0.07 (−2.2 to 2.2) Community PS ES = 0.38 (−2.0 to 2.5)
		Social Skills Rating Scale by quality (teacher rated)	C	Quality, no difference
Head Start (Magnuson et al., 2007)	Early Childhood Longitudinal Study, Kindergarten Class 1998/1999	Social Skills Rating Scale (teacher rated)	C	Kindergarten: Self control (ES): pre-K = −0.12 $p < 0.01$, PS = −0.08 $p < 0.05$, Head Start = −0.09 $p < 0.05$, other non-parental = 0.07 $p > 0.05$

Table 7.3 (cont.)

Study name	Data source	Social outcome measure	Age group	Results (95% confidence interval)	Overall direction of association
				Externalizing behavior (ES): pre-K = 0.19 p < 0.01, PS = 0.14 p < 0.01, Head Start = 0.11 p < 0.01, other non-parental = −0.12 p < 0.01 Grade 1: Self control (ES): pre-K = −0.13 p < 0.01, PS = −0.11 p < 0.01, Head Start = −0.14 p < 0.01, other non-parental = 0.04 p > 0.05 Externalizing behavior (ES): pre-K = 0.21 p < 0.01, PS = 0.14 p < 0.01, Head Start = 0.14 p < 0.01, other non-parental = −0.03 p > 0.05	
Head Start (Lee et al., 1990)	Head Start Longitudinal Study	California Preschool Competency Test	C	ES = 0.34 (p ≤ 0.05)	+
Perry Preschool Study (Weikart et al., 1978)	Perry Preschool Study	Ypsilanti Rating Scale	C	Social development ES = 0.25 (−0.18 to 0.69) Emotional adjustment ES = 0.39 (−0.06 to 0.8)	
Early Training project (Gray et al., 1983)	Longitudinal follow-up of experimental study	School counsellor completed social competence scale	C	Control males more productive, experimental females more social competence across leadership, productivity, social adjustment and participation (p ≤ 0.05), details not reported	

Study	Design	Outcome	Direction	Results
Swedish Day Care study (Andersson, 1992)	Longitudinal cohort (of existing day care services)	Social competence by age of entry (teacher rated)	C	Age 8 (mean score): 0–1 Year = 12.28 (se 0.33) 1–2 year = 12.28 (se 0.44) 2+ year = 11.67 (se 0.44) Home care = 11.58 (0.42), (0–1 > home care, p = 0.01) Age 13 (mean score): 0–1 year = 28.66 (se 0.9) 1–2 year = 27.23 (se 1.19) 2+ year = 26.37 (se 1.21) Home care = 24.82 (se 1.23), (0–1 > home care, p = 0.01)
Head Start Project Star (Kaminski et al., 2002)	Longitudinal follow-up of experimental study	Social competence (Child Behavior Checklist Peer Rejection; Parent Perceived Social Competence Scale Pro-social Communication Skills; Social Competence and Behavior Evaluation Questionnaire Social Competence)	C	Social competence greater in intervention groups F= 6.68 p < 0.05
Chicago Child–Parent Centre study (Reynolds, 1994)	Longitudinal quasi-experimental cohort	Teacher rating of school adjustment	C	ES = 0.12 p > 0.05
Head Start (Zhai et al., 2011)	Fragile Families and Child Well being Study	Adaptive Social Behavior Inventory Express Subscale	C	ES = 0.24 (0.09–0.40)

Key: + beneficial direction of outcome for intervention group, – adverse direction of outcome for intervention group, mixed uncertain, either beneficial or adverse outcome, = no difference between intervention and control
RR relative risk, ARD absolute risk difference, OR odds ratio, ES Cohen's d, se standard error

used data from large national cohort studies of usual center-based care services, examining outcomes up to 15 years old. These results were unchanged when examined by quality of the intervention received (Belsky et al., 2007; Bryant et al., 1993) or intensity of exposure (Belsky et al., 2007; Vandell et al., 2010).

Mental health related behaviors and diagnoses

Five studies examined depression and anxiety problems (Table 7.4) in childhood (Caputo, 2004; Hyman, 2011b; Peters et al., 2003; Raine et al., 2003; Weikart et al., 1978). There was no association between preschool attendance and depression at 8 years in the BBBF study (Peters et al., 2003) and from 14 years in the Caputo and Hyman Head Start studies (Caputo, 2004; Hyman, 2011b); however, there was a reduction in symptoms of anxiety in the Better Beginnings Better Futures (BBBF) study (Cohen's d = 0.47, $p <$ 0.01) (Peters et al., 2003). The low risk of bias Mauritius and Perry Preschool studies found no difference between intervention and control groups on symptoms of anxiety (Raine et al., 2003) or social-emotional status (Weikart et al., 1978).

In adulthood, depression was assessed by two studies using the Center for Epidemiological Studies Depression Scale (Caputo, 2004; Palfrey et al., 2005), and the complete Brief Symptom Inventory was used by one study (McLaughlin et al., 2007), and in part by another (Reynolds et al., 2007). The high-quality Abecedarian study reported some evidence for improved symptoms of depression at 21 years old when using a continuous scale, but not for a diagnosis of depression, with a moderate Cohen's d effect size of 0.44 (95 percent CI −3.3 to 2.4 percent) (McLaughlin et al., 2007). Furthermore, when considering the impact of childhood home environment quality measured by the Home Observation for Measurement of the Environment tool on depression symptoms, the intervention group had reduced symptoms of depression (regression coefficient, gender adjusted T scores with a mean of 50 and standard deviation of 10, b = 11.26, t = 0.70, p = 0.48) and the control group increased symptoms of depression (b = −34.61, t = 2.17, p = 0.03), indicating the intervention was able to overcome the negative impact of a poor-quality home environment on depression. The only non-US based study, set in Mauritius and which included nutritional supplementation, found reduced schizotypal symptoms at age 17 but not at age 23, except for those who were malnourished as children (Cohen's d effect size −0.42, $p <$ 0.05) (Raine et al., 2003).

Twenty studies examined externalizing problems in childhood using a behavioral scale, with thirteen of these studies showing no effect of preschool on externalizing behaviors. These behaviors included conflict,

Table 7.4 *Mental health outcomes associated with center-based preschool.*

Study name	Data source	Mental health outcome measure	Age group	Result (95% confidence interval)	Overall direction of association
Depression					
Head Start (Caputo, 2004)	National Longitudinal Survey of Youth (NLSY79) and the National Longitudinal Survey's Child–Mother study	Centre for Epidemiological Studies Depression Scale	C	Head Start exposure (mean): mother and child = 4.33, child only = 5.29, control = 4.75 F = 1.92 $p > 0.05$	=
Head Start (Caputo, 2004)	National Longitudinal Survey of Youth (NLSY79) and the National Longitudinal Survey's Child–Mother study	Centre for Epidemiological Studies Depression Scale	C	Head Start exposure: mother and child = 4.33, child only = 5.29, control = 4.75 F = 1.92 $p > 0.05$	
Head Start (Hyman, 2011b)	National Longitudinal Survey of Youth (NLSY79) and the National Longitudinal Survey's Child–Mother study	Centre for Epidemiological Studies Depression Scale	C	ES = 0.03 (se 0.07)	
Better Beginnings Better Futures (Peters et al., 2003)	Longitudinal follow-up of quasi-experimental cohort	Ontario Child Health Study questionnaire (anxiety and depression subscales)	C	Anxiety ES = 0.47 (reduction) $p < 0.01$ Depression – no difference, details not reported	
Chicago Child Parent Centre study (Reynolds et al., 2007)	Longitudinal quasi-experimental cohort	Brief Symptom Inventory (in part)	A	RR = 0.74 ARD = –4.6% (–9.5 to 0.3%)	+
Abecedarian (McLaughlin et al., 2007)	Longitudinal experimental cohort	Brief Symptom Inventory	A	Cohen's d = –0.44 (–3.3 to 2.4)	
Brookline Early Education Project (Palfrey et al., 2005)	Longitudinal quasi-experimental cohort	Centre for Epidemiological Studies Depression Scale	A	(Suburban) Cohen's d = –0.01 (–1.8 to 1.7) (Urban) Cohen's d = –0.64 (–3.8 to 5.0)	

Table 7.4 (cont.)

Study name	Data source	Mental health outcome measure	Age group	Result (95% confidence interval)	Overall direction of association
Behavior					
Mauritius study (Raine et al., 2003)	Longitudinal follow-up of quasi-experimental cohort	Self report questionnaire Revised Behavior Problem Check List	C	Age 17: Positive schizotypal personality ES = −0.29 $p < 0.04$ Disorganization ES = −0.34 $p < 0.02$, malnourished ES = −0.71 $p = 0.003$ Conduct disorder ES = −0.44 $p = 0.003$, malnourished ES = −0.63 $p = 0.004$ Psychotic behavior ES = −0.31 $p < 0.04$ Anxious withdrawn ES = −0.01 $p > 0.05$ Attention problems ES = 0.07 $p > 0.05$	+
			A	Age 23: Schizotypal personality Cohen's d = −0.02 (−3.1 to 1.6) Schizotypal personality (malnourished) Cohen's d = −0.42 $p < 0.05$	
Usual services (Loeb et al., 2005)	Early Childhood Longitudinal Study – Kindergarten 1998/1999	Behavior composite (? source)	C	Centre care ES = −0.09 (se 0.026) $p \leq 0.01$ Head Start ES = −0.12 (se 0.041) $p \leq 0.01$	=

Study	Design	C	Measure	Results	
		C	Behavior composite by age of entry	0–1 years ES = −0.29 (se 0.044) $p \le 0.01$ 1–2 years ES = −0.209 (se 0.048) $p \le 0.01$ 2–3 years ES = −0.16 (se 0.038) $p \le 0.01$ 3–4 years ES = −0.085 (se 0.03) $p \le 0.01$ 4–5 years ES = −0.026 (se −0.03) $p > 0.1$	–
		C	Behavior composite by intensity of exposure	15–30 h/week, 9 months ES = −0.10 (se 0.030) $p \le 0.01$ At least 30 h/week, 9 months ES = −0.25 (se 0.028) $p \le 0.01$	–
Day Care study (Bates et al., 1994)	Retrospective cohort	C	Behavior composite by age of entry (from Teacher's Report Form and the Teacher Checklist)	Negative adjustment: 4–5 years $\beta = 0.01$ ($p \ge 0.1$), 1–4 years $\beta = 0.13$ ($p < 0.01$), 0–1 years $\beta = 0.07$ ($p < 0.1$) Positive adjustment: 4–5 years $\beta = 0.01$ ($p \ge 0.1$), 1–4 years $\beta = -0.04$ ($p \ge 0.1$), 0–1 years $\beta = -0.15$ ($p < 0.005$)	=
Early Provision of Preschool Education Project (Sammons et al., 2007)	Longitudinal cohort (of existing preschool services)	C	Strengths and Difficulties Questionnaire (teacher rated) Record of conduct/emotional problems (school records)	Hyperactivity, self-regulation – no difference (details not reported) Pro-social behavior: ES = 0.19, $p \le 0.05$ Antisocial behavior, no difference	=
		C	Behavior by high educational quality preschool vs. no preschool:	Self regulation ES = 0.25 $p \le 0.05$ Pro-social behavior ES = 0.23 Hyperactivity ES = 0.02 $p \le 0.05$ Antisocial behavior ES = −0.2 (for all $p \le 0.05$)	+

Table 7.4 (cont.)

Study name	Data source	Mental health outcome measure	Age group	Result (95% confidence interval)	Overall direction of association
Chicago Child Parent Centre study (Reynolds, 1998)	Longitudinal quasi-experimental cohort	Socially resilient (Teacher Child Rating Scale + teacher reported delinquency)	C	RR = 1.0 ARD = 0.2% (−7.8 to 8.2%)	=
Perry Preschool study (Weikart et al., 1978)	Longitudinal follow-up of experimental study	Pupil Behavior Inventory	C	Classroom conduct ES = 0.52 (0.22 to 0.8) Socio-emotional status ES = 0.16 (−0.17 to 0.44) Behavior ES = 0.14 (−0.09 to 0.36) Teacher dependence ES = 0.16 (−0.12 to 0.44)	Mixed
Head Start (Lee et al., 1990)	Head Start Longitudinal Study	Schaefer Classroom Behavior Inventory	C	ES = −0.14 p > 0.05	=
Turkish early enrichment project (Kagitcibasi, Stormshale, and Good 2001)	Longitudinal follow-up of experimental study	Parental Acceptance–Rejection Questionnaire (parent assessment)	C	Aggression subscale (mean higher score = lower aggression) E (HV) = 19.88, E (no HV) = 17.12, home care (HV) = 17.94, home care (no PP) = 18.48 Self concept subscale (mean): E (HV) = 30.96 E (no HV) = 29.6, day care (HV) = 29.76 day care (no HV) = 29.0, home care (HV) = 31.25 home care (no HV) = 30.58	+

Study	Study description	Measure		Results	
Comprehensive Child Development Program (Goodson et al., 2000)	Longitudinal follow-up of experimental study	Child Behavior Checklist	C	Dependency subscale (mean): E (HV) = 14.21 E (no HV) = 11.60, home care (HV) = 11.88 home care (no HV) = 11.93 E less negative behavior than home care $p = 0.01$ ES = −0.03 (−0.58 to 0.5)	=
		Kindergarten Developmental Check List	C	ES = 0.07 (−0.23 to 0.36)	=
Usual services (Belsky et al., 2007; Vandell et al., 2010)	National Institute of Child Health and Human Development Study	Child Behavior Checklist (teacher reported) and Student–Teacher Relationship Scale by child care quality	C	Age 12: Externalizing behavior ES = −0.01 $p > 0.05$ Teacher–child conflict ES = −0.00 $p > 0.05$ Age 15: Externalizing behavior ES = −0.09 $p < 0.05$	=
		Child Behavior Checklist and Student–Teacher Relationship Scale by quantity of care/week	C	Externalizing behavior ES = −0.03 $p > 0.05$ Teacher–child conflict ES = −0.02 $p > 0.05$ Age 15: Externalizing behavior ES = 0.04 $p > 0.05$	=
		Child Behavior Checklist and Student–Teacher Relationship Scale by centre care	C	Externalizing behavior ES = 0.08 $p < 0.01$ Teacher–child conflict ES = 0.03 $p > 0.05$ Age 15: Externalizing behavior ES = 0.02 $p > 0.05$	=
Georgia pre-K study (Henry et al., 2004)	Georgia Early Childhood Study	Composite of classroom behaviors (scale of 1–7)	C	Pre-K coefficient = 0.17 $p > 0.05$	=

Table 7.4 (cont.)

Study name	Data source	Mental health outcome measure	Age group	Result (95% confidence interval)	Overall direction of association
Day care – Learning games (Haskins, 1985)	Longitudinal follow-up of experimental study	Classroom Behavior Inventory (scale 1 low–5 high)	C	Aggressive act e.g. hit ES = 0.14 (−0.46 to 0.67), kick ES = 0.49 (−0.1 to 0.95), push ES = −0.19 (−0.78 to 0.35) Verbal aggression e.g. threaten ES = 0.24 (−0.47 to 0.82), tease ES = 0.32 (−0.24 to 0.85) argue ES = −0.29 (−0.92 to 0.21)	–
		Classroom Behavior Inventory by amount of day care attendance	C	Aggressive act (5 years versus 0–18 months) e.g. hit ES = 0.33 (0.06 to 0.86), kick ES = 0.47 (0.17 to 0.89), push ES = 0.69 (0.38 to 1.25) Verbal aggression e.g. threaten ES = 0.52 (0.14 to 1.08), tease ES = 0.29 (−0.05 to 0.95) argue ES = 0.33 (0.02 to 0.87)	–
Head Start Project Star (Kaminski et al., 2002)	Longitudinal follow-up of experimental study	Self regulation (Eyberg Child Behavior Inventory Problem Score and Intensity Score; Child Behavior Checklist Attention Problems and Aggressive Behavior Scale; Parent Perceived Social	C	Self regulation, no difference F = 0.24, $p > 0.05$	=

Study	Sample		Measure	Results	Direction
Head Start (Roy, 2003)	Children of National Longitudinal Survey of Youth – 1979, National Longitudinal Survey of Youth – 1979	C	Competence Scale Emotion Regulation Scale; ADHD Rating Scale; Social Competence and Behavior Evaluation Questionnaire Externalizing Scale) Behavior Problems Index	Head Start (coefficient) = −10.45 (se 5.27) $p \le 0.05$ Preschool (coefficient) = 6.05 (se 4.62) $p > 0.05$	+
Head Start (Hyman, 2011b)	Children of National Longitudinal Survey of Youth – 1979, National Longitudinal Survey of Youth – 1979	C	Behavior Problems Index Delinquent behavior	ES = −0.04 (se 0.05) ES = 0.14 (se 0.07)	=
Philadelphia study (Beller, 1983)	Longitudinal follow-up of experimental study	C	Behavior, aggression	Observed classroom behavior in grade 1 (aggression, mean): E = 4.54, C1 = 3.56, C2 = 3.44 F–ratio = 4.59 $p = 0.05$	−
Child Health and Education Study (Osborn & Milbank, 1987)	Cohort, nationally representative (linkage)	C	Rutter A scale Rutter B scale Connors Teacher Rating Scale	Conduct disorder (10 years): Government: nursery school ES = −0.02, nursery class ES = 0.08, day care ES = 0.2, Private: nursery school ES = 0.2, day care ES = 0.19, C ES = −0.05, $p < 0.005$	mixed
Head Start (Aughinbaugh, 2001)	NLSY-97 cohort, nationally representative	C	Parental report of school suspensions	Head Start coefficient = 0.286 (se 0.049), AD = 9.1% $p \le 0.01$ Centre Care coefficient = 0.059 (se 0.018), AD = 1.8% $p > 0.05$	–

Table 7.4 (cont.)

Study name	Data source	Mental health outcome measure	Age group	Result (95% confidence interval)	Overall direction of association
Four preschool comparison study (Miller & Bizzell, 1984)	Longitudinal follow-up of experimental study	Self report school suspensions	C	Males: BE ES = −0.3 (−0.93 to 0.32) DARCEE ES = 0.1 (−0.48 to 0.72) Montessori ES = −0.4 (−1.17 to 0.25) Traditional ES = 0.5 (−1.25 to 1.18) Females: BE ES = −0.5 (−0.78 to 0.54) DARCEE ES = −0.3 (−0.86 to 0.81) Montessori ES = −0.3 (−1.03 to 0.78) Traditional ES = −0.2 (−0.67 to 0.88)	+
Chicago Child–Parent Centre study (Reynolds et al., 2001)	Longitudinal quasi-experimental cohort	Criminal records	C	Any juvenile arrest RR = 0.67 AD = −8.2% (−12.7 to −3.7%) Any violent arrest RR = 0.59 AD = −6.3% (−10.0 to −2.6%) Any non-violent arrest RR = 0.75 AD = −4.8% (−9.0 to −0.64%)	+
Chicago Child–Parent Centre study (Reynolds et al., 1998)	Longitudinal quasi-experimental cohort	Delinquency School records 13–16 years Self report grade 10–11	C	School records: Age 13–14 RR = 1.0 ARD = 0.2% (−22 to 22%)	=

Study	Design	Measure		Findings
Perry Preschool Study (Schweinhart & Weikart, 1980)	Longitudinal follow-up of experimental study	Self rated school conduct (higher score better conduct)	C	Age 15–16 RR = 0.88 ARD = −2.8% (−15 to 21%) Self report: Arrests ARD = −1.9% (−45 to 49%) School conduct score 30–36 RR = 1.3 AD = 7% (−26.8 to 40.8%) + School conduct score 22–29 RR = 1.04 AD = 2% (−26.9 to 31.0) School conduct score 14–21 RR = 0.8 AD = −5% (−40.0 to 29.6%) School conduct score 10–13 RR = 1.5 AD = −1% (−42.2 to 44.3%) Self reported delinquent behavior non-offenders + 1× offender RR = 1.7 AD = 18% (−0.57 to 36.6%) Self reported delinquent behavior 5+ offenders RR = 0.69 AD = −16% (−35.4 to 3.4%)
Syracuse Family Development Research Program (Lally et al., 1988)	Longitudinal follow-up of experimental study	Court records Teacher questionnaire	C	Delinquency: RR = 0.27 ARD = −16% (−28.5 to −3.5%) + Teacher ratings: Positive attitude toward self and others, control of aggression: E > C in girls, no difference with boys (details not reported)

Table 7.4 (cont.)

Study name	Data source	Mental health outcome measure	Age group	Result (95% confidence interval)	Overall direction of association
Tulsa Pre-K program and Head Start (Gormley et al., 2011)	Tulsa Pre-K longitudinal study	Adjustment Scales for preschool Intervention	C	Tulsa Pre-K: Disobedient ES = 0.02 $p > 0.05$ Aggressive ES = 0.04 $p > 0.05$ Attention seeking ES = −0.09 $p > 0.05$ Apathetic ES = −0.09 $p > 0.05$ Timid ES = −0.15 $p < 0.05$ Head Start: Disobedient ES = 0.15 $p > 0.05$ Aggressive ES = 0.02 $p > 0.05$ Attention seeking ES = −0.05 $p > 0.05$ Apathetic ES = −0.01 $p > 0.05$ Timid ES = −0.27 $p > 0.05$	=
Head Start (Zhai et al., 2011)	Fragile Families and Child Well-being Study	Child Behavior Checklist	C	Attention problems ES = −0.10 (se 0.09) Internalizing problems ES = −0.06 (se 0.08) Externalizing problems ES = −0.07 (se 0.08)	=

Key: + beneficial direction of outcome for intervention group, − adverse direction of outcome for intervention group, mixed uncertain, either beneficial or adverse outcome, = no difference between intervention and control

RR relative risk, ARD absolute risk difference, OR odds ratio, ES Cohen's d, se standard error

aggression, and antisocial behavior (Belsky et al., 2007; Goodson et al., 2000; Gormley et al., 2011; Henry et al., 2004; Hyman, 2011b; Kaminski et al., 2002; Lee et al., 1990; Loeb et al., 2005; Osborn and Milbank, 1987; Reynolds, 1998; Sammons et al., 2007; Vandell et al., 2010; Zhai et al., 2011). Five studies, all of which were interventions in children aged 3 or older, found a reduction in externalizing problems, including the methodologically low risk of Perry bias Preschool Project (Schweinhart and Weikart, 1980; Weikart et al., 1978) and Mauritius study (Raine et al., 2003), and two methodologically high risk of bias studies, the Turkish Early Enrichment Project (Kagitcibasi, Sunar, and Bekman, 2001) and the Roy evaluation of Head Start (Roy, 2003). Two small experimental studies found a small to moderate negative effect on externalizing in the intervention group (e.g., Cohen's d range 0.23 to 0.32: Haskins, 1985).

Four studies described above examined externalizing problems on a behavioral scale by intensity of exposure, with two studies (one methodologically moderate and one high risk of bias) finding increasingly adverse effects as intensity of exposure increased (Haskins, 1985; Loeb et al., 2005) and one moderate risk study finding no effect by intensity of exposure at age 12 and then at 15 years (Belsky et al., 2007; Vandell et al., 2010). The moderate risk of bias study by Loeb and colleagues (2005) found greater adverse effects on externalizing problems for children commencing the intervention at a younger age of entry, and the Bates et al. Day Care study found a reduction in positive adjustment at kindergarten for children who commenced day care at a younger age (Bates et al., 1994). Only two moderate-risk studies considered the effect on behavior by measured quality of the intervention. The Early Provision of Preschool Education Project found improved self-regulation and pro-social behavior if children attended a high-quality center-based service, and the Belsky et al. study of usual care in the USA found no effect overall, regardless of intervention quality (Belsky et al., 2007).

Six studies examined school suspensions and adolescent crime. There were conflicting findings for the two methodologically high-risk studies that reported on school suspensions. One study that used parental report found an increased risk of school suspensions for preschool participants (Aughinbaugh, 2001) and the other study that used self-report of school suspensions found a reduced risk (Miller and Bizzell, 1984). Three of the four studies that examined crime found a reduced risk of crime for preschool participants. The 1998 Chicago Child Parent Centers study that found a null effect used school and self-report as the delinquency outcome (e.g., arrests ARD −1.9 percent, 95 percent CI −45 to 49 percent) (Reynolds and Temple, 1998), but when a later study examined objective documented crime it found a reduction in delinquency (e.g., arrest ARD −8.2 percent, 95 percent CI −12.7 to −3.7 percent) (Reynolds et al., 2001).

In summary, there was no clear effect of interventions on self-esteem, but some evidence for a small positive effect on social skills for the higher-quality interventions. The evidence suggests that preschool interventions have negligible effects on externalizing behavior problems except possibly for adverse effects for interventions that start from the first year of life. High-quality interventions may have small beneficial effects on behavior. There was, however, consistent evidence for a benefit regarding crime and delinquency reduction in childhood, and for depression reduction in adulthood.

Outcomes primarily related to parenting programs and a healthier home environment

Physical activity

The five studies (one in childhood: Gietzen and Vermeersch, 1980, and four in adulthood: Anderson, Foster, and Frisvold, 2004; Campbell et al., 2002; Campbell et al., 2008; D'Onise et al., 2011) that examined physical activity found preschool participants did more physical activity, with the greatest effect seen in the small randomized Project CARE study (ARD 52 percent, 95 percent CI 22.9 to 81.1 percent, Table 7.2) (Campbell et al., 2008). The Anderson et al. Head Start study that had a number of methodological problems found more physical activity benefits for the intervention group for those who had more than two years of Head Start participation (Anderson et al., 2004).

Safety behaviors

Health related safety behaviors in childhood were assessed by three studies (Table 7.2) (Goodson et al., 2000; Peters et al., 2003; Vandell et al., 2010). The low risk of bias BBBF study found no difference in the parental report of use of bicycle helmets, or traffic safety between preschool and non-preschool control groups by age 8 years (Goodson et al., 2000; Peters et al., 2003; Vandell et al., 2010). The moderate risk of bias Comprehensive Child Development Program (CCDP) study found no difference between intervention and control groups in the number of injuries requiring hospitalization or the severity of injuries at 5 years (Goodson et al., 2000).

The high-quality Perry Preschool study and Abecedarian studies both found more people from the intervention group wore a seatbelt usually or always than the control group in adulthood (25 percent and 8 percent respectively) (Campbell et al., 2008; Meunnig et al., 2009). Conversely,

Project CARE found a reduced prevalence of seatbelt use in the center-based intervention group (ARD −16 percent, 95 percent CI −50.0 to 17.0 percent: Anderson et al., 2004; Campbell et al., 2008; D'Onise et al., 2011); however, this was based on small numbers, with five people in the intervention group and eleven in the control group. The Brookline Early Education Program (BEEP) study found greater condom use and health behaviors measured by a composite index which included drug and alcohol use, safety behaviors, diet, and health service use in the urban but not the suburban cohort (Palfrey et al., 2005).

Anthropometry and diet
Five studies examined anthropometric and diet related outcomes in childhood, ages most likely to be influenced by the home environment (Table 7.2) (Currie and Thomas, 1995; Frisvold, 2007; Gietzen and Vermeersch, 1980; Peters et al., 2003; Zhai, 2008). There was no difference in growth (measured height for age) or dietary quality in the methodologically strong BBBF study. The Frisvold study was an observational cohort that examined adult-recalled attendance at Head Start in relation to researcher-measured obesity outcomes in children aged 5 to 19 years, and found a 44 percent absolute reduction in risk (95 percent CI −56.0 to −30.3 percent) of obesity for the African American sub-cohort of children. For children older than 10 years, the effect of Head Start participation on obesity was smaller and the confidence interval included a null effect (ARD 35 percent, 95 percent CI −104.3 to 34.5 percent) (Frisvold, 2007). The reduction in effect with increasing age was consistent with findings from the randomized Perry Preschool study, which found a slightly increased risk of self-reported overweight but not obesity at age 40 (Schweinhart et al., 2005). It is also consistent with the generally null effects seen on fruit and vegetable intake seen in four studies.

General health
General health measures were assessed by three studies in childhood, three in adulthood and one Head Start study that evaluated general health measures at age 14 to 21 years (Table 7.2) (Anderson et al., 2004; Caputo, 2004; Gietzen and Vermeersch, 1980; Henry et al., 2004; Meunnig et al., 2009; Palfrey et al., 2005; Peters et al., 2003). Four studies assessed self-reported general health using a rating from poor to excellent, a well-accepted measure of health that has also been associated with outcomes such as mortality and is independent of health service access. There was no evidence of benefit from preschool programs except in a sub-cohort in the BEEP (Palfrey et al., 2005) study and possibly in the Perry Preschool program at age 40 years (Meunnig et al., 2009).

Other measures used to indicate general health varied widely across studies. For example, in childhood, a potential high risk of bias study found Head Start participants had reduced sick days as recorded in school records compared with Free School Lunch children (Cohen's d = −0.7, 95 percent CI −2.0 to 1.7) (Gietzen and Vermeersch, 1980). The low-risk BBBF (Peters et al., 2003) study found a greater improvement in general health rating over time for those in the intervention group at 8 years (Cohen's d = 0.37, $p < 0.05$). The Perry Preschool program at 40 years old found a reduced risk in the intervention group (ARD −12 percent, 95 percent CI −30.4 to 6.4 percent) of having lost one or more weeks from work in the previous fifteen years for health reasons (Schweinhart et al., 2005).

Mortality

Mortality was examined by two studies in childhood (one moderate risk, one high risk of bias) with both finding no effect of the intervention on this rare outcome at up to 9 years, although the effects were in the beneficial direction (e.g., ARD −0.25 percent, 95 percent CI −0.95 to 0.45 percent) (Goodson et al., 2000; Ludwig and Miller, 2006). Mortality in adulthood was evaluated by the Perry Preschool study by 40 years with an ARD of 8 percent less mortality in the intervention cohort ($p = 0.06$) (Meunnig et al., 2009).

In summary, there was inconsistent evidence for beneficial outcomes in the primary school years of an improved home environment with regards to health, except for a reduced risk of obesity in two Head Start studies which notably include a strong emphasis on comprehensive nutrition programs. In adulthood, there was some evidence for greater physical activity in intervention groups but conflicting evidence regarding safety behaviors. The benefit on obesity risk in childhood was no longer apparent by age 40 years in the Perry Preschool study, although there was a suggestion that there was reduced mortality for preschool participants.

Enhanced access to health services – direct health service provision and promotion to parents

Health service use

Direct indicators of health service use were examined by four studies in childhood (Currie and Thomas, 1995; Goodson et al., 2000; Peters et al., 2003; Roy, 2003) and three in adulthood (Meunnig et al., 2009; Palfrey et al., 2005; Schweinhart et al., 1993) (Table 7.5). Across all ages, there was no consistent evidence of an association between preschool participation and enhanced health service use, with some studies showing

Table 7.5 *Health service use outcomes associated with center-based preschool interventions.*

Health measure	Study	Outcome measurement	Age	Results (95% confidence interval)	Overall direction of association
Health service use	Comprehensive Child Development Program (St. Pierre et al., 1997)	Parental report	C	Preventive medical visits/year: ES = 0.01 (−0.05 to 0.07) Dental visits/year: ES = 0.0 (−0.03 to 0.03)	=
	Better Beginnings Better Futures BBBF (Peters et al., 2003)	Parental report	C	Health care worker, no consistent differences Optometrist, no difference Dentist, no difference Emergency room visits E > C Doctor, no consistent pattern of effects	
	Smart Start (Kropp et al., 2001)	Health provider report	C	Regular place of health care OR = 1.5 p = 0.05	
	Head Start (Roy, 2003)	Parental report	C	Routine doctor check up past 11 months (coefficient): Head Start = 0.37 (se 0.69) $p > 0.05$ Routine dental check up past 11 months (coefficient): Head Start = 1.55 (se 0.69) $p \leq 0.05$	
	Perry Preschool (Meunnig et al., 2009; Schweinhart et al., 1993; Schweinhart et al., 2005)	Self report	A	No routine physician visit last 12 months (27 years) ARD = 2% p = 0.87 No routine physician visit last 12 months (40 years) ARD = 7% p = 0.32 No Ophthalmology visit in last 12 months ARD = −17% p = 0.10 No dental visit last 12 months ARD = −12% p = 0.22 Emergency visit last 12 months RR = 1.05 AD = 1% (−14.2 to 16.2%)	=

Table 7.5 (cont.)

Health measure	Study	Outcome measurement	Age	Results (95% confidence interval)	Overall direction of association
	Brookline Early Education Project (Palfrey et al., 2005)	Self report	A	Doctor visit last 12 months (suburban) RR = 1.0 AD = 0.6% (−11.5 to 12.7%) (urban) RR = 0.87 AD = −11.7% (−31.7 to 8.3%) Regular source of health care (suburban) RR = 0.97 AD = −2% (−14 to 10%) (urban) RR = 1.17 AD = 13% (−8.2 to 34.2%) Gynaecology visit in last 5 years (suburban) RR = 1.07 AD = 6% (−0.14 to 12.1%) (urban) RR = 1.0 AD = 0 (−12.1 to 12.1%) Mental health visit in last 5 years (suburban) RR = 0.90 AD = −3% (−15.7 to 9.7%) (urban) RR = 0.5 AD = −16% (−39.3 to 7.3%) Dental visit last 12 months (suburban) RR = 1.11 AD = 7.5% (−5.3 to 20.3%) (urban) RR = 0.87 AD = −8.5% (−35.5 to 18.5%)	
Immunization	Head Start (Currie & Thomas, 1995)	Parental report	C	Head Start (white) ARD = 8.2% (2.3 to 14.1%) Head Start (African American) ARD = 9.4% (2.9 to 15.9%) Preschool (white) ARD = 12.3% (7.6 to 17.0%) Preschool (African American) ARD = 5% (−1.7 to 11.7%)	mixed
	Smart Start (Kropp et al., 2001)	Health provider report	C	DTP immunization OR 4.5 ($p = 0.008$) Last vaccination on time OR = 1.3 $p = 0.06$ 5 other vaccines, no difference	
	Better Beginnings Better Futures (Peters et al., 2003)	Parental report	C	Immunization, no consistent difference	

benefits for one sub-group only (BEEP: Palfrey et al., 2005) and measured with low precision, and others finding no or a negative effect. There was a suggestion that Head Start participation enhanced dental visits for children (Currie and Thomas, 1995) and the Perry Preschool intervention enhanced both dental and ophthalmology visits (Meunnig et al., 2009). There was also no consistent evidence on the increased requirement for hospitalization which presumably indicates an increased probability of disease. At age 27 in the Perry Preschool study, there was a relative risk of 2.0 for those in the intervention group being hospitalized, which had reversed by age 40 (ARD −23 percent p = 0.36) (Schweinhart et al., 2005).

Timely receipt of immunizations is an indirect marker of health service use. Only one study with a high potential risk of bias found evidence for improved immunization uptake for Head Start participants at 8 to 9 years (Currie and Thomas, 1995), with the Smart Start study (moderate risk of bias) finding benefits for some vaccines but not others at 5 years (Kropp et al., 2001). The low risk of bias BBBF study found no consistent differences in immunization between the intervention and control groups at 8 years (Peters et al., 2003).

Diagnosed physical illness

In order for a disease to have been doctor diagnosed it is necessary that a health service was accessed, that screening (for diseases such as hypertension) or diagnosis (for diseases such as asthma) occurred, and additionally that the information was understood and retained by the study participant. Chronic disease diagnosis therefore is a marker of health service access but also for factors such as health literacy and increased preventive health behaviors (Nutbeam, 2000).

Three studies examined diagnosed physical illness in childhood (Table 7.2) (Goodson et al., 2000; Kropp et al., 2001; Peters et al., 2003). The moderate risk of bias CCDP study found no difference between intervention and control groups in diagnosed physical illnesses at 8 years (Goodson et al., 2000). This was consistent with findings from the moderate risk of bias Smart Start program and low risk of bias BBBF program that both found no difference in illness including asthma diagnosis and hospitalizations between intervention and control groups (Kropp et al., 2001; Peters et al., 2003).

Five studies examined chronic disease outcomes in adulthood (Table 7.2) (Anderson et al., 2004; Caputo, 2004; Frisvold, 2007; Meunnig et al., 2009; Palfrey et al., 2005). The Perry Preschool study with follow-up at 40 years reported doctor diagnosed diabetes mellitus risk was double in the intervention group, although the overall numbers were small, with four cases in the intervention and two cases in the control group (numbers calculated from original study report) (Meunnig et al., 2009). The Perry Preschool study found a 15 percent higher prevalence of self-reported hypertension in the intervention group (p = 0.12), which was also seen in the Anderson et al. Head Start study that had a number of methodological issues, although with a smaller effect size (ARD 6.2 percent, 95 percent CI −4.0 to 16.4 percent) (Anderson et al., 2004; Meunnig et al., 2009). The hypertension effect in the Head Start study with a young age of follow-up (18–35 years) was reduced for those who participated in Head Start for more than two years (ARD 2.2 percent, 95 percent CI −20.3 to 24.7 percent) (Anderson et al., 2004).

In summary, there is no clear evidence that attendance at preschool improves health service access. Chronic disease diagnoses in adulthood have not been adequately assessed and so no conclusion regarding intervention effects on chronic disease can be made.

Summary of results

The majority of beneficial health outcomes were reported from studies evaluating comprehensive interventions that included parenting components and direct educational services to children, with the majority of null effects in the preschool only interventions. This finding is consistent with the evidence from other outcomes associated with ECDIs such as school achievement, where greater effects are seen with a combination of center-based services for children and a parenting component (Gomby et al., 1995; Karoly et al., 2005). There was no clear evidence that preschool programs that included health services had greater positive health outcomes. Beneficial effects were seen in interventions such as the Perry Preschool study that did not include health services, and for large-scale government demonstration projects such as the BBBF study and CCDP that included health services there were generally null effects across a range of health outcomes.

Further, the majority of the positive effects on health were seen in those health outcomes most likely to be influenced by direct educational services to children. These include better mental health outcomes from childhood through to adulthood, as well as an indication of greater social competency. There was less delinquency in childhood, which is also likely to be a factor in the strong evidence for less tobacco and marijuana smoking in adulthood, given smoking uptake in adolescence is associated with delinquent or socially marginalized behavior. There were uncertain effects on alcohol drinking and other illicit drug use.

Health outcomes related to the parenting programs and the home environment had less evidence of beneficial effects. There was possibly an early beneficial effect on obesity which was gone by adulthood and no clear evidence of an effect on health promoting behaviors except for enhanced physical activity. There was, however, a suggestion that there was reduced mortality for preschool participants from childhood through to adulthood, although this was based on small numbers given the relatively young ages of follow-up.

There was no clear evidence that attendance at preschool improves health service access, and the effects on chronic disease diagnoses in adulthood have not been adequately assessed to enable a firm conclusion to be made.

Overall, while beneficial effects were seen across a minority of health outcomes, there was no consistent evidence of harmful effects on health. The majority of the health outcomes assessed had no evidence of effect.

Limitations

It is important to recognize that the findings of this review are limited by a number of factors that should be considered when interpreting the results. It may be, for example, that the majority null effects are the result of a range of methodological issues, rather than a "true" effect of the intervention being evaluated. These limitations and the potential consequences of them are outlined below.

Selection bias and confounding
The majority of the studies were at risk of confounding bias. That is, those child and family characteristics that lead to a desire to send children to center-based preschool may also lead to more positive health outcomes, compared with those who do not choose to send their child to preschool (Rothman, 2002). This will have the effect of making the preschool program appear to improve health outcomes. For example, parents with a higher education level may be more likely to send children to preschool. Further, higher education in parents is more likely to lead to better health outcomes for their children. Thus it may appear that those children who went to preschool had better health than those who did not, but at least some of that association may be explained by the parents having a higher education level. In randomized studies, having random allocation to either the intervention (preschool group) or the non-intervention group will reduce the risk of confounding bias, particularly in larger studies. The majority of non-randomized studies did, however, adjust for a range of potential factors that could have led both to the decision to participate in a preschool program and to better health outcomes, such as socio-demographic factors in early childhood. As such, while the risk of this bias

affecting the results should be kept in mind, the low and moderate risk of bias studies in particular are likely to represent a reasonably accurate reflection of the "true" findings.

Likewise, many of the studies were at risk of selection bias. That is, the characteristics of those who chose to participate in the study/preschool program were different from the characteristics of those who did not participate in a way that also had an effect on health outcomes (Rothman, 2002). Selection bias can also be introduced when people who once participated in a study drop out (known as attrition), so that those who stayed in the study are different from those who left the study. These biases can lead to results that are not "true" findings. For the better-quality studies, however, there was remarkably good follow-up which limits the effect of attrition on the findings presented here.

Negative health outcomes are rare

A difficulty that most of the studies had was assessing preschool effects on health outcomes that are uncommon. For example, diabetes is relatively uncommon in the general population (8.3 percent prevalence in the US: Centers for Disease Control and Prevention, 2011), but is even more uncommon among 40-year-old people, which was the oldest age followed up in this review. The rarity of the outcome at this age makes it difficult to find any effect of preschool when the sample size studied is small, as there are insufficient numbers to reliably and validly conduct statistical tests. Importantly, the best randomized studies have small sample sizes and so they may not be suitable to examine preschool effects on rarer chronic disease outcomes in adulthood.

Limited range of health outcomes and the use of self-report

The majority of the health outcomes studied were limited in scope largely because these ECDIs were not primarily intended as studies of health outcomes. The studies included health behaviors such as smoking, drug and alcohol use, and exercise. The Perry Preschool study was the only study to examine chronic disease outcomes (at age 40) diabetes mellitus, arthritis, and asthma (Schweinhart et al., 2005). Mental health outcomes were also relatively limited in scope, with the outcomes depression, anxiety, and schizotypal personality disorder reported. Thus, the health outcomes in this review represent a limited picture of the potential positive adult health effects of center-based preschool interventions, given the much wider array of diseases and their risk factors associated with social disadvantage (for example, chronic diseases such as cardiovascular disease).

The vast majority of the studies used self-reported health outcomes. Self-report measures were used for outcomes such as health service utilization and illicit drug use, and additionally the Perry Preschool study used self-report of doctor diagnosis of diabetes mellitus, asthma, arthritis, and hypertension (Schweinhart et al., 2005). A particular problem with the use of self-reported prior doctor diagnosis for asymptomatic diseases such as diabetes mellitus is that the results may reflect other factors, for example health literacy and access to health services in addition to disease outcomes (Kickbusch, 2008; Zhang et al., 2008). For measures such as preventive health service use and illicit drug use, social desirability may be an influencing factor in the reporting of previous use (Johnson and Fendrich, 2005). All of these factors can lead to errors in measurement of the health outcome with the potential to falsely increase the apparent benefits of preschool but also potentially to falsely reduce beneficial effects of preschool attendance.

The measures used across the studies were often simply dichotomous indicators of outcomes. For example, report of current smoking was indicated with a "yes/no" response, rather than pack-years, or age at commencement/cessation of smoking. Smoking is a complex behavior that is influenced by a range of factors that are likely to be different in childhood (when smoking generally commences) than in adulthood (where it is maintained or when quitting occurs). Dichotomous outcomes in reducing complex health outcomes also likely lead to measurement error in the outcomes. The potential importance of preschool for adult health warrants a more in-depth analysis to better understand any potential effects.

Comparison groups
The majority of the studies involved a comparison group potentially exposed to a wide array of alternate educational, health, and social services directed to children and parents. For example, 15 percent of the control group in the Chicago Child–Parent Centers had participated in Head Start (Reynolds et al., 2007), and the control group in the Abecedarian study included children who had access to a range of child care and preschool services available in the community (Campbell et al., 2002; Campbell et al., 2008; McLaughlin et al., 2007). This has the effect of making the control group more like the preschool group and so any benefit of preschool attendance is reduced in comparison. However, this is the nature of conducting evaluations of ECDIs or any intervention in more "real world" settings (Hawe, Shiell, and Riley, 2004), and it means that the study findings can be more realistically applied in the real world.

Design of research, future directions
There are two major methodological challenges to be overcome in the study design to evaluate the effects of ECDIs on adult health. The first is a potential for residual or unmeasured confounding of an association

between ECDI participation and the outcome by family factors that lead to the decision to send a child to a preschool program also leading to benefits for future long-term health. This issue is common to all outcomes and has been addressed in the ECDI research by randomized controlled studies such as the Perry Preschool study and Abecedarian study. While these studies have described social gains from model preschool programs they have a sample size that is likely to be too small (less than 100 in intervention and control groups) to assess health outcomes into the future which tend to be uncommon. The other major issue relates to the long time period between the intervention in early childhood and measurement of the health outcome in late adulthood when it is most likely to be apparent (although it is possible to measure risk factors such as blood pressure and serum lipids early in adulthood which can identify individuals at risk of future hypertension, at increased cost of research). This leads to problems of attrition and practical concerns in waiting over fifty years for a study to be complete. In this regard, retrospective cohort studies may become increasingly important to enable evaluation of health outcomes in a timely manner. These designs are, however, limited by problems of recall bias (particularly for studies spanning many years) and measurement error as well as problems relating to unmeasured or residual confounding as outlined above.

Novel study designs are required to assess these research questions further. For example, health outcomes of participants of Head Start (a program that was widely implemented in the US with large numbers of participants over time) could be assessed by linking Head Start participation with health datasets such as hospitalization records, comparing them with health outcomes for those from a similar population who did not attend Head Start. This design has the advantage of having a large sample size (in some cases the complete population) which increases the power of the study to analyze rarer health outcomes, objectively measured and standardized outcomes, and timeliness and the findings are not subject to recall bias. Linking to administrative datasets may also provide a wealth of data that can be used to control for confounding by background family factors.

This line of research will also be progressed by a better understanding of potential pathways of effect. ECDI studies with long-term follow-up should be assessed for all potential pathways of health effect using the large amount of data collected over time, as was recently done in the Chicago Child–Parent Centers study for education and crime outcomes (Reynolds, Temple, and Ou, 2010). This would enable future intervention studies to be assessed for likely health effects (according to the proposed pathway of effect) using intermediate measures that can be evaluated in the short term.

Policy implications

Generalizability

The interventions in this review may not be appropriate or effective in different settings. The majority of the interventions occurred in relatively homogeneous, disadvantaged populations in the USA, and so the same effects may not be seen in other populations and in different countries.

A key question when assessing the policy implications of this research relates to the modern-day relevance of preschool programs that were conducted twenty to fifty years ago, as in the case for studies following through to adulthood. This is particularly the case for population health outcomes which are relevant to the social context in which they are implemented (Rychetnik et al., 2002). An example of this was seen in the Kindergarten Union study, with older males having a greater risk of smoking when smoking was more socially acceptable and less likely to take up smoking as more information on the risks of smoking became available.

Quality

It is likely that certain quality factors will remain important over time, as there was consistent evidence from interventions conducted in different decades of certain features of quality. For example, factors such as highly trained educators, the quality of the curriculum, and including parents in the intervention are principles that have not changed over time (Gomby et al., 1995). The studies that found positive effects on smoking were high-quality interventions, which may have been an important factor in bringing about health benefit. Likewise, the wide range of studies with varying level of quality of intervention may have played a role in the generally null findings in this review.

The best social and educational outcomes for preschool programs have been reported in the single-site researcher-led interventions (such as the Perry Preschool study: Schweinhart et al., 2005), rather than the widely implemented community or government run preschool programs (such as Head Start: Anderson et al., 2004). This is also likely to be the case for any health effects. For example, for the small number of smoking and illicit drug use benefits evident from this review, the most methodologically rigorous assessment of a large-scale government funded program, the Chicago Child–Parent Center study, demonstrated only modest benefits compared with those from the experimental programs. In part the reduced benefit of large-scale programs may reflect challenges in measuring and adjusting for all relevant confounders, or the difficulties involved in ensuring program fidelity and quality across multiple sites in a population-wide approach to providing early childhood development programs. For population health effects ECDIs would need to be implemented on a wide scale and as such the more realistic benefits to health will be of a smaller effect size than reported in the researcher-led interventions.

Perhaps the most important effect of ECDIs on health is the consistently demonstrated large reduction in the risk of smoking, which accounts for 12 percent of male deaths and 6 percent of female deaths world-wide (World Health Organization, 2009). Further, given the findings of a reduction in ever smoking (i.e., never taking up smoking), ECDIs may offer a reduction in the high smoking related individual and health care costs through primary prevention of smoking, rather than through costly and inefficient quitting programs (Stead, Bergson, and Lancaster, 2008).

Conclusion

There is mounting evidence that early childhood is an important period for establishing future health (Kuh and Ben-Shlomo, 2004). While there is a great expectation that ECDIs will improve child and then adult health (Irwin, Siddiqi, and Hertzman, 2007), this review has found limited evidence of beneficial health outcomes from center-based preschool interventions for children aged 3–4. A wide array of health outcomes was assessed by the different studies and for the majority there was no effect of center-based preschool programs. Across the spectrum of health outcomes there was, however, a general trend toward beneficial effects, with particularly beneficial effects for smoking and drug use, physical activity, mental health, social competency, and crime prevention. Importantly, there was no evidence of harmful effects, which is an important consideration in implementing wide-scale programs across a population.

The differing effect on health outcomes may relate to differing origins of diseases and pathways of effect between preschool and health. The limitations of the reviewed studies for health outcomes suggest that further research is required to better understand the policy potential of ECDIs for population health. This research warrants greater engagement by population health researchers as although the benefits appear to be more narrow in scope than hypothesized, they (in particular reduction in smoking) are of great public health importance and have the potential to reduce morbidity and mortality due to chronic diseases across the population.

References

Anderson, K., Foster, J., and Frisvold, D. (2004). *Investing in health: the long-term impact of Head Start*. Nashville: Vanderbilt University Press.

Andersson, B. (1992). Effects of day-care on cognitive and socioemotional competence of thirteen-year-old Swedish schoolchildren. *Child Development*, 63(1), 20–36.

Armstrong, R., Waters, E., Jackson, N., Oliver, S., Popay, J., Shepherd, J. et al. (2007). *Guidelines for systematic reviews of health promotion and public health interventions*. Melbourne University Press.

Aughinbaugh, A. (2001). Does Head Start yield long-term benefits? *Journal of Human Resources*, 36(4), 641–665.

Ball, T. M., Holberg, C. J., Aldous, M. B., Martinez, F. D., and Wright, A. L. (2002). Influence of attendance at day care on the common cold from birth through 13 years of age. *Archives of Pediatric and Adolescent Medicine*, 156(2), 121–126.

Bates, J. E., Marvinney, D., Kelly, T., Dodge, K. A., Bennett, D. S., and Pettit, G. S. (1994). Child care history and kindergarten adjustment. *Developmental Psychology*, 30(5), 690–700.

Batty, G. D., and Dreary, I. (2004). Early life intelligence and adult health. *British Medical Journal*, 329, 585–586.

Beller, E. (1983). The Philadelphia study: the impact of preschool on intellectual and socioemotional development. In The Consortium for Longitudinal Studies (ed.), *As the twig is bent: lasting effects of preschool programs*. Hillsdale, NJ: Lawrence Erlbaum Associates.

Belsky, J., Burchinal, M., McCarteny, K., Vandell, D., Clarke-Stewart, K., and Owen, M. (2007). Are there long-term effects of early child care? *Child Development*, 78(2), 681–701.

Bennett, J., and Tayler, C. (2006). *Starting strong II: early childhood education and care*. Paris: OECD.

Borger, J., Bezruczko, N., Cohen, D., Eckert, K., O'Neill, P., and Wood, J. (1994). *Illinois initiatives for educational reform: evaluation of the 1993 State Prekindergarten Program*. Chicago Public Schools, Department of Research, Evaluation and Planning.

Bryant, D. M., Peisner-Feinberg, E., and Clifford, R. (1993). *Evaluation of public preschool programs in North Carolina*. Chapel Hill, NC: Frank Porter Graham Child Development Center.

Calvin, C. M., Dreary, I. J., Fenton, C., Roberts, B., Der, G., Leckenby, N., and Batty, D. G. (2011). Intelligence in youth and all-cause-mortality: systematic review with meta-analysis. *International Journal of Epidemiology*, 40, 626–644.

Campbell, F. A., Ramey, C. T., Pungello, E., Sparling, J., and Miller-Johnson, S. (2002). Early childhood education: young adult outcomes from the Abecedarian Project. *Applied Developmental Science*, 6(1), 42–57.

Campbell, F., Wasik, B., Pungello, E., Burchinal, M., Barbarin, O., Kainz, K. et al. (2008). Young adult outcomes of the Abecedarian and CARE early childhood educational interventions. *Early Childhood Research Quarterly*, 23(4), 452–466.

Caputo, R. K. (2003). Head Start, other preschool programs, and life success in a youth cohort. *Journal of Social Society and Welfare*, 30(2), 105–126.

(2004). The impact of intergenerational Head Start participation on success measures among adolescent children. *Journal of Family Economic Issues*, 25(2), 199–223.

Centers for Disease Control and Prevention (2011). *National diabetes fact sheet: national estimates and general information on diabetes and prediabetes in the United States, 2011.* Atlanta, GA: US Department of Health and Human Services, Centers for Disease Control and Prevention.

Currie, J., and Thomas, D. (1995). Does Head Start make a difference? *American Economic Review*, 20(3), 341–364.

D'Onise, K., Lynch, J., and McDermott, R. (2010). Can attending preschool reduce the risk of tobacco smoking in adulthood? The effects of Kindergarten Union participation in South Australia. *Journal of Epidemiology and Community Health*, 65(12), 1111–1117.

D'Onise, K., McDermott, R., Lynch, J., and Esterman, A. (2011). The beneficial effects of preschool attendance on adult cardiovascular disease risk. *Australian and New Zealand Journal of Public Health*, 35(3), 278–283.

Effective Public Health Practice Project (EPHPP) (2008). Quality assessment tool for quantitative studies. Available from www.myhamilton.ca/NR/rdonlyres/6B3670AC-8134-4F76-A64C-9C39DBC0F768/0/QATool.pdf.

Egger, M., Davey Smith, G., and Altman, D. (2001). *Systematic reviews in health care: meta-analysis in context.* London: BMJ Publishing Group.

Elkan, R., Kendrick, D., Hewitt, M., Robinson, J., Tolley, K., Blair, M. et al. (2000). The effectiveness of domiciliary health visiting: a systematic review of international studies and a selective review of the British literature. *Health Technology Assessments*, 4(13).

Engle, P. L., Black, M. M., Behrman, J. R., Cabral de Mello, M., Gertler, P. J., Kapiriri, L. et al. (2007). Strategies to avoid the loss of developmental potential in more than 200 million children in the developing world. *The Lancet*, 369(9557), 229–242.

Fergusson, D. M., Horwood, L. J., Boden, J. M., and Jenkin, G. (2007). Childhood social disadvantage and smoking in adulthood: results of a 25-year longitudinal study. *Addiction*, 102(3), 475–482.

Frisvold, D. (2007). *Head Start participation and childhood obesity.* Michigan: Early Childhood Research Collaborative.

Galobardes, B., Lynch, J., and Davey Smith, G. (2004). Childhood socioeconomic circumstances and cause-specific mortality in adulthood: systematic review and interpretation. *Epidemiology Reviews*, 26, 7–21.

Garber, H. (1988). *The Milwaukee Project: preventing mental retardation in children at risk.* Washington, DC: American Association on Mental Retardation.

Geesaman, P. (1970). The health status of project Head Start children and non-project Head Start children from the same socioeconomic level. *Dissertation Abstracts*, 31, 5453.

Gietzen, D., and Vermeersch, J. (1980). Health status and school achievement of children from Head Start and Free School Lunch Programs. *Public Health Reports*, 95(4), 362–369.

Gomby, D. (1999). Home visiting: recent program evaluations – analysis and recommendations. *Future Child*, 9(1), 4–26.

Gomby, D., Larner, M., Stevenson, C., Lewit, E., and Behrman, R. (1995). Long-term outcomes of early childhood programs: analysis and recommendations. *Future Child*, 5(3), 6–24.

Goodson, B. D., Layzer, J. I., St. Pierre, R. G., Bernstein, L. S., and Lopez, M. (2000). Effectiveness of a comprehensive, five-year family support program for low-income children and their families: findings from the comprehensive child development program. *Early Childhood Research Quarterly*, 15(1), 5–39.

Gormley, W. T., Jr., Phillips, D., Newmark, K., Welti, K., and Adelstein, S. (2011). Social-emotional effects of early childhood education programs in Tulsa. *Child Development*, 82(6), 2095–2109.

Government of South Australia (2008). Community children's centres: learning together every day. Retrieved July 27, 2010, from www.sachildcare.com.au/.

Gray, S., Ramsey, B., and Klaus, R. (1983). The Early Training Project 1962–1980. In The Consortium for Longitudinal Studies (ed.), *As the twig is bent: lasting effects of preschool programs*. Hillsdale, NJ: Lawrence Erlbaum Associates.

Haskins, R. (1985). Public school aggression among children with varying day-care experience. *Child Development*, 56, 68–703.

Hawe, P., Shiell, A., and Riley, T. (2004). Complex interventions: how "out of control" can a randomised controlled trial be? *British Medical Journal*, 328(7455), 1561–1563.

Heckman, J., and Masterov, D. (2004). *The productivity argument for investing in young children*. Washington, DC: Committee for Economic Development.

Henry, G., Rickman, D., Ponder, B., Henderson, L., Mashburn, A., and Gordon, C. (2004). *The Georgia Early Childhood Study, 2001–2004*. Georgia State University, Andrew Young School of Policy Studies.

Hickman, L. (2006). Who should care for our children: the effects of home versus center care on child cognition and social adjustment. *Journal of Family Issues*, 27(5), 652–684.

Hyman, J. (2011). Identifying the channels through which Head Start affects long-term outcomes. Retrieved December 2, 2011, from www.eric.ed. gov/ERICWebPortal/search/detailmini.jsp?_nfpb=true&_&ERICExtSear ch_SearchValue_0=ED517845andERICExtSearch_SearchType_0=no&acc no=ED517845.

Irwin, L., Siddiqi, A., and Hertzman, C. (2007). *Early child development: a powerful equalizer. Final Report of the Commission on Social Determinants of Health*. Geneva: Early Child Development Knowledge Network, World Health Organization.

Johnson, T., and Fendrich, M. (2005). Modeling sources of self-report bias in a survey of drug use epidemiology. *Annals of Epidemiology*, 15(5), 381–389.

Kagitcibasi, C., Sunar, D., and Bekman, S. (2001). Long-term effects of early intervention: Turkish low-income mothers and children. *Journal of Applied Developmental Psychology*, 22, 333–361.

Kaminski, R. A., Stormshak, E. A., Good, III, R. H., and Goodman, M. R. (2002). Prevention of substance abuse with rural Head Start children and families: results of project STAR. *Psychology of Addictive Behavior*, 16(4), S11–S26.

Karoly, L., Kilburn, R., and Cannon, J. (2005). *Early childhood interventions: proven results, future promise*. Santa Monica: RAND Corporation.

Kendrick, D., Elkan, R., Hewitt, M., Dewey, M., Blair, M., Robinson, J. et al. (2000). Does home visiting improve parenting and the quality of the home environment? A systematic review and meta analysis. *Archives of Disease in Childhood*, 82(6), 443–451.

Kickbusch, I. (2008). Health literacy: an essential skill for the twenty-first century. *Health Education*, 108(2), 101–104.

Kotchabhakdi, N. J. (1999). Impact of a community-based program on early childhood development. *Journal of Pediatric Health Care*, 13(3, Part 2), S17–S20.

Kropp, N., Kotch, J., Harris, S., and UNC-FPG Smart Start Evaluation Team (2001). *The effect of Smart Start health interventions on children's health and access to care*. Chapel Hill: University of North Carolina.

Kuh, D., and Ben-Shlomo, Y. (2004). *A life course approach to chronic disease epidemiology* (2nd edn). Oxford University Press.

Lally, J., Mangione, P., and Honig, A. (1988). The Syracuse University Family Development Program: long-range impact of early intervention with low-income children and their families. In D. Powell (ed.), *Parent education as early childhood intervention: emerging directions theory research and practice* (pp. 79–104). Westport, CT: Greenwood.

Lee, V. E., Brooks-Gunn, J., Schnur, E., and Liaw, F.-R. (1990). Are Head Start effects sustained? A longitudinal follow-up comparison of disadvantaged children attending Head Start, no preschool, and other preschool programs. *Child Development*, 61(2), 495.

Loeb, S., Bridges, M., Bassok, D., Fuller, B., and Rumberger, R. (2005). How much is too much? The influence of preschool centers on children's social and cognitive development. *Economics of Education Review*, 26, 52–66.

Lu, N., Samuels, M., Shi, L., Baker, S., Glover, S., and Sanders, J. (2004). Child day care risks of common infectious diseases revisited. *Child: Care, Health and Development*, 30(4), 361–368.

Ludwig, J., and Miller, D. (2006). *Does Head Start improve children's life chances? Evidence from a regression discontinuity design*. Bonn: Institute for the Study of Labor.

Magnuson, K., Ruhm, C., and Waldfogel, J. (2007). Does prekindergarten improve school preparation and performance? *Economics of Education Review*, 26, 33–51.

McLaughlin, A. E., Campbell, F. A., Pungello, E. P., and Skinner, M. (2007). Depressive symptoms in young adults: the influences of the early home environment and early educational child care. *Child Development*, 78(3), 746–756.

Meunnig, P., Schweinhart, L. J., Montie, J., and Neidell, M. (2009). Effects of a prekindergarten educational intervention on adult health: 37-year follow up results of a randomized controlled trial. *American Journal of Public Health*, 99(8), 1431–1437.

Miller, L. B., and Bizzell, R. P. (1984). Long-term effects of fourth preschool programs: ninth and tenth-grade results. *Child Development*, 55(4), 1570.

Nutbeam, D. (2000). Health literacy as a public health goal: a challenge for contemporary health education and communication strategies into the 21st century. *Health Promotion International*, 15(3), 259–267.

Office of Head Start (2008). Retrieved December 2, 2008, from www.acf.hhs.gov/programs/ohs/.

Ontario Early Years Centres (2007). A place for parents and their children. Retrieved December 2, 2008, from www.gov.on.ca/children/oeyc/en/index.html.

Osborn, A., and Milbank, J. (1987). *The effects of early education: a report from the Child Health and Education Study.* Oxford: Clarendon Press.

Palfrey, J. S., Hauser-Cram, P., Bronson, M. B., Warfield, M. E., Sirin, S., and Chan, E. (2005). The Brookline Early Education Project: a 25-year follow-up study of a family-centered early health and development intervention. *Pediatrics*, 116(1), 144–152.

Peters, R. D., Petrunka, K., and Arnold, R. (2003). The Better Beginnings, Better Futures Project: a universal, comprehensive, community-based prevention approach for primary school children and their families. *Journal of Clinical Child and Adolescent Psychology*, 32(2), 215–227.

Raine, A., Mellingen, K., Liu, J., Venables, P., and Mednick, S. A. (2003). Effects of environmental enrichment at ages 3–5 years on schizotypal personality and antisocial behavior at ages 17 and 23 years. *American Journal of Psychiatry*, 160(9), 1627–1635.

Reynolds, A. J. (1994). Effects of a preschool plus follow-on intervention for children at risk. *Developmental Psychology*, 30(6), 787–804.

(1998). Resilience among black urban youth: prevalence, intervention effects and mechanisms of influence. *American Journal of Orthopsychiatry*, 68(1), 84–100.

Reynolds, A. J., Chan, H., and Temple, J. A. (1998). Early childhood intervention and juvenile delinquency: an exploratory analysis of the Chicago Child–Parent Centers. *Evaluation Reviews*, 22(3), 341–372.

Reynolds, A. J., and Temple, J. A. (1998). Extended early childhood intervention and school achievement: age thirteen findings from the Chicago Longitudinal Study. *Child Development*, 69(1), 231–246.

Reynolds, A. J., Temple, J. A., and Ou, S.-R. (2010). Preschool education, educational attainment, and crime prevention: contributions of cognitive and non-cognitive skills. *Child and Youth Services Reviews*, 32(8), 1054–1063.

Reynolds, A. J., Temple, J. A., Ou, S.-R., Arteaga, I., and White, B. (2011). School-based early childhood education and age-28 well-being: effects by timing, dosage, and subgroups. *Science*, 333, 360–364.

Reynolds, A. J., Temple, J. A., Ou, S.-R., Robertson, D. L., Mersky, J. P., Topitzes, J. W., et al. (2007). Effects of a school-based, early childhood intervention on adult health and well-being: a 19-year follow-up of low-income families. *Archives of Pediatric and Adolescent Medicine*, 161(8), 730–739.

Reynolds, A. J., Temple, J. A., Robertson, D. L., and Mann, E. A. (2001). Long-term effects of an early childhood intervention on educational achievement and juvenile arrest: a 15-year follow-up of low-income children in public schools. *Journal of the American Medical Association*, 285(18), 2339–2346.

Rivara, F. P., DiGuiseppi, C., Thompson, R. S., and Calonge, N. (1989). Risk of injury to children less than 5 years of age in day care versus home care settings. *Pediatrics*, 84(6), 1011.

Rothman, K. (2002). *Epidemiology: an introduction.*Oxford University Press.

Roy, A. (2003). *Evaluation of the Head Start Program: additional evidence from the NLSCM79 data.* New York: University of Albany.

Rychetnik, L., Frommer, M., Hawe, P., and Shiell, A. (2002). Criteria for evaluating evidence on public health interventions. *Journal of Epidemiology and Community Health,* 56(2), 119–127.

Sammons, P., Sylva, K., Melhuish, E., Siraj-Blatchford, I., Taggart, B., Barreau, S., et al. (2007). *Effective Pre-school and Primary Education 3–11 Project (EPPE 3–11): Influences on children's development and progress in key stage 2; social/behavioural outcomes in Year 5.* University of London Press.

Schweinhart, L., Barnes, H., and Weikart, D. (1993). *Significant benefits: the High/Scope Perry Preschool Study through age 27.* Ypsilanti, MI: The High/Scope Press.

Schweinhart, L., Montie, J., Ziang, Z., Barnett, W., Belfield, C. R., and Nores, M. (2005). *Lifetime effects: the High/Scope Perry Preschool Study through age 40.* Ypsilanti, MI: High/Scope Press.

Schweinhart, L. J., and Weikart, D. (1980). *Young children grow up: the effects of the Perry Preschool Program on youths through age 15.* Ypsilanti, MI: High/Scope Educational Research Foundation.

Shonkoff, J., Boyce, W., and McEwen, B. (2009). Neuroscience, molecular biology, and the childhood roots of health disparities: building a new framework for health promotion and disease prevention. *Journal of the American Medical Association,* 301(21), 2252–2259.

St. Pierre, R. G., Layzer, J. I., Goodson, B. D., and Bernstein, L. S. (1997). *National impact evaluation of the Comprehensive Child Development Program.* Washington, DC: Administration on Children, Youth and Families, US Department of Health and Human Services.

Stead, L., Bergson, G., and Lancaster, T. (2008). Physician advice for smoking cessation (review). *Cochrane Database System Review* (2), CD000165. DOI: 000110.001002/14651858.CD14000165.pub14651853.

Sterne, J. A. C., Smith, G. D., and Cox, D. R. (2001). Sifting the evidence: what's wrong with significance tests? Another comment on the role of statistical methods. *British Medical Journal,* 322(7280), 226–231.

Sure Start (2008). Retrieved December 2, 2008, from www.surestart.gov.uk/sure-startservices/settings/introduction/.

Tonge, B. (1998). Common child and adolescent psychiatric problems and their management in the community. *Medical Journal of Australia,* 168(5), 241–248.

Vandell, D. L., Belskey, J., Burchinal, M., Steinberg, L., Vandergrift, N., and NICHD Early Child Care Research Network (2010). Do effects of early child care extend to age 15 years? Results from the NICHD Study of Early Child Care and Youth Development. *Child Development,* 81(3), 737–756.

Weikart, D., Bond, J., and McNeil, J. (1978). *The Ypsilanti Perry Preschool Project: preschool years and longitudinal results through fourth grade.* Ypsilanti, MI: High/Scope Educational Research Foundation.

World Health Organization (2009). *Global health risks: mortality and burden of disease attributable to selected major risks.* Geneva: World Health Organization.

Zhai, F. (2008). *Effects of Head Start on the outcomes of participants.* New York: Columbia University Press.

Zhai, F., Brooks-Gunn, J., and Waldfogel, J. (2011). Head Start and urban children's school readiness: a birth cohort study in 18 cities. *Developmental Psychology*, 47(1), 134–152.

Zhang, X., Geiss, L. S., Cheng, Y. J., Beckles, G. L., Gregg, E. W., and Kahn, H. S. (2008). The missed patient with diabetes: how access to health care affects the detection of diabetes. *Diabetes Care*, 31(9), 1748–1753.

Zigler, E., Piotrkowski, C., and Collins, R. (1994). Health services in Head Start. *Annual Reviews of Public Health*, 15, 511–534.

8   The Head Start REDI Project and school readiness

Karen L. Bierman, Robert L. Nix, Celene E. Domitrovich, Janet A. Welsh, and Scott D. Gest

National statistics suggest that, on average, 16 percent of American children enter school without the readiness skills they need for success (Rimm-Kaufman, Pianta, and Cox, 2000). Children growing up in poverty are particularly vulnerable; over 40 percent of these children demonstrate delayed language skills and social skills at school entry, and over 20 percent exhibit high rates of disruptive behavior problems that undermine school adjustment (Macmillan, McMorris, and Kruttschnitt, 2004). Children who begin school unprepared for the learning and behavioral demands typically remain low achievers throughout elementary school, and are more likely than their more advantaged peers to experience learning disabilities, conflictual relationships with teachers and peers, grade retention, early school drop-out, and long-term underemployment (Ryan, Fauth, and Brooks-Gunn, 2006). Rates of child poverty are on the rise in the United States, with nearly one in four preschoolers living in poverty and nearly one in two preschoolers living in low-income families (200 percent of poverty; National Center for Children in Poverty, 2010), making the problem of understanding and promoting school readiness a national priority.

Delays in school readiness are part of a larger set of health and mental health disparities associated with low socioeconomic status (SES), which confers elevated health risks in diverse areas, including cardiovascular disease, hypertension, arthritis, diabetes, and cancer, as well as overall

The REDI Project was supported by National Institute of Child Health and Human Development grants HD046064 and HD43763. Appreciation is expressed to the teachers, students, parents, and program personnel who served as partners in this project in the Huntingdon, Blair, and York County Head Start Programs of Pennsylvania. In addition, this work reflects the particular efforts and talents of Gloria Rhule, Harriet Darling, Julia Gest, the REDI intervention staff, and the entire REDI research team. Reprint requests can be sent to Karen Bierman, The Pennsylvania State University, 251 Moore Building, University Park, PA 16802 (phone: 814–865–3879; fax:814–863–7002, kb2@psu.edu).

higher mortality (Adler and Newman, 2002). The link between SES and child risk for mental illness is well established, evident particularly in elevated rates of depressive and anxiety disorders, conduct problems, and attention deficit hyperactivity disorder (ADHD) among children growing up in poverty (Ritsher et al., 2001). Although multiply determined, the negative impact of low SES on child mental health appears driven in part by parental education, maternal depression, and single-parenthood, all of which are associated with SES and affect the quality of parenting and parent–child interaction and support (Ritsher et al., 2001).

Remediating delays in school readiness, although only one facet of SES-related disadvantage, may be highly strategic, given the likelihood that improved educational outcomes have the potential to leverage upward socioeconomic mobility and promote corresponding improvements in adult health and well-being (Adler and Newman, 2002). Logically, investing in early education makes sense, as education shapes future occupational opportunities and earning potential, provides knowledge and life skills that allow better-educated persons to gain more ready access to information and resources to promote health, and allows individuals to live in better resourced, less polluted, and less stressful neighborhoods (Adler and Newman, 2002; Winkleby, Cubbin, and Ahn, 2006). In addition, past research on model preschool programs, such as the High/Scope Perry Preschool curriculum, suggests that optimal school readiness support can promote long-term benefits for children, including higher rates of high school graduation, fewer crimes, and better employment outcomes (Schweinhart et al., 2005).

The challenge, however, is to "go to scale" with optimal preschool programming. Head Start, which has been referred to as the nation's premier federally sponsored early childhood education program, has proven somewhat effective in promoting some aspects of school readiness, but has not attained the kind of impact promised by model programs such as Perry Preschool, nor demonstrated a consistent capacity to improve social-emotional and behavioral readiness for school (USDHHS, 2005). Two factors likely limit its impact. First, programming often does not take advantage of recent research that might increase its effectiveness. The majority of Head Start programs in the nation use either the High/Scope curriculum, first developed in 1962, or the Creative Curriculum for Preschool, first developed in 1978. Since then, both models have upgraded programming; however, evidence-based curriculum components are often lacking when these programs are used in the field. Second, an ongoing challenge is achieving the high-fidelity implementation of evidence-based practice or model programs in the field. For example, when "typical" Head Start programs use High/Scope, the fidelity of curriculum implementation is often weak, and the quality of parent-focused home visits, teacher training, and organizational support falls far short of that used in the model Perry Preschool program (Schweinhart, 2004). Overall, Head Start centers often lack the research expertise, financial resources, and technical assistance necessary to integrate new research-based strategies effectively and with high implementation fidelity into their local programs, which results in lower-impact programming and less benefit for participating children (Iutcovich et al., 1997).

In this chapter, we review recent research describing the impact of early disadvantage on the developing brain, and identify the implications for the strategic design of enriched preschool interventions that have the capacity to remediate early delays. We also review research on the challenges of "going to scale" with evidence-based preschool programming, and the critical role of professional development and support to promote high-fidelity implementation of quality preschool curricula and teaching practices. We then describe the implementation and outcomes of the Head Start REDI (Research-Based, Developmentally Informed) preschool enrichment program, which was designed to facilitate the integration of research-based practices into Head Start classrooms by providing teachers with manualized enrichment curricula and mentored professional development opportunities, targeting improvements in the dual domains of child language-literacy skills and social-emotional well-being. We conclude that evidence-based preschool programming has considerable potential to enhance the school readiness of vulnerable and disadvantaged children, but that reaching that potential requires strategic and sustained investment in curriculum enrichment and professional development support.

The impact of early disadvantage on children's development

Language and emergent literacy skills

Research accumulating since the 1990s leaves no doubt concerning the importance of early cognitive development, particularly the acquisition of oral language and emergent literacy skills for school readiness (Lonigan, 2006). A meta-analysis conducted by the National Early Literacy Panel (2005) demonstrated that, when measured at school entry, a child's phonological sensitivity (the capacity to detect and manipulate sounds and parts of words) and alphabet knowledge are robust predictors of their later reading decoding and comprehension skills, with correlations ranging from .39 to .50. Oral language skills, including vocabulary, syntax (understanding of various grammatical forms), and narrative (being able to sequence events when describing experiences or retelling a story) also support school success (Catts, Fey, Zhang, and Tomblin, 1999). In addition to providing essential support for reading comprehension, oral language skills form the basis for understanding information and directions provided in class, and for developing and maintaining positive relations with teachers and peers (Catts et al., 1999). Children who are delayed in their development of these critical language and emergent literacy skills often struggle to learn to read in elementary school and rarely catch up to their non-impaired peers, sometimes suffering lifelong reading disabilities and underachievement.

Relative to socio-economically advantaged children, children growing up in poverty often show delays in oral language development and emergent literacy skills (Hart and Risley, 1995). To a large degree, the negative impact of family poverty on child development and school readiness reflects lower-quality learning opportunities within the home and in early child care and preschool settings that are associated with low SES (Duncan, Brooks-Gunn, and Klebanov, 1994). The frequency and quality of parent–child verbal interaction dramatically affects children's oral language skills and early literacy development, as does the quality of language use in child care and early school setting (Hart and Risley, 1995). For example, family SES is associated with exposure to books and other print materials, the frequency of parent–child reading, and adult language use that includes complex oral vocabulary and syntax. In families with higher SES, parents are more likely to engage in interactive reading approaches with their children, discussing stories in ways that expand vocabulary and foster story comprehension and narrative skills, and children are more likely to be in child care and preschools that reinforce and enrich this language exposure (Senechal, 2006). In part, the lower frequency and quality of parent–child conversation, reading, and learning activities associated with low SES reflects low levels of parent education, but it also reflects the high rates of parental depression and stress experienced by families living in poverty, as well as financial and environmental factors that limit access to high-quality child care and preschool opportunities (Duncan et al., 1994).

Mental health and related social-emotional skills

In addition to its negative impact on cognitive development, poverty takes a toll on children's mental health, delaying social-emotional and behavioral development. The World Health Organization defines mental health as: "a state of well-being in which an individual realizes his or her own abilities, can cope with the normal stresses of life, can work productively and is able to make a contribution to his or her community" (WHO, 2010). In early childhood, mental health is reflected in the developing social, emotional, and behavioral skills that foster a child's capacity for effective interpersonal interaction, learning, and adaptation. Developing mental health is dependent upon skills in three interrelated domains that play a critically important role in school readiness and school success (Blair, 2002): (1) social skills that support positive interpersonal relations, (2) emotional skills that allow children to understand and manage their feelings, and feel empathy for others, and (3) self-control and social-problem solving skills that foster the child's ability to comply with societal expectations regarding behavioral control (i.e., inhibit aggression, follow dictions), manage conflicts peacefully, and approach learning tasks with interest and concentration.

Social skills

Developing the capacity for social collaboration represents a critical developmental task of the preschool years and an important marker of mental health and school readiness. Normatively, first friendships are established during the preschool years, and most preschool children take great pleasure in cooperative and shared fantasy play with peers (Bierman and Erath, 2006). In order to sustain friendly exchanges, children must learn to negotiate, cooperate, and compromise – requiring the development of prosocial skills, such as helping, sharing, and taking turns. In order to contribute to elaborated play, they must develop play skills that include an understanding of the "scripts" of various play activities, and they must follow through by enacting complementary social roles and social routines. In addition to the behaviors needed for effective social collaboration, positive peer interactions motivate and support the development of perspective-taking skills, communication skills, and flexible problem solving (Coolahan et al., 2000).

Although teachers and parents provide some explicit guidance (e.g., "don't hit," "use your words," "share"), social skills develop primarily through implicit learning (i.e., observing how individuals treat each other) and experience. The degree to which parents and other child care givers are able to provide stable, warm, sensitive, and responsive caregiving fosters prosocial skill development. Conversely, the frequent use of harsh and punitive discipline practices predicts low levels of prosocial skill development and elevated oppositional and aggressive behavior problems, which in turn predict problematic school adjustment (Campbell, 2006). Positive, well-supervised peer experiences are also important, so that children have the opportunity to practice developing social skills in a supportive context (Bierman and Erath, 2006).

Emotional awareness and management

In addition to social skills, emotional understanding and emotion regulation skills are important for adaptive development. Poor emotional understanding and low levels of frustration tolerance are often associated with elevated aggressive and oppositional behavior in preschool and elementary school (Ladd, Buhs, and Seid, 2000). The preschool years represent an important period for the development of emotional understanding; normatively, empathy and altruism emerge in preschool, as children recognize and differentiate a broader array of emotions and begin to understand that their actions can cause feelings in other people that are different from their own (Fabes and Eisenberg, 1992).

Emotional awareness fosters social development and aggression control in several ways. First, the capacity to use language to describe internal affective states allows children to redirect emotional arousal into adaptive activity, and thus facilitates the inhibition of reactive aggressive behavior (Izard, 2002). Second, the ability to share feelings verbally with others fosters the capacity for negotiation and peaceful conflict management. In addition, being able to identify unpleasant arousal with specific labels empowers children to identify cause–effect sequences associated with those feelings, promoting anticipatory problem solving.

Emotional understanding and corresponding language skills also allow children to better understand the feelings of others, allowing them to be more sensitive and responsive in their peer interactions. Positive peer exchanges further motivate children to inhibit impulsive and aggressive behaviors that might alienate their peers. Conversely, low levels of emotional understanding increase the likelihood that children will fail to understand or will misinterpret the actions of others, thus fueling interpersonal conflicts and supporting negative attributional biases (Bierman and Erath, 2006).

Executive functioning and self-control

Intertwined with the development of oral language skills, social skills, and emotional management skills are the self-control skills that foster adaptive approaches to learning in school, including the capacity to participate cooperatively in classroom activities, follow teacher directions, focus attention, control behavior, and sustain task involvement (Ladd et al., 2000; McClelland, Acock, and Morrison, 2006). Kindergarten teachers list these self-control skills high on the list of competencies they believe are necessary for successful school adjustment (Rimm-Kaufman et al., 2000).

During the preschool years, growth in the executive regulatory system plays a central role in supporting the preschool child's acquisition of these self-control skills (Blair, 2002). Specific skills that are part of the executive regulatory system include: (1) working memory, which allows children to hold ideas and information in mind, so they can think about and manipulate the information in new ways, (2) inhibitory control, which allows children to delay impulsive or habitual responding in order to consider alternative, strategic responses, and (3) attention set-shifting, which allows children to strategically focus attention, maintain concentration, and ignore distractions (Blair, Zelazo, and Greenberg, 2005). Supported by neural processes located in the prefrontal cortex, the executive regulatory system modulates arousal, and regulates attention and emotion (Blair et al., 2005). Functionally, these skills enhance children's capacity for goal-oriented learning and flexible problem solving, and support the acquisition of emergent literacy and math skills (Welsh et al., 2010). Conversely, delays in executive functioning skill development increase a child's risk for adjustment difficulties and poor mental health in the elementary school context.

Although the development of the executive regulatory system and corresponding self-control skills depends upon biological maturation, the process appears heavily influenced by environmental experiences and input. Exposure to early adversity has a negative impact on the development of the executive regulatory system, and children who experience extreme adversity in their early years, such as maltreatment or severe neglect, show increased levels of attention problems, emotion dysregulation, and language delays (Cicchetti, 2002). Exposure to adversity and threat requires "fight or flight" reactivity, modulated by neuroendocrine and autonomic stress responses, which increases demands on the executive regulatory system and diverts resources that might otherwise be employed for goal-oriented learning (Cicchetti, 2002).

Summary

In summary, SES disadvantage is associated with developmental impairments in both cognitive and mental health domains of school readiness. Relative to socio-economically advantaged children, children growing up in poverty exhibit lower levels of prosocial skills, emotional awareness, self-regulated behavior, and adaptive approaches to learning, and they display elevated rates of inattention and disengaged behavior at school entry. To a large extent, the delays in both language skills and these social-emotional skills reflect low levels of cognitive stimulation during early childhood, reduced exposure to sensitive-responsive caregiving, and fewer opportunities for guided exploration of the social and physical environment (Lengua, Honorado, and Bush, 2007). Poverty, and the factors associated with it, reduces access to high-quality child care and preschool experiences, which further contributes to delays in both cognitive and social-emotional development (Lengua et al., 2007).

Improving preschool quality

The positive news is that research has demonstrated the capacity of early intervention to make a difference. In addition to studies which show that high-quality preschool programs can reduce the SES gap in cognitive skills at school entry (Barnett, 1995), a rapidly growing research base suggests that social-emotional competencies (in areas of prosocial behaviors, emotional understanding, self-control, and social problem solving skills) can also be enhanced via the use of systematic instructional approaches in the classroom (Consortium on the School-Based Promotion of Social Competence, 1994).

In recent years, efforts to promote school readiness for children growing up in poverty have focused primarily on improving the instructional content of Head Start and public pre-kindergarten programs, in order to enhance children's acquisition of key emergent literacy skills, such as letter identification and phonemic sensitivity (Lonigan, 2006). Although this is an important area of focus, a failure to also address the mental health needs of these vulnerable children may be one factor that has limited the impact of school-based programs. Several recent studies suggest that preschool interventions designed to enhance social-emotional learning and self-regulation skills have the potential to strengthen neuro-cognitive executive functioning as it develops, which should support both academic and behavioral readiness for school (Diamond et al., 2007; Riggs et al., 2006). The practical question to address is whether teachers are able to integrate multiple research-based curriculum components at the same time, enriching the support they are providing to children in both cognitive and social-emotional domains, and whether a dual emphasis has synergistic effects on child outcomes.

Enriching preschool curricula with evidence-based approaches that address the social-emotional as well as the cognitive needs of dis-advantaged children is an important step in improving the quality of their preschool experience. However, introducing evidence-based lesson plans without including sufficient professional development to support high-quality implementation and teaching practices is unlikely to produce optimal effects. A growing body of research suggests that proximal features of teaching quality, including teachers' instructional practices and the quality of teacher–student relationships, play a primary role in fostering child skill development and school readiness (Pianta, 2003).

Preschool teachers exert strong socialization influences on young children, affecting their learning in both formal and informal ways (Denham and Burton, 2003). Hence, to maximize the benefits of preschool for disadvantaged children, it is important to enrich both the curriculum and more general teaching practices with evidence-based approaches. In terms of evidence-based teaching quality, two domains are important: the quality of instructional support and language use, and the quality of social-emotional support and classroom management strategies (La Paro and Pianta, 2003; Pianta, 2003).

Learning is enhanced when teachers organize classroom activities in ways that maximize children's opportunities to receive guidance as they explore instructional materials, extend their knowledge, practice higher-order thinking and problem solving skills, and receive high-quality feedback (Pianta, 2003). Children's linguistic development is fostered by teacher–student verbal interactions that include rich and varied vocabulary, back and forth exchanges between teacher and students, and decontextualized and cognitively challenging talk. In particular, teachers enhance children's syntax skills when they build upon students' communications by expanding or recasting children's utterances using new words or grammatical structures that fit the context of the ongoing activity and are just slightly beyond children's current skill levels (Nelson and Welsh, 1998).

Teachers who interact with students in a warm, sensitive, and responsive style validate their students' emotional experiences and foster a sense of security that supports active engagement in classroom learning activities (Pianta, 2003). In addition, several specific teaching strategies promote children's emotional understanding and social competence. These include "emotion coaching," which involves empathic and nonjudgmental responses to children's emotional expressions, and the use of social problem solving dialogue, which provides children with "on line" support to manage conflicts by identifying problems and associated feelings, generating alternative solutions, and selecting solutions that are acceptable to all parties (Denham and Burton, 2003). When teachers reduce their reliance on directives and negative consequences and instead focus on clear expectations, predictable and appropriate routines (La Paro et al., 2004), and induction strategies involving social feedback, they are most likely to encourage and support children's self-control efforts (Bierman, 2004).

Fostering improvements in teaching quality

Workshop training, which is the most common form of professional development activity, is of limited utility in improving teaching quality.

However, research has demonstrated that teaching quality can be improved with a more strategic and sustained set of professional development activities, including a combination of: (1) specific and targeted workshop training, with (2) opportunities for practice in classroom contexts with feedback, and (3) adequate supervision time for teachers to reflect on and evaluate their own practices and set future goals (see Domitrovich et al., 2009). In order to provide opportunities for guided and reflective practice in high-quality teaching, a number of studies have included mentoring with in-class coaching and individual meetings. For example, Raver and colleagues (Raver et al., 2008) provided Head Start teachers with five six-hour training sessions throughout the school year and weekly coaching from mental health consultants in behavior management strategies. Results indicated significantly higher levels of positive climate, teacher sensitivity, and behavior management in intervention classrooms at the end of the year. In another study using mentoring to support improved teaching quality, Wasik and colleagues (Wasik, Bond, and Hindman, 2006) introduced a language and literacy intervention in Head Start classrooms that combined interactive reading (i.e., asking questions, making connections, and explicitly teaching target vocabulary words while reading) with professional development designed to enhance general teacher language use (i.e., coaching in explicit routines and strategies to expand on children's utterances, foster listening, encourage conversations, and model rich language). Teachers attended nine monthly, two-hour workshops and received in-class coaching sessions in which a mentor modeled the strategy, observed the teacher using the strategy, and provided the teacher with written and oral feedback. Post-intervention observations indicated that intervention teachers talked significantly more than control teachers, posed more open-ended questions, and used more conversational strategies.

Rather than piecemeal approaches to improving the benefits of preschool to disadvantaged children, these findings suggest a comprehensive and integrated approach is needed. We need to focus on building language and emergent literacy skills and promoting social-emotional skills, and we need to do that by combining the enrichment provided by evidence-based curriculum components with intensive professional development support.

The Head Start REDI Project

The goal of the REDI intervention was to improve children's school readiness and associated academic and mental health outcomes by supplementing Head Start programs with evidence-based curriculum components and enhancing teaching quality. REDI was designed to enrich and complement the broad educational programming provided by High/Scope or Creative Curriculum, increasing the systematic emphasis teachers placed on a set of target skills that research has linked with school success. As described in more detail below, the REDI intervention included specific curriculum components targeting children's language, emergent literacy, and social-emotional development, and also utilized professional development activities designed to improve the quality of teacher's language use, emotional support, and positive behavioral management strategies in the classroom. To evaluate its effectiveness, the REDI Project employed a randomized trial design, assigning forty-four classrooms to intervention or "usual practice" conditions. A large, ethnically diverse group of 4-year-old children was pre-tested as they entered these Head Start classrooms and assessed again at the end of the year. In the next sections, the intervention is described, followed by a review of the research findings.

Intervention design

The REDI intervention is delivered by Head Start lead and assistant teachers and integrated into their ongoing classroom programs. It includes curriculum-based lessons, center-based extension activities, and training in teaching strategies to use throughout the day. A major goal of REDI is to assist teachers with the integration of evidence-based practices in their classrooms, by providing teachers with manualized enrichment curricula, consisting of brief lessons, "hands on" extension activities, and specific instructional strategies, all arranged strategically to address a scope and sequence of language/emergent literacy and social-emotional skills.

Language and emergent literacy skill enrichment

Four language and emergent literacy skills are targeted in REDI: (1) vocabulary, (2) syntax, (3) phonological awareness, and (4) print awareness. Three program components target these skills. First, an interactive reading program uses an approach developed by Wasik and colleagues (Wasik et al., 2006) and by Whitehurst and colleagues (Whitehurst et al., 1994) that encourages active and engaging discussion with children during book-reading activities. When done interactively, book-reading provides an ideal setting for the types of conversational exchanges that appear most central to supporting oral language skill development. The reading technique, labeled dialogic reading by Whitehurst and colleagues, shifts the child role from being one of passive listener to one of active participant in the reading experience. By asking questions, and prompting children to describe the pictures and events in the stories, the goal is to enhance the children's comprehension and reasoning skills, building vocabulary, and enhancing narrative understanding. The REDI curriculum includes two books per week, which are scripted with interactive questions, to help teachers focus on the main points of the story and provide exemplars of the interactive style of reading. Each book has a list of targeted vocabulary words, presented with the aid of physical props and illustrations. In addition to presenting these materials in a systematic way during the week, teachers also received mentoring in the use of "language coaching" strategies, such as expansions and grammatical recasts, to provide a general scaffold for language development in the classroom. The overall goal is to improve teachers' strategic use of language in order to increase children's oral language skills, including vocabulary, narrative, and syntax.

REDI also targets phonological awareness skills with a set of "Sound Games" that helps children recognize and manipulate different sounds, based on the work of Adams and colleagues(1998). The games are organized developmentally, progressing through increasingly challenging skills during the year, from listening, to rhyming, to alliteration, to word-play, and finally to the manipulation of syllables and phonemes. In REDI, teachers use a ten-minute Sound Game at least three times per week.

Third, REDI includes developmentally sequenced activities and materials to be used in alphabet centers to promote letter knowledge. These materials include letter stickers, a letter bucket, Letter Wall supplies, and craft materials for various letter-learning activities. Teachers are asked to make sure that each child visits the alphabet center several times per week, and are given records to track the children's acquisition of letter names.

Social-emotional skill enrichment

To promote children's social-emotional skills, REDI uses the Preschool PATHS curriculum (Domitrovich et al., 1999). This curriculum targets four domains: (1) prosocial friendship skills, (2) emotional understanding and emotional expression skills, (3) self-control (i.e., the capacity to inhibit impulsive behavior and organize goal-directed activity), and (4) problem solving skills, including interpersonal negotiation and conflict resolution skills. The curriculum is divided into thirty-three lessons that are delivered by teachers during circle time. These lessons include modeling stories and discussions, and utilize puppet characters, photographs, and teacher role-play demonstrations. Each lesson includes extension activities (e.g., cooperative projects and games) that provide children with opportunities to practice the target skills with teacher support.

Teachers conduct one PATHS lesson and one extension activity each week. Generalized teaching strategies are encouraged with mentoring, including positive classroom management, use of specific teacher praise and support, emotion coaching, and induction strategies to promote appropriate self-control.

The Preschool PATHS curriculum was designed specifically to foster neuro-cognitive developmental control by improving emotional understanding and social problem solving skills, and increasing children's capacity to use language effectively in the service of emotion regulation (see also Riggs et al., 2003). It has proven effective at promoting more socially competent behavior among children attending Head Start (Domitrovich, Cortes, and Greenberg, 2007). In addition, Riggs and colleagues (2006) found that PATHS improved the executive function skills of second and third grade children, suggesting that it may also strengthen the developing executive function skills of preschool children.

A central objective of REDI was to maximize the integration of the social-emotional and language/emergent literacy intervention components that comprised the enrichment program. Each week, one of the books used in the interactive reading program focused on the PATHS theme for that week (e.g., friendship, feelings, self-control, and social problem solving), and feeling words were included in the vocabulary prompts. Additionally, PATHS extension activities incorporated language and emergent literacy skills.

Teacher support and parent take-home materials

For the evaluation trial of REDI, teachers received detailed manuals and kits containing all materials needed to implement the intervention. A three-day professional training was conducted in August, prior to initiating the intervention, and a one-day booster training session was conducted in January. Teachers also received weekly mentoring support provided by local "REDI trainers," experienced master teachers who were supervised by two project-based senior educational consultants. The weekly mentoring was intended to enhance the quality of implementation through modeling, coaching, and providing ongoing feedback regarding program delivery. REDI trainers spent an average of three hours per week in each classroom observing, demonstrating, or team teaching lessons. They also met with the head and assistant teacher for one hour each week outside of class.

Finally, to help parents understand and reinforce what children were learning in REDI, three "take-home" packets were mailed during the course of the year, each containing a modeling videotape with parenting tips and learning activities to use at home. In addition, the PATHS curriculum included handouts for parents, with suggestions for home activities. Children also took home letter stickers and compliment pages to prompt their parents to ask them about their school day and provide positive support at home.

REDI research evaluation

In this section of the chapter, we review the findings from the research evaluation of the REDI program. Head Start programs in three counties participated in the research trial. Using a stratified randomization process, classrooms were divided into groups based on demographics, location (e.g., central or southeastern Pennsylvania), and length of school day (e.g., full-day or half-day). Within stratified groups, centers were randomly assigned to intervention or control conditions. Although classrooms contained 3- and 4-year-old children, only 4 year olds participated in this evaluation. Teachers were studied as they implemented the intervention for the first time, and 4-year-old children were assessed after receiving one year of REDI intervention. Teachers in the comparison classrooms continued to teach "as usual."

Participants

Participants included 356 children (17 percent Hispanic, 25 percent African American, 42 percent European American; 54 percent girls) in forty-four Head Start classrooms. Families were recruited via brochures sent home at the beginning of the school year. Only fourteen eligible families declined to participate, but an additional forty families were unable to complete the assessments (e.g., could not be reached or withdrew early from Head Start). Overall, 86 percent of the eligible children participated. At the beginning of the Head Start year, children were, on average, 4.49 years old (SD = .31, range = 3.72–5.65). On the Block Design scale of the WPPSI – III, a measure of non-verbal cognitive ability that is highly correlated with Full Scale IQ (r = .72; Wechsler, 2002), children received an average standard score of 7.98 (SD = 2.88), approximately two-thirds of a standard deviation below the national mean of 10 and comparable to similar samples of children growing up in poverty.

Data collection procedures

Child assessments were conducted at school by trained assessors, during two individual "pull-out" sessions (30–45 minutes each). Baseline assessments began three weeks after school started, and continued through the end of October. End-of-year child assessments were conducted in March and April. In April, teachers were asked to complete ratings on each child in the study. Each child also was observed during two 12–15 minute play sessions. In addition, parents provided ratings of their children's social-emotional skills and behavior problems at the start and end of the year.

Intervention implementation

The first question we addressed involved the feasibility of REDI program implementation, which required teachers to integrate multiple new curriculum components into their daily activities and to adjust their teaching in new ways in order to optimize support for children's language development and social-emotional development. Monitoring of program implementation indicated that teachers were able to deliver the intervention with relatively high levels of fidelity (see Bierman, Domitrovich et al., 2008 for details.) On average, teachers reported implementing each week: 6.08 dialogic reading activities, 2.57 sound game activities, 3.56 alphabet center activities, and 1.77 PATHS lessons and extension activities. In addition, teachers answered ten questions using three-point scales to describe the quality of their implementation (e.g., Were you able to complete the lesson as written? How well did the children understand the lesson?). The average rating of 2.78 indicated that, from the teachers' perspective, the curriculum was being delivered with fidelity and children were engaged in the lessons.

On a monthly basis, REDI trainers assessed the fidelity and quality of implementation of program components, based on their own observations in the classrooms, using a six-point Likert scale. Their average implementation quality ratings were 4.39 for dialogic reading activities, 4.52 for sound game activities, 4.70 for alphabet center activities, and 4.61 for PATHS lessons and extension activities. Scores of 4–5 reflected descriptions of "adequate" to "strong."

REDI effects on teaching quality

A second important question was whether the REDI professional development focus led to improvements in the quality of teacher language use, instructional support, positive classroom management, and emotional support in the classroom. In order to evaluate the impact on teaching quality, research assistants who were blind to study condition visited intervention and "usual practice" comparison classrooms, and coded teachers on general dimensions of Emotional Support (e.g., positive climate, negative climate, teachers' sensitivity, and behavior management) and Instructional Support (e.g., productivity, concept development, instructional learning formats, and the quality of feedback provided to children) using the *Classroom Assessment Scoring System* (CLASS; La Paro and Pianta, 2003). In addition, observers rated the degree to which teachers used Positive Discipline (e.g., specific praise, reinforcement, redirection, and the absence of negative discipline) and Positive Classroom Management (e.g., teacher's preparedness, use of consistent routines, and effective control and limit-setting), and maintained a Positive Emotional Climate (e.g., support for student emotion regulation, and emotion modeling) using the *Teaching Style Rating Scale* (TSRS; Domitrovich, Cortes, and Greenberg, 2000). Finally, research assistants conducted time sampling counts of language use (e.g., directives, questions, statements, decontextualized talk) and completed ratings of language quality, including richness of teacher talk (e.g., vocabulary, elaboration, cognitive challenge) and sensitivity (e.g., availability, warmth, balance, responsiveness) with the *Classroom Language and Literacy Environment Observation* (CLEO; Holland-Coviello, 2005).

Compared to the "usual practice" comparison group, research assistants rated intervention teachers significantly or marginally significantly higher on dimensions of Positive Emotional Climate, Positive Classroom Management, and Instructional Support. A full account of these findings is available in Domitrovich et al., 2009; a summary is provided in Table 8.1. Moreover, REDI teachers talked with children more frequently and in more cognitively complex ways. Overall, these findings indicate that the REDI intervention successfully improved teaching quality in dimensions associated with school readiness.

REDI effects on child outcomes

Next, we examined the impact of REDI on children's skill acquisition in the targeted domains of language and emergent literacy skill development and social-emotional skills. These child outcomes are reported in full in Bierman, Domitrovich et al., 2008 and Bierman, Nix et al., 2008. Our summary here highlights the significant or marginally significant findings on children's vocabulary, using the Expressive One Word Vocabulary Test (Brownell, 2000), and emergent literacy skills, using the Blending, Elision, and Print Awareness scales of the Test of Preschool Early Literacy (Lonigan et al., 2007). The summary also includes direct assessments of children's social-emotional skills, including emotion knowledge, using the Assessment of Children's Emotion Skills (Schultz, Izard, and Bear, 2004); emotion recognition, using the Emotion Recognition Questionnaire (Ribordy et al., 1988); and aggressive and competent social

Table 8.1 *Impact of Head Start REDI on broad summary scales of teaching quality.*

	Control group mean (SD)	Intervention mean (SD)	Effect size
Emotional-behavioral support			
Positive emotional climate (TSRS)	2.52 (1.05)	3.18 (1.24)	.69*
Emotional support (CLASS)	5.65 (.81)	5.97 (.45)	.39
Classroom management (TSRS)	4.09 (.71)	4.32 (.67)	.60**
Positive discipline (TSRS)	3.91 (.91)	4.39 (.72)	.65
Cognitive-linguistic support			
Instructional support (CLASS)	3.76 (.72)	4.14 (.68)	.45+
Statements (CLEO)	5.77 (1.78)	7.03 (1.58)	.82***
Questions (CLEO)	2.98 (1.15)	3.95 (1.20)	.89***
Decontextualized utterances (CLEO)	.61 (.64)	1.06 (.86)	.68**
Language richness-sensitivity (CLEO)	3.07 (.53)	3.41 (.44)	.67**

$^+p < .10$, $^*p < .05$, $^{**}p < .01$, $^{***}p < .001$

Note: Because modal values were near scale extremes for the TSRS, random-effects ordered probit models were used to analyze treatment differences. For these outcomes, Vargha and Delaney's A is presented rather than Cohen's d, as the latter is sensitive to deviations from normality in variable distribution. An A of .56, .64, and .71 corresponds to a small, medium, and large effect size, respectively (Vargha and Delaney, 2000).

problem solving, using the Challenging Situations Task (Denham, Bouril, and Belouad, 1994). The summary includes teacher, parent, and observer ratings of children's social competence and aggression, using the Social Health Profile (Conduct Problems Prevention Research Group, 1995) and Teacher Observation of Child Adaptation-Revised (Werthamer-Larsson, Kellam, and Wheeler, 1991), respectively. Finally, the summary includes an assessment of children's executive functioning, using the Dimensional Change Card Sort (Frye, Zelazo, and Palfai, 1995), which measures working memory, inhibitory control, and set shifting. We also report on interviewer ratings of the child's task orientation, using the Preschool Self-Regulation Assessment Ratings (Smith-Donald et al., 2007), which measures the ability to sustain concentration and behavioral control while engaging in challenging work.

To examine REDI effects on child outcomes, we estimated a series of hierarchical linear models that accounted for the nesting of children within classrooms and controlled for factors such as child sex, child race, Head Start center location, and baseline assessment of the outcome, when available. As shown in Table 8.2, positive effects for REDI were found on children's growth in vocabulary and emergent literacy skills.

Table 8.2 *Impact of Head Start REDI on child skills and behaviors.*

	Control group mean (SD)	Intervention group mean (SD)	Effect size (*p*-value)
Language and emergent literacy skills			
Vocabulary	41.03 (11.24)	42.79 (11.55)	.15*
Blending	13.04 (4.30)	14.71 (4.33)	.39***
Elision	9.61 (3.58)	11.19 (4.02)	.35***
Print awareness	16.49 (12.59)	18.84 (12.84)	.16+
Social-emotional skills			
Emotion knowledge	7.12 (2.28)	7.45 (2.36)	.21+
Emotion recognition	1.52 (.26)	1.61 (.24)	.23*
Aggressive social problem solving	2.06 (2.55)	1.53 (2.21)	−.21*
Competent social problem solving	2.29 (2.05)	3.16 (2.55)	.35**
Behavior			
Social competence (teacher ratings)	3.98 (.88)	4.15 (.82)	.24+
Social competence (parent ratings)	3.66 (.84)	3.73 (.80)	.09
Social competence (observer ratings)	2.21 (.53)	2.36 (.49)	.26+
Aggression (teacher ratings)	4.12 (1.70)	3.69 (1.52)	−.28*
Aggression (parent ratings)	2.86 (.97)	2.71 (.99)	−.13+
Aggression (observer ratings)	.37 (.34)	.30 (.31)	−.19
Self-regulation skills			
Executive functioning	.63 (.45)	.71 (.39)	.20+
Task orientation	2.61 (.49)	2.72 (.49)	.28*

$^+p < .10$, $^*p < .05$, $^{**}p < .01$, $^{***}p < .001$

Similarly, positive effects for REDI were found for children's emotion knowledge and recognition, as well as in their ability to generate non-aggressive and competent solutions to hypothetical social problems. In terms of behavior, teachers, parents, and observers rated children in REDI classrooms as displaying higher levels of social competence and lower levels of aggression than children in "usual practice" Head Start classrooms.

The REDI findings show that evidence-based instruction and positive classroom management can accelerate the pace of learning for children in Head Start classrooms. It can increase the rate at which they acquire critically important emergent literacy and social-emotional skills during the pre-kindergarten year, and thereby enhance their school readiness. The REDI findings also demonstrate the utility of a dual-domain focus on the promotion of cognitive skills as well as social-emotional competencies in preschool programs serving children who have experienced early adversity. Because of the relations over time among language skills, social competence, self-regulation, and learning engagement (Bierman et al.,

2009; Welsh et al., 2010), we suspect that the broad focus of the REDI intervention may have generated synergistic effects in enhancing school readiness across domains.

Implications for practice and policy

Too often child mental health needs are viewed as separate and distinct from their academic needs; yet, they are intertwined developmentally. Both are affected adversely by early exposure to the high stress and low support that so often affect children growing up in poverty. Evidence-based practices are available that can reduce the school readiness gaps associated with early disadvantage; however, rarely are they implemented in a comprehensive manner with high quality. Additional efforts to improve the quality of preschool programming with evidence-based practice are needed.

The most important finding from the REDI project was that evidence-based practices produced simultaneous – and perhaps synergistic – gains in child school readiness in the dual domains of language/emergent literacy and social-emotional skills. Compared with their peers in "usual practice" classrooms, children in REDI classrooms made greater gains in areas of vocabulary, phonological awareness, print knowledge, emotion recognition, and social problem solving skills. Behavioral improvements were documented as well, with children in REDI classrooms showing higher levels of social competence and engaging in less aggression. A prior study (Bierman, Nix, et al., 2008) indicated that the provision of the REDI intervention was particularly beneficial to children who started the year with low levels of behavioral inhibitory control (e.g., difficulties delaying motor responding and sustaining effortful task engagement). REDI also demonstrated that preventive intervention can foster the development of self-regulation. REDI promoted improvements on measures of executive function and task orientation, which is notable because these capacities enable children to approach learning tasks more effectively and efficiently, thus facilitating learning and social-emotional adjustment to school.

One of the factors that has limited current efforts to improve preschool programming is that evidence-based curricula are often "piecemeal" and focus on reducing gaps in highly specific cognitive skills, such as phonological awareness or language delays. Although very important, efforts that focus only on the cognitive skills of disadvantaged children ignore the serious impact that early adversity has on children's mental health, and on the development of the social-emotional and self-regulatory skills needed for goal-oriented learning and school success. Academic achievement requires the development of adaptive learning behaviors as well as the acquisition of content knowledge (Blair, 2002). In addition, a successful life benefits from social skills, emotion regulation abilities, and self-control, all core components of mental health. To strengthen impact, preschool programs designed for socio-economically disadvantaged children need to adapt evidence-based practices that support developing social-emotional skills and mental health, as well as promoting cognitive development.

In addition, to promote the widespread implementation of evidence-based practice, more must be done to support teachers in their efforts to learn and implement evidence-based practices with fidelity. Head Start teachers often report feeling overwhelmed by the dual demands of implementing curriculum improvements designed to close the achievement gap, while also effectively managing behaviorally challenging children who lack the self-regulation and social skills needed for engaged learning (Iutcovich et al., 1997). Current practice, which typically involves introducing new curriculum approaches during brief workshops, is not sufficient to provide teachers with the knowledge and skills needed to implement evidence-based curricula effectively. Even when teachers are provided with a complete curriculum, their capacity to integrate it effectively into their classrooms and to utilize effective teaching strategies is limited (Pianta, 2003). More intensive professional development efforts are needed, including opportunities for guided practice in classroom contexts, and adequate mentoring time to allow teachers to reflect on their own practices, set goals, and receive performance feedback (Domitrovich et al., 2009).

The REDI intervention was designed to evaluate the feasibility and impact of enriching Head Start programs with a comprehensive set of evidence-based curriculum components, targeting emergent literacy as well as social-emotional skills. To support teachers in mastering these multiple curriculum components and to improve their language use and emotional support in the classroom, REDI provided sustained professional development, including workshop training and in-class coaches who observed and mentored teachers over the course of a year.

The approach was successful. By the end of the year, when compared to teachers in "usual practice" classrooms, Head Start REDI teachers talked with children more frequently and in more cognitively complex ways, using richer vocabulary and asking more questions in a manner that was more sensitive and responsive to children. They also established a more positive classroom climate, and used more preventive behavior management strategies. The changes in multiple domains of teaching quality by REDI teachers reflect the importance and value of an intensive professional development support model provided during the first year of implementation of a new evidence-based curriculum. Head Start REDI also made it easier for teachers to incorporate evidence-based instruction by providing teachers with a well-specified enrichment curriculum. The specific and scripted REDI curricula provided a useful scaffold, assisting teachers by providing lesson plans and organizing skill presentation along a scope and sequence, thereby reducing teacher preparation time and providing teachers with a platform for skill coaching throughout the day. The REDI results document that, with well-developed curriculum guides and effective professional development support, Head Start teachers can incorporate comprehensive evidence-based practices, and improve instructional and emotional support in their classrooms.

Although the coaching model used in REDI was highly effective, a key limitation is that it is not easily portable or sustainable without additional resources. Hence, a key challenge for the future will be the development of more cost-effective means of providing similar levels of professional development support for teachers. The use of technology-assisted platforms to deliver professional development may be very useful in this regard. In a recent project, Pianta and his colleagues (Pianta et al., 2008) used an innovative web-based platform to deliver teacher professional development support. The My Teaching Partner (MTP) program includes an array of web-based professional development resources, including video exemplars and lesson plans. In addition, web-mediated consultation was provided, in which teachers met regularly with an "on-line" coach. Teachers shared videotaped excerpts of their classroom lessons, and received positive support, feedback, and suggestions from their on-line MTP coach. Teachers who received the full MTP program, with full access to web-based resources along with on-line coaching showed the greatest improvement in teaching quality (relative to those who had access to the web resources but no coaching), and these effects were most pronounced in classrooms serving a high proportion of socio-economically disadvantaged children (Pianta et al., 2008).

"Going to scale" with comprehensive evidence-based preschool programming that addresses the cognitive and social-emotional needs of disadvantaged children remains a future goal. The REDI project findings validate the importance of this goal, the potential benefits to children, and the critical need to further develop and disseminate the curriculum guides and professional development support systems that enable the widespread adoption and high-quality implementation of evidence-based preschool programs and practices.

References

Adams, M. J., Foorman, B. R., Lundberg, I., and Beeler, T. (1998). *Phonological sensitivity in young children: a classroom curriculum*. Baltimore: Paul H. Brookes Publishing.

Adler, N. E., and Newman, K. (2002). Socioeconomic disparities in health: pathways and policies. *Health Affairs*, 21, 60–76.

Barnett, S. (1995). Long-term effects of early childhood programs on cognitive and school outcomes. *Future of Children*, 5, 25–50.

Bierman, K. L. (2004). *Peer rejection: developmental processes and intervention strategies*. New York: Guilford.

Bierman, K. L., Domitrovich, C. E., Nix, R. L., Gest, S. D., Welsh, J. A., Greenberg, M. T., Blair, C., Nelson, K., and Gill, S. (2008). Promoting academic and social-emotional school readiness: the Head Start REDI Program. *Child Development*, 79, 1802–1817.

Bierman, K. L., and Erath, S. A. (2006). Promoting social competence in early childhood: classroom curricula and social skills coaching programs. In K. McCartney and D. Phillips (eds.), *Blackwell handbook on early childhood development* (pp. 595–615). Malden, MA: Blackwell.

Bierman, K. L., Nix, R. L., Greenberg, M. T., Blair, C., and Domitrovich, C. E. (2008). Executive functions and school readiness intervention: impact, moderation, and mediation in the Head Start REDI Program. *Development and Psychopathology*, 20, 821–843.

Bierman, K. L., Torres, M. M., Domitrovich, C. E., Welsh, J. A., and Gest, S. D. (2009). Behavioral and cognitive readiness for school: cross-domain associations for children attending Head Start. *Social Development*, 18, 305–323.

Blair, C. (2002). School readiness: integrating cognition and emotion in a neuro-biological conceptualization of child functioning at school entry. *American Psychologist*, 57, 111–127.

Blair, C., Zelazo, P. D., and Greenberg, M. T. (2005). The measurement of executive function in early childhood. *Developmental Neuropsychology*, 28, 561–571.

Brownell, R. (2000). *Expressive One-Word Picture Vocabulary Test manual*. Novato, CA: Academic Therapy Publications.

Campbell, S. B. (2006). Maladjustment in preschool children: a developmental psychopathology perspective. In K. McCartney and D. Phillips (eds.), *The Blackwell handbook of early childhood development* (pp. 358–378). London: Blackwell.

Catts, H. W., Fey, M. E., Zhang, X., and Tomblin, J. B. (1999). Language basis of reading and reading disabilities: evidence from a longitudinal investigation. *Scientific Studies of Reading*, 3, 331–361.

Cicchetti, D. (2002). The impact of social experience on neurobiological systems: illustration from a constructivist view of child maltreatment. *Cognitive Development*, 17, 1407–1428.

Conduct Problems Prevention Research Group (1995). *Social health profile*. Unpublished measure available at www.fasttrackproject.org.

Consortium on the School-Based Promotion of Social Competence (1994). The school-based promotion of social competence: theory, research, practice, and policy. In R. J. Haggerty, L. R. Sherrod, N. Garmezy, and M. Rutter (eds.), *Stress, risk, and resilience in children and adolescents: processes, mechanisms, and interventions* (pp. 268–316). Cambridge University Press.

Coolahan, K., Fantuzzo, J., Mendez, J., and McDermott, P. (2000). Preschool peer interactions and readiness to learn: relationships between classroom peer play and learning behaviors and conduct. *Journal of Educational Psychology*, 92, 458–465.

Denham, S., Bouril, B., and Belouad, F. (1994). Preschoolers' affect and cognition about challenging peer situations. *Child Study Journal*, 24, 1–21.

Denham, S. A., and Burton, R. (2003). *Social and emotional prevention and intervention programming for preschoolers*. New York: Kluwer-Plenum.

Diamond, A., Barnett, W. S., Thomas, J., and Munro, S. (2007). Preschool program improves cognitive control. *Science*, 318, 1387–1388.

Domitrovich, C. E., Cortes, R., and Greenberg, M. T. (2000). The Teacher Style Rating Scale technical report. Unpublished manuscript. Pennsylvania State University.

  (2007). Improving young children's social and emotional competence: a randomized trial of the preschool PATHS curriculum. *Journal of Primary Prevention*, 28, 67–91.

Domitrovich, C. E., Gest, S. D., Gill, S., Bierman, K. L., Welsh, J., and Jones, D. (2009). Fostering high quality teaching in Head Start classrooms: experimental evaluation of an integrated curriculum. *American Education Research Journal*, 46, 567–597.

Domitrovich, C. E., Greenberg, M. T., Cortes, R., and Kusche, C. (1999). *Manual for the Preschool PATHS Curriculum*. Pennsylvania State University.

Duncan, G. J., Brooks-Gunn, J., and Klebanov, P. K. (1994). Economic deprivation and early childhood development. *Child Development*, 65, 296–318.

Fabes, R. A., and Eisenberg, N. (1992). Young children's coping with interpersonal anger. *Child Development*, 63, 116–128.

Frye, D., Zelazo, P. D., and Palfai, T. (1995). Theory of mind and rule-based reasoning. *Cognitive Development*, 10, 483–527.

Hart, B., and Risley, T. R. (1995). *Meaningful differences in the everyday experience of young American children*. Baltimore, MD: Brookes Publishing.

Holland-Coviello, R. (2005). *Language and literacy environment quality in early childhood classrooms: exploration of measurement strategies and relations with children's development*. Unpublished doctoral dissertation, Pennsylvania State University.

Iutcovich, J., Fiene, R., Johnson, J., Koppel, R., and Langan, F. (1997). *Investing in our children's future: the path to quality child care through the Pennsylvania child care/early childhood development training system*. Erie, PA: Keystone University Research Corporation.

Izard, C. E. (2002). Translating emotion theory and research into preventive interventions. *Psychological Bulletin*, 128, 796–824.

La Paro, K. M., and Pianta, R. C. (2003). *CLASS: Classroom Assessment Scoring System*. Charlottesville: University of Virginia.

La Paro, K., Pianta, R., and Stuhlman, M. (2004). Classroom assessment scoring system (CLASS): findings from the pre-k year. *Elementary School Journal*, 104, 409–426.

Ladd, G. W., Buhs, E. S., and Seid, M. (2000). Children's initial sentiments about kindergarten: is school liking an antecedent of early childhood classroom participation and achievement. *Merrill-Palmer Quarterly*, 46, 255–279.

Lengua, L. J., Honorado, E., and Bush, N. R. (2007). Contextual risk and parenting as predictors of effortful control and social competence in preschool children. *Journal of Applied Developmental Psychology*, 28, 40–55.

Lonigan, C. J. (2006). Development, assessment, and promotion of preliteracy skills. *Early Education and Development*, 17, 91–114.

Lonigan, C. J., Wagner, R. K., Torgesen, J. K., and Rashotte, C. A. (2007). *TOPEL: Test of Preschool Early Literacy*. Austin, TX: PRO-ED, Inc.

Macmillan, R., McMorris, B. J., and Kruttschnitt, C. (2004). Linked lives: stability and change in maternal circumstances trajectories of antisocial behavior in children. *Child Development*, 75, 205–220.

McClelland, M. M., Acock, A. C., and Morrison, F. J. (2006). The impact of kindergarten learning-related skills on academic trajectories at the end of elementary school. *Early Childhood Research Quarterly*, 21, 471–490.

National Center for Children in Poverty (2010). Basic facts about low-income children, 2009. http://nccp.org/publications/pub_975.html.

National Early Literacy Panel (2005). *Report on a synthesis of early predictors of reading*. Louisville, KY.

Nelson, K. E., and Welsh, J. A. (1998). Progress in multiple language domains by deaf children and hearing children: discussions with a rare event transactional model. In R. Paul (ed.), *The speech/language connection* (pp. 179–225). Baltimore, MD: Brookes Publishing.

Pianta, R. C. (2003). *Experiences in p-3 classrooms: the implications of observational research for redesigning early education*. New York: Foundation for Child Development.

Pianta, R. C., Mashburn, A. J., Downer, J. T., Hamre, B. K., and Justice, L. M. (2008). Effects of web-mediated professional development resources on teacher–child interactions in pre-kindergarten classrooms. *Early Childhood Research Quarterly*, 23, 431–451.

Raver, C. C., Jones, S. M., Li-Grining, C. P., Metzger, M., Smallwood, K., and Sardin, L. (2008). Improving preschool classroom processes: preliminary findings from a randomized trial implemented in Head Start settings. *Early Childhood Research Quarterly*, 23, 10–26.

Ribordy, S., Camras, L., Stafani, R., and Spacarelli, S. (1988). Vignettes for emotion recognition research and affective therapy with children. *Journal of Clinical Child Psychology*, 17, 322–325.

Riggs, N. R., Blair, C. B., and Greenberg, M. T. (2003). Concurrent and 2-year longitudinal relations between executive function and the behavior of 1st and 2nd grade children. *Child Neuropsychology*, 9, 267–276.

Riggs, N. R., Greenberg, M. T., Kusche, C. A., and Pentz, M. A. (2006). The meditational role of neurocognition in the behavioral outcomes of a social-emotional prevention program in elementary school students: effects of the PATHS Curriculum. *Prevention Science*, 7, 91–102.

Rimm-Kaufman, S., Pianta, R. C., and Cox, M. (2000). Teachers' judgments of problems in the transition to school. *Early Childhood Research Quarterly*, 15, 147–166.

Ritsher, J., Warner, E. B., Johnson, J. G., and Dohrenwend, B. P. (2001). Inter-generational longitudinal study of social class and depression: a test of social causation and social selection models. *British Journal of Psychiatry*, 178, 84–90.

Ryan, R. M., Fauth, R. C., and Brooks-Gunn, J. (2006). Childhood poverty: implications for school readiness and early childhood education. In B. Spodek and O. N. Saracho (eds.), *Handbook of research on the education of children* (2nd edn, pp. 323–346). Mahwah, NJ: Erlbaum Associates.

Schultz, D., Izard, C. E., and Bear, G. (2004). Children's emotion processing: relations to emotionality and aggression. *Development and Psychopathology*, 16, 371–387.

Schweinhart, L. J. (2004). The High/Scope Perry Preschool Study through age 40: summary, conclusions, and frequently asked questions. www.highscope.org/ Research/PerryProject/perrymain.htm.

Schweinhart, L. J., Montie, J., Xiang, Z., Barnett, W. S., Belfield, C. R., and Nores, M. (2005). *Lifetime effects: the High/Scope Perry Preschool study through age 40*. Monographs of the High/Scope Educational Research Foundation 14. Ypsilanti, MI: High/Scope Press.

Senechal, M. (2006). Testing the Home Literacy Model: parent involvement in kindergarten is differentially related to grade 4 reading comprehension, fluency, spelling, and reading for pleasure. *Scientific Studies on Reading*, 10, 59–87.

Smith-Donald, R., Raver, C. C., Hayes, T., and Richardson, B. (2007). Preliminary construct and concurrent validity of the Preschool Self-Regulation Assessment (PSRA) for field-based research. *Early Childhood Research Quarterly*, 22, 173–187.

US Department of Health and Human Services (2005). *Head Start Impact Study: first year findings*. Washington, DC. www.acf.hhs.gov/programs/opre/hs/ impact_study/reports/.

Vargha, A., and Delaney, H. D. (2000). A critique and improvement of the CL common language effect size statistics of McGraw and Wong. *Journal of Educational and Behavioral Statistics*, 24, 101–132.

Wasik, B. A., Bond, M. A., and Hindman, A. (2006). The effects of a language and literacy intervention on Head Start children and teachers. *Journal of Educational Psychology*, 98, 63–74.

Wechsler, D. (2002). *Wechsler Preschool and Primary Scale of Intelligence – III*. San Antonio, TX: Psychological Corporation.

Welsh, J. A., Nix, R. L., Blair, C., Bierman, K. L., and Nelson, K. E. (2010). The development of cognitive skills and gains in academic school readiness for children from low income families. *Journal of Educational Psychology*, 102, 43–53.

Werthamer-Larsson, L., Kellam, S., and Wheeler, L. (1991). Effect of first-grade classroom environment on shy behavior, aggressive behavior, and concentration problems. *American Journal of Community Psychology*, 19, 585–602.

Whitehurst, G. J., Arnold, D., Epstein, J. N., Angell, A. L., Smith, M., and Fischel, J. E. (1994). A picture book reading intervention in daycare and home for children from low-income families. *Developmental Psychology*, 30, 679–689.

Winkleby, M., Cubbin, C., and Ahn, D. (2006). Effects of cross-level interaction between individual and neighborhood socioeconomic status on adult mortality rates. *American Journal of Public Health*, 96(12), 2145–2153.

World Health Organization (2010). *Mental health: strengthening our response.* Retrieved October 5, 2010 from www.who.int/mediacentre/factsheets/fs220/en/.

9 Early Head Start: mental health, parenting, and impacts on children

Catherine C. Ayoub, Jessica Dym Bartlett,
Rachel Chazan-Cohen, and Helen Raikes

Early Head Start (EHS) is a federally funded community-based program for low-income pregnant women and families with infants and toddlers. As one of the largest early intervention programs in the US, EHS focuses on promoting healthy prenatal outcomes for pregnant women, enhancing the development of very young children, and supporting healthy family functioning. The program was established in 1994 as part of the re-authorization of Head Start, a federal initiative responding to mounting scientific evidence that a child's earliest years of life constitute a critical period of human development and a key determinant of individual health and well-being over the lifespan (Carnegie Corporation of New York, 1994; National Scientific Council on the Developing Child, 2005; Shonkoff and Phillips, 2000). It had become increasingly clear that, because individual developmental processes both influence and are influenced by early environments (Bronfenbrenner, 1979), intervention efforts would need to attend to infant–caregiver relationships and family well-being as the primary contexts in which a child's development unfolds (Ainsworth, 1973; Bowlby, 1969). Programs have indeed had demonstrable positive effects on parent–child interaction in the early years (Brooks-Gunn, Berlin, and Fuligni, 2000; Brooks-Gunn and Markman, 2005). In line with an ecological view of child development, the Advisory Committee on Services for Families with Infants and Toddlers (ACSFIT, 1994) formed by the US Secretary of Health and Human Services recommended that the EHS program address the needs of low-income parents and young children based on four cornerstones of practice: (1) supporting child development, (2) empowering families, (3) building communities, and (4) enhancing staff quality.

In 1995 and 1996, the US Department of Health and Human Services' Administration on Children, Youth and Families (ACYF) launched the first 143 EHS programs under the umbrella of its predecessor, Head Start, to serve low-income pregnant women and families with children under age 3. EHS grew quickly, to over 700 programs by 2004 serving approximately 60,000 children and families. In 2009, expansion under the American Recovery and Reinvestment Act increased capacity (more programs, additional children within programs) to over 1,000 programs nationwide serving over 110,000 children and families. EHS programs were designed to provide and coordinate comprehensive services for the whole child, and to produce outcomes in four domains: child development (health, resilience, social, cognitive, and language), family development (parenting, relationships with children, home environment, family functioning, family health, and economic self-sufficiency), staff development (professional development and relationships with parents), and community development (child care quality, community collaboration, and integration of services for families with young children) (USDHHS, 2002). Program involvement addresses children's cognitive development directly through specific child-focused cognitive and language promotion activities offered during regular home visits and through the provision of high-quality center-based child care experiences, and indirectly through parenting education and support services. Additional services include visits by the child's teacher and other EHS staff, and bi-monthly socialization experiences. EHS programs can be home-based, center-based, or a combination of the two (Administration for Children and Families [ACF], 2006b).

Concomitant with implementing EHS nationwide, ACYF selected seventeen programs across the country to participate in a congressionally mandated rigorous, large-scale, random-assignment evaluation. The initial evaluation aims of the Early Head Start Research and Evaluation Project (EHSREP) were to document program services and impact. Programs in EHSREP were chosen to represent a range of rural and urban settings, diverse family backgrounds, and variations in program approach (Love et al., 2005; USDHHS, 2002). Between July 1996 and September 1998, a total of 3,001 families that applied to enroll in an EHS program were randomly assigned either to a program group (participation in EHS) or to a control group (access to any services in their communities with the exception of EHS). Families in both groups participated in interviews with primary caregivers, direct child assessments, observations of the home environment, and parent–child interactions that were videotaped and later coded when the children were approximately 14, 24, and 36 months old. Two follow-up assessments were conducted in the spring prior to when children enrolled in kindergarten and when children were in the fifth grade (Vogel et al., 2010).

Rare are opportunities to explore the impact of interventions of this magnitude and timing on outcomes for children and families, and EHSREP has been fertile ground for developmental scientists interested in studying an array of subjects including: home visiting, child care, school readiness, parenting, family engagement, special needs, social and emotional development, cognitive and language development, prenatal health, child health, infant and early childhood mental health, and parental mental health. The impact study showed modest but promising results from the very beginning. Several notable effects comparing the program and control groups emerged when children were enrolled in EHS:

- Children in EHS scored higher on standardized measures of cognitive and language development at 24 and 36 months in relation to their peers in the comparison group, although their performance still trailed the national norms. A program offering a mix of home- and center-based services quadrupled a child's chance of performing well on assessments of cognitive development, receptive vocabulary, and sustained attention to objects relative to children in the control group.
- Children in EHS showed benefits in social-emotional development. They were rated lower on aggressive behavior problems at 24 and 36 months than those in the control group. At 36 months children also were observed to be more attentive to objects, less negative, and better able to engage their parents during play.
- Children in EHS exhibited gains in language development (receptive language) at 24 months, which they had sustained when assessed again at age 3.
- Parents of children in EHS exhibited more support for language and learning and were more likely to read to their children daily compared to non-EHS parents.
- Parents in EHS were more emotionally supportive, spanked less, and used less punitive discipline when children were 36 months old than non-EHS parents.
- Mothers in EHS were more likely to be in education or job training programs.
- In a subset of twelve sites that participated in a study of fathers, EHS showed positive impacts on fathers' interactions with their children, including less spanking and intrusiveness. Their children also were observed to be more engaged and attentive during play than those who were not in EHS (Love et al., 2002; Love et al., 2005).

Important to the topic of this chapter, there was little indication that the program had an impact on family well-being. At age 2, the program did show a reduction in parenting stress, but there was no impact on maternal depression or family use of mental health services (according to parent report). In the follow-up two years after the end of the program, EHS had continued impacts in the realm of child social emotional functioning, specifically reduced aggressive and problem behaviors and improved approaches toward learning, and parenting, mostly in the area of parent support for learning in the home. And, for the first time EHS mothers reported fewer symptoms of depression than those in the control group (Chazan-Cohen et al., 2007). The follow-up in fifth grade (age 10) indicated that EHS did not show the "broad pattern of impacts for child and family outcomes seen at early ages" (Vogel et al., 2010: xii), yet positive impacts remained for children's social emotional well-being, the domain with the most consistent effects while children were in the program.

Patterns of impact also differed for subgroups of children and families. These findings were especially noteworthy for policymakers and program staff interested in determining what types of programs work for what types of families under what conditions:

- For families where mothers reported elevated symptoms of depression at enrollment (50 percent of the sample) EHS had favorable impacts for children and for parent-child interactions. It appeared to buffer children from the effects of maternal depression.
- Programs that fully implemented the Head Start Performance Standards and provided a flexible mix of home- and center-based services had the greatest impacts on children's development and family functioning (Love et al., 2005; Vogel et al., 2010).
- Favorable impacts were especially pronounced for children whose mothers enrolled while still pregnant (Vogel et al., 2010).
- Impacts of EHS were especially strong for African American families, with positive effects for children's social-emotional development, parent involvement in children's education, and parental mental health (i.e., fewer depressive symptoms, less alcohol use: Love et al., 2002; Vogel et al., 2010).
- The impact of EHS varied by a family's risk status. Demographic risk factors (single parent, public assistance, neither employed nor in school or job training, adolescent parent) were assessed and families were assigned to low, moderate, and high risk groups. Positive impacts were most consistent for the moderate-risk group.

While in the program, favorable effects for families overall included children's language and cognitive development, parent and child behaviors during play, parent support for learning, parental well-being, and self-sufficiency. Two years later, positive impacts included parent support for learning, parental well-being, and child social-emotional development. Two years after the program ended, the highest-risk group showed positive impacts on mothers' report of abuse, and for living with someone with a drug or alcohol problem. There was a *negative* pattern of impacts on children's math and vocabulary outcomes, a trend at age 3 that achieved significance at the two follow-up assessments (Vogel et al., 2010).

A comprehensive review of the results of EHS research and evaluation is beyond the scope of this chapter. Instead, we discuss findings salient to one of our collective interests and areas of expertise, namely, the effects of adult mental health and parenting on child outcomes. We submit that, in the course of studying parenting and parental mental health in EHS, researchers have unearthed compelling findings on the potential of early intervention programs to improve child outcomes. A "magic bullet" did not emerge, but there are valuable lessons to be learned from EHSREP on how interventions aimed at engaging families on parenting and mental health issues during the prenatal period and first three years of a child's life increase the chances that children follow resilient life trajectories.

For families in Early Head Start, there were three key impacts on children's development related to parenting. First, parents in EHS had less stress related to the tasks of parenting. Second, they interacted with their children in ways that better stimulated children's cognitive development. And third, when parents interacted insensitively with their children, this insensitivity caused less harm to children in EHS than to comparison children (Ayoub, Vallotton, and Mastergeorge, 2011). These results demonstrate that EHS interventions can positively influence children's development both directly and indirectly by protecting the family from stress and by promoting positive parent–child relationships despite exposure to stressors. That is, the intervention both protects parenting and buffers children from the effects of demographic risks, parenting stress, and depression, in turn supporting parents in raising healthy children. The results have particular weight, as early intervention can impart benefits that reverberate throughout life, and families may be especially receptive to intervention when children are very young (Howard and Brooks-Gunn, 2009). Prior to further discussion of EHSREP findings we consider the overall "picture" of parental mental health in EHS.

Parental mental health in Early Head Start

Impoverished adults are at high risk for experiencing mood, anxiety, and substance abuse disorders (Fryers, Melzer, and Jenkins, 2003; Lorant et al., 2007; Sareen et al., 2011). Moreover, low-income minority women carry an undue burden of mental illness, as they are less likely than white women to seek or receive adequate mental health care (Young et al., 2001). Mothers of young children living in poverty face substantial risk for mental health problems (Lanzi et al., 1999; Loeb et al., 2004). Estimates suggest that from one-quarter to over one-half of poor mothers with young children suffer from depression (Chazan-Cohen et al., 2007; Knitzer, 2001). Many of these families encounter considerable obstacles to accessing appropriate treatment, such as a lack of transportation, child care, and health care coverage. Given the low energy and motivation that characterize depression, as well as the social stigma of mental illness, parents with mental health issues may not have the personal, social, or financial resources to obtain care (Beeber et al., 2004; Love et al., 2005).

Findings from EHSREP were consistent with prior research establishing a high incidence of stress, depression, and anxiety in families with certain demographic risk factors, many of which characterize the EHS eligible population (e.g., low income, parenting young children, minority background). Almost half (48 percent) of mothers reported moderate to severe depressive symptoms at the time of enrollment. For a number of women (12 percent), depression was chronic when their children were 1 and 3 years of age (ACF, 2006a). In addition, 18 percent of fathers reported clinically significant levels of depressive symptoms when children were 2 years old, and 16 percent met the criteria when children were 3 years old (Love et al., 2002). Pregnant women reported especially high levels of psychological distress: 68 percent had clinically significant depressive symptoms, 39 percent were emotional stressed, 32 percent exhibited irritability, and 21 percent reported anxiety (ACF, 2006a). On average, Hispanic parents reported more parenting stress than other parents, and white parents reported more substance abuse.

Taken together, these figures are alarming in light of mounting evidence that parental psychological distress impairs parenting and causes disturbance in family functioning that, in turn, may lead to cognitive, social, emotional, and behavioral deficits in children (for review see National Research Council and Institute of Medicine [NRC and IOM], 2009). The underlying mechanisms of these associations continue to be hotly debated by experts, but there is ample evidence that parental stress, anxiety, and depression impacted the quality of parent–child relationships in EHS (Chazan-Cohen et al., 2007; Malik et al., 2007; McKelvey et al., 2002; Vogel et al., 2011). How children faired depended in large part upon other personal and environmental resources (McKelvey et al., 2002).

Parental mental health and child outcomes in Early Head Start

Studies on children reared by parents with symptoms of mental illness strongly suggest that they are more likely than other children to exhibit problems with school adjustment, aggression, conduct disorders, speech and learning difficulties, and depression (NRC and IOM, 2009). Moreover, early childhood is a sensitive period during which exposure to parental mental health problems may be more harmful than during subsequent developmental stages (Bureau, Easterbrooks, and Lyons-Ruth, 2009;

Murray, Cooper, and Hipwell, 2003). In EHS, toddlers living in families with two or more psychological risk factors (i.e., moderate or severe depressive symptoms, parenting stress, substance abuse) were at higher risk for problems with fine motor development, gross motor development, and problem solving at age 1 than toddlers living in families with a single psychological risk factor. They also experienced more economic risk, had poorer birth outcomes, scored lower on a measure of general health, were less likely to be insured, and were more likely to be spanked by caregivers. Parents with more psychological risk factors more frequently reported that toddlers had social-emotional problems than did parents with one risk factor.

There are a number of pathways that might explain the toll parental mental health problems take on children. There may be *direct* effects on child outcomes, such as when a caregiver's depression negatively impacts a child's development (Cicchetti, Rogosch, and Toth, 1998; Cummings, Keller, and Davies, 2005), or *indirect* effects, such as when adversities present in the child's environment mediate the link between parental depression and child functioning (Dawson et al., 2003; Malik et al., 2007). Multiple pathways also may be in operation at once. For example, a study by Cummings and colleagues (2005) found both a direct relationship between maternal depression and child behavior in kindergarten, and also that marital satisfaction partially mediated this association. Other studies indicate that the negative impacts of parental mental health symptoms on children may be fully explained by extrinsic factors. An investigation on the effect of maternal depression on preschool-aged children's behavior (Dawson et al., 2003) determined that a composite score for contextual risk (i.e., negative life events, parenting stress, marital satisfaction, family emotional climate, and social support) fully mediated the relation between the associations. Findings from the EHSREP generally support the existence of multiple pathways from poor psychological functioning in parents to compromised development in their children (Chazan-Cohen et al., 2007; Malik et al., 2007; Rowe, Pan, and Ayoub, 2005; Vogel et al., 2011).

Influence of parents and environments on child outcomes

Direct effects of parental psychological impairment on child functioning have been apparent in EHS families. For example, a study using one local EHS sample discovered that children's language was adversely impacted by a mother's depression (Rowe et al., 2005). Specifically, maternal depression was related to amount of maternal talk, although not to the diversity of maternal vocabulary, replicating findings from other studies. Given the symptoms of disengagement, withdrawal, and lethargy commonly associated with depression, it follows that such symptoms would result in a decrease in maternal talk. The symptoms of depression often lead to slowed speech and increased periods of silence between phrases that result in the reduction of talk. Furthermore, talk such as fillers or repetitions that is not as essential to the communicative exchange, particularly in the context of communicating animated and positive emotion, is often missing in maternal–child exchanges with depressed mothers (Cohn and Tronick, 1989; Field, 1995). Depressive symptoms would not, however, be expected to impact the basic sophistication in the mothers' vocabulary use.

In keeping with earlier research on the mediating role of contextual factors, Malik et al. (2007) used an ecological model to examine the indirect effects of SES and family functioning on maternal depression and child aggression in a multiethnic cross-site study in EHS. They found that maternal depression directly predicted child aggression, but when child aggression was tested as a predictor of either maternal depression or parenting stress, the relationship was mediated by family factors (i.e., parenting stress, partner support). In both models, environmental factors had important contributions to the outcome. In EHSREP there also were clear links between a parent's psychological distress and ineffective parenting in absence of an explicit link to negative sequelae in children (McKelvey et al., 2002).

These findings are consistent with other researchers' observations that mothers experiencing depression are less attuned to their infants, more neglectful or withdrawn, display high levels of irritable or negative mood, show little capacity to module behavior and affect, and talk less with their children during parent–child interactions compared to their non-symptomatic peers (Carter et al., 2001; National Institute of Child Health and Development [NICHD] Child Care Research Network, 2005). A study on spanking in EHS families (Berlin et al., 2009), for instance, noted a significant positive association between maternal depression when children were age 1 and more frequent spanking when children were both age 1 and age 2. Spanking in turn predicted child aggression and cognitive development at age 3.

Another investigation of 105 low-income mother–infant dyads enrolled in EHS (McKelvey et al., 2002) showed that mothers were less able to engage in positive interactions with their infants when they perceived high levels of life stress. The investigators hypothesized that coping would shield children from the effects of stress on mother–infant interaction, but this finding was not significant. The main effect of life stress suggested that mothers who were less stressed were more sensitive to infants' cues, more responsive to their signals of distress, and better able to support their social-emotional development.

Although the impact of parent characteristics and contextual factors on infants' and toddlers' well-being has been the subject of much scientific attention, there is evidence to suggest that the child also has a role in parenting quality. A small number of EHSREP studies highlight this aspect of parenting and child outcomes within the context of an early intervention (Berlin et al., 2009; Raikes et al., 2007).

Influence of child characteristics on child outcomes

EHS research builds on prior evidence of the reciprocity of parent–child relationships (Brazelton, Koslowski, and Maine, 1974; Tronick, 1982) by pointing to the importance of child characteristics to parenting, such as temperament and self-regulation. Berlin and colleagues (2009), for instance, identified a link between child fussiness when children were 1 year of age and an increased likelihood of their parents spanking them at ages 1, 2, and 3. In addition, the follow-up study at grade five (Chazan-Cohen et al., 2007) revealed that children's ability to regulate their behavior had a durable effect on their mothers' depression, such that women whose children had better self-regulatory skills had consistently lower levels of depression. Women who had more demographic risks during pregnancy had consistently higher levels of depression throughout the course of their child's first twelve years of life. These findings were indicative of persistent maternal mental health difficulties; children of depressed mothers in this sample continued to be disregulated, and the extent of their disregulation increased when mothers remained depressed through the first twelve years of the their lives.

Taken together, the findings from Early Head Start on relations between parenting and child outcomes are consistent with an ecological view of human development (Bronfenbrenner, 1979) and parenting determinants (Belsky, 1984), in that they implicate multiple interacting forces in the quality of caregiving children receive and the nature of their development over time. Research conducted from this vantage point has helped to advance the field of early intervention by helping to expand scientific inquiry beyond how parents influence their children to how extrinsic factors (e.g., poverty, social support, early intervention) might help to explain these associations (mediators) and differentiate processes for different groups of families (moderators). This information can be leveraged to help steer families with young children in the right direction. In this way, the results of the EHS impact study suggest avenues for early intervention to improve outcomes for families, even among families experiencing the highest level of personal and environmental risk.

Impacts of Early Head Start for families experiencing parental mental health challenges

Some of the most common parental mental health problems also are the most amenable to treatment. Depression, for example, is one of the most remediable of all mental health conditions (Golden, Hawkins, and Beardslee, 2011). Young children of parents who receive appropriate treatment early on (e.g., during the prenatal period or first few years of a child's life) are far less likely than children of untreated parents to experience adverse consequences during their lifetime, such as developing mental illness themselves (NRC and IOM, 2009; Shonkoff, Boyce, and McEwen, 2009). However, since impaired parenting has been seen in depressed mothers even when symptoms have decreased, the parent's symptom trajectory throughout childhood may be an important factor in ameliorating or preventing adverse effects (Seifer et al., 2001).

An encouraging discovery from the EHSREP was that the rate of mental health services usage was higher for families in which a mother was depressed, although less than one-quarter (23 percent) of EHS families accessed mental health services by the time their children aged out of the program. White families were the most likely to use mental health services (34 percent), followed by Hispanic families (27 percent) and African American families (17 percent). EHS parents who accessed mental health services generally were in greater need, reporting more parental depressive symptoms, family conflict, and child aggression than other families in the intervention group (Vogel et al., 2010). The differences between EHS and the control group families in the level of services they received were smaller when a primary caregiver was at risk for depression. Parental stress and substance use problems were not significantly related to the probability of receiving mental health services (Vogel et al., 2011).

Some research indicates that high-risk groups of parents, such as mothers who have few psychological resources, are particularly likely to benefit from early intervention (e.g., Olds et al., 2004). And yet, a growing literature from evaluation studies suggests that parental depression and related adversities not only limit a parent's ability to provide a child with sensitive and responsive care (Beardslee et al., 2010), but also attenuate early intervention effectiveness (Ammerman et al., 2010; Ayoub et al., 2011; Bartlett, Ayoub, and Beardslee, 2013; Easterbrooks et al., 2012). There are a number of possible explanations for limited program success with depressed families. Caregivers who are depressed may be less able to identify appropriate mental health resources or to accept help than their non-depressed counterparts (Stevens, Ammerman, Putnam, and VanGinkel, 2002). Depressed mothers also may be more likely to endorse parenting beliefs and behaviors that are harmful to their children, such as a belief in physical punishment, that limit a program's ability to promote healthy parenting (Jacobs et al., 2005; Mitchell-Herzfeld et al., 2005). In addition, early intervention staff report having difficulty engaging these parents (Ammerman et al., 2010; Bartlett et al., 2013). Lecroy and Whittaker (2005) interviewed ninety-one home visitors and noted that 78.5 percent of home visitors had encountered a parent with mental illness in the past month; 44 percent felt they were unprepared to work successfully with families suffering from mental illness. EHS staff also report that working with mothers who were depressed was challenging (Love et al., 2002, p. 325). What seems clear is that early childhood interventions continue to struggle to work with these families effectively, whether they lack knowledge, skills, an adequate community network, or other supports.

Program impacts on parental depression

Chazan-Cohen and colleagues (2007) asserted: "Given the environmental contributions to depression, a two-generation supportive intervention aimed at improving both child and parent outcomes might expect to have an impact on reducing depressive symptoms" (p. 153). And yet, given evidence that post-partum depression may extend across several years for a significant number of women, the discovery that EHS did not have a statistically significant impact on maternal or paternal depression upon program completion was not entirely unexpected, since there was no intensive, targeted, evidence-based relational or cognitive behavioral treatment for parents embedded in the program. Furthermore, despite EHS programs' nearly universal efforts to connect families with a range of mental health services in their communities, the program did not have an impact on families' service usage by the time children were age 3 (Love et al., 2002). However, a noteworthy discovery was that children in EHS were buffered from the negative effects of maternal depression. A follow-up EHSREP study in the spring prior to the children entering kindergarten demonstrated a significant positive program impact for reducing maternal depression (Chazan-Cohen et al., 2007). The results showed that earlier program impacts on children and parents – when children were 2 and 3 years of age – mediated, or led to, the delayed impact on maternal depression. One conclusion that may be drawn from these findings is that the universal support system of EHS offers an important milieu for change, but that coordination of these services with targeted parental mental health interventions has the potential to yield more immediate reductions in maternal depression. One example of this positive interface between EHS programing and depression treatment is seen in the work of Linda Beeber (Beeber et al., 2009; Beeber et al., 2010); this research demonstrates a significant and lasting reduction in depression in mothers engaged in time-limited, cognitive-relational treatment embedded in an EHS program.

Understanding adversity and the buffering effects of Early Head Start

Several members of the EHS Research Consortium further assessed findings in their own local samples and expanded our knowledge related to demographic risk, parenting stress, and maternal depression. For example, researchers at Harvard University (Ayoub and Pan, 2002) partnered with Early Education Services in Brattleboro, Vermont, to collect and analyze longitudinal data to supplement national findings and to inform practice at the local level. The results provided a closer look at parenting stress and children's language skills. Findings showed that, over time, parenting stress decreased for families in both the program and comparison groups, with the highest stress typically reported in infancy. By the time their child was 14 months old, families receiving Early Head Start services showed lower levels of parenting stress than comparison families, and these differences were maintained through age 3. For Vermont families, EHS participation reduced parenting stress and assisted parents in feeling more competent as parents. For children, participation in EHS had many benefits, including the development of a larger vocabulary by ages 2 and 3, a critical predictor for later literacy development. Parents were found to be a good source of information about their children's current language skills, an asset that program staff can use in monitoring children's development (Pan et al., 2004).

In another recent study (Ayoub et al., 2011), the interaction between demographic risks, parenting stress (combination of anxiety, isolation, and depression), and mother–child interaction were examined in the context of child language and self-regulatory outcomes with children in EHS and a non-EHS comparison group. The authors used dynamic skill theory to explain the multiple mechanisms and mediating processes influencing development of self-regulatory and language skills in children at 14, 24, and 36 months of age. While children began with the same risks, families in EHS changed in ways that were different from those who did not receive the intervention. For all children, general stress reduced child language and self-regulation skills, but for children in EHS the negative effects of demographic family risks on parenting stress were buffered by involvement in the program. In the face of family demographic risks and stress, EHS protected children's language acquisition from the negative effects of parental insensitivity and supported positive parent–child interactions by bolstering parents' intentional teaching of children in everyday interactions. Ayoub and colleagues concluded that there is a strong need to bolster parents' intentional teaching of their children during everyday interactions in the face of family risks and stress.

Cognitive development: the importance of parental risk, protection, and Early Head Start

Parental mental health and well-being can not only impact the social and emotional development of their young child, but also have a lasting effect on the child's cognitive skills. Another national study (Ayoub et al., 2009) on the same EHS sample examined associations between risk factors and the cognitive performance from 1 to 3 years of age of children living in poverty, and investigated the protective and/or promotive effects of EHS on children's cognitive skill performance. There were four main findings. First, children's cognitive skill scores decreased significantly from 1 to 3 years of age in comparison with national norms. Second, children whose families were on government assistance, children whose mothers had less than a high school education, children who received lower levels of cognitive and language stimulation at home, and children who had higher levels of negative emotionality evidenced more rapid rates of decline. Third, children in families who received government assistance, children whose parents were unemployed, and children whose mothers had less than a high school education had lower cognitive skill scores at 3 years of age. Fourth, children who were enrolled in EHS had higher cognitive skill scores at 3 years of age than their peers who were not in the program.

Implications of these findings for policy may be that intervention and prevention programs that work toward decreasing socioeconomic risk and supporting parent–child interactions and enhancing cognitive and language stimulation in the home may be effective at supporting the cognitive skill development of children in poverty as well as their social-emotional health. In addition, the promotive effect of EHS on children's cognitive skills signals the importance of intervening very early in childhood with all children living in poverty, regardless of additional risks. Early interventions may have the potential to reduce the early achievement gap between children living above and below the poverty line.

The EHS program may serve as one model for targeted interventions for children with special needs. Additional targeted services for different groups of children and their families may be more effective if offered in the larger context of a comprehensive extended two-generational programming effort. Because coordination of services has value above that of the individual service, specialty services embedded in comprehensive early childhood systems hold promise. However, the variation in cognitive skills predicted over time is in significant part predicted by the multiple risks that are present in each family; these risks include distant and unengaged parent–child interactions patterns and emotional negativity in the child. These two mental health/relational issues are important components of a picture of risk. These findings reinforce the need for continuing development of interventions to address multiple co-occurring risk factors, including emotional and parenting issues in early childhood. These findings also have implications for early childhood education. Children enrolled in EHS received early education services including center-based child care and child-based home visits beginning in the first year of life. It is likely that positive effects of EHS participation on children's cognitive skills are attributable in part to these experiences.

Summary of program effects on parenting, parental mental health, and child outcomes

Wide-ranging positive effects of EHS on parenting and child outcomes were detected by the end of the program when children were age 3, and a number of these were evident two years later, prior to kindergarten entry. At age 5, salutogenic effects for children and their families were noted for parenting, parent well-being, and children's social-emotional development. Impacts varied for subgroups; for instance, African American children exhibited the most impacts across domains. The majority of favorable impacts for young children and parents were no longer significant at the fifth grade follow-up, but a positive effect for children's social-emotional development was sustained, and impacts were again found for subgroups of families. Statistically significant effects were found mostly for African American fifth graders, although Hispanic families continued to demonstrate the parental self-sufficiency observed when chidren were 3 and 5. Family participation in home-based programs was associated with positive findings for family well-being and mental health, as well as economic self-sufficiency (Vogel et al., 2010). The results of EHSREP research support the two-generation approach of EHS, offering evidence that the program's attention to parental well-being helps safeguard children from parents' psychological distress and reduces depression, even if effects cannot be seen until after the program ends (Chazan-Cohen et al., 2007). At the same time, it is evident that the program could do more for families at high risk and those with identified mental health problems while they are enrolled.

Conclusions and implications for research, policy, and practice

Parenting has a powerful influence on children's development that surpasses the influence of early care experiences or interventions alone (Belsky et al., 2007; Shonkoff and Phillips, 2000). Viewed from this perspective, evidence that parental mental health and well-being help to shape child outcomes makes intuitive sense (Bartlett et al., 2013). That is, one might expect poor parental functioning to be associated with cognitive, emotional, and behavioral disturbances in children (NRC and IOM, 2009) and, conversely, that healthy nurturing caregiving relationships would support children's movement along adaptive pathways (Shonkoff and Phillips, 2000; National Research Council and Institute of Medicine, 2012). Given both an instinctive and an evidence-based case for linking the well-being of parents to the well-being of their offspring, it follows that improving parenting in the service of raising children who thrive is the "holy grail" of early childhood policy and practice. Similarly, exposing the processes by which parenting quality can be enhanced through early intervention is the fundamental aim of applied developmental research and program evaluation.

Public recognition of the mental health needs of parents and young children remains woefully inadequate to mount an effective campaign to address mental health challenges among families living in poverty. To the extent that research and evaluation in EHS have helped propel these issues into the public discourse, the work makes a valuable contribution to the field. Furthermore, the program's wide-ranging effects on parenting and child outcomes during program enrollment (Love et al., 2005) offer hope that successful early intervention is an attainable goal. The data suggest this may be especially true for families at the most demographic risk (Vogel et al., 2010; Vogel et al., 2011).

Research from neuroscience on the effects of early relationships on the architecture of the human brain leaves little room for interpretation regarding the importance of intervening early to promote healthy parenting as an essential means of helping vulnerable infants and toddlers become happy, productive citizens (Shonkoff and Phillips, 2000; IOM and NRC, 2012). Exactly how programs such as Early Head Start can produce long-term gains for young children and their families is less clear, and the limited measurable impact of EHS in grade five is enough to give us pause. Evaluations of pioneering programs (e.g., Abecedarian Project, Perry Preschool Project) nevertheless indicate that more distal benefits are possible, reducing children's achievement disparities in school and promoting positive development that extends into adulthood (Ludwig and Miller, 2007; Pianta et al., 2009; Reynolds et al., 2001).

The results of EHSREP have led EHS and Head Start (HS) to clarify and increase their focus, targeting families with depression in both EHS and HS programs, instituting system-wide preventive programming around mental health consultation and training, and piloting programs that offer time limited home-based interventions for depression to women with children in EHS. Beeber and colleagues (Beeber et al., 2004; Beeber et al., 2009; Beeber et al., 2010), for example, found that a nurse-delivered short-term in-home psychotherapeutic intervention tailored to the needs of Latina mothers reduced maternal depression in EHS families. Interestingly, Latina mothers derived some of the most essential mental health benefits from parent–provider relationships. Another example of intervention development in response to EHS research findings is Family Connections, a systems-wide preventive mental health consultation and training program aimed at increasing staff's ability to deal with depression and related adversities in their encounters with young children and families. The intervention proves to be both feasible to deliver and successful in increasing staff's capacity to work with families affected by depression (Beardslee et al., 2010).

Federal law states that early intervention must be provided in natural environments (e.g., home, early education settings) and EHS programs are practical places to provide screening and treatment connections for parents with mental health issues. Yet given scarce economic resources and gaps in our current knowledge about how best to help different types of families parent effectively, further specificity is essential for guiding policy and practice. Results from the EHSREP indicate that extending services to young children and families living in poverty by providing intensive, specialized services in natural environments and focusing on families with the greatest number of demographic risk factors may be a good approach, especially when services begin early (e.g., during pregnancy) and are implemented fully (Love et al., 2005; Vogel et al., 2010). However, longitudinal follow-up studies are needed to establish what aspects of programming and specialized services increase the chances of favorable long-term effects for different groups of families with particular constellations of risk factors.

In some ways, the policy implications of findings from EHSREP are quite clear – intervene early, offer flexible and quality programing that can be tailored to the needs of diverse groups of families, and add targeted services for children and families with specific mental health or relational difficulties. To do so will require a workforce that is well trained and culturally competent, as well as program capacity to establish collaborative partnerships within communities to meet the mental health needs of poor families (Zeanah, 2007). This necessitates a considerable investment, and fully funding EHS is an important start – at present, EHS serves only 4 percent of eligible families (Office of Head Start, 2012a).

The Advisory Committee on Head Start Research and Evaluation (ACHSRE, 2012), an assembly of scientists and leading practitioners that developed a science-based vision and recommendations for Head Start, made four recommendations with respect to families' health and mental health: (1) connect and coordinate timely follow-up services for all children, (2) utilize evidence-based practices emphasizing collaboration with the health professionals in the community, (3) clarify how programs meet different health, nutrition, and mental health requirements, linking these approaches to educational, health and mental health outcomes, and using this information to develop tools for programs to use in formative evaluation, and (4) increase collaboration among all HS stakeholders to leverage local resources and improve consistency of messages and services for local HS programs (ACHSRE, 2012, p. 82). We concur with the Committee's recommendations and additionally assert that parental mental health should be front and center upon implementing such a plan. Findings across both the national and the local samples from EHSREP highlight the need to more fully address the toll parental difficulties take on child well-being within the context of early intervention policy and programs.

In addition, an ever-growing body of knowledge related to mental health consultation in early care settings has been pioneered through Early Head Start and Head Start programs (Cohen and Kaufman, 2005; Hunter and Hemmeter, 2009) and the professional standards for professionals working with families in HS/EHS have been revised with attention to professionalizing this workforce (OHS, 2012b). Both of these practice activities illustrate the increased attention raised in part from the EHS research on parenting and depression. The harmful effects of depression and other mental health challenges may be buffered by EHS, but programs will need more comprehensive strategies to make a difference in the lives of families experiencing mental health problems. Policies that support systems-wide integration of screening, mental health consultation, reflective practice and supervision, and the establishment of community partnerships (ACF, 2008; Bartlett et al., 2013; Fenichel, 1992; Parlakian, 2001), as well as targeted initiatives aimed at reducing depression and related adversities in families of infants and toddlers, will be critical to their success.

Researchers also have an important role to play in generating the scientific evidence base to promote families' mental health. The Early

Promotion and Intervention Consortium (E-PIRC) was formed recently to develop and test approaches to support the mental health of infants and toddlers and their families in Early Head Start (Beeber et al., 2007). Their joint work resulted in the publication of research materials that extended evidence-based practice (Beeber et al., 2004; Beeber et al., 2009; Beeber et al., 2010) as well as practice-based guidance for implementation of mental health practice in HS/EHS programs (Summers and Chazan-Cohen, 2011; Malik et al., 2007). Continued partnerships between research and intervention evaluation and practice programming are critical to the continued development and improvement of systems of care for families with young children. If nothing else, research on Early Head Start has shown us that every person in a young child's life, regardless of personal or professional role, has an important part to play in supporting parental mental health with the ultimate goal of promoting lifelong resilience in children.

References

Administration for Children and Families (2006a). *Research to practice: depression in the lives of Head Start families*. Washington, DC: US Department of Health and Human Services, Administration for Children and Families.

    (2006b). *Research to practice: program models in Early Head Start*. Washington, DC: US Department of Health and Human Services, Administration for Children and Families.

    (2008). *Research to practice: lessons learned from interventions to address infant mental health in Early Head Start*. Washington, DC: US Department of Health and Human Services, Administration for Children and Families.

Advisory Committee on Head Start Research and Evaluation (2012). *Advisory Committee on Head Start Research and Evaluation: final report*. Washington, DC: US Department of Health & Human Services.

Advisory Committee on Services for Families with Infants and Toddlers (1994). *The statement of the Advisory Committee on Services for Families with Infants and Toddlers*. Washington, DC: US Department of Health and Human Services.

Ainsworth, M. D. S. (1973). The development of infant–mother attachment. In B. Cardwell and H. Ricciuti (eds.), *Review of child development research* (vol. 3, pp. 1–94). University of Chicago Press.

Ammerman, R. T., Putnam, F. W., Bosse, N. R., Teeters, A. R., and Van Ginkel, J. B. (2010). Maternal depression in home visitation. *Aggression and Violent Behavior*, 15(3), 191–200.

Ayoub, C., O'Connor, E., Rappolt-Schlichtmann, G., Raikes, H., Chazan-Cohen, R., and Vallotton, C. (2009). Losing ground early: protection, risk and change in poor children's cognitive performance. *Early Childhood Research Quarterly*, 24, 289–305.

Ayoub, C., and Pan, B. A. (2002). Early Head Start impacts on parental stress and harsh parenting attitudes among rural families. In *Making a difference in the lives of infants and toddlers and their families: the impacts of early Head Start.*

Volume III: Local contributions to understanding the programs and their impacts. Final report (pp. 15–22). Washington, DC: US Department of Health and Human Services.

Ayoub, C., Vallotton, C., and Mastergeorge, A. (2011). Developmental pathways to integrated social skills: the roles of parenting and early intervention in raising healthy children. *Child Development*, 82(2), 583–600.

Bartlett, J. D., Ayoub, C., and Beardslee, W. (2013). *Family well-being and parental depression*. Boston, MA: Office of Head Start National Center on Parent, Family, and Community Engagement, Boston Children's Hospital.

Beardslee, W., Avery, M., Ayoub, C., and Watts, C. (2009). Family connections: helping Early Head Start/Head Start staff and parents make sense of mental health challenges. *Journal of Zero to Three*, 29(6), 34–43.

Beardslee, W. R., Ayoub, C. A., Avery, M. W., Watts, C. L., and O'Carroll, K. L. (2010). Family connections: an approach for strengthening early care systems facing depression and adversity. *American Journal of Orthopsychiatry*, 80(4), 482–495.

Beeber, L., Chazan-Cohen, R., Squires, J., Harden, B. J., Boris, N. W., Heller, S. S., and Malik, N. M. (2007). The early promotion and intervention research consortium E-PIRC: five approaches to improving infant/toddler mental health in Early Head Start. *Infant Mental Health Journal*, 28(2), 130–150.

Beeber, L. S., Holditch-Davis, D., Belyea, M. J., Funk, S. G., and Canuso, R. (2004). In-home intervention for depressive symptoms with low-income mothers of infants and toddlers in the United States. *Health Care for Women International*, 25(6), 561–580.

Beeber, L. S., Holditch-Davis, D., Perreira, K., Schwartz, T. A., Lewis, V., Blanchard, H., . . . and Goldman, B. D. (2010). Short-term in-home intervention reduces depressive symptoms in Early Head Start Latina mothers of infants and toddlers. *Research in Nursing and Health*, 33(1), 60–76.

Beeber, L. S., Lewis, V. S., Cooper, C., Maxwell, L., and Sandelowski, M. (2009). Meeting the "now" need: PMH-APRN interpreter teams provide in-home mental health intervention for depressed Latina mothers with limited English proficiency. *Journal of the American Psychiatric Nurses Association*, 15(4), 249–259.

Belsky, J. (1984). The determinants of parenting: a process model. *Child Development*, 55, 83–96.

Belsky, J., Vandell, D., Burchinal, M., Clarke-Stewart, K. A., McCartney, K., and Owen, M. NICHD Early Child Care Research Network (2007). Are there long-term effects of early child care? *Child Development*, 78, 681–701.

Berlin, L. J., Ispa, J. M., Fine, M. A., Malone, M. S., Brooks-Gunn, J., Christy Brady-Smith, . . . and Bai, Y. (2009). Correlates and consequences of spanking and verbal punishment for low-income White, African American, and Mexican American toddlers. *Child Development*, 80(5), 1403–1420.

Bowlby, J. (1969). *Attachment and loss*, vol. 1: *Attachment*. New York: Basic Books.

Brazelton, T. B., Koslowski, B., and Maine, M. (1974). The origin of reciprocity: the early mother–infant interaction. In M. Lewis and L. Rosenblum (eds.), *The effect of the infant on its caregiver* (pp. 49–76). New York: Wiley.

Bronfenbrenner, U. (1979). *Ecology of human development.* Cambridge, MA: Harvard University Press.

Brooks-Gunn, J., Berlin, L. J., and Fuligni, A. S. (2000). Early childhood intervention programs: what about the family? In J. P. Shonkoff and S. J. Meisels (eds.), *Handbook on early childhood intervention* (pp. 549–588). Cambridge University Press.

Brooks-Gunn, J., and Markman, L. (2005). The contribution of parenting to ethnic and racial gaps in school readiness. *Future of Children,* 15(1), 138–167.

Bureau, J. F., Easterbrooks, M. A., and Lyons-Ruth, K. (2009). Maternal depression in infancy: critical to children's depression in childhood and adolescence? *Development and Psychopathology,* 21(2), 519–537.

Carnegie Corporation of New York (1994). *Starting points: meeting the needs of our youngest children.* New York: Carnegie Corporation.

Carter, A. S., Garrity-Rokous, F. E., Chazan-Cohen, R., Little, C., and Briggs-Gowan, M. J. (2001). Maternal depression and comorbidity: predicting early parenting, attachment security, and toddler social-emotional problems and competencies. *Journal of the American Academy of Child and Adolescent Psychiatry,* 40(1), 18–26.

Chazan-Cohen, R., Ayoub, C., Pan, B. A., Roggman, L., Raikes, H., McKelvey, L., and Hart, A. (2007). It takes time: impacts of Early Head Start that lead to reductions in maternal depression two years later. *Infant Mental Health Journal,* 28(2), 151–170.

Cicchetti, D., Rogosch, F. A., and Toth, S. L. (1998). Maternal depressive disorder and contextual risk: contributions to the development of attachment insecurity and behavior problems in toddlerhood. *Development and Psychopathology,* 10, 283–300.

Cohen, E., and Kaufmann, R. (2005). *Early childhood mental health consultation.* Rockville, MD: Center for Mental Health Services, Substance Abuse and Mental Health Services Administration.

Cohn, J. F., and Tronick, E. Z. (1989). Specificity of infants' response to mothers' affective behavior. *Journal of the American Academy of Child and Adolescent Psychiatry,* 28, 242–248.

Cummings, E. M., Keller, P. S., and Davies, P. T. (2005). Towards a family process model of maternal and paternal depressive symptoms: exploring multiple relations with child and family functioning. *Journal of Child Psychology and Psychiatry,* 46(5), 479–489.

Dawson, G., Ashman, S. B., Panagiotides, H., Hessel, D., Self, J., Yamada, E., and Embry, L. (2003). Preschool outcomes of children of depressed mothers: role of maternal behavior, contextual risk, and children's brain activity. *Child Development,* 74(4), 1158–1175.

Easterbrooks, M. A., Jacobs, F. H., Bartlett, J. D., Goldberg, J., Contreras, M. M., Kotake, C., ... and Chaudhuri, J. H. (2012). *Initial findings from a randomized, controlled trial of Healthy Families Massachusetts: early program impacts on young mothers' parenting.* Washington, DC: Pew Charitable Trusts.

Fenichel, E. (1992). *Learning through supervision and mentorship to support the development of infants, toddlers, and their families.* Washington, DC: Zero to Three.

Field, T. (1995). Infants of depressed mothers. *Infant Behavior and Development*, 18, 1–13.

Fryers, T., Melzer, D., and Jenkins, R. (2003). Social inequalities and the common mental disorders: a systematic review of the evidence. *Social Psychiatry & Psychiatric Epidemiology*, 38, 229–237.

Golden, O., Hawkins, A., and Beardslee, W. (2011). *Home visiting and maternal depression: seizing the opportunities to help mothers and young children.* Washington, DC: The Urban Institute.

Howard, K. S., and Brooks-Gunn, J. (2009). The role of home-visiting programs in preventing child abuse and neglect. *Future of Children*, 19(2), 119–146.

Hunter, A., and Hemmeter, M. L. (2009). Addressing challenging behavior in infants and toddlers. *Zero to Three*, 29(3), 5–12.

Jacobs, F., Easterbrooks, M. A., Brady, A., and Mistry, J. (2005). *Healthy Families Massachusetts: final report.* Massachusetts Healthy Families Evaluation, Tufts University.

Knitzer, J. (2001). Caring for infants and toddlers: federal and state efforts to improve care for infants and toddlers. *Future of Children*, 11, 79–97.

Lanzi, R. G., Pascoe, J. M., Keltner, B., and Ramey, S. L. (1999). Correlates of maternal depressive symptoms in a national Head Start program sample. *Archives of Pediatrics & Adolescent Medicine*, 153(8), 801–807.

Lecroy, C. W., and Whitaker, K. (2005). Improving the quality of home visitation: an exploratory study of difficult situations. *Child Abuse & Neglect*, 29, 1003–1013.

Loeb, S., Fuller, B., Kagan, S. L., and Carrol, B. (2004). Child care in poor communities: early learning effects of type, quality, and stability. *Child Development*, 75(1), 47–65.

Lorant, V., Croux, C., Weich, S., Deliege, D., Mackenbach, J., and Ansseau, M. (2007). Depression and socioeconomic risk factors: 7-year longitudinal population study. *British Journal of Psychiatry*, 190, 293–298.

Love, J. M., Kisker, E. E., Ross, C., Raikes, H., Constantine, J., Boller, K., . . . and Vogel, C. (2005). The effectiveness of Early Head Start for 3-year-old children and their parents: lessons for policy and programs. *Developmental Psychology*, 41(6), 885–901.

Love, J. M., Kisker, E. E., Ross, C. M., Schochet, P. Z., Brooks-Gunn, J., Paulsell, D., . . . and Brady-Smith, C. (2002). *Making a difference in the lives of infants and toddlers and their families: the impacts of early Head Start*, vols. I–III: *Final technical report and appendixes and local contributions to understanding the programs and their impacts.* Washington, DC: Office of Planning, Research and Evaluation, US Department of Health and Human Services, Administration for Children and Families.

Ludwig, J., and Miller, D. L. (2007). Does Head Start improve children's life chances? Evidence from a regression-discontinuity design. *Quarterly Journal of Economics*, 122(1), 159–208.

Malik, N. M., Boris, N. W., Heller, S. S., Harden, B. J., Squires, J., Chazan-Cohen, R., . . . and Kaczynski, K. J. (2007). Risk for maternal depression and child aggression in Early Head Start families: a test of ecological models. *Infant Mental Health Journal*, 28(2), 171–191.

McKelvey, L. M., Fitzgerald, H. E., Schiffman, R. F., and von Eye, A. (2002). Family stress and parent–infant interaction: the mediating role of coping. *Infant Mental Health Journal*, 23, 164–181.

Mitchell-Herzfeld, S., Izzo, C., Greene, R., Lee, E., and Lowenfels, A. (2005). *Evaluation of Healthy Families New York (HFNY): first year program impacts.* Rensselaer, NY: New York State Office of Children and Family Services.

Murray, L., Cooper, P., and Hipwell, A. (2003). Mental health of parents caring for infants. *Archives of Women's Mental Health*, 6, 71–77.

National Institute of Child Health and Development [NICHD] Early Child Care Research Network (2005). *Child care and child development.* New York: Guilford.

National Research Council and Institute of Medicine [NRC and IOM] (2009). *Depression in parents, parenting and children: opportunities to improve identification, treatment, and prevention efforts.* Washington, DC: National Academies Press.

National Research Council. (2012). *From neurons to neighborhoods: an update. Workshop summary.* Washington, DC: National Academies Press.

National Scientific Council on the Developing Child (2005). *Excessive stress disrupts the architecture of the developing brain.* Working Paper 3. Retrieved January 3, 2013 from www.developingchild.net.

Office of Head Start (2012a). *Early Head Start program facts: Fiscal Year 2011.* Washington, DC: US Department of Health & Human Services, Administration for Children & Families. Retrieved January 23, 2013 from www.ehsnrc.org/PDFfiles/ehsprogfactsheet.pdf.

(2012b). *Head Start and Early Head Start relationship-based competencies for staff and supervisors who work with families.* Washington, DC: US Department of Health & Human Services, Administration for Children & Families. Retrieved January 23, 2013 from www.eclkc.ohs.acf.hhs.gov/hslc/tta-sys tem/family/FamilyandCommunityPartnerships/FamilyServices/ ProfessionalDevelopment/ohs-rbc.pdf.

Olds, D. L., Robinson, J., Pettitt, L., Luckey, D. W., Holmberg, J., Ng, R. K., . . . and Sheff, K. (2004). Effects of home visits by paraprofessionals and by nurses: age-four follow-up of a randomized trial. *Pediatrics*, 114, 1560–1568.

Pan, B., Rowe, M., Spier, E., and Tamis-LeMonda, C. S. (2004). Measuring productive vocabulary of toddlers in low-income families: concurrent and predictive validity of three sources of data. *Journal of Child Language*, 31(3), 587–608.

Parlakian, R. (2001). *The power of questions: building quality relationships with families.* Washington, DC: Zero to Three Press.

Pianta, R. C., Barnett, W. S., Burchinal, M., and Thornburg, K. R. (2009). The effects of preschool education: what we know, how public policy is or is not aligned with the evidence base, and what we need to know. *Psychological Science in the Public Interest*, 10, 49–88.

Raikes, A., Robinson, J., Bradley, R., Raikes, H., and Ayoub, C. (2007). Developmental trends in self-regulation among low income toddlers. *Social Development*, 16(1), 128–149.

Reynolds, A. J., Temple, J. A., Robertson, D. L., and Mann, E. A. (2001). Long-term effects of an early childhood intervention on educational achievement and juvenile arrest: a 15-year follow-up of low-income children in public schools. *Journal of the American Medical Association*, 285, 2339–2346.

Rowe, M., Pan, B., and Ayoub, C. (2005). Predictors of variation in maternal talk to children: a longitudinal study of low-income families. *Parenting: Science & Practice*, 5(3), 285–310.

Sareen, J., Afifi, T. O., McMillan, K. A., and Asmundson, G. J. G. (2011). Relationship between household income and mental disorders: findings from a population-based longitudinal study. *Archives of General Psychiatry*, 68(4), 419–427.

Seifer, R., Dickstein, S., Sameroff, A. J., Magee, K. D., and Hayden, L. C. (2001). Infant mental health and variability of parental depression symptoms. *Journal of the American Academy of Child and Adolescent Psychiatry*, 40, 1375–1382.

Shonkoff, J. P., Boyce, W. T., and McEwen, B. S. (2009). Neuroscience, molecular biology, and the childhood roots of health disparities: building a new framework for health promotion and disease prevention. *Journal of the American Medical Association*, 301(21), 2252–2259.

Shonkoff, J., and Phillips, D. A. (2000). *From neurons to neighborhoods: the science of early childhood development.* Washington, DC: National Academies Press.

Stevens, J., Ammerman, R., Putnam, F., and VanGinkel, J. (2002). Depression and trauma history in first-time mothers receiving home visitation. *Journal of Community Psychology*, 30, 551–564.

Summers, S. J., and Chazan-Cohen, R. (eds.) (2011). Understanding early childhood mental health: a practical guide for professionals. Baltimore, MD: Brookes.

Tronick, E. (1982). *Social interchange in infancy: affect, cognition, and communication.* Baltimore, MD: University Park Press.

Vogel, C. A., Boller, K., Yange, Y., Blair, R., Aikens, N., Burwick, A., ... and Stein, J. (2011). *Learning as we go: a first snapshot of Early Head Start programs, staff, families, and children.* Washington, DC: Office of Planning, Research, and Evaluation, Administration for Children and Families, US Department of Health and Human Services.

Vogel, C. A., Xue, Y., Moiduddin, E. M., Kisker, E. E., and Carlson, B. L. (2010). *Early Head Start children in grade 5: long-term follow-up of the Early Head Start Research and Evaluation Study sample.* Washington, DC: Office of Planning, Research, and Evaluation, Administration for Children and Families, US Department of Health and Human Services.

Young, A. S., Klap, R., Sherbourne, C., and Wells, K. (2001). The quality of care for depressive and anxiety disorders in the United States. *Archives of General Psychiatry*, 58(1), 55–61.

Zeanah, C. H. (2007). Infant mental health and Early Head Start: the glass is half full. *Infant Mental Health Journal*, 28(2), 252–254.

10 Health outcomes of the Abecedarian, Child–Parent Center, and HighScope Perry Preschool programs

Michelle M. Englund, Barry White, Arthur J. Reynolds, Lawrence J. Schweinhart, and Frances A. Campbell

Researchers examining data from three longitudinal studies of high-quality preschool programs provided to preschoolers from low-income families – the Carolina Abecedarian Project, the Chicago Child–Parent Centers, and the HighScope Perry Preschool Program – have identified positive long-term effects of early educational interventions on adult outcomes including education attainment, criminal behavior, and economic well-being (e.g., Campbell et al., 2002; Campbell et al., 2012; Reynolds and Ou, 2011; Reynolds et al., 2001; Schweinhart, Barnes, and Weikart, 1993; Schweinhart et al., 2005). Furthermore, cost-benefit analyses of these early childhood education programs have documented the existence of social benefits that far exceed the costs of the interventions (Barnett and Masse, 2007; Heckman et al., 2010; Reynolds et al., 2011; Schweinhart et al., 2005). The current chapter extends this previous research by investigating the effects of early childhood education on adult health using data from all three of these longitudinal studies.

Prior research indicates a link between socioeconomic status (SES), education, and health (see, for example, Cutler and Lleras-Muney, 2012; Molla, Madans, and Wagener, 2004; Topitzes et al., 2009; Turrell et al., 2007). More specifically, higher SES and educational attainment are associated with better health outcomes in adulthood and investigators have confirmed the lifelong health consequences of early disadvantage (Luo and Waite, 2005; Melchior et al., 2007; Pascall, Flewelling, and Faulkner, 2000; Topitzes et al., 2009). Furthermore, research on the effects of early intervention suggests that participation in a high-quality preschool program is associated with higher educational attainment among individuals from low-income families (Campbell et al., 2002; Campbell et al., 2012; Consortium for Longitudinal Studies, 1983; Currie and Thomas, 2000; Garces, Thomas, and Currie, 2002; Reynolds et al., 2001; Reynolds et al., 2010; Schweinhart et al., 1993; Schweinhart et al., 2005). Additionally, some studies have found a positive direct effect of preschool participation on specific health outcomes in early adulthood (Anderson, Foster, and Frisvold, 2010; Muennig et al., 2011; Reynolds et al., 2007; Topitzes et al., 2009). Other evidence suggests, however, that the influence of preschool involvement on health and health compromising behaviors in early adulthood is not direct, but, rather, that preschool involvement affects health outcomes via its influence on intervening educational factors, including educational attainment (D'Onise et al., 2010; Muennig et al., 2009).

Research examining the effects of education on health outcomes, however, is not as well defined, with outcomes as well as effects varying across studies, and few studies systematically examining intervening educational variables (Braveman, 2011; Matthews and Gallo, 2011). In order to gain a more thorough understanding of the impact of education on adult health outcomes, a multi-study analysis is needed, examining the influence of not only preschool involvement and educational attainment on health outcomes in adulthood but also intervening educational factors. The current study uses longitudinal data from three preschool intervention programs conducted at different points in time and in different locations and examines similar factors across interventions and time. Specifically, we investigate the effect of participation in a high-quality preschool program, school-age educational factors, and educational attainment at age 21 on health and health compromising behaviors in adulthood. This inquiry provides an exploration of whether involvement in a high-quality preschool program directly affects health and health behaviors in adulthood or whether it "sets the stage" for a lower likelihood of engaging in health compromising behaviors with other intervening educational factors directly influencing later health behaviors.

Low SES and health outcomes

The association between low SES and health problems has long been noted by researchers (Braveman, 2011; Matthews and Gallo, 2011). Morbidity rates for many diseases and other health problems, including stroke (Heeley et al., 2011; Kerr et al., 2011), cardiovascular disease (Clark et al., 2009), heart failure (Hawkins et al., 2012), and chronic obstructive pulmonary disease (COPD; Gershon et al., 2012), increase with a decrease in SES. Furthermore, accumulating evidence indicates that disparities in health between low-income and higher-income individuals are evident as early as adolescence (Frytak, Harley, and Finch, 2003). It is possible that health disparities among SES levels are at least partially due to higher levels of engagement in health compromising behaviors by low-income individuals. For example, smoking is more prevalent among lower-income individuals (Barkley, 2008; Hiscock et al., 2012), and a recent meta-analysis (Lemstra et al., 2008) revealed higher rates of use for both marijuana and alcohol among low SES adolescents compared to higher SES youth.

In addition to a concurrent association between SES and health, low SES in childhood is also a risk factor for poor health in adulthood (Braveman, 2011; Brisbois, Farmer, and McCargar, 2012; Galobardes, Lynch, and Smith, 2004; Matthews and Gallo, 2011; Tamayo, Christian, and Rathmann, 2010). These results have been found consistently in both retrospective and prospective investigations, even after accounting for the influence of adult SES (Galobardes et al., 2004; Melchior et al., 2007; Poulton et al., 2002). What have not been clearly identified, however, are the mechanisms by which childhood socioeconomic circumstances influence adult health (Braveman, 2011; Matthews and Gallo, 2011; Melchior et al., 2007).

Education and health

Education, and especially educational attainment, may provide a key to potential mechanisms by which childhood SES influences adult health. Educational attainment is linked to both SES and health; economically disadvantaged young people are more likely to have lower educational attainment than individuals from higher-income families (Day and Newburger, 2002; Iceland, 2000; Ross et al., 2012), and individuals with lower levels of educational attainment are more likely to have poorer health (Cutler and Lleras-Muney, 2012). Lower levels of educational attainment are associated with malnutrition in poor countries and obesity in wealthier countries (Cutler and Lleras-Muney, 2012). Additionally, educational attainment has been found to be inversely related to a number of health outcomes, including depression, diabetes mellitus, hypertension, stroke, and premature death (Baker, Leon, Smith Greenaway, Collins, and Movit, 2011; Cutler and Lleras-Muney, 2012; Kautzky-Willer et al., 2012; Lee, 2011; Ma et al., 2012; Non, Gravlee, and Mulligan, 2012). Furthermore, educational attainment is negatively associated with health compromising behaviors; individuals with lower levels of education are more likely to smoke and engage in heavy drinking in both the US and the UK compared to their counterparts with higher levels of education (Cutler and Lleras-Muney, 2012).

Recently researchers have uncovered an association between preschool participation and desirable health outcomes in adulthood. For instance, Muennig and colleagues (2011) examining data from the Carolina Abecedarian Project, a randomized control trial of a preschool intervention program, found a direct effect for preschool education and health outcomes such that the preschool intervention group had significantly better overall health and engaged in lower levels of health compromising behaviors at 21 years compared to the control group. Furthermore, an investigation using data from the Panel Study of Income Dynamics (Anderson et al., 2009) found that the risk of cigarette smoking in adulthood was significantly lower among Head Start participants compared to their siblings. Aside from these noteworthy studies, however, there is limited evidence of a direct effect from preschool participation to health outcomes in adulthood (D'Onise et al., 2010). Results from these studies raise the question of how preschool participation affects adult health.

Numerous studies (Campbell et al., 2002; Consortium for Longitudinal Studies, 1983; Currie and Thomas, 2000; Garces et al., 2002; Reynolds et al., 2001; Reynolds et al., 2010; Schweinhart et al., 1993; Schweinhart et al., 2005) have found that preschool education leads to higher levels of educational attainment in early adulthood; so it may be that preschool involvement affects later health outcomes through its effects on intervening educational factors, including educational attainment. This is supported by results from the Chicago Longitudinal Study, a quasi-experimental study of the Chicago Child–Parent Centers, indicating that involvement in this preschool intervention program significantly increased high school completion by 21 years, which, in turn, led to significantly lower rates of tobacco and substance use, and lower depression scores (Topitzes et al., 2009). Additional results from the HighScope Perry Preschool Program suggest that preschool participation increased educational attainment levels which then were related to a decrease in overall substance use in adulthood (Muennig et al., 2009). Few studies, however, have examined preschool involvement, educational attainment in early adulthood, and intervening educational factors that may contribute to the relationship between preschool education and health outcomes in adults who experienced economic disadvantages as children.

Present study

The current study begins to fill this gap in the research literature by examining data from three preschool intervention programs that have studied low SES participants from program entry to adulthood: the Carolina Abecedarian Project (ABC), the Chicago Child–Parent Centers (CPC), and the HighScope Perry Preschool Program (PPP). Our study addressed the following questions:

1. Does involvement in a high-quality preschool program and later educational attainment decrease the likelihood of low SES participants

engaging in health compromising behaviors and having poor health in adulthood?
2. Do intervening educational factors add to the prediction of health outcomes in early adulthood?
3. Can we identify common predictors of health outcomes in early adulthood across the three studies?

We chose to examine the ABC, CPC, and PPP studies for a number of reasons. First, all three studies are longitudinal investigations of high-quality preschool intervention programs provided to low-income participants and include both an intervention group and a comparison control group. Second, the three studies could be matched on not only preschool intervention, but also outcome and intervening variables at similar points in time. Third, the studies vary in scale, geographic location, and decade of preschool delivery, as well as intervention curriculum and services, providing an opportunity for greater generalizability of similar findings.

METHODS

Program and sample descriptions

All three of the programs provided high-quality early childhood education to at-risk children. The programs, however, were conducted in different areas of the United States and samples were obtained during different decades.

The Abecedarian Project (ABC; Ramey, Campbell, and Blair, 1998; Ramey et al., 2000) provided an early childhood intervention beginning at 6 weeks of age and continuing through preschool age (5 years, full-time, year round) from 1972 to 1977 at the Frank Porter Graham Child Development Center at the University of North Carolina-Chapel Hill. The children came from low SES homes, and nearly all were African American (98 percent). The study included 111 families; 57 children were randomly assigned to the intervention group (average age at entry was 8.7 weeks) and 54 children were in the control group. The program was intended to promote optimal child development and emphasized language and social development; medical and nutritional services were also provided. The control group families had community access to low-cost medical services and received iron-fortified formula for the first 15 months to control for possible deficits in very early nutrition. For the infant portion of the program, the child:staff ratio was 3 to 1, in year 2 and 3 it was 3.5 to 1, and during preschool it was 6 to 1.

The Child–Parent Center program (CPC; Reynolds, 2000; Reynolds et al., 2001) is a federally funded preschool program for 3 and 4 year olds offered in Chicago public schools; the program impact study, the Chicago Longitudinal Study (CLS), included the cohort of children who began attending preschool at age 3 in 1983–84 or age 4 in 1984–85. The intervention group of the CLS consisted of all children who attended the preschool program and completed kindergarten in the spring of 1986 (N = 989), and 550 children who attended all-day kindergarten programs for children at risk were the control group. All children in the study were from low-income families, 93 percent of the children were African American and 7 percent were Hispanic. The CPC program, offered in twenty-four centers in Chicago at the time of the study, provided comprehensive family-support and educational services to children and their families; the curriculum emphasized language and social development. The child:staff ratio was 8.5 to 1.

The Perry Preschool Program (PPP; Schweinhart et al., 1993) served 3- and 4-year-old children in Ypsilanti, Michigan. All of the children were African American, had IQs in the 70–85 range, and were from low-income families. Five consecutive cohorts from 1962–67 were included in the impact study for a total of 123 participants, 58 of whom were randomly assigned to the intervention group, and 65 of whom stayed at home and served as controls. The PPP followed the HighScope curriculum model, which has a Piagetian cognitive focus and is based on child-initiated learning. Classes were half-day, five days per week, and averaged 22 children per classroom, yielding a child-staff ratio of 5.7 to 1.

Measures

A comparison of the measures used in this study across the three programs is presented in Table 10.1. Frequencies of each measure investigated are provided in Table 10.2. Outcome, covariate, and predictor variables were chosen in order to correspond across the three studies in terms of the constructs examined and the age range of measurement.

Predictor measures

Preschool participation
Whether or not participants attended the preschool program offered by each of the three programs was coded as 0 = control group, 1 = preschool group.

Cognitive advantage
Three different measures of cognitive advantage were included in the analyses: IQ/achievement at kindergarten entry, reading achievement at

Table 10.1 *Comparison measures for three preschool programs.*

Construct	Variable	Abecedarian	Chicago Child–Parent Centers	Perry Preschool
PREDICTORS:				
Preschool participation	**Preschool program enrollment**	Educational day care vs. none; control group in home care but received some well-baby care services	Preschool vs. no preschool; 15% of controls enrolled in Head Start and 100% in full-day K (60% for CPC)	Preschool vs. no preschool; control group in home care
Cognitive advantage	**IQ/achievement (kindergarten/5 years)**	WPPSI IQ (60 mos.); standard score	ITBS cognitive composite (kindergarten entry); standard-score	Stanford-Binet (5 years); standard score
	Reading achievement (14/15 yrs)	Woodcock-Johnson Reading (age 15; ninth or eighth grade)	Iowa Test of Basic Skills Reading Comprehension (age 14; eighth or seventh grade)	California Achievement Tests Reading (age 14; eighth or seventh grade)
	Ever retained or in special education	Through age 15	Through age 15	Through age 15
Social adjustment	**Elementary Social Adjustment (teacher rated)**	CBI: Social Adjustment 1–2 averaged	SEMAT (socio-emotional Maturity) 1–3 averaged	Public Behavior Inventory: socio-emotional adjustment 1–3 averaged
	Adolescent social Adjustment: delinquent behavior–juvenile	Arrested prior to age 19	Any juvenile petition or self-report arrest (arrested prior to age 18)	Any arrest as juvenile (arrested prior to age 19)
Family support	**Parental involvement with school/education**	HOME (8 years) parental involvement second grade	Parent involvement with school (teacher rating) 1–3 averaged	Mother's participation with school (teacher rating–Ypsilanti Rating Scale) 1–3 averaged
Motivation	**Elementary motivation (teacher rated)**	CBI: motivation K/1 averaged	Motivation K/1 averaged	Public Behavior Inventory: Academic Motivation (teacher ratings) K/1 averaged

Table 10.1 (cont.)

Construct	Variable	Abecedarian	Chicago Child–Parent Centers	Perry Preschool
School support	**School mobility**		# of different schools fourth grade through eighth grade	# of different schools through eighth grade
	School quality		attended magnet school (grades 4–8) or 40% + above grade level in reading in fifth grade	Ypsilanti vs. non-Ypsilanti School (age 14)
Educational Attainment	Last grade completed (21 years)	21 years	21 years	21 years
OUTCOMES: Health compromising behaviors	Frequent/heavy drug use	30 years	16–26 years	by age 27 years
	Daily/regular tobacco use	30 years	22–24 years	27 years
	Frequent/heavy alcohol use	30 years	22–24 years	27 years
	Two or more indicators of health compromising behavior	30 years	22–24 years	27 years
Mental health	Depressive symptoms	30 years	22–24 years	na
COVARIATES:	**Gender** (1 = girls)	Gender	Gender	Gender
	Father present in home	Father in home (birth)	Single parent (study entry)	Father in home (study entry – 3 years)
	Mother's education – graduated from high school or not	(birth)	(birth or study entry)	(study entry – 3 years)

Table 10.2 *Frequencies.*

Measure	Valid	Range	Mean	S.D.	Frequency
PREDICTORS:					
Preschool					
Preschool participation					
Abecedarian	104	0/1			No preschool = 51 Preschool = 53
Child–Parent Centers	1531	0/1			No preschool = 543 Preschool = 988
Perry Preschool	123	0/1			No preschool = 65 Preschool = 58
Cognitive advantage					
IQ/achievement (5 years)					
Abecedarian (WPPSI)	97	71–125	97.49	12.70	
Child–Parent Centers (SSREADY imputed)	1531	28–83	47.39	8.79	
Perry Preschool (Stanford-Binet)	121	60–134	88.31	12.26	
Reading achievement eighth Grade/age 14					
Abecedarian (Woodcock Johnson Standard Score)	104	69–113	91.53	10.40	
Child–Parent Centers (SS Reading Comprehension)	1344	77–212	144.72	21.76	
Perry Preschool (CAT)	95	10–59	28.73	11.40	
Either special ed. or retained by eighth grade/age 14					
Abecedarian	102	0/1			No = 42 Either special ed or retained = 60
Child–Parent Centers	1531	0/1			No = 1029 Either special ed or retained = 502
Perry Preschool	112	0/1			No = 42 Either special ed or retained = 70

Table 10.2 (cont.)

Measure	Valid	Range	Mean	S.D.	Frequency
Social adjustment					
Elementary school social adjustment					
Abecedarian (Social Adjustment scale derived from the CBI, average grades 1–2)	91	16.00–31.75	24.30	2.68	
Child–Parent Centers (Social Emotional Maturity [SEMAT], average grades 1–3 new variable 2–4–05)	1430	7–30	19.12	4.82	
Perry Preschool (PBI socio-emotional adjustment, average grades 1–3)	116	1.25–5.00	3.55	.75	
Adolescent social adjustment: juvenile arrests					
Abecedarian (arrested or not by age 19)	103	0/1			Not arrested = 68 Ever arrested = 35
Child–Parent Centers (arrested or not by age 18)	1404	0/1			Not arrested = 1112 Ever arrested = 292
Perry Preschool (arrested or not as a teenager–juvenile arrests)	121	0/1			Not arrested = 96 Ever arrested = 25
Family support					
Parent involvement					
Abecedarian (derived from the HOME Stimulation Scale 8 years)	85	1–4	3.02	.73	1 = 1 2 = 18 3 = 44 4 = 22
Child–Parent Centers (average grades 1–3)	1414	1–5	2.58	1.02	
Perry Preschool (average grades 1–3)	120	1–7	4.04	1.68	
Motivation					
Abecedarian (motivation scale derived from CBI, average K-1)	90	25.50–42.00	34.08	3.92	
Child–Parent Centers (motivation–new scale 6–18–07, average K-1, z-score)	1203	-3.17–1.79	.0035	.93	
Perry Preschool (PBI academic motivation, average grades K-1)	121	1.11–4.78	3.07	.78	

School support
School mobility

	N	Range	Mean	SD	Distribution
Child–Parent Centers (# of school moves–grades 4–8)	1361	0–4	.97	.99	0 = 536 1 = 477 2 = 220 3 = 115 4 = 13
Perry Preschool (# of different schools through eighth grade–minus 1 to account for junior high transition)	112	0–5	1.64	.97	0 = 4 1 = 60 2 = 26 3 = 17 4 = 4 5 = 1

School quality

	N	Range	Mean	SD	Distribution
Child–Parent Centers (if attended magnet school [grades 4–8] or 40% or more above grade level in reading in fifth grade–imputed)	1531	0/1			Attended magnet school = 156 Did not attend magnet school = 1375
Perry Preschool (School at age 14–Ypsilanti vs. others)	100	0/1			Ypsilanti = 76 Other = 24

Educational attainment
Highest grade completed at 21 years

	N	Range	Mean	SD	Distribution
Abecedarian	103	8–16	11.92	1.51	8 = 2 9 = 4 10 = 12 11 = 12 12 = 46 13 = 12 14 = 10 15 = 4 16 = 1
Child–Parent Centers	1296	7–14	11.14	1.81	7 = 22 8 = 156 9 = 144

Table 10.2 (cont.)

Measure	Valid	Range	Mean	S.D.	Frequency
Perry Preschool	123	7–16	11.40	1.54	10 = 110 11 = 91 12 = 419 13 = 352 14 = 2 7 = 1 8 = 3 9 = 11 10 = 24 11 = 13 12 = 38 13 = 31 14 = 1 16 = 1
OUTCOMES:					
Frequent or heavy drug use					
Abecedarian	100	0/1			No = 87 Yes = 13
Child–Parent Centers	1473	0/1			No = 1160 Yes = 313
Perry Preschool [a]	116	0/1			No = 51 Yes = 65
Daily or regular tobacco use					
Abecedarian	100	0/1			No = 49 Yes = 51
Child–Parent Centers	1125	0/1			No = 899 Yes = 226
Perry Preschool	117	0/1			No = 58 Yes = 59

Frequent or heavy alcohol use

Abecedarian	100	0/1			No = 80
					Yes = 20
Child–Parent Centers	1123	0/1			No = 930
					Yes = 193
Perry Preschool	116	0/1			No = 91
					Yes = 25

Composite measure of health compromising behaviors (0–3 scale)

Abecedarian	100	0–3	.84	.88	0 = 42
					1 = 38
					2 = 14
					3 = 6
Child–Parent Centers	1199	0–3	.61	.85	0 = 705
					1 = 304
					2 = 142
					3 = 48
Perry Preschool	117	0–3	1.32	.95	0 = 25
					1 = 45
					2 = 32
					3 = 15

Two or more health compromising behaviors

Abecedarian	100	0/1			No = 80
					Yes = 20
Child–Parent Centers	1199	0/1			No = 1009
					Yes = 190
Perry Preschool	117	0/1			No = 70
					Yes = 47

Depressive symptoms

Abecedarian	104	0/1			No = 71
					Yes = 33
Child–Parent Centers	1134	0/1			No = 960
					Yes = 174

Table 10.2 (cont.)

Measure	Valid	Range	Mean	S.D.	Frequency
COVARIATES:					
Gender					
Abecedarian	104	0/1			Male = 51
					Female = 53
Child–Parent Centers	1531	0/1			Male = 761
					Female = 770
Perry Preschool	123	0/1			Male = 72
					Female = 51
Father present in home at entry					
Abecedarian	104	0/1			No = 74
					Yes = 30
Child–Parent Centers	1482	0/1			No = 1120
					Yes = 362
Perry Preschool	123	0/1			No = 58
					Yes = 65
Mother's education – graduated from high school or not					
Abecedarian	101	0/1			Non-completion of high school = 66
					Graduated high school = 35
Child–Parent Centers	1475	0/1			Non-completion of high school = 796
					Graduated high school = 679
Perry Preschool	123	0/1			Non-completion of high school = 97
					Graduated high school = 26

[a] Defined as any drug use.

14/15 years, and ever retained or in special education through age 15 years.

IQ/achievement at kindergarten entry

Either IQ or academic achievement was obtained at 5 years of age (kindergarten entry) for all three programs. For the ABC this measure was the Wechsler Preschool and Primary Scale of Intelligence (WPPSI; Wechsler, 1967), for the CPC this measure was the Iowa Test of Basic Skills (Hieronymus, Lindquist, and Hoover, 1982) cognitive composite, and for the PPP this measure was the Stanford-Binet (Terman and Merrill, 1960).

Reading achievement at 14/15 years

A measure of reading achievement was administered in all three projects when the participants were ages 14/15 years old. For the ABC this was the Woodcock Johnson Test of Achievement–Reading Comprehension (Woodcock and Johnson, 1989), for the CPC this was the Iowa Test of Basic Skills (Hieronymus et al., 1982) Reading Comprehension scale, and for the PPP this was the California Achievement Test–Reading Comprehension (Tiegs and Clark, 1963; 1971).

Special education/retention by 15 years

A binary measure was derived for each project indicating whether a participant had received special education or had been retained by age 15 years. This variable was coded 0 if the participant had not received special education services or been retained between kindergarten and age 15 years and was coded 1 if the participant had received special education services or was retained at any time between kindergarten and 15 years.

Social adjustment

Two measures of social adjustment were included in the analyses for each of the studies, a measure of elementary social emotional adjustment at ages 7–9 years and a measure of juvenile arrests.

Elementary social adjustment

A teacher-rated measure of social adjustment was completed between the ages of 7 and 9 years in each of the three projects. For the ABC, a derived eight-item measure was obtained from the Classroom Behavior Inventory measure (Schaefer, Edgerton, and Aaronson, 1978) acquired at ages 7–8 years. The items were added together and an average score for ages 7–8 years was obtained. For the CPC a six-item measure of social-emotional maturity was averaged for ages 7–9 years. The Pupil Behavior Inventory social-emotional adjustment scale (Vinter et al., 1966) completed at ages 7–9 years was used as the social adjustment measure for the PPP.

Juvenile arrests

Juvenile arrests data were collected from administrative data and coded as 0 for no arrests and 1 for any arrests for all three studies.

Family support

Parent involvement with the school/education was coded for all three studies when the participants were 7–9 years old. A derived measure of parental involvement in education was coded from the Caldwell HOME (Home Observation for Measurement of the Environment) Stimulation Scale (Caldwell and Bradley, 1984) for the ABC. This measure was obtained when the participants were 8 years old; the newly created variable combined four items from the HOME (child has a library card, and family arranges for child to go to library once a month; parent reads to, or listens to child read, once a week; child is encouraged to read on his or her own; and parent will offer help if child is frustrated by a task). For the CPC, teacher questionnaires were completed when the participants were 7–9 years old; the measure of parental involvement in school is an average rating of first through third grade teachers' responses to parental involvement questions. The PPP study utilized the Ypsilanti Rating Scale, completed by teachers, which included a measure of parental involvement with school. This measure was averaged across ages 7–9 years.

Motivation

Teacher rated measures of child motivation were completed in all three studies when the children were in kindergarten and first grade; an average rating of motivation was derived for age 6–7 years in all three studies. The academic motivation scale of the Pupil Behavior Inventory (Vinter et al., 1966) was used as a measure of motivation for the PPP. Based on this measure, we identified similar items on the Classroom Behavior Inventory (Schaefer et al., 1978) for the ABC, and from teacher surveys for the CPC. Where required, these items were reverse coded, and scores from each item were added together. Z-scores were derived for both kindergarten and first grade for the CPC as some questions differed across the two years; all analyses used the averaged z-score. For both the ABC and PPP, motivation scores were averaged for the two years.

School support
For both the CPC and PPP, two measures of school support were included in the analyses: school mobility and school quality. For the ABC, there was no available measure of school mobility and the school quality measure lacked variability in this study.

School mobility
The number of schools that participants attended from fourth grade to eighth grade was used as the measure of school mobility for the CPC. For the PPP, the number of schools that participants attended from kindergarten through eighth grade (minus one move from elementary to junior high school) was used as the school mobility measure.

School quality
A dichotomous variable was created for both the CPC and PPP studies to measure school quality. For the CPC, this variable was based on whether a participant had attended a magnet school at any time between fourth and eighth grades or if they attended a school during this time where 40 percent or more of the students were above grade level in reading during fifth grade. For the PPP, school quality was indicated by whether participants had attended Ypsilanti schools at age 14 or not.

Educational attainment
This measure was the last grade that participants completed by the age of 21 years.

Outcome measures: health compromising behaviors in adulthood

Frequent or heavy drug use
A measure of frequent or heavy drug use in adulthood was included as an outcome variable for each of the programs. For the ABC, the data are from interviews completed by age 30 years. If a participant indicated that they had smoked marijuana ten or more times in the past 30 days and/or used harder drugs three or more times in the last 30 days,[1] this variable was then coded as a 1 (yes). For the CPC, this construct is measured from an early adult interview/questionnaire collected at age 22/24 years; a 1 (yes) was indicated by an affirmative response on any of the following: any self-reported substance abuse treatment, any

---

[1] No Abecedarian Project participants reported using drugs harder than marijuana more than once in the past 30 days.

self-reported personal substance abuse problem, smoking marijuana almost every day at present, and/or using drugs harder than marijuana a few times a week or more at present. The data were supplemented with administrative data on drug related convictions by age 26, so that if a participant had been convicted of a drug related offense by 26 years the participant also received a score of 1. The format of the PPP interview questions regarding substance use did not allow for a comparable measure. Therefore, for the PPP frequent or heavy drug use is defined as ever using marijuana or harder drugs by age 27/28 years. Over 56 percent of PPP program and comparison group participants reported ever using illegal substances by age 27/28 years. Although estimated intervention effects on frequent substance use are reported for the PPP, the definitions employed for the CPC and the ABC are believed to more appropriately measure frequent use among the participants.

Tobacco use

Tobacco use data are from self-reports at various ages[2] and are coded as no (0) or yes (1). For the ABC, the measure is defined as smoking one or more cigarettes per day during the past 30 days or ever smoking one or more cigarettes per day for a period of 30 days or more. For the CPC and PPP, the measure of tobacco use is defined as smoking and/or using other tobacco products daily at present. Overall, 20 percent, 50 percent, and 51 percent of CPC, PPP, and ABC participants were assumed to be daily users of tobacco, respectively.

Frequent or heavy alcohol use

For the CPC frequent or heavy alcohol use is defined as drinking alcohol "a few times a week or more" at present. For the PPP, the measure is defined as drinking alcohol "several times a week or more" at present. The overall rates of what is assumed to indicate "frequent or heavy alcohol use" for the CPC and PPP are 17 percent and 22 percent, respectively.

For the ABC, the measure of frequent or heavy alcohol use is defined as drinking at least one drink for ten or more days in the past 30 days and/or drinking five or more drinks for three or more days in the past 30 days.[3] In

---

[2] Child–Parent Center tobacco use data are from ages 22–24. HighScope Perry Preschool data are from age 27. Abecedarian Project data are from age 30.
[3] Binge drinking for males is commonly defined as 5 or more drinks on one occasion. Binge drinking for females is defined as 4 or more drinks on one occasion; however, all participants (male and female) were asked to report the number of occasions they consumed 5 or more consecutive drinks in the past 30 days. Females were not asked to report the number of occasions they consumed 4 or more consecutive drinks.

defining frequent or heavy alcohol use for the ABC, the objective was to create a measure consistent with the CPC and PPP measures of alcohol use. Approximately 20 percent of ABC participants (both program and comparison groups) reported consuming alcohol ten or more days in the past 30 days and/or consuming five or more drinks on three or more occasions in the past 30 days.

Two or more health compromising behaviors

For each of the studies discussed, a binary measure of health compromising behavior was created indicating whether participants engaged in two or more of the three common indicators of health compromising behavior (drug use, daily or regular tobacco use, and frequent or heavy alcohol use as defined above). To the degree that the definitions of the individual measures of health compromising behavior across the three studies differ, there is variation in the definitions of this composite measure.

Outcome measures: depressive symptoms in adulthood

Between ages 22 and 24, program and comparison group participants of the CPC rated how often in the past month they felt depressed, helpless, lonely, and/or that life is not worth living. A dichotomous measure indicates the frequent presence of one or more symptoms defined at levels ranging from "a few times a month" to "almost every day." For the ABC, depression (depressive symptoms) at a mean age of 21 years was assessed using the Brief Symptoms Inventory, consisting of six items (BSI; Derogatis, 1993). Participants rated the degree to which each item (e.g., "feeling blue," "feeling no interest in things") applied to themselves in the past 7 days. Response categories ranged from "not at all" to "extremely." Raw scores were converted to gender-adjusted T scores, and depression in early adulthood was defined as a T score of 63 or higher.

Covariates

The following covariates were included in the analysis for all three studies: gender of the child, single-parent status, and mother's educational level. The single-parent measure varied somewhat by project as follows: for the ABC the measure was whether the father was living in the home at the child's birth; for the CPC it was whether the parent was not single at any point in time between the child's birth and 3 years of age; and for the PPP it was whether the father was living in the home at program entry.

Mother's educational status was coded as 0 = did not graduate from high school or 1 = graduated from high school.

RESULTS

The research strategy in this chapter has three main components. First correlations were computed for each study. The correlations show the association between the variables; especially of interest are the associations with preschool education and the correlations with the outcomes under investigation. We then conducted two sets of probit regressions. Our first set of regressions examined the main effect of preschool on health and health compromising behaviors controlling for gender, single-parent status, and mother's educational level. This analysis illuminates the differences between the preschool intervention groups and the comparison groups on our adult health related outcomes. We then added educational attainment at age 21 into our models. This allowed us to examine how much of the estimated effect of preschool education is accounted for by educational attainment in early adulthood. Our second set of regressions examines common predictors of the health outcomes across the three studies (preschool education, educational variables in childhood and adolescence, and educational attainment). This analysis provides information as to which variables add significant contributions to the variance predicted in the health outcomes for each study and provides insight as to whether common predictors of the health outcomes can be identified.

Correlations

For each study, Polychoric correlations are calculated. Missing values were imputed through multiple imputation procedures using the EM algorithm. The correlations indicate an association between preschool participation, educational attainment by age 21, and health compromising behavior and depressive symptoms in adulthood. Polychoric correlations using imputed data for the ABC, CPC, and PPP studies are included in Tables 10.3, 10.4, and 10.5, respectively. Preschool participation was significantly correlated with highest grade completed at age 21 and two or more health compromising behaviors for all three studies. Furthermore, preschool participation was significantly correlated with depressive symptoms for both ABC and CPC. In addition, preschool participation was significantly associated with frequent or heavy drug use in the ABC study, all of the outcome measures for the CPC study, and frequent or heavy alcohol use in the PPP study.

Table 10.3 *Abecedarian Project correlation table (polychoric correlations – imputed data).*

	1	2	3	4	5	6	7	8	9	10	11	12	13	14
1. Preschool participation	–													
2. WPPSI (60 months)	0.41	–												
3. Reading Woodcock-Johnson reading (14 years)	0.34	0.43	–											
4. Ever retained or special ed. through eighth grade	–0.23	–0.55	–0.60	–										
5. Child Behavior Index derived scale 1–2 averaged	–0.04	0.26	0.26	–0.41	–									
6. Any juvenile arrest by age 19	–0.12	–0.05	–0.20	0.41	–0.14	–								
7. Motivation: Child Behavior Index derived scale K-1 averaged	0.26	0.51	0.37	–0.47	0.29	–0.26	–							
8. Parent involvement derived from HOME (age 8)	0.06	0.23	–0.00	–0.50	0.16	–0.05	0.18	–						
9. Educational attainment: highest graded completed by age 21	0.30	0.33	0.34	–0.45	0.11	–0.49	0.31	0.26	–					
10. Daily/regular tobacco use	–0.10	–0.18	–0.11	0.25	0.07	0.52	–0.14	–0.11	–0.68	–				
11. Frequent/heavy drug use	–0.33	–0.26	–0.33	0.46	0.00	0.46	0.12	–0.42	–0.38	0.68	–			
12. Frequent/heavy alcohol use	–0.04	0.16	0.09	–0.04	0.16	0.25	0.08	0.02	–0.23	0.25	0.57	–		
13. Two or more health compromising behaviors	–0.21	–0.14	–0.14	0.24	0.06	0.42	0.16	–0.22	–0.51	0.79	0.77	0.86	–	
14. Depressive symptoms	–0.22	–0.26	0.05	0.24	–0.20	–0.07	–0.05	–0.27	–0.33	0.09	0.25	–0.13	0.18	–

Note: correlations at $r = .20$ are significant at $p < .05$; correlations at $r = .26$ are significant at $p < .01$; correlations at $r = .32$ are significant at $p < .001$

Table 10.4 *Child–Parent Centers correlation table (polychoric correlations – imputed data).*

	1	2	3	4	5	6	7	8	9	10	11	12	13	14	15	16
1. Preschool participation	—															
2. ITBS Cognitive Composite (Kindergarten)	0.36	—														
3. ITBS Reading Comprehension (eighth grade)	0.20	0.42	—													
4. Ever retained or special ed. through eighth grade	-0.28	-0.41	-0.63	—												
5. SEMAT average gr. 1–3	0.18	0.37	0.61	-0.60	—											
6. Any juvenile petition or self-reported arrest by 18	-0.19	-0.11	-0.35	0.33	-0.32	—										
7. Motivation	0.13	0.36	0.45	-0.48	0.65	-0.21	—									
8. Parent involvement average grades 1–3	0.24	0.25	0.37	-0.38	0.54	-0.32	0.37	—								
9. # of schools moves grades 4–8	-0.21	-0.17	-0.23	0.24	-0.19	0.30	-0.14	-0.24	—							
10. Attended magnet school (grades 4–8) or 40% + above grade level reading in fifth grade	0.30	0.37	0.36	-0.21	0.17	-0.26	0.16	0.22	-0.27	—						
11. Educational attainment: highest graded completed by age 21	0.12	0.16	0.38	-0.36	0.38	-0.51	0.23	0.32	-0.27	0.29	—					
12. Daily/regular tobacco use	-0.09	-0.03	-0.19	0.10	-0.20	0.42	-0.15	-0.14	0.20	-0.29	-0.35	—				
13. Frequent/heavy drug use	-0.11	-0.02	-0.28	0.28	-0.28	0.67	-0.19	-0.23	0.24	-0.25	-0.43	0.51	—			
14. Frequent/heavy alcohol use	-0.07	0.03	-0.18	0.18	-0.24	0.36	-0.15	-0.11	0.16	-0.14	-0.26	0.43	0.63	—		
15. Two or more health compromising behaviors	-0.14	-0.06	-0.30	0.29	-0.28	0.56	-0.22	-0.22	0.23	-0.32	-0.38	0.81	0.92	0.89	—	
16. Depressive symptoms	-0.13	-0.17	-0.25	0.15	-0.26	0.34	-0.17	-0.18	0.20	-0.21	-0.27	0.37	0.35	0.32	0.43	—

Note: correlations at $r = .06$ are significant at $p < .05$; correlations at $r = .08$ are significant at $p < .01$; correlations at $r = .10$ are significant at $p < .001$

Table 10.5 *Perry Preschool Project correlation table (polychoric correlations – imputed data).*

	1	2	3	4	5	6	7	8	9	10	11	12	13	14	15
1. Preschool participation	–														
2. Stanford-Binet 5 years	0.57	–													
3. Reading CAT eighth grade	0.26	0.44	–												
4. Ever retained or special ed. through eighth grade	0.02	-0.18	-0.48	–											
5. Socio-emotional adjustment 1–3 averaged	0.10	0.21	0.42	-0.38	–										
6. Any juvenile arrest	-0.28	-0.10	-0.12	-0.23	0.09	–									
7. PBI academic motivation K-1 averaged	0.21	0.45	0.66	-0.45	0.53	-0.09	–								
8. Parent involvement 1–3 averaged	0.03	0.29	0.29	-0.34	0.43	-0.14	0.43	–							
9. # of different schools through eighth grade	-0.05	0.03	-0.16	0.19	-0.22	0.20	0.05	-0.19	–						
10. Ypsilanti vs. non-Ypsilanti school at 14 years	0.35	0.04	-0.05	-0.45	-0.17	0.05	-0.22	-0.10	0.01	–					
11. Educational attainment: highest graded completed by age 21	0.21	0.31	0.39	-0.56	0.25	-0.20	0.37	0.40	-0.18	0.16	–				
12. Daily/regular tobacco use	-0.19	-0.20	-0.22	0.09	0.01	0.24	-0.12	-0.13	0.08	0.08	-0.40	–			
13. Any drug use	-0.10	0.13	-0.02	0.06	0.06	-0.03	-0.04	0.06	-0.11	-0.11	-0.05	0.14	–		
14. Frequent/heavy alcohol use	-0.21	0.02	-0.26	0.26	-0.10	-0.08	-0.19	-0.07	-0.06	0.18	-0.12	0.40	0.46	–	
15. Two or more health compromising behaviors	-0.29	-0.06	-0.23	0.14	0.02	0.09	-0.13	-0.03	-0.00	-0.06	-0.36	0.84	0.76	0.90	–

Note: correlations at $r = .20$ are significant at $p < .05$; correlations at $r = .26$ are significant at $p < .01$; correlations at $r = .32$ are significant at $p < .001$

Probit regressions

Main effects of preschool on health and health compromising behaviors

The main effects of preschool participation on selected health compromising behaviors as well as depressive symptoms are presented in Table 10.6. Estimated effects are from probit regressions of health related outcomes (frequent or heavy drug use, daily or regular tobacco use, frequent or heavy alcohol use, and depressive symptoms) in adulthood on preschool participation, gender of the child, single-parent status, and mother's education level. In addition to main effects of preschool, rates of participation in health compromising behavior as well as rates of indicated depressive symptoms among program and comparison group participants are presented in Table 10.6. The only significant difference ($p < .05$) between program participation and comparison group participants was for frequent or heavy drug use in the CPC program; participants who attended a CPC were 4.5 percentage points less likely to report frequent drug use (14.8 percent vs. 19.3 percent, $p = 0.03$). The current analysis did reveal, however, several marginal, but practical differences between program and comparison group participants in all three studies. ABC participation was associated with an 11.1 percentage point reduction in the rate of frequent drug use (6.8 percent vs. 17.9 percent, $p = 0.10$) at age 30. At age 21, 39.7 percent of ABC program group participants and 54.4 percent of comparison group participants described themselves as regular smokers ($p = 0.15$). Nearly ten years later (at age 30), the estimated rates among ABC program and comparison group participants were 48.3 percent and 53.8 percent, respectively (not statistically different). Furthermore, marginal effects were found for the CPC where preschool program participants were 4.7 percentage points less likely to report daily tobacco use (18.0 percent vs. 22.7 percent, $p = 0.06$) at ages 22–24 compared with the control group. For the PPP, there are practical differences in the rates of daily tobacco use (11.3 percentage point reduction) and frequent or heavy alcohol use (8.9 percentage point reduction) at age 27.

Furthermore, there is evidence that preschool participation is associated with reduced incidences of combined health compromising behaviors. Participants exhibiting multiple health compromising behaviors are expected to be at relatively high risk for undesirable health outcomes. A significant difference was found for the PPP, wherein program participation was associated with an 18.8 percentage point reduction in the probability of engaging in two or more health compromising behaviors

Table 10.6 *Estimated intervention effects on health related outcomes.*

	Abecedarian Project			Child–Parent Center			Perry Preschool		
	PreK	Comp.	Diff.	PreK	Comp.	Diff.	PreK	Comp.	Diff.
Frequent/heavy drug use, %[a]	6.82	17.90	−11.08[+]	14.75	19.25	−4.50[*]	53.07	59.24	−6.17
Tobacco use (daily or regular use), %	48.34	53.78	−5.44	17.99	22.66	−4.67[+]	44.56	55.86	−11.30
Frequent/heavy alcohol use, %	19.09	19.86	−0.77	14.27	15.40	−1.13	16.62	25.47	−8.85
Two or more indicators of health compromising behaviors, %	14.57	24.10	−9.53	10.31	13.84	−3.53[+]	30.29	49.06	−18.77[*]
Depressive symptoms, %	26.46	37.19	−10.73	13.58	17.90	−4.32[+]	na	na	na

[+] $p < 0.10$, [*] $p < 0.05$, [**] $p < 0.01$, [***] $p < 0.001$

Estimates are adjusted for gender, single-parent status, and mother's education level.

[a] Defined as any drug use for the Perry Preschool Program

PreK = preschool intervention group

Comp. = comparison group

na = not available.

(30.3 percent vs. 49.1 percent; $p = 0.04$). Program participation in a CPC marginally predicted a decreased likelihood of engaging in two or more health compromising behaviors such that program participants were 3.5 percentage points less likely to exhibit two or more health compromising behaviors in adulthood (10.3 percent vs. 13.8 percent, $p = 0.07$). Although the estimated effect of the ABC is not statistically significant at the 5 percent level, it is clearly suggestive; ABC participation was associated with a 9.5 percentage point reduction in the likelihood of exhibiting two or more health compromising behaviors (14.6 percent vs. 24.1 percent; $p = 0.24$).

Main effects on symptoms of depression in early adulthood are reported in previous analyses of the CPC and ABC (McLaughlin et al., 2007; Reynolds et al., 2007). Overall, 15 percent of CPC and 32 percent of ABC program and comparison group participants satisfied the respective definitions of depression. Controlling for gender, single-parent status, and mother's education level, participation in a CPC is associated with a 4.3 percentage point reduction in the probability of the frequent presence of one or more depressive symptoms at age 22–24 (13.6 percent vs. 17.9 percent; $p = 0.06$). The ABC is associated with a 10.7 percentage point reduction in the likelihood of meeting the clinical cut point for identifying depression (gender-adjusted T score of 63; 26.6 percent vs. 37.1 percent; $p = 0.25$).

Further regression analysis included adding highest grade completed by age 21 in the model after entering program participation and the covariates. Across the three studies, educational attainment by age 21 accounts for a sizable portion of the main effect of preschool participation on health compromising behaviors. For the ABC, educational attainment by age 21 accounts for 20 percent of the main effect of preschool on frequent or heavy drug use, 100 percent of the main effect on tobacco use, and 30 percent of the main effect on depressive symptoms. For the CPC, educational attainment accounts for 75 percent of the main effect of preschool on frequent drug use, 71 percent of the main effect on daily tobacco use, and 7 percent of the main effect on depressive symptoms. For the PPP, educational attainment accounts for 37 percent of the main effect on daily tobacco use and 7 percent of the main effect on frequent or heavy alcohol use. Approximately 43 percent of the main effect of the CPC on the probability of exhibiting two or more health compromising behaviors is accounted for by educational attainment. Similarly, educational attainment by age 21 accounts for 40 percent and 19 percent of the main effect of the ABC and PPP on the likelihood of participating in multiple health compromising behaviors in adulthood, respectively.

Common predictors

The contribution of preschool education, cognitive, social, motivational, family and school support factors, and educational attainment in early adulthood to the prediction of health related outcomes in adulthood is also assessed. Probit regressions of health compromising behaviors across the three studies as well as depressive symptoms among CPC and ABC participants on preschool participation, childhood predictor measures, educational attainment by age 21, and the covariate measures are presented in Tables 10.7 and 10.8. These analyses allowed us to examine the significance of the effects of each of the variables on health compromising

Table 10.7 *Probit regression of two or more health compromising behaviors on selected predictors.*

	Perry Preschool		Abecedarian		Child–Parent Centers	
	β	Marginal effect	β	Marginal effect	β	Marginal effect
Preschool	−0.27*	−0.24*	−0.05	−0.03	−0.03	−0.01
Gender (female)	−0.04	−0.04	−0.21	−0.12	−0.35***	−0.16***
Mother completed high school	0.19	0.21	−0.04	−0.03	0.04	0.02
Father in home	−0.05	−0.05	−0.04	−0.02	0.10*	0.06*
Cognitive skills	0.25[+]	0.009[+]	−0.14	−0.003	0.08[+]	0.002[+]
Reading achievement	−0.30[+]	−0.013[+]	−0.04	−0.001	−0.12*	−0.001*
Ever retained or in special ed.	−0.03	−0.03	−0.03	−0.01	−0.01	−0.01
Social adjustment	0.20	0.12	0.05	0.01	0.05	0.00
Delinquent behavior	−0.04	−0.04	0.14	0.09	0.15**	0.10**
Motivation	−0.01	−0.01	0.48**	0.04**	−0.09[+]	−0.02[+]
Parent involvement	0.01	0.00	−0.13	−0.05	−0.03	−0.01
School mobility	−0.12	−0.06	–	–	0.08[+]	0.02[+]
School quality	0.09	0.10	–	–	−0.10[+]	−0.05[+]
Highest grade completed by age 21	−0.40**	−0.12**	−0.49**	−0.09**	−0.16***	−0.02***
n	117		100		1056	
Pseudo R2	0.1359		0.2644		0.2464	

[+]$p < 0.10$, *$p < 0.05$, **$p < 0.01$, ***$p < 0.001$

Table 10.8 *Probit regression of depressive symptoms on selected predictors.*

	Abecedarian		Child–Parent Centers	
	β	Marginal effect	β	Marginal effect
Preschool	−0.14	−0.11	−0.03	−0.02
Gender (female)	0.04	0.03	0.07	0.03
Mother completed high school	0.04	0.04	−0.01	−0.00
Father in home	−0.10	−0.08	−0.05	−0.03
Cognitive skills	−0.24	−0.008	−0.06	−0.002
Reading achievement	0.31[+]	0.012[+]	−0.05	−0.001
Ever retained or in special ed.	0.10	0.08	−0.09	−0.04
Social adjustment	−0.21	−0.03	−0.17*	−0.01*
Delinquent behavior	−0.10	−0.08	0.14**	0.10**
Motivation	0.13	0.01	0.01	0.00
Parent involvement	−0.11	−0.06	−0.00	−0.00
School mobility	–	–	0.09[+]	0.02[+]
School quality	–	–	−0.06	−0.04
Highest grade completed by age 21	−0.32*	−0.09*	−0.10*	−0.01*
n	104		1007	
Pseudo R2	0.1380		0.0790	

[+]$p < 0.10$, *$p < 0.05$, **$p < 0.01$, ***$p < 0.001$

behaviors and depressive symptoms across the studies and to identify common predictors of the health outcomes.

As seen in Table 10.7, the patterns of results for each study are similar across the individual measures of health compromising behaviors. For the ABC, there is evidence that motivation contributes to the prediction of health compromising behavior in adulthood. Interestingly, motivation in kindergarten and first grade is positively associated with the likelihood of exhibiting two or more health compromising behaviors. Furthermore, the magnitude of the coefficients for cognitive skills at kindergarten entry, parent involvement in early elementary school, and delinquent behavior in adolescence, although not statistically significant, potentially show a practical effect on health compromising behaviors in adulthood. For the CPC, there is evidence that cognitive advantage, social adjustment, motivation, and school support all add to the prediction of multiple health compromising behaviors in adulthood. The analysis suggests that, all else equal, a one standard deviation increase in reading achievement at age 14 among CPC program and comparison group participants is associated with a 0.12 standard deviation decrease in the likelihood of exhibiting two or more health compromising behaviors in adulthood. In addition, CPC participants petitioned to juvenile court by the age of 18 are 9.6 percentage points more likely to exhibit two or more health compromising behaviors in adulthood. For the PPP, both cognitive skills at age 5 and reading achievement at age 14 add to the prediction of health compromising behaviors. Across the three studies, an additional year of education at age 21 is associated with between a 1.9 and 12.1 percentage point reduction in the likelihood of exhibiting two or more health compromising behaviors. In sum, results from all three studies point to the importance of educational attainment in the prediction of health compromising behaviors in adulthood such that higher levels of educational attainment lead to lower levels of health compromising behaviors. Furthermore, there are indications in two of the studies (PPP and CPC) that cognitive skills at kindergarten entry and reading achievement at 14/15 years of age, and motivation (ABC and CPC), are also important predictors of health outcomes in adulthood.

Table 10.8 presents the probit regressions for the prediction of depressive symptoms for ABC and CPC. Reading achievement at age 15 adds to the prediction of depressive symptoms among ABC participants, although the association appears to be positive. For the ABC, an additional year of education is associated with an 8.5 percentage point reduction in the probability of being identified as exhibiting depressive symptoms. Both measures comprising the social adjustment hypothesis add to the prediction of depressive symptoms among CPC participants. Participants who petition to juvenile court are 9.7 percentage points more likely to exhibit depressive symptoms in adulthood. School mobility also appears to add to the prediction of depressive symptoms among CPC participants. Each school move between fourth and eighth grade is associated with a 2.2 percentage point increase in the probability of being identified as exhibiting depressive symptoms. For the CPC, an additional year of education at age 21 is associated with a 1.4 percentage point reduction in the probability of being identified as exhibiting depressive symptoms. Across both studies, those individuals with lower levels of education are more likely to exhibit depressive symptoms in adulthood.

DISCUSSION

The current study examined: preschool participation; childhood cognitive, social adjustment, family support, motivation, and school support measures; and educational attainment at 21 years, in predicting health and health compromising behaviors in early adulthood for low-income participants in the ABC, CPC, and PPP preschool intervention programs. More specifically, we examined whether participation in one of these high-quality preschool programs decreased the likelihood of individuals engaging in health compromising behaviors in early adulthood and whether intervening educational factors, including educational attainment at 21 years, significantly predicted health outcomes in early adulthood.

Our findings indicate that participation in a high-quality preschool program decreased the likelihood of involvement in health compromising behaviors for participants in all three programs at a significant or practical level after controlling for gender, single-parent status, and mother's educational level. Participants in all three programs were less likely to engage in two or more indicators of health compromising behavior compared to the comparison groups. For the ABC and CPC, the two programs where we had measures of depressive symptoms in adulthood, preschool program participants were less likely to have depressive symptoms compared to the control groups. These findings support previous research (Anderson et al., 2010; Muennig et al., 2011) indicating that participation in preschool interventions has a direct effect on adult health compromising behaviors.

Further analysis reveals, however, that intervening educational factors, especially educational attainment at age 21 years, are also robust predictors of health outcomes in early adulthood. The highest grade completed by age 21 significantly predicted health compromising behaviors for all three studies and depressive symptoms for the ABC and, marginally, for CPC. Individuals with higher educational attainment were less likely to engage in health compromising behaviors and less likely to have depressive symptoms in early adulthood. Cognitive advantage was also a notable predictor; reading achievement in early adolescence predicted health compromising behaviors significantly for the CPC and marginally for the PPP, cognitive skills in kindergarten marginally added to the prediction of two or more health compromising behaviors for both the CPC and the PPP, and reading achievement in early adolescence significantly predicted depressive symptoms in early adulthood for the ABC. Individuals with greater levels of cognitive skills were less likely to engage in health compromising behaviors in the CPC and the PPP and less likely to have depressive symptoms in early adulthood in the ABC. For the CPC, social adjustment was also an important predictor of both health compromising behaviors and depressive symptoms; higher levels of social adjustment in elementary school and lower levels of delinquent activity through adolescence predicted lower levels of health compromising behaviors and depressive symptoms in adulthood.

Results suggest that educational attainment and cognitive advantage measures as well as social adjustment measures for CPC add to the prediction of health outcomes over and above participation in a high-quality preschool program. These results support the perspective that high-quality preschool intervention programs predict positive health outcomes in adulthood both directly and through the programs' influence on intervening variables that then directly affect health behaviors in early adulthood. Thus, although there are direct main effects from preschool participation, participation in preschool also sets the stage for positive health outcomes in adulthood by providing a cognitive advantage to preschool participants throughout elementary and high school and for CPC greater social adjustment, both of which lead to greater educational attainment in early adulthood (Reynolds et al., 2010). In conjunction with a cognitive advantage and better social adjustment, a higher level of educational attainment appears to be a strong deterrent to engagement in health compromising behaviors later in adulthood, at least for the low income participants, in all three of these preschool intervention studies. Participation in a high-quality preschool program appears to set in motion a process whereby children gain a cognitive advantage early in school that continues throughout elementary and high school, encouraging better social adjustment in early elementary school and lower levels of engagement in delinquent acts in adolescence. Cognitive advantage and positive social adjustment provide a basis for higher educational attainment in early adulthood further contributing to lower levels of health compromising behaviors and depressive symptoms in adulthood.

Despite the noteworthy contribution of this study to furthering understanding of the longitudinal influence of preschool participation on adult health outcomes, there are limitations to our research. The estimated main effects reported are not always statistically significant at the 5 percent level. This may be due to the small sample sizes for the ABC and PPP; it should be noted, however, that many of the main effects are practically significant. Additionally, health data for the three studies were limited. Our analyses focused on available measures of health compromising behavior; although health compromising behaviors associated with undesirable health outcomes, there is also a need to examine physical health data (e.g., blood pressure, BMI, diseases, health problems), especially as the participants age. A further limitation is that the measures across the studies are not entirely the same. We have attempted to define measures consistently across the three studies; although there are differences in the definitions, the direction of the main effects are similar. Furthermore, given the amount of variance in both health compromising behaviors and depressive symptoms that has not been accounted for by the variables included in the model ranges from 74 percent (ABC two or more health compromising behaviors) to 92 percent (CPC depressive symptoms), there are clearly other factors that also contribute to the prediction of these outcomes.

Regardless, the current analysis does provide information regarding the potential mechanisms through which early educational interventions affects health outcomes in adulthood. For the low-income individuals investigated in the current study, preschool participation appears to set in motion pathways leading to less likelihood of engaging in health compromising behaviors and of depressive symptoms in early adulthood via the influences of preschool education, educational attainment, and intervening educational factors, especially greater cognitive skills and academic achievement. Given program differences in terms of services, geographic location, and time, these results reveal some commonality in the potential mechanisms by which early childhood education programs influence adult health. Furthermore, as found with our examination of the effects of preschool participation on educational attainment in early adulthood in these three studies (Reynolds et al., 2010), the pathways may be complex. Although educational attainment was a strong indicator across all three studies, factors that were not analyzed here appear to be in play as well.

Results from our study provide further support for investments in early childhood education. High-quality preschool programs not only affect children in the short term by developing school readiness skills and increasing their cognitive abilities, but also affect children in the long term. In addition to the positive long-term effects of preschool participation found in previous studies (e.g., higher levels of educational attainment, lower likelihood of engaging in criminal activities), these analyses suggest that participation in a high-quality preschool program also decreases engagement in health compromising behaviors and depressive symptoms into early adulthood. This research has direct implications for health care costs, and indicates that increased investment in early childhood education would contribute to lower health care expenditures in the future. Overall, this study provides support for the generalizability of potential pathways leading from preschool participation to health outcomes in adulthood. Future research will involve path analysis to gain a better understanding of the mechanisms that mediate the relation between preschool and health related outcomes in adulthood. Future research not only should attempt to identify other factors that may account for additional proportions of the effects of early childhood education on later health outcomes, but should also examine the effects of preschool participation on physical health outcomes in adulthood.

References

Anderson, K. H., Foster, J. E., and Frisvold, D. E. (2010). Investing in health: the long-term impact of Head Start on smoking. *Economic Inquiry*, 48, 587–602.

Baker, D. P., Leon, J., Smith Greenaway, E. G., Collins, J., and Movit, M. (2011). The education effect of population health: a reassessment. *Population and Development Review*, 37(2), 307–332.

Barkley, G. S. (2008). Factors influencing health behaviors in the National Health and Nutritional Examination Survey, III (NHANES III). *Social Work in Health Care*, 46(4), 57–79.

Barnett, W. S., and Masse, L. N. (2007). Comparative benefit–cost analysis of the Abecedarian program and its policy implications. *Economics of Education Review*, 26, 113–125.

Braveman, P. (2011). Accumulating knowledge on the social determinants of health and infectious disease. *Public Health Reports*, 126 (Suppl. 3), 28–30.

Brisbois, T. D., Farmer, A. P., and McCargar, L. J. (2012). Early markers of adult obesity: a review. *Obesity Reviews*, 13, 347–367.

Caldwell, B. M., and Bradley, R. H. (1984). *HOME observation for measurement of the environment* (rev. edn). Little Rock: Center for Child Development and Education, University of Arkansas at Little Rock.

Campbell, F. A., Pungello, E. P., Burchinal, M., Kainz, K., Pan, Y., Wasik, B. H., ... and Ramey, C. T. (2012). Adult outcomes as a function of an early childhood educational program: an Abecedarian Project follow-up. *Developmental Psychology*, 48, 1033–1043.

Campbell, F. A., Ramey, C. T., Pungello, E., Sparling, J., and Miller-Johnson, S. (2002). Early childhood education: young adult outcomes from the Abecedarian Project. *Applied Developmental Science*, 6(1), 42–57.

Clark, A. M., DeseMeules, M., Luo, W., Duncan, A. S., and Wielgosz, A. (2009). Socioeconomic status and cardiovascular disease: risks and implications for care. *Nature Reviews Cardiology*, 6, 712–722.

Consortium for Longitudinal Studies (1983). *As the twig is bent: lasting effects of preschool programs*. Hillsdale, NJ: Erlbaum.

Currie, J., and Thomas, D. (2000). School quality and the longer-term effects of Head Start. *Journal of Human Resources*, 35(4), 755–774.

Cutler, D. M., and Lleras-Muney, A. (2012). *Education and health: insights from international comparisons*. NBER Working Paper No. 17738, National Bureau of Economic Research. Retrieved January from www.nber.org/papers/w17738.

Day, J. C., and Newburger, E. C. (2002). *The big payoff: educational attainment and synthetic estimates of work-life earnings*. US Census Bureau, Current Population Reports, No. P23–210. Washington, DC: US Government Printing Office.

Derogatis, L. R. (1993). *Brief symptom inventory: administration, scoring and procedures manual*. Minneapolis, MN: National Computer Systems Inc.

D'Onise, K., Lynch, J. W., Sawyer, M. G., and McDermott, R. A. (2010). Can preschool improve child health outcomes? A systematic review. *Social Science and Medicine*, 70, 1423–1440.

Frytak, J. R., Harley, C. R., and Finch, M. D. (2003). Socioeconomic status and health over the life course: capital as a unifying concept. In J. T. Mortimer and

M. J. Shanahan (eds.), *Handbook of the life course* (pp. 623–643). New York: Kluwer Academic/Plenum.

Galobardes, B., Lynch, J. W., and Smith, G. D. (2004). Childhood socioeconomic circumstances and cause-specific mortality in adulthood: systematic review and interpretation. *Epidemiologic Reviews*, 26, 7–21.

Garces, E., Thomas, D., and Currie, J. (2002). Longer term effects of Head Start. *American Economic Review*, 92(4), 999–1012.

Gershon, A. S., Dolmage, T. E., Stephenson, A., and Jackson, B. (2012). Chronic obstructive pulmonary disease and socioeconomic status: a systematic review. *Journal of Chronic Obstructive Pulmonary Disease*, 9(3), 216–226.

Hawkins, N. M., Jhund, P. S., McMurray, J. J., and Capewell, S. (2012). Heart failure and socioeconomic status: accumulating evidence of inequality. *European Journal of Heart Failure*, 14(2), 138–146.

Heckman, J. J., Moon, S. H., Pinto, R., Savelyev, P., and Yavitz, A. (2010). A new cost-benefit and rate of return analysis for the Perry Preschool Program: a summary. In A. J. Reynolds, A. J. Rolnick, M. M. Englund, and J. A. Temple (eds.), *Childhood programs and practices in the first decade of life: a human capital integration* (pp. 366–380). Cambridge University Press.

Heeley, E. L., Wei, J. W., Carter, K., Islam, M. S., Thrift, A. G., Hankey, G. J., … and Anderson, C. S. (2011). Socioeconomic disparities in stroke rates and outcome: pooled analysis of stroke incidence studies in Australia and New Zealand. *Medical Journal of Australia*, 195, 10–14.

Hieronymus, A. N., Lindquist, E. F., and Hoover, H. D. (1982). *Iowa Tests of Basic Skills: manual for school administrators*. Chicago: Riverside.

Hiscock, R., Bauld, L., Amos, A., Fidler, J. A., and Munafò, M. (2012). Socioeconomic status and smoking: a review. *Annals of the New York Academy of Sciences*, 1248, 107–123.

Iceland, J. (2000). *Poverty among working families: findings from experimental poverty measures*. US Census Bureau, Current Population Reports, No. P23–203. Washington, DC: US Government Printing Office.

Kautzky-Willer, A., Dorner, T., Jensby, A., and Rieder, A. (2012). *BMC public health*, 12, 392. Retrieved from www.biomedcentral.com/1471–2458/12/.

Kerr, G. D., Slavin, H., Clark, D., Coupar, F., Langhorne, P., and Stott, D. J. (2011). Do vascular risk factors explain the association between socioeconomic status and stroke incidence: a meta-analysis. *Cerebrovascular Diseases*, 31, 57–63.

Lee, J. (2011). Pathways from education to depression. *Journal of Cross Cultural Gerontology*, 26, 121–135.

Lemstra, M., Bennett, N. R., Neudorf, C., Kunst, A., Nannapaneni, U., Warren, L. M., … and Scott, C. R., (2008). A meta-analysis of marijuana and alcohol use by socioeconomic status in adolescents aged 10–15 years. *Canadian Journal of Public Health*, 99(3), 172–177.

Luo, Y., and Waite, L. J. (2005). The impact of childhood and adult SES on physical, mental and cognitive well-being in later file. *Journals of Gerontology Series B., Psychological Sciences and Social Sciences*, 60, S93–S101.

Ma, J., Xu, J., Anderson, R. N., and Jemal, A. (2012). Widening educational disparities in premature death rates in twenty six states in the United States, 1993–2007. *PLOS One*, 7(7), e41560.

Matthews, K. A., and Gallo, L. C. (2011). Psychological perspectives on pathways linking socioeconomic status and physical health. *Annual Reviews in Psychology*, 62, 501–530.

McLaughlin, A. E., Campbell, F. A., Pungello, E. P., and Skinner, M. (2007). Depressive symptoms in young adults: the influences of the early home environment and early educational child care. *Child Development*, 78(3), 746–756.

Melchior, M., Moffitt, T. E., Milne, B. J., Poulton, R., and Caspi, A. (2007). Why do children from socioeconomically disadvantaged families suffer from poor health when they reach adulthood? A life-course study. *American Journal of Epidemiology*, 166, 966–974.

Molla, M. T., Madans, J. H., and Wagener, D. K. (2004). Differentials in adult mortality and activity limitation by years of education in the United States at the end of the 1990s. *Population and Development Review*, 30, 625–646.

Muennig, P., Robertson, D., Johnson, G., Campbell, F., Pungello, E. P., and Neidell, M. (2011). The effects of an early education program on adult health: the Carolina Abecedarian Project randomized control trial. *American Journal of Public Health*, 101, 512–516.

Muennig, P., Schweinhart, L., Montie, J., and Neidell, M. (2009). Effects of a prekindergarten educational intervention on adult health: 37-year follow-up results of a randomized controlled trial. *American Journal of Public Health*, 99, 1431–1437.

Non, A. L., Gravlee, C. C., and Mulligan, C. J. (2012). Education, genetic ancestry, and blood pressure in African Americans and whites. *American Journal of Public Health*, 102, 1559–1565.

Pascall, M. J., Flewelling, R. L., and Faulkner, D. L. (2000). Alcohol misuse in young adulthood: effects of race, educational attainment, and social context. *Substance Use and Misuse*, 35, 1485–1506.

Poulton, R., Caspi, A., Milne, B. J., Thomson, W. M., Taylor, A., Sears, M. R., and Moffitt, T. E. (2002). Association between children's experience of socioeconomic disadvantage and adult health: a life-course study. *The Lancet*, 360, 1640–1645.

Ramey, C. T., Campbell, F. A., and Blair, C. (1998). Enhancing the life course for high risk children: results from the Abecedarian Project. In J. Crane (ed.), *Social programs that work* (pp. 163–183). New York: Russell Sage.

Ramey, C. T., Campbell, F. A., Burchinal, M., Skinner, M. L., Gardner, D. M., and Ramey, S. L. (2000). Persistent effects of early intervention on high-risk children and their mothers. *Applied Developmental Science*, 1, 2–14.

Reynolds, A. J. (2000). *Success in early intervention: the Chicago Child–Parent Centers*. Lincoln: University of Nebraska Press.

Reynolds, A. J., Englund, M., Ou, S., Campbell, F. A., and Schweinhart, L. J. (2010). Paths of effects of preschool participation to educational attainment at age 21: a 3-study analysis. In A. J. Reynolds, A. J. Rolnick, M. M. Englund, and J. A. Temple (eds.), *Childhood programs and practices in the first decade of life: a human capital integration* (pp. 415–412). Cambridge University Press.

Reynolds, A. J., Temple, J. A., Ou, S., Robertson, D. L., Mersky, J. P., Topitzes, J. W., and Niles, M. D. (2007). Effects of a school-based, early childhood intervention on adult health and well-being: a 19-year follow-up of low-income families. *Archives of Pediatrics & Adolescent Medicine*, 161(8), 730–739.

Reynolds, A. J., Temple, J. A., Robertson, D. L., and Mann, E. A. (2001). Long-term effects of an early childhood intervention on educational achievement and juvenile arrest: a 15-year follow-up of low-income children in public schools. *Journal of the American Medical Association*, 285(18), 2339–2346.

Reynolds, A. J., Temple, J. A., White, B. A., Ou, S., and Robertson, D. L. (2011). Age 26 cost–benefit analysis of the Child–Parent Center Early Education Program. *Child Development*, 82, 379–404.

Ross, T., Kena, G., Rathbun, A., KewalRamani, A., Zhang, J., Kristapovich, P., and Manning, E. (2012). *Higher education: gaps in access and persistence study* (NCES 2012–046). US Department of Education, National Center for Education Statistics. Washington, DC: US Government Printing Office.

Schaefer, E. S., Edgerton, M., and Aaronson, M. (1978). *Classroom Behavior Inventory, revised*. Chapel Hill: University of North Carolina.

Schweinhart, L. J., Barnes, H. V., and Weikart, D. P. (1993). *Significant benefits: the High/Scope Perry Preschool study through age 27*. Ypsilanti, MI: High/Scope Press.

Schweinhart, L. J., Montie, J., Xiang, Z., Barnett, S. W., Belfield, C. R., and Nores, M. (2005). *Lifetime effects: the High/Scope Perry Preschool study through age 40* (Monographs of the High/Scope Educational Research Foundation 14). Ypsilanti, MI: High/Scope Press.

Tamayo, T., Christian, H., and Rathmann, W. (2010). Impact of early psycho-social factors (childhood socioeconomic factors and adversities) on future risk of type 2 diabetes, metabolic disturbances and obesity: a systematic review. *BMC Public Health*, 10, 525. Retrived from www.biomedcentral.com/1471–2548/10/525.

Terman, L. M., and Merrill, M. A. (1960). *Stanford-Binet Intelligence Scale Form L-M: manual for the third revision*. Boston: Houghton-Mifflin.

Tiegs, E. W., and Clark, W. W. (1963). *California Achievement Tests: complete battery* (1957 edn). Monterey Park: California Test Bureau McGraw-Hill.

 (1971). *California Achievement Tests* (1970 edn). Monterey Park: California Test Bureau McGraw-Hill.

Topitzes, J., Godes, O., Mersky, J. P., Ceglarek, S., and Reynolds, A. J. (2009). Educational success and adult health: findings from the Chicago Longitudinal Study. *Prevention Science*, 10, 175–195.

Turrell, G., Lynch, J. W., Leite, C., Raghunathan, T., and Kaplan, G. A. (2007). Socioeconomic disadvantage in childhood and across the life course and all-cause mortality and physical function in adulthood: evidence from the Alameda County Study. *Journal of Epidemiology and Community Health*, 61, 723–730.

Vinter, R. D., Sarri, R. C., Vorwaller, D. J., and Schafer, W. E. (1966). *Pupil Behavior Inventory*. Ann Arbor: University of Michigan Press.

Wechsler, D. (1967). *Wechsler Preschool and Primary Scale of Intelligence*. New York: Psychological Corporation.

Woodcock, R. W., and Johnson, M. B. (1989). *Woodcock-Johnson Psycho-Educational Battery – revised*. Allen, TX: DLM Teaching Resources.

11 Preschool instructional approach and adult well-being

Momoko Hayakawa and Arthur J. Reynolds

Introduction

Historically, early childhood education programs were developed to promote children's cognitive, literacy, and social-emotional development for school entry and beyond and to counteract the negative effects of poverty that are transmitted from generation to generation. In response to President Lyndon B. Johnson's War on Poverty, preschool programs, such as the federally funded Head Start, emerged in the 1960s with the belief that environmental context can have an impact on children's cognitive and social-emotional development (Condry, 1983). After several decades of research, there is now strong evidence documenting that investments aimed at improving school readiness for economically disadvantaged children are an effective strategy to prevent problems before they arise (Duncan and Murnane, 2011).

Since the emphasis on early childhood education interventions proposed in the 1960s, American society has come to rely on its schools to reduce the achievement gap particularly among children born into poverty (Duncan and Murnane, 2011). Currently, a large variety of curricula under the broad framework of several instructional approaches have been developed and implemented in response to the multiple perspectives of best practices for promoting early childhood learning. However, with so many curricula and instructional approaches in existence, early education researchers, teachers, and policymakers have questioned which preschool instructional approach is most effective and whether or not gains due to preschool programs are sustained over time.

Furthermore, there has been a dearth of research examining long-term effects of preschool instruction, particularly those examining adult academic and social outcomes. This is because research on the long-term impact of preschool instruction requires longitudinal data on the effectiveness of a variety of preschool instructional approaches, in addition to a large sample size. The Chicago Longitudinal Study (CLS) of the Child–Parent Center preschool program, which has followed 989 children from preschool into adulthood, provides data that allow researchers to address long-term questions about the effectiveness of instructional approaches. Utilizing data from the CLS, the present study examines the differential impact of teacher-directed and child-initiated instructional approaches on adult education, crime, and health outcomes.

Instructional approach

Teacher-directed instructional approaches

One method to quantitatively study preschool instructional approach is to reconceptualize the analysis of curriculum styles. Two dimensions existing on a continuum will be discussed. The first dimension, teacher-directed instructional approaches, includes curricula that emphasize direct instruction that occurs via structured and scripted lessons. While this style proposes specific concepts that must be taught, the child's interest and abilities determine the content and extent to which a concept is taught at a particular time (Anderson and Bereiter, 1972). It focuses on teaching basic academic skills – such as phonological awareness and literacy – that are thought to provide the foundation for development in other domains. In this approach, the teacher is responsible for creating and presenting the lessons in a structured format. The teacher-directed instructional approach typically includes components such as: (1) large-group, teacher-directed instruction with blocks of time set aside to learn specific content, (2) workbooks, ditto sheets, flashcards, and other two-dimensional learning, (3) memorization and drills as learning strategies and (4) direct teaching of letter recognition, reciting the alphabet, and being instructed in the correct formation of letters (Hyson, 1991). The Direct Instruction System for Teaching Arithmetic and Reading (DISTAR) curriculum and the Demonstration and Research Center for Early Education (DARCEE) instructional program are examples of the teacher-directed approach. In these structured programs, every moment during preschool has a carefully designed instructional purpose to meet an established objective (Miller and Camp, 1972). Advocates of this approach emphasize that the formal enrichment children are exposed to early on in their development provides a valuable early start to schooling (Eastman and Barr, 1985).

Child-initiated instructional approaches

Another dimension, child-initiated teaching styles, involves the child independently selecting instructional activities that are provided by the teacher. This approach emphasizes a flexible schedule for preschoolers where the preschool day is centered around large blocks of time during which children move freely from one age-appropriate activity to another around the classroom (Crosser, 1996). With this teaching style, the teacher helps the child to construct his own knowledge from feedback from objects and through his own reasoning with objects, as opposed to learning external behavior or final answers to questions directly from the teacher (Kamii, 1972). Some specific examples of aspects of child-initiated classrooms include: (1) children self-selecting activities among a variety of learning areas presented by the teacher, (2) learning activities closely related to children's daily life experiences, (3) children using a variety of media in ways of their own choosing for an eclectic experience, and (4) teachers using redirection, positive reinforcement, and encouragement as guidance and discipline techniques (Hyson, 1991). This is thought to nurture self-awareness, self-regulation, and other meta-cognitive abilities that lay the foundation for acquiring academic skills. This type of instruction is often labeled as the "traditional" or "nursery school" approach. Montessori, Reggio Emilia, and High/Scope curricula exemplify this type of approach and are characterized by constructivist approaches to learning. Originally explored by Montessori and later expanded by Piagetian perspectives of child development, the teacher's role in the child-initiated approach is to enable the child to create knowledge, as opposed to transmitting knowledge (Kamii, 1972). Proponents of this child-initiated approach believe that through allowing children to select their activities, the program promotes enthusiasm for school, self-confidence, and creativity (Hirsh-Pasek, 1991).

Both styles of instructional approaches have advantages. According to Parker and Day (1972), advantages of teacher-directed programs are: (1) the child is directly taught basic skills deemed necessary for its educational development, (2) the child is provided with adult models for behavior rather than discovering through trial and error appropriate behavior, and (3) the teacher can offer immediate feedback to the child's actions. However, there are also advantages to the child-initiated approach, for example: (1) autonomy encourages the development of initiative, (2) the approach ensures a child's interest in its chosen activity and thus provides intrinsic motivation for its learning experience, (3) the approach increases the likelihood that the material the child selects is developmentally appropriate, and (4) the child-initiated approach allows the child an opportunity to discover relationships and principles on her own, rather than being told the information by the teacher. Both styles of instruction have their respective strengths that can justifiably aid children's cognitive and social-emotional development. More importantly, these styles of instruction may not be mutually exclusive in practice.

Despite the dichotomous perception of instructional approach in the literature as teacher-directed or child-initiated, preschool programs can have both teacher-directed and child-initiated program components. For example, once a child independently selects an activity, a teacher can direct the student's learning using developmentally appropriate strategies. More recently, preschool curricula, such as Building Blocks (Clements and Sarama, 2007), Research Based Developmentally Informed (REDI) (Bierman et al., 2008), and Evidence Based Program for the Integration of Curricula (EPIC) (Fantuzzo et al., 2003), have been developed with this idea of incorporating both teacher-directed and child-initiated approaches. Building Blocks is a mathematics curriculum mixing individual, small-group, and large-group activities. This program includes both instructional approaches through embedding mathematical concepts in preschoolers' daily lives. REDI and EPIC are also programs that incorporate both types of instructional approaches, particularly through emphasizing child-centered approaches to learning that draw on resources surrounding the classroom, home, and learning community. Developmentally appropriate and empirically validated components of curriculum are integrated across the school day in the REDI and EPIC programs, such as using a mixture of individual, small-group, and large-group activities.

Current findings from longitudinal preschool instruction studies

As reported by Graue and colleagues (2004), previous research has found that instruction classified as primarily teacher-directed activities (direct instruction) produced the most academic gains as measured by IQ and standardized achievement tests. While these cognitive gains were imme-diate, the effects typically dissipated after third grade (e.g., Dale and Cole, 1988; Karnes, Shwedel, and Williams, 1983; Karnes, Teska, and Hodgins, 1970; Miller and Dyer, 1975; Schweinhart, Weikart, and Larner, 1986). Marcon (2002) reported differential effects by various preschool instruc-tions on report cards, grade retention, and special education. By the end of preschool, children who had experienced child-initiated programs demonstrated greater mastery of basic skills, and by the end of fourth grade they had better grades than their counterparts in teacher-directed classrooms. In an analysis of forty-two classrooms across a variety of programs, Stipek and colleagues (1998) found that structured programs encouraging basic skills that used teacher-directed approaches were less nurturing and responsive to individual children, provided children with fewer choices, and used more negative strategies to control children's behaviors. After a two-year follow-up, children who experienced child-initiated instruction had maintained better scores on cognitive measures over children from teacher-directed instruction. Furthermore, Golbeck (2002) has also reported differential findings of preschool instructional approaches and has found that children in more academically oriented programs seem to fare better short-term on achievement tests, but had lower motivation and self-confidence than children in child-initiated programs.

To our knowledge, very few longitudinal studies have examined children's long-term outcomes of various instructional approach effects in early intervention programs. Schweinhart and Weikart (1997) assessed differential program effectiveness among High/Scope (i.e., a child-initiated instructional approach), teacher-directed programs, and traditional nursery schools. Results suggested that, at age 23, people who experienced the teacher-directed group were more likely to have engaged in criminal activity and to have emotional disturbances than the High/Scope curriculum group. Although results did not distinguish between the High/Scope group and the traditional nursery group, both of which adopted the child-initiated approach, there were clear advantages to being in either one of those programs over a teacher-directed approach. Thus, this study highlighted significant long-term benefits to being in a child-initiated preschool instruction over a teacher-directed preschool instruction.

Despite research indicating support for child-initiated instruction, a recent review of preschool intervention programs by Camilli and colleagues (2010) suggests that teacher-directed instruction accompanied by small-group instruction promoted children's academic success. Of note, however, they advise that successful programs focus on developmentally appropriate explicit instruction rather than rely only on direct instruction as a method of teaching.

Moreover, examining longitudinal effects of instructional approaches, Cole and colleagues (2002) compared the effects of child-initiated programs and direct instruction on social development and found no differences on any social outcomes at age 15. Jenkins et al. (2006) randomly assigned preschoolers in special education to either direct instruction or mediated learning (child-initiated) groups. At age 19, they also found that there were no differential instruction effects on achievement or special education placement during any point of the study. However, Nelson, Westhues, and Macleod (2003), examined thirty-four studies between 1970 and 2000 and found that long-term (through eighth grade) cognitive impact was largest for preschool programs with a direct teaching component.

The numerous and contradictory impacts of child-initiated versus teacher-directed approaches reported thus far in the literature lead us to investigate whether differences on long-term impacts by instructional approaches do exist and, if so, how the effects of instructional approach differ in adults across a variety of outcomes. Moreover, as Stipek and colleagues (1995) encouraged, a dichotomous analysis is inadequate in characterizing the complexity of instruction type. Thus, further research considering both domains simultaneously is beneficial in examining preschool instruction effectiveness.

Graue and colleagues (2004) examined the impact of instructional approaches in the Child–Parent Center (CPC) preschool program for outcomes measured from kindergarten to high school. The study found that a combination of high teacher-directed and high child-initiated programs was consistently associated with children's achievement during childhood – school readiness at kindergarten, reaching achievement in grade school, and avoidance of grade retention. This blended approach was consistently and significantly associated with children's educational achievement. Instructional approaches focusing on only teacher-directed or child-initiated activities were less strongly associated with children's academic performance. However, differences emerged between short- and long-term effects. The teacher-directed approach with low levels of child-initiated activities was associated with kindergarten achievement in word analysis and mathematics but a child-initiated approach was more associated with high school completion by age 22 than any other instructional approach. Other than high school completion, outcomes were assessed during childhood and adolescence.

Further investigation is needed on the extent to which instructional approach impacts adult well-being. Previous studies have found that CPC participation promotes health in adulthood, for example through improved self-perceived health status and behavior, and lower rates of depression. More recent studies have also found that CPC participation is associated with other general indicators of adult well-being, such as higher education and socioeconomic status and lower involvement in the criminal justice system (Reynolds et al., 2007; Reynolds, Temple, and Ou, 2010; Reynolds et al., 2011). One plausible explanation of the observed multifaceted adult outcomes may be due to the contribution of effective preschool instructional approaches. Child-initiated and activity-based instructional approaches are designed to promote exploration, self-regulation, and achievement motivation (Schweinhart and Weikart, 1988; Stipek et al., 1995), which are expected to strengthen later self-efficacy and perceived control leading to greater aspirations, educational attainment, and ultimately positive health and well-being (Braveman and Barclay, 2009; Schweinhart et al., 1993; Singh-Manoux et al., 2004).

The present study expands upon the earlier studies by examining the role of preschool instructional approach on life-course outcomes in early adulthood for children participating in CPC preschool programs. Following the same participants into early adulthood, this study will examine the role of instructional approach on later adult outcomes, including educational attainment, criminal history, and health status. Three questions are addressed. What is the impact that instructional approach has on (1) educational outcomes, (2) adult criminal activity, and (3) adult health status? Based on previous studies, we expect that instructional approaches blending teacher-direction and child-initiated activities will be most positively associated with later outcomes.

Methodology

Sample and intervention

The study includes 989 children in the Chicago Longitudinal Study (Reynolds, 1999) who attended the Chicago Child–Parent Centers (CPC) at age 3 or 4. Study children (93% of whom are African American) resided in low-income families and were raised in neighborhoods with the highest poverty levels in Chicago. Because the focus of the present study was on children in the preschool program, the 550 children in the non-CPC comparison group were excluded.

Table 11.1 displays the child and family characteristics of the study sample. The CPC preschool group was gender balanced. Among socioeconomic characteristics, over 90% were eligible for the subsidized school lunch program. Approximately one half resided in single-parent families and in families in which parents were not employed full- or part-time. Furthermore, approximately half the sample participated in CPC preschool for two years beginning at age 3, 60 percent attended full-day kindergarten programs in the centers, and 69 percent attended the CPC school-age program for at least one year.

The CPC program is an early educational intervention providing comprehensive educational and family services to children between the ages of 3 and 9 (preschool to third grade) and their families living in poverty. The program practices and structures are based on the assumptions that development is optimized in rich, stable learning environments where parents are heavily involved in the process of learning. Four components comprise the program: early intervention, parent involvement, a structured language/basic skills learning approach, and program continuity between preschool and elementary school.

The CPC program is a combination of standardization and local control, while highlighting the importance of academic and social-emotional development. The core instructional philosophy emphasizes the acquisition of

Table 11.1 *Descriptive statistics for CPC preschool participants in the Chicago Longitudinal Study by Curriculum.*

	HT/HC n = 387		HT/LC n = 63		LT/HC n = 363		LT/LC n = 176	
	n	%	n	%	n	%	n	%
African American	384	99.2	62	98.4	313	86.2	158	89.9
Boys	201	51.9	37	58.7	190	52.3	84	47.7
Low birth weight (< 2500 grams)	37	9.6	7	11.1	47	12.9	17	9.7
Mother completed high school, child age 0–3	197	50.9	25	39.7	183	50.4	80	45.5
Mother attended some college	53	13.7	4	6.3	56	15.4	20	11.4
Mother not employed full time, child age 0–3	266	68.7	44	69.8	238	65.6	118	67.0
Mother single parent, child age 0–3	314	81.1	51	81.0	264	72.7	130	73.9
Mother less than 18 years at child's birth	63	16.3	10	15.9	55	15.2	26	14.8
TANF participation, child age 0–3	249	64.3	47	74.6	217	59.8	111	63.1
Eligible for free lunch, child age 0–3	322	83.2	55	87.3	306	84.3	150	85.2
< 4 children in household, child age 0–3	69	17.8	7	11.1	52	14.3	30	17.0
Child welfare services	8	2.1	3	4.8	16	4.4	4	2.3
Missing on any indicator	69	17.8	7	11.1	52	14.3	18	10.2
Living in a neighborhood with 60%+ poverty (mean)	72.0		100.0		69.0		100.0	
% of low-income families in school area (mean)	68.8		72.9		60.1		72.2	
Number of years of preschool								
1 year	170	43.9	23	36.5	177	48.8	85	48.3
2 years	217	56.1	40	63.5	186	51.2	91	51.7

basic skills and knowledge in literacy and mathematics through relatively structured but diverse learning experiences that range from whole class, small group, learning centers, individual work, and fieldtrips. Affective learning is embedded within the academic content. This core is shared across centers but is adapted to reflect local needs. Suggested instructional activities are provided (Chicago Board of Education, 1988) and supplemented with other literacy materials, such as Houghton Mifflin, DISTAR, and Peabody Language Development kits. The child-to-staff ratio is limited to 17 to 2 in preschool and 25 to 2 in kindergarten, although parent volunteers reduced these numbers further. The centers make considerable efforts to involve parents in the education of their children, requiring at least half a day per week of parent involvement in the program (Reynolds, 2000).

Explanatory measures

Instructional approach

Teachers rated the extent to which the centers emphasized basic skills, small- or large-group activities, formal reading instruction, learning centers, fieldtrips, and child- and teacher-directed activities. The teaching philosophy of the center and specific instructional materials in use were reported retrospectively through open-ended questions by head teachers of the Child–Parent Centers in 1995 (Reynolds, 2000). From these data, each Child–Parent Center was classified as relatively high or low on two dimensions of preschool instruction: teacher-directed instructional activities and child-initiated instructional activities. Centers rated high on *teacher-directed* (HT) activities used direct instruction materials that emphasized phonics and pencil-and-paper activities (e.g., Houghton Mifflin). HT classrooms frequently use large-group activities, emphasize basic skills for learning, and implement formal reading instruction. As defined earlier, these characteristics were identified as supportive of teacher-directed instructional approaches according to previous literature (e.g., Hyson, 1991). In teacher-directed activities, the content is identified and sequenced by the teacher. Centers low in teacher-directed activities (LT) used activity-based approaches or materials emphasizing using language in context (e.g., labeling, comparing, storytelling, remembering) such as the Peabody Language Development kits.

Use of a *child-initiated* approach identified by CPC head teachers was based on ratings of the extent to which centers utilized child-focused instructional approaches including (1) fieldtrips, (2) small-group learning centers, and (3) child-initiated activities. Centers were rated as having a high emphasis on child-initiated activities (HC) if each of the three approaches was used "often" (on a scale of never, sometimes, often). As mentioned previously in our description of child-initiated instructional approaches, these characteristics are representative of HC activities, as they are planned in general by the teachers but function under the assumption that play and children's choice of activity is developmentally appropriate to facilitate learning. Remaining centers were rated as low on child-initiated activities (LC). Detailed information and descriptive statistics about the approach used in the classification of instructional approaches, with an identical CLS sample, are documented by Graue et al. (2004).

Children in the present study were categorized into one of four instructional groups: (1) high teacher-directed instruction and high child-initiated instruction (HT+HC; n = 387), (2) high teacher-directed instruction and low child-initiated instruction (HT+LC; n = 63), (3) low teacher-directed instruction and high child-initiated instruction (LT+HC; n = 363), and (4) low teacher-directed instruction and low child-initiated instruction (LT+LC; n = 176). Of importance, the LT/LC instructional style was low in teacher direction and child initiation relative to the other three curricula. The LT/LC approach did include some teacher-directed and child-initiated activities that the other groups used, but a clear instructional style was not evident.

Assessment of inter-rater reliability, based on three raters, for assignment into teacher-directed and child-initiated instructional approaches produced a Kappa = .75. This measure of agreement is significant and substantial (Landis and Koch, 1977). Although the classification was based largely on retrospective reports, to minimize reporting bias we relied most heavily on the teaching philosophy and specific instructional materials used in the centers in determining the classifications. This information was verifiable with reports by head teachers (directors) of all CPC sites (Graue et al. 2004).

Covariates

Measures of preprogram attributes were obtained through birth records, CLS parent survey and self-report participant surveys, and administrative records provided by the Illinois Department of Child and Family Services, the Illinois Department of Health and Family Services, and the Chicago Public Schools.

> *CPC Program Participation:* A dichotomous indicator identified whether children enrolled in the CPC program for two years beginning at age 3 or for one year at age 4.
>
> *Race/ethnicity of child:* African American children were coded 1 and Hispanic children were coded 0.
>
> *Sex of child:* Boys were coded 1 and girls were coded 0.
>
> *Child welfare services:* Having any child welfare history is a dichotomous indicator of any substantiated abuse or neglect report on the child by the child's fourth birthday.
>
> *Indicators of background risk:* Eight dichotomous sociodemographic measures are included as indicators of preprogram family risk status. These were selected based on their well-known associations with child and family well-being (Bendersky and Lewis, 1994) and include maternal education, the single-parent status of the child's mother, teen-parent status of the child's mother, family size, free school lunch eligibility, family public aid recipient (AFDC or TANF), parent employment status, and

residence in a school neighborhood in which 60 percent or more of children are in low-income families.

Maternal education: Maternal education by the child's fourth birthday was identified using two variables collected through administrative data: mother's high school completion status and mother's college attendance status. Mother's high school completion status is a dichotomous variable indicating whether or not the mother completed high school or received a GED credential. Mother's college attendance is a dichotomous variable which indicates whether or not the mother had attended any college.

Outcome measures

Items used to assess adult outcomes were collected retrospectively throughout adulthood from a variety of sources (e.g., self-report, public data).

Educational attainment

The sample used to predict educational attainment includes youth whose educational attainment could be determined by August 2004 (mean age is 24) (n = 892). Four measures were used as indicators of educational attainment: (1) high school completion, (2) highest grade completed, (3) on-time graduation, and (4) four-year college attendance. High school completion is a dichotomous variable indicating whether youths completed their secondary education by earning an official high school diploma or passing the General Education Development test (GED) by age 24. If they completed high school or received a GED they were coded as 1, and all others as 0. On-time graduation is a dichotomous variable indicating whether a participant graduated high school on-time or not. Four-year college attendance is a dichotomous variable indicating whether a participant attended (and earned college credit at) any four-year college. These measures were extracted from administrative records in all schools youths attended and were supplemented by interviews with family members.

Adult crime

The sample used to predict adult criminal behavior (n = 918) includes all participants who completed the CLS age 22–24 adult survey, whose criminal records were available through administrative records, or whom various administrative sources identified as adult (over 18) residents of Illinois. Three measures were used as indicators of criminal behavior between the ages of 18 and 24 years: (1) incarceration or jail, (2) felony arrest, and (3) conviction.

Physical and mental health

Five measures were used as indicators of participants' health and mental well-being: teenage parenting, substance use, health insurance coverage, disability status, and depressive symptoms.

Teenage parenting

Teenage parenting (n = 512) was determined for all female participants. If the participant had a child before the age of 18, the variable was coded as 1, and 0 if otherwise. This information was obtained through self-report measures collected in the CLS age 22–24 adult survey as well as public administrative records.

Health insurance coverage

Health insurance coverage (n = 837) from either a public or a private (employer-based) source was assessed between ages 22 and 24 years. Public insurance coverage data came from state-level Medicaid records and the CLS age 22–24 adult survey (e.g., "Do you get health benefits from your employer?") and were supplemented with records from the Illinois Department of Employment Security.

Substance use

Substance use (n = 777) was a dichotomous variable that included self-reported drug abuse problems and administrative adult drug arrest records by age 24. Adult drug arrest records included drug possession, drug manufacturing/delivery, and drug conspiracy, collected from official court reports of criminal records at the county, state, and federal level. Any affirmative response for any of these variables received a code of 1.

Disability status

Disability status (n = 961) measured receipt of disability assistance (i.e., from Social Security Disability Insurance or Supplemental Security Income) since age 18 years from either the Illinois Department of Health and Human Services records or the adult survey. Teenage parenting was a dichotomous variable indicating whether girls gave birth before age 18. Data were from the adult survey and public aid records (n = 512).

Depressive symptoms

Depressive symptoms also were reported in the self-report CLS adult survey at age 22–24. Participants rated how often in the past month they felt (1) depressed, (2) helpless, (3) lonely, (4) that life is not worth living, and (5) very sad (0 = not at all, 5 = almost every day). To maximize reliability, we used a dichotomous variable indicating the frequent presence of one or more symptoms defined at levels ranging from a few times a month to almost every day.

Results

Mean comparisons

Means were calculated for each instructional group and for each outcome measure as the first step to examine whether long-term outcomes differed by instructional approach. To determine the effects of controlling for various risk and demographic factors on the outcomes, mean values were adjusted for demographic factors: gender, ethnicity, child abuse/neglect, and preschool length as well as preprogram risk indicators.

Educational attainment

F tests revealed significant differences between groups for high school completion and four-year college attendance, even after accounting for the covariates. There were no other statistically significant differences between groups for the other educational attainment outcomes. No significant differences among instructional approaches were found in the post hoc pairwise comparisons.

Adult crime

Differences between groups for all the adult crime outcomes were significant, controlling for covariates. Results from the Tukey-Kramer pairwise comparisons indicate that both the high child-initiated approaches had significantly lower rates of felony arrests and incarceration, compared to either of the low child-initiated instructional approaches. As for convictions of criminal activity, children from low child-initiated programs did not significantly differ from each other, and had higher rates of criminal conviction than other instructional approaches. However, the mean of children from the high teacher-directed/low child-initiated approach did not significantly differ from criminal conviction means of any other instructional approach. Moreover, the lowest rates of criminal conviction were among the high child-initiated instructional approaches. This finding is consistent across multiple adult crime related outcomes.

Table 11.2 *Adjusted means for preschool curriculum – age 24 young adult outcomes.*

Outcomes measures	Preschool curriculum				
	HT/HC	HT/LC	LT/HC	LT/LC	Chi^2
Educational attainment by age 24					
High school completion, %	83.67	76.92	80.58	74.6	5.68*
Highest grade completed	12.06	11.79	12.04	11.92	F = .709
On time graduation, %	47.95	40.19	45.08	41.67	2.15
4-year college attendance, %	13.89	7.82	11.26	7.77	4.81*
Adult crime by age 24					
Any incarceration or jail, %	3.13[b]	18.60[a]	3.43[b]	12.85[a]	26.54***
Felony arrest, %	7.29[b]	22.09[a]	7.30[b]	22.28[a]	24.57***
Any conviction, %	14.77[cd]	24.8[abc]	14.02[bd]	26.82[a]	10.48***
Health and mental health by age 24					
Had child before age 18 (females), %	26.60	32.61	25.50	24.88	1.89
Drug abuse and conviction age 24, %	16.48	25.02	17.00	25.30	4.58
Any health insurance, %	61.61	55.82	70.15	58.69	.64
Public insurance, %	18.31	17.88	27.19	30.79	7.86**
Private insurance, %	37.80	34.59	37.65	23.70	8.28**
Any disability, %	4.25	8.48	5.61	7.30	2.52
If reported any depression symptom, %	17.33	11.21	12.29	18.39	2.07

Note: *p < .10, **p < .05, ***p < .01. Superscripts a, b, c, and d denote significant adjusted mean differences from Tukey-Kramer post hoc pairwise comparisons. Values adjusted for: gender, ethnicity, child welfare services ages 0–3, preschool length, missing any risk indicators, and eight indicators of preprogram risk status (child age 0–3): 60% + poverty in school area, mother did not complete high school, public assistance (TANF/AFDC), mother not employed, single parent status, mother less than 18 years old at child's birth, four or more children in the household, eligible for free lunch.

Health and mental health

F values for private insurance use and public insurance use were significant when means differences were adjusted with covariates. There were no other significant differences for any other physical or mental health outcomes.

Hierarchical regression models[1]

Key outcomes based on the analyses of group difference means were entered into a hierarchical model to further address our first question in

---

[1] Hierarchical regressions examining the impact of two instructional approaches (i.e., teacher-directed approach and child-initiated approach) in conjunction with its interaction of teacher-directed × child-initiated approach on adult outcomes were also examined. The

understanding to what extent adult outcomes are associated with various types of preschool instructional approaches. To account for clustering of students by CPC centers, standard errors, and thus p-values, have been adjusted by center. Main effects from probit regressions, adjusted standard errors, and p-values are displayed in Table 11.3. Outcomes of interest included high school completion, felony arrests, and public insurance use.

High school completion by age 24

In model 1, the LT/LC group showed marginally significant and negative associations in predicting high school completion (b = −.080, $p < .052$). In model 2, instructional approach was no longer significant, and instead, African American status (b = −.138, $p < .001$), gender (b = −.106, $p < .005$), free lunch eligibility (b = − .084, $p < .049$), public aid participation (b = − .104, $p < .017$), and mother's incompletion of high school (b = − .077, $p < .046$) significantly predicted high school completion (pseudo R^2 = .084). In model 1, instructional approach explained 0.7 percent of the variance while model 2 explained 8.4 percent of the variance in high school completion.

Felony arrests by age 24

In model 1, the HT/LC group and LT/LC group both significantly and positively predicted felony arrest (b = .145, $p < .001$; b = .166, $p < .001$, respectively). In model 2, the HT/LC group and LT/LC group remained positively significant (b = .170, $p < .001$; b = .156, $p < .001$, respectively), as did other covariates such as gender (b = .257, $p < .001$) and public aid participation (b = .056, $p < .020$). In model 1, instructional approach explained 3.6% of the variance while model 2 explained 26.4 percent of the variance in felony arrests (pseudo R^2 = .264).

Public insurance by age 24

Instructional approach was not a significant predictor of public insurance in model 1. In model 2, HT/HC was approaching significance and negatively predicted public insurance use (b = −.060, $p < .082$). Covariates such as gender (b = −.305, $p < .001$), mother's incompletion of high school (b = .146, $p < .001$), and mother's single-parent status at participant's birth (b = .141, $p < .002$) significantly positively predicted public insurance use. In model 1, instructional approach explained 0.6 percent of the variance while model 2 explained 14.5 percent of the variance in high school completion. The pseudo R squared change from model 1 to model 2

interaction term was non-significant for all adult outcomes. We suspect that it is not necessarily the blended teacher-directed/child-initiated approach that is effective but rather the high child-initiated approach.

Table 11.3 *Hierarchical logistic regression models predicting long-term outcomes.*

	High school completion		Felony arrests		Public insurance	
	B (s. e.)	p	B (s. e.)	p	B (s. e.)	p
Model 1 (unadjusted)						
HT/HC	.003 (.061)	.955	.004 (.041)	.91	-.047 (.029)	.110
HT/LC	-.082 (.059)	.146	.145 (.037)	.001	.008 (.022)	.714
LT/LC	-.080 (.052)	.110	.166 (.046)	.001	.060 (.035)	.082
Pseudo R²	.007		.036		.006	
Wald Chi²	4.05		29.77		9.60	
Model 2 (adjusted)						
HT/HC	.031 (.046)	.506	-.001 (.022)	.976	-.066 (.030)	.025
HT/LC	-.031 (.052)	.536	.170 (.039)	.001	-.062 (.028)	.033
LT/LC	-.054 (.056)	.307	.156 (.039)	.001	.070 (.043)	.097
African American	-.138 (.020)	.001	-.001 (.029)	.969	-.015 (.048)	.752
Gender	-.106 (.040)	.005	.257 (.027)	.001	-.305 (.033)	.001
Child welfare	-.073 (.085)	.348	.074 (.059)	.105	.134 (.117)	.226
Missing indicator	.015 (.037)	.678	-.018 (.019)	.396	-.013 (.062)	.832
Years of CPC prekindergarten	-.001 (.031)	.979	-.024 (.016)	.162	.028 (.030)	.353
% of low income families in school region	-.018 (.50)	.722	-.039 (.027)	.126	-.003(.043)	.940

Free lunch eligibility	−.084 (.037)	.049		.020 (.018)	.292		−.028 (.056)	.616
Mother not employed	.013 (.041)	.744		−.030 (.023)	.151		−.004 (.049)	.941
Public aid participation	−.104 (.041)	.017		.056 (.020)	.004		.087 (.058)	.138
Four or more children	−.123 (.046)	.003		.036 (.022)	.055		−.003 (.048)	.950
Mother not complete high school	−.077 (.038)	.046		.002 (.018)	.929		.146 (.025)	.001
Teenage mother	.017 (.028)	.554		.008 (.019)	.672		−.072 (.048)	.156
Single parent	−.055 (.035)	.122		.001 (.021)	.956		.141 (.042)	.002
Pseudo R^2	.084			.264			.145	
Wald Chi^2	776.46			396.84			462.95	

Note: Marginal effects from probit regressions are reported.

Standard errors and *p*-values are adjusted for clustering by CPC center

OR predicting high school completion: HT/HC = 1.237; HT/LC = .700; LT/LC = .665

OR predicting felony arrests: HT/HC = .620; HT/LC = 1.931; LT/LC = 2.689

OR predicting public insurance: HT/HC = .734; HT/LC = 1.077; LT/LC = 1.454

(pseudo R^2 = .145) indicates a modest increase in variance explained with the addition of predictors for public insurance usage rates.

Discussion

This study builds upon earlier studies examining the long-term effects of preschool instruction on academic and social outcomes (Graue et al., 2004; Reynolds, 2000). Previous results indicated the long-term benefits of instructional approaches that incorporated a high teacher-directed and high child-initiated approach. The results of the present study are consistent with the findings on high school completion from previous studies, but also extend beyond the previous study by demonstrating that preschool instructional approach links to measures of adult well-being at age 24, including involvement in the criminal justice system and health insurance coverage, as well as educational attainment. Compared to relatively low child-initiated approaches, a high child-initiated instructional approach was associated with significantly lower rates of official felony arrest, conviction, and incarceration. The rates of felony arrest for the high child-initiated instructional groups, for example, were one-third of those of the low child-initiated groups (7.3 percent vs. 22.3 percent; Table 11.3). Furthermore, our results indicate that instructional approaches low in child-initiated activities (i.e., HT/LC and LT/LC) are significantly and positively associated with higher criminal activity. This finding suggests the importance of child-initiated activities in promoting lifelong skills.

These preventive benefits highlight the efficacy of high child-initiated instructional approaches and their long-term benefits, particularly on criminal behavior. Specifically, high child-initiated approaches have consistently been associated with positive long-term outcomes such as differences in adult crime outcomes, high school completion rates, and college attendance (Schweinhart et al., 1993; Schweinhart and Weikart, 1997). Furthermore, we also have found significantly lower rates of incarceration and felony arrests for boys who experienced high child-initiated instruction. As noted by Camilli et al. (2010), however, there is no evidence indicating that teacher-directed approaches should be avoided. What this study highlights instead is the significant long-term benefits of a child-initiated approach – especially in conjunction with an instruction high in teacher-directed activities. The addition of the teacher-directed approach may enhance the benefits of the child-initiated instruction.

Our results are consistent with literature in child development – instructional approaches relying heavily on activities initiated by the child are developmentally appropriate, particularly for the preschool period.

These activities enhance children's independent interest in school – an important factor for children to acquire basic social-emotional skills necessary for learning during this age. Perhaps these early and basic skills form the foundation for later well-being. Our results suggest a continued association between child-initiated instructional approaches in preschool and reductions in involvement with crime as adults. These findings are supported by previous studies examining child-initiated versus teacher-directed instructional approaches. Schweinhart and Weikart (1997) in their examination of the long-term impact of preschool instruction in the High/Scope curriculum found that the child-initiated instructional approaches were associated with early adult outcomes such as fewer felony arrests, fewer arrests for property crime, fewer reports of misconduct, and more engagement in volunteer work.

In our study, however, the association between instructional approach and educational outcomes was not observed into adulthood. This finding is consistent with previous literature which has documented short-term associations between teacher-directed preschool instruction and achievement which disappear by the third grade (e.g., DeVries, Reese-Learned, and Morgan, 1991; Hirsh-Pasek, Hyson, and Rescorla, 1990; Schweinhart and Weikart, 1997). We suspect that the lack of a significant association between instructional approach and educational outcomes in our study is due to our question addressing main effects, and not to meditational or generative mechanisms. We would expect other factors, such as achievement across childhood, to have direct impacts on long-term educational outcomes.

Contributions to preschool instruction research

A unique feature of the study is the longitudinal comparisons of preschool instructional approach on measures of adult well-being. Our study is one of the first to examine preschool instructional effects on general well-being including health status and behavior, mental health, and many measures of education and socioeconomic status. Furthermore, this study elaborates upon the Preschool Curriculum Evaluation Research (PCER) study, a large-scale national attempt to address the question of effective instructional approach. The PCER study assessed the effectiveness of an array of early education programs, through fifteen implementations of early education programs across the United States (2008). Although the PCER study provides a comprehensive review of the potential benefits of various programs, first it did not allow for cross-curriculum comparisons due to differing control groups and disparate populations assessed, and second it did not examine long-term effects of the various programs. Third, and most importantly, due to the nature of the question – comparing different types of curricula – the results did not provide conclusive answers about the best *instructional approach* to inform practitioners.

The effectiveness of assessing instructional approaches, rather than curricula, is supported by our research as well as by others. Karnes and colleagues (1983) also suggest that program effects may be delayed and examine long-term effects of instructional approaches dimensionally, as opposed to by curriculum comparisons. In their assessment of instructional approaches, they found that at the end of first grade, children in the structured, teacher-directed curricula academically outperformed children in child-initiated programs, such as Montessori. However, at later follow-up they found that children who experienced the Montessori program were more likely to complete high school, compared to children from the teacher-directed approach. As such, examining preschool programs by instructional approach over a long period of time has the greatest benefits for practitioners and policymakers in discerning the most critical components for an effective preschool programs with long-lasting positive gains.

Because the CPC program is routinely implemented in the Midwest, the generalizability of the findings is greater than for many previous studies, which were largely limited to efficacy trials designed to test curricular effects in small samples and outside of public schools. Consequently, the findings have relevance for other Title I funded programs, state-funded prekindergarten, and Head Start. For example, the expansion of the CPC program or core instructional and organizational elements of the CPC program may help strengthen currently operating programs, especially those whose effects are modest. Although the CPC program has been implemented well for decades within a comprehensive-service mission, the instructional philosophy can be applied to other programs and expansion efforts without sacrificing quality and flexibility of implementation.

Implications

Our findings highlight the importance of having a pre-established instructional approach. Preschools implementing a specified instructional framework created under theories of child development (e.g., Piagetian theories of development) enhance the quality of the program by providing a system in place. For example, teachers certified to teach a child-initiated preschool program have opportunities to interact with other likeminded teachers to form a community with shared styles of teaching. This produces a system where consistent child-initiated instruction is promoted and implemented.

Furthermore, after assessing effective preschool programs, specific advantages of instructional approaches have been identified. Principles of effective instructional characteristics include small class size, certified teachers, high teacher–student ratio, professional development opportunities, and history of implementation. It is critical to examine the principles of effectiveness of programs to better understand both short- and long-term program effects.

Our findings highlight the importance of including a system with a concretely defined instructional approach integrating both teacher-directed and child-initiated activities. This blended approach would allow the implementation of a program that affords an opportunity for advantageous long-term impacts in social and academic performance. These components can be vital elements in promoting early learning for children at risk and are potentially powerful factors in predicting adult social outcomes. Literature in child development has documented early childhood as a particularly promising period for efficient interventions (Nelson and Sheridan, 2011). We must take advantage of this opportunity and develop and assess effective early childhood programs to effectively reduce the expanding income achievement gap in America.

References

Anderson, V., and Bereiter, C. (1972). Extending direct instruction to conceptual skills. In R. Parker (ed.), *The preschool in action: exploring early childhood programs* (pp. 339–352). Boston: Allyn and Bacon.

Bendersky, M., and Lewis, M. (1994). Environmental risk, biological risk, and developmental outcome. *Developmental Psychology*, 30, 484–494.

Bierman, K. L., Domitrovich, C. E., Nix, R. L., Gest, S. D., Welsh, J. A., Greenberg, M. T., Blair, C., Nelson, K., and Gill, S. (2008). Promoting academic and social-emotional school readiness: the Head Start REDI program. *Child Development*, 79, 1802–1817.

Braveman, P., and Barclay, C. (2009). Health disparities beginning in childhood: a life-course perspective. *Pediatrics*, 124, S163–S175.

Camilli, G., Vargas, S., Ryan, S., and Barnett, W. S. (2010). Meta-analysis of the effects of early education interventions on cognitive and social development. *Teachers College Record*, 112(3), Article 15440.

Chicago Board of Education (1988).*Chicago EARLY: instructional activities for ages 3 to 6*. Vernon Hills, IL: ETA.

Clements, D. H., and Sarama, J. (2007). Effects of a preschool mathematics curriculum: summary research on the Building Blocks project. *Journal for Research in Mathematics Education*, 38, 136–163.

Cole, K. N., Mills, P. E., Jenkins, J. R., and Dale, P. S. (2002). Early intervention curricula and subsequent adolescent social development: a longitudinal examination. *Journal of Early Intervention*, 27(2), 71–82.

Condry, S. (1983). History and background of preschool intervention programs and the Consortium for Longitudinal Studies. In Consortium for

Longitudinal Studies (ed.), *As the twig is bent: lasting effects of preschool programs* (pp. 1–31). Hillsdale, NJ: Lawrence Erlbaum Associates.

Crosser, S. (1996). The butterfly garden: developmentally appropriate practice defined. *Early Childhood NEWS*, 8, 20–24.

Dale, P. S., and Cole, K. N. (1988). Comparison of academic and cognitive programs for young children. *Exceptional Children*, 54, 439–447.

DeVries, R., Reese-Learned, H., and Morgan, P. (1991). Sociomoral development in direct-instruction, eclectic, and constructivist kindergartens: a study of children's enacted interpersonal understanding. *Early Childhood Research Quarterly*, 6(4), 473–517.

Duncan, G. J., and Murnane, R. J. (2011). Introduction: the American Dream, then and now. In G. J. Duncan and R. J. Murnane (eds.), *Whither Opportunity?* (pp. 3–23). New York: Russell Sage Foundation.

Eastman, P., and Barr, J. L. (1985). *Your child is smarter than you think*. London: Jonathan Cape.

Fantuzzo, J. W., Gadsden, V., McDermott, P. A., Frye, D. A., and Culhane, D. (2003). Evidence based program for the integration of curricula (EPIC): a comprehensive initiative for low-income preschool children (School Readiness Grant No. R01HD46168–01). Washington, DC: National Institute of Child Health and Human Development.

Golbeck, S. L. (2002). *Instructional models for early childhood education* (ERIC Document Reproduction Service No. ED 468565). Retrieved August, 26, 2011 from ceep. crc.uiuc.edu/eecearchive/digests/2002/golbeck02.pdf.

Graue, E., Clements, M. A., Reynolds, A. J., and Niles, M. D. (2004). More than teacher directed or child initiated: preschool curriculum type, parent involvement, and children's outcomes in the child–parent centers. *Education Policy Analysis Archives*, 12(72), 1–38.

Hirsh-Pasek, K. (1991). Pressure or challenge in preschool? How academic environments affect children. *New Directions for Child Development*, 53, 39–45.

Hirsh-Pasek, K., Hyson, M. C., and Rescorla, L. (1990). Academic environments in preschool: do they pressure or challenge young children? *Early Education and Development*, 1(6), 401–423.

Hyson, M. C. (1991). The characteristics and origins of the academic preschool. *New Directions for Child Development*, 53, 21–29.

Jenkins, J. R., Dale, P., Mill., P., Cole, K., Pious, C., and Ronk, J. (2006). How special education preschool graduates finish: status at age 19. *American Educational Research Journal*, 43(4), 737–781.

Kamii, C. (1972). An application of Piaget's theory to the conceptualization of a preschool curriculum. In R. Parker (ed.), *The preschool in action: exploring early childhood programs* (pp. 91–131). Boston: Allyn and Bacon.

Karnes, M. B., Shwedel, A. M., and Williams, M. B. (1983). A comparison of five approaches for educating young children from low-income homes. In Consortium for Longitudinal Studies (ed.), *As the twig is bent: lasting effects of preschool programs* (pp. 133–169). Hillsdale, NJ: Lawrence Erlbaum Associates.

Karnes, M. B., Teska, J. A., and Hodgins, A. S. (1970). The effects of four programs of classroom intervention on the intellectual and language development of

4-year-old disadvantaged children. *American Journal of Orthopsychiatry*, 40(1), 58–76.

Landis, J. R., and Koch, G. G. (1977). The measurement of observer agreement for categorical data. *Biometrics*, 33, 159–174.

Marcon, R. A. (2002). Moving up the grades: relationship between preschool model and later school success. *Early Childhood Research and Practice*, 4, 1–23.

Miller, J., and Camp, J. (1972). Toward individual competency – a curriculum in the child's ecology. In R. Parker (ed.), *The preschool in action: exploring early childhood programs* (pp. 380–407). Boston: Allyn and Bacon.

Miller, L. B., and Dyer, J. L. (1975). *Four preschool programs: their dimensions and effects*. Monographs of the Society for Research in Child Development, 40(5–6, Serial No. 162). New York: Wiley.

Nelson III, C. A., and Sheridan, M. A. (2011). Lessons from neuroscience research for understanding causal links between family and neighborhood characteristics and educational outcomes. In G. J. Duncan and R. J. Murnane (eds.), *Whither Opportunity?* (pp. 27–46). New York: Russell Sage Foundation.

Nelson, G., Westhues, A., and MacLeod, J. (2003). A meta-analysis of longitudinal research on preschool prevention programs for children. *Prevention and Treatment*, 6(31), 16–71.

Parker, R., and Day, M. (1972). Comparisons of preschool curricula. In R. Parker (ed.), *The preschool in action: exploring early childhood programs* (pp. 465–508). Boston: Allyn and Bacon.

Preschool Curriculum Evaluation Research Consortium (2008). *Effects of preschool curriculum programs on school readiness* (NCER 2008–2009). Washington, DC: National Center for Education Research (ERIC Document Reproduction Service No. ED502153).

Reynolds, A. J. (1999). Educational success in high-risk settings: contributions of the Chicago Longitudinal Study. *Journal of School Psychology*, 37(4), 345–354.

(2000). *Success in early intervention: the Chicago Child–Parent Centers*. Lincoln: University of Nebraska Press.

Reynolds, A. J., Temple, J. A., and Ou, S. (2010). Preschool education, educational attainment, and crime prevention: contributions of cognitive and non-cognitive skills. *Children and Youth Services Review*, 32, 1054–1063.

Reynolds, A. J., Temple, J. A., Ou, S., Robertson, D. L., Mersky, J. P., Topitzes, J. W., and Niles, M. D. (2007). Effects of a school-based, early childhood intervention on adult health and well-being: a 19-year follow-up of low-income families. *Archives of Pediatrics and Adolescent Medicine*, 161(8), 730–739.

Reynolds, A. J., Temple, J. A., White, B., Ou, S., and Robertson, D. L. (2011). Age-26 cost-benefit analysis of the Child–Parent Center early education program. *Child Development*, 82(1), 379–404.

Schweinhart, L. J., Barnes, H. V., and Weikart, D. P. (1993). *Significant benefits of the High/Scope Perry Preschool study through age 27*. Ypsilanti, MI: High/Scope Press.

Schweinhart, L. J., and Weikart, D. P. (1988). Education for young children living in poverty: child-initiated learning or teacher-directed instruction? *Elementary School Journal*, 89, 213–225.

Schweinhart, L. J., and Weikart, D. P. (1997). *Lasting differences: the High/Scope Preschool Curriculum Comparison study through age 23*. Monographs of the High/Scope Educational Research Foundation, 12. Ypsilanti, MI: High/Scope Press.

Schweinhart, L. J., Weikart, D. P., and Larner, M. B. (1986). Consequences of three preschool curriculum models through age 15. *Early Childhood Research Quarterly*, 1, 15–45.

Singh-Manoux, A., Ferrie, J. E., Chandola, T., and Marmot, M. (2004). Socioeconomic trajectories across the life course and health outcomes in midlife: evidence for the accumulation hypothesis? *International Journal of Epidemiology*, 33, 1072–1079.

Stipek, D., Feiler, R., Byler, P., Ryan, R., Milburn, S., and Salmon, J. (1998). Good beginnings: what difference does the program make in preparing young children for school? *Journal of Applied Developmental Psychology*, 19, 41–66.

Stipek, D., Feiler, R., Daniels, D., and Millburn, S. (1995). Effects of different instructional approaches on young children's achievement and motivation. *Child Development*, 66(1), 209–223.

Part III

Effects of health and education policy
on child development

Commentary: Patient Protection and Affordable
Care Act and health outcomes

Samuel A. Kleiner

The Patient Protection and Affordable Care Act (PPACA) of 2010 was arguably one of the most sweeping pieces of health care legislation in decades. Included in its provisions are reforms intended to expand health insurance coverage, improve health care quality and system performance, and contain costs. While the included reforms are likely to affect access and care provision across the age spectrum, a number of key terms in the legislation are particularly relevant to the health and well-being of children. Under PPACA, beginning in 2014, health insurance coverage will be mandated, and in many states Medicaid eligibility will be extended to all non-Medicare-eligible individuals with family incomes up to 133 percent of the federal poverty level (FPL). In addition, the legislation extends funding for the Children's Health Insurance Program (CHIP), a program enacted in 1997 to cover children from low- and moderate-income families through the year 2015, and protects the program through the year 2019 (Kenney and Pelletier, 2010). These provisions combined are expected to result in an increase in both Medicaid and CHIP enrollment of 13 million persons (The Lewin Group, 2010) and reduce the number of uninsured children from 7.2 million to 4.2 million (Kenney et al., 2011).

While a number of provisions in the legislation will potentially affect the coverage and treatment of children specifically, in what follows I discuss some of the main research findings on the effects of insurance expansions on utilization and health, including studies that focus on children. The overall effects of insurance expansions will depend in part on the demand response of the newly insured, as well as on whether the acquisition of insurance through PPACA will improve health outcomes. However, supply-side responses to these expansions are of considerable importance as well. For example, insurance coverage expansions could lead to a significant increase in the demand for medical care, resulting in difficulty accessing health care providers. Furthermore, public insurance programs pay considerably less than those insured through the private market (Zuckerman, Williams, and Stockley, 2009). Thus, providers may be reluctant to accept large numbers of the newly insured, and quality of care for these individuals may suffer if high-priced, high-quality providers become less accessible.

Utilization and outcomes

There is consistent evidence in the economics literature documenting the utilization effects of insurance expansions for various populations. Buchmueller et al. (2005) provide a review of this literature (which I partially summarize here) and note that most studies indicate that extending insurance coverage results in significant increases in all types of medical care utilization. As noted in Buchmueller et al. (2005), a number of studies indicate that this increase in utilization applies to youth as well. Specifically, while having insurance increases outpatient utilization for adults by between one to two visits per year, insured children are shown to increase outpatient utilization by roughly one visit per year. Inpatient utilization has also been shown to be responsive to the presence of insurance coverage. Currie and Gruber (1996a) find that eligibility for Medicaid increases the probability of hospitalization for children by approximately 4 percentage points, while Dafny and Gruber (2005) show that most of the increase in inpatient utilization for newly eligible children is due to conditions classified as unavoidable.

However, increased access to care due to insurance does not ensure improvement in health. Specifically, a number of studies have shown that more medical treatment is not necessarily productive on the margin. For example, Fisher et al. (2003) and Fisher et al. (2004) show no association between increased treatment intensity and patient outcomes.[1] Thus, these insurance expansions could potentially have two competing effects. First, they could have an "efficiency effect," wherein greater access to care enables the avoidance of severe health conditions, thereby improving health and lowering overall health care costs. However, lower out-of-pocket costs for the newly insured may lead to an "access effect," wherein individuals consume more health care, which could lead to increased costs and no improvement in health, if the additional consumption is unproductive.

Evidence on the effects of expansions on health in the adult population has mostly shown a beneficial effect of insurance on health status. In the elderly population, Lichtenberg's (2002) analysis indicates that the increased utilization of care due to Medicare eligibility lowers mortality, while Card, Dobkin,

---

[1] Almond et al. (2010) and Doyle (2011) respectively study newborns and Medicare patients and have found evidence of a causal relationship between treatment intensity and patient outcomes.

and Maestas (2009) find a mortality reduction for hospitalized patients of approximately 20 percent for the severely ill. Evidence for the privately insured by Kolstad and Kowalski (2010) shows that in Massachusetts the 2006 reform that decreased uninsurance by 28 percent led to a reduction in hospitalization rates for preventable conditions of 1.7 percent.

Most studies that focus on children show health benefits of insurance for both infants and older children. For example, the implementation of universal coverage in Canada during the 1960s and 1970s was shown by Hanratty (1996) to reduce infant mortality by 4 percent, while the 30 percentage point increase in Medicaid eligibility for women of childbearing age during the 1979–1992 period in the United States was associated with an 8.5 percent reduction in infant mortality (Currie and Gruber, 1996b). The incidence of low birthweight babies also declined by 1.3 percent in Canada after the implementation of universal coverage (Hanratty, 1996), though a study by Haas, Udvarhelyi, and Epstein (1993) shows no effect on outcomes of a 1985 Massachusetts insurance expansion that targeted low-income pregnant women. Studies that include older children find effects as well; Currie and Gruber's (1996a) analysis of childhood mortality finds that the 15 percentage point increase in insurance eligibility during the 1980s and early 1990s decreased childhood mortality by 5 percent, while Aizer's (2007) study of California Medicaid enrollment in the late 1990s finds that an increase in enrollment of 10 percent results in a 2–3 percent decrease in avoidable hospitalizations for children.

Supply-side and access

An important consideration in the aforementioned studies is the extent to which supply-side factors respond to insurance expansions. The impact of the PPACA expansions will depend largely on the intermediate inputs used to produce health. As Buchmueller et al. (2005) note, the utilization and health outcome effects associated with the additional large number of newly insured individuals could be constrained by existing short-run provider capacity, and thus not all health care demand created by the insurance expansion may be accommodated. For example, Hofer, Abraham, and Moscovice (2011) estimate that in order to accommodate the predicted increase in demand for primary care visits of 7.9 percent, nearly 7,000 additional primary care providers will be needed. Such an increase may be difficult, as salaries for primary care physicians are traditionally lower than in other specialties (Leigh, 2010), and, as Nicholson (2002) has shown, physicians are particularly responsive to expected income differences across specialties.

Furthermore, because many of the insurance expansions will be through Medicaid, which offers the least generous payments as compared to Medicare and private insurers (Zuckerman et al., 2009), provider availability for the newly insured may be limited, since physicians have been shown by Decker (2007) to accept fewer Medicaid patients in response to payment reductions. Access issues are likely to apply to non-physician providers as well, as Buerhaus, Auerbach, and Staiger (2009) project a shortage of nurses of over a quarter-million individuals by 2025, and these projections do not account for the likelihood of additional utilization that will likely occur as a result of PPACA. Given that nurses have been shown to be integral to the quality of care received in inpatient facilities (Bartel et al., 2011; Gruber and Kleiner, 2012), a further shortage of high-quality nurses is likely to have deleterious effects on patient outcomes.

The quality of care received by those affected by the PPACA provisions may also be affected depending on whether the PPACA results in the "crowd-out" of insurance coverage (the extent to which insurance expansions reduce private insurance coverage) or "crowd-down" (where a switch to a less generous insurance plan restricts the beneficiaries to providers that may be of lower quality). For example Koch's (2009) study of children's health outcomes shows that a crowd-out induced loss of superior-quality private insurance adversely affects health for children. Specifically, he finds that the availability of public health insurance decreases self-reported measures of health, lowers the probability that a child has a usual source of care, and increases emergency room utilization. Currie and Gruber (1997) find that these expansion effects are likely to vary depending on the proximity of a high-quality provider, as their findings indicate that the beneficial effects of expansions on outcomes for newborns are likely to be the greatest for individuals who live close to a technologically advanced hospital that has a neonatal intensive care unit on the premises. Furthermore, the competitive environment in which a nearby hospital operates is likely to be a factor on the health effects of these expansions, as Gaynor (2006) has shown that hospital quality is higher in competitive markets.

Will there be long-term effects?

As briefly reviewed here, much research suggests that health insurance expansions increase utilization and improve health for all populations, including children. Thus if the predicted increase in insurance rates for children under PPACA are able to allow for access to high-quality providers, previous research suggests an improvement in short-term health outcomes. Additionally, recent studies have shown evidence that these positive effects may be more long-lived. Specifically, Levine and

Schanzenbach's (2009) study examines the impact of public health insurance expansions through both Medicaid and SCHIP on children's educational outcomes. Their findings indicate that test scores in reading increased for those children affected at birth by increased health insurance eligibility (though math scores show no significant change in their analysis). This result is consistent with Currie, Decker, and Lin's (2008) assertion that, for children's outcomes, eligibility when young puts children on a better health trajectory, resulting in improved health at older ages. Thus, the long-term effects of reform may translate to improved outcomes for young children on dimensions other than health, though analysis of these effects will likely not be feasible in the near future.

References

Aizer, Anna (2007). Public health insurance, program take-up, and child health. *Review of Economics and Statistics*, 89(3), 400–415.

Almond, Douglas, Doyle, Joseph, Kowalski, Amanda, and Williams, Heidi (2010). Estimating marginal returns to medical care: evidence from at-risk newborns. *Quarterly Journal of Economics*, 125(2), 591–634.

Bartel, Ann P., Phibbs, Ciaran S., Beaulieu, Nancy, and Stone, Patricia (2011). *Human capital and organizational performance: evidence from the healthcare sector*. Cambridge, MA: NBER Working Paper No. 17474.

Buchmueller, Thomas C., Grumbach, Kevin, Kronick, Richard, and Kahn, James (2005). The effect of health insurance on medical care utilization and implications for insurance expansion: a review of the literature. *Medical Care Research and Review*, 62(1), 3–30.

Buerhaus, Peter I., Auerbach, David I., and Staiger, Douglas O. (2009). The recent surge in nurse employment: causes and implications. *Health Affairs*, 28(4), w657–w668. Published online June 12, 2009; 10.1377/hlthaff. 28.4.w657.

Card, David, Dobkin, Carlos, and Maestas, Nicole (2009). Does medicare save lives? *Quarterly Journal of Economics*, 124(2), 597–636.

Currie, Janet, Decker, Sandra, and Lin, Wanchuan (2008). Has public health insurance for older children reduced disparities in access to care and health outcomes? *Journal of Health Economics*, 27(6), 1567–1581.

Currie, Janet, and Gruber, Jonathan (1996a). Health insurance eligibility, utilization of medical care, and child health. *Quarterly Journal of Economics*, 111(2), 431–466.

(1996b). Saving babies: the efficacy and cost of recent changes in the Medicaid eligibility of pregnant women. *Journal of Political Economy*, 104(6), 1263–1296.

(1997). *The technology of birth: health insurance, medical interventions, and infant health*. Cambridge, MA: NBER Working Paper No. 5985.

Dafny, Leemore S., and Gruber, Jonathan (2005). Public insurance and child hospitalizations: access and efficiency effects. *Journal of Public Economics*, 89(1), 109–129.

Decker, Sandra (2007). Medicaid physician fees and the quality of medical care of Medicaid patients in the USA. *Review of Economics of the Household*, 5(1), 95–112.

Doyle, Joseph J. (2011). Returns to local-area health care spending: evidence from health shocks to patients far from home. *American Economic Journal: Applied Economics*, 3(3), 221–243.

Fisher, Elliott S., Wennberg, David E., Stukel, Thérèse A., and Gottlieb, Daniel J. (2004). Variations in the longitudinal efficiency of academic medical centers. *Health Affairs*, Web Exclusive, VAR19–32. http://content.healthaffairs.org/cgi/reprint/hlthaff.var.19v1.

Fisher, Elliott S., Wennberg, David E., Stukel, Thérèse A., Gottlieb, Daniel J., Lucas, F. L., and Pinder, Étoile L. (2003). The implications of regional variations in Medicare spending, part 2: health outcomes and satisfaction with care. *Annals of Internal Medicine*, 138(4), 288–298.

Gaynor, Martin (2006). Competition and quality in health care markets. *Foundations and Trends in Microeconomics*, 2(6), 441–508.

Gruber, Jonathan, and Kleiner, Samuel A. (2012). Do strikes kill? Evidence from New York State. *American Economic Journal: Economic Policy*, 4(1), 127–157.

Haas, Jennifer S., Udvarhelyi, Steven, and Epstein, Arnold M. (1993). The effect of health coverage for uninsured pregnant women on maternal health and the use of cesarean section. *Journal of the American Medical Association*, 270, 61–64.

Hanratty, Maria J. (1996). Canadian national health insurance and infant health. *American Economic Review*, 86(1), 276–284.

Hofer, Adam N., Abraham, Jean Marie, and Moscovice, Ira (2011). Expansion of coverage under the Patient Protection and Affordable Care Act and primary care utilization. *Millbank Quarterly*, 89(1), 69–89.

Kenney, Genevieve M., Buettgens, Matthew, Guyer, Jocelyn, and Heberlein, Martha (2011). Improving coverage for children under health reform will require maintaining current eligibility standards for Medicaid and CHIP. *Health Affairs*, 30(12), 2371–2381.

Kenney, Genevieve, and Pelletier, Jennifer E. (2010). *How will the Patient Protection and Affordable Care Act of 2010 affect children?* Washington, DC: Urban Institute.

Koch, Thomas G. (2009). Public insurance, crowd-out and health care utilization. Unpublished paper, Economics Department, University of California, Santa Barbara.

Kolstad, Jonathan T., and Kowalski, Amanda E. (2010). *The impact of health care reform on hospital and preventive care: evidence from Massachusetts*. Cambridge, MA: NBER Working Paper No. 16012.

Leigh, J. Paul, Tancredi, Daniel, Jerant, Anthony, and Kravitz, Richard L. (2010). Physician wages across specialities: informing the physician reimbursement debate.

Levine, Philip, and Schanzenbach, Diane (2009). The impact of children's public health insurance expansions on educational outcomes. *Forum for Health Economics and Policy*, 12(1), Article 1.

The Lewin Group (2010). Patient Protection and Affordable Care Act (PPACA): long-term costs for governments, employers, families and providers. Published online at www.lewin.com/~/media/lewin/site_sections/publications/lewingroupanalysis-patientprotectionandaffordablecareact2010.pdf.

Lichtenberg, Frank R. (2002). The effects of Medicare on health care utilization and outcomes. In Alan M. Garber (ed.), *Frontiers in Health Policy Research* (vol. 5, pp. 27–52). Cambridge, MA: MIT Press. Available online at www.nber.org/chapters/c9857.

Nicholson, Sean (2002). Physician specialty choice under uncertainty. *Journal of Labor Economics*, 20(4), 816–847.

Zuckerman, Stephen, Williams, Aimee F., and Stockley, Karen E. (2009). Trends in Medicaid physician fees, 2003–2008. *Health Affairs*, 28(3), w510–w519.

12 The ABCs of children's health: potential impact of the Patient Protection and Affordable Care Act

Jean Marie Abraham, Pinar Karaca-Mandic, and Sung J. Choi Yoo

Introduction

In 2010, US health care spending reached approximately $2.59 trillion, or $8,402 per person (Centers for Medicare and Medicaid Services, 2012). Despite greater per capita spending relative to other industrialized nations, the United States has lower performance on several health outcome measures for both the child and the adult populations (OECD, 2011). In 2009–10, in an effort to reform the US health care system, the Obama Administration made health care top domestic policy priority. After a long and contentious debate in Congress the Patient Protection and Affordable Care Act (ACA) was passed on March 23, 2010.

As implementation proceeds, provisions within the ACA have begun to alter the financing and delivery of health care for millions of Americans, the most noteworthy being a large-scale expansion of affordable coverage options for lower-income children and adults beginning in 2014. The ACA is a comprehensive piece of legislation and is expected to affect *access* to health insurance by children and adults, their health care related spending and financial *burden*, and their *consumption* of medical care – in other words, their ABCs.

This chapter focuses on identifying the potential effects of the Affordable Care Act for children. For each of the ABCs – access, burden, and consumption – we summarize current knowledge from the research literature and then identify and briefly describe important provisions from the ACA that are expected to influence these outcomes.

Access to coverage by children and their families

Children's health outcomes depend on a broad set of factors, including having access to health care. The concept of *access* is a complex one that reflects the financial means to pay for medical care as well as non-financial factors, including transportation and the capacity of providers to care for new patients. In the United States, financial access to health care is improved dramatically by having health insurance. The most common way through which US children obtain access to health insurance is through a working parent who is offered this fringe benefit as part of his or her compensation package. For children in low-income families, a large proportion are able to qualify for public insurance programs such as Medicaid or the Children's Health Insurance Program (CHIP), but income eligibility requirements vary considerably by state. Among children who lack access to employer-sponsored insurance and live in families with incomes that are too high to qualify for public insurance, their primary source for obtaining coverage is the individual market. Based on 2010 estimates from the Current Population Survey, 55 percent of US children were covered by employer-sponsored insurance, 5.7 percent were covered by a policy purchased directly from an insurer, 38 percent were covered by public insurance programs such as Medicaid or CHIP, and 10 percent were uninsured (DeNavas-Walt, Proctor, and Smith, 2011).[1]

To examine the demographic and economic factors associated with being uninsured among children, we analyzed the Medical Expenditure Panel Survey (MEPS) Household Component for years 2003 to 2007. The MEPS is nationally representative of the civilian non-institutionalized US population. We estimated a binary logit model of the probability that a child (0–18 years of age) was reported as being uninsured for the full year. Our explanatory variables included age categories (0–5, 6–12, and 13–17), whether the child was female, indicators for race (white, black, Asian, other (reference)) and Hispanic ethnicity, whether or not the child lives in a family with married adults, the number of family members, family income (specified as a percentage of the 2010 Federal Poverty Level (FPL)), geographic census regions (Northeast, Midwest, South, and West (reference)), and year indicators. The MEPS utilizes a complex survey design and thus regression estimates were weighted accordingly.

Table 12.1 provides the results. Estimates suggest that older children between 13 and 17 years of age are 5.4 percent more likely to be full-year uninsured relative to children 5 years of age and younger. We also find evidence of differences by ethnicity. Hispanic children are 5.6 percent more likely to lack coverage throughout the year relative to non-Hispanics. One of the most important factors associated with the probability of a child being uninsured is family income. Compared to children in families with

---

[1] Percentages do not sum to 100 since individuals may have more than one type of insurance throughout the year.

incomes above 400 percent of FPL, children in families with annual income below 200 percent of FPL are 4.5 percent more likely to be uninsured and those between 200–400 percent FPL are 2.6 percent more likely to be uninsured.[2] Thus, children in lower-income families are less likely to have coverage, often because working parents in these families do not have access to employer-based coverage or because private insurance options are deemed unaffordable (Abraham, DeLeire, and Royalty, 2009).

Table 12.1 *Binary logit model of the probability of child being uninsured full-year.*

Variable	Marginal effect	Standard error	z
Child 0–5	reference	reference	–
Child 6–12	0.0272996	0.00409	6.67
Child 13–17	0.0538483	0.0054	9.98
Female	−0.0005378	0.00315	−0.17
White	0.0052726	0.0085	0.62
Black	−0.0128431	0.00928	−1.38
Asian	0.009514	0.01267	0.75
Other race	reference	reference	–
Hispanic	0.0560252	0.007	8.01
Married family	0.0087774	0.00667	1.32
Family size	−0.0042712	0.00199	−2.14
Income < 133% FPL	0.0449849	0.00812	5.54
Income 133–200% FPL	0.0444999	0.00706	6.31
Income 200–400% FPL	0.0263859	0.00544	4.85
Income > 400% FPL	reference	reference	–
Full-time worker	0.0049962	0.007	0.71
Northeast	−0.0246353	0.00762	−3.23
Midwest	−0.008839	0.00858	−1.03
South	0.0114743	0.00807	1.42
West	reference	reference	–
Metropolitan Statistical Area	0.0190858	0.00589	3.24
Year 2007	0.0076693	0.00653	1.17
Year 2006	−0.0081635	0.00542	−1.51
Year 2005	−0.0084688	0.00542	−1.56
Year 2004	0.0029326	0.00489	0.6
Year 2003	reference	reference	–

[2] To clarify, here we have defined a family as a health insurance eligibility unit in the MEPS. An HIEU is a sub-family relationship unit constructed to include adults plus those family members who would typically be eligible for coverage under private family plans, including spouses, unmarried natural or adopted children who are age 18 or under, and children under age 24 who are full-time students.

The ACA and children's access to coverage

A primary policy objective of the ACA is to reduce the number of US children and adults who lack health insurance. Estimates from the US Bureau of the Census for 2010 indicate that 49.9 million individuals within the United States lack health insurance, including 7.3 million children under the age of 18 (DeNavas-Walt et al., 2011). As Guendelman and Pearl (2004) note, the vast majority of children who are uninsured also have parents who lack health insurance, according to their analyses using the National Health Interview Survey.

Shortly after the ACA legislation was signed into law in March 2010, implementation began on several new insurance market regulations affecting individuals' access to private insurance, including employer-sponsored and individual plans. Historically, insurers in forty-five states have been able to medically underwrite applicants for individual policies, leading to coverage with exclusions for pre-existing conditions, and in some cases full denials of coverage for individuals who had been diagnosed with a very serious disease such as cancer. For policies issued later than March 23, 2010, the ACA prohibits health insurers from denying benefits or coverage for particular services for children under 19 years of age with pre-existing health conditions. In 2014, this provision will expand to include the adult population as well.[3]

Also in 2014, the two major coverage expansions will go into effect. The first of these is going to occur through an expansion of the Medicaid program. Specifically, the ACA calls for states to expand eligibility to individuals in families earning up to 133 percent of the FPL. However, given a standard 5 percent income disregard, the effective eligibility threshold will be 138 percent of FPL. In 2012, this amount corresponds to $31,809 for a family of four living in the continental United States.

In a complex decision handed down on June 28, 2012, the US Supreme Court upheld the constitutionality of the Affordable Care Act, but it struck down parts of the Medicaid expansion. The language within the ACA had indicated that states that failed to expand eligibility would lose federal matching dollars for their existing Medicaid programs. The Supreme Court ruling implied that the existing Medicaid program and the expansion under the ACA could be treated as two separate programs. It further noted that the federal government cannot force a state to participate in a new federal program and it cannot threaten the state with the loss of funding under one federal program because it refuses to participate in a separate program (Rosenbaum and Westmoreland, 2012).

[3] See www.healthcare.gov for detailed language regarding this provision.

There is still much uncertainty as to whether all states will proceed with expanding Medicaid eligibility, despite strong financial incentives to do so. If one assumes that all states expand their Medicaid programs in 2014, then children in twenty states would be directly affected by this new threshold based on an evaluation of state Medicaid eligibility guidelines in force in 2009. The ACA also allocates additional resources for states to expand enrollment and outreach activities, since many currently uninsured children are eligible for coverage but simply not enrolled.

In 2014, individuals in families that do not have access to employer-sponsored insurance and have annual income of between 100 and 400 percent of FPL will be able to qualify for subsidized individual coverage sold in newly created Exchanges, which are organized marketplaces to facilitate the purchase of plans for individuals as well as small employer groups. For an individual, subsidies in the form of a premium assistance credit will be determined on a sliding scale based on his or her family income. The actual size of the credit is the difference between the total premium charged for the second-lowest cost "silver" plan offered in an Exchange and a maximum percentage of income that a family would pay, based on their income relative to the FPL.[4] The maximum percentages range from 2 percent for a family earning 100 percent of FPL to 9.5 percent for a family earning between 300 and 400 percent of FPL. Thus, for a family of four earning 138 percent of FPL, the maximum they would pay out-of-pocket is 3 percent of income or roughly $954 (2012 dollars) to obtain health insurance for their family.

While children's access to coverage is expected to improve further as a result of the Affordable Care Act, several implementation challenges remain, as documented by McMorrow, Kenney, and Coyer (2012). First, some children may have working parents with an offer of employer-sponsored insurance as part of their compensation package. However, that offer may not include dependent coverage. As a result, there may be uncertainty regarding the children's eligibility for subsidies should the parent obtain an employee-only policy, but seek subsidized Exchange-based coverage for them. A second issue arises for families that have mixed citizenship and documentation status, given eligibility provisions for the Medicaid expansion and Exchange subsidies. In 2014, lawfully residing immigrants will be eligible for Medicaid under the expansion, but many will continue to be subject to a five-year waiting period before they may enroll in coverage. For Exchange-based plans, subsidies will be available for US citizens and legal immigrants only. Undocumented

---

[4] A silver plan is defined in the legislation as a plan having a 70 percent actuarial value.

immigrants will be ineligible under both coverage expansion mechanisms. Third, children who have one parent residing outside of the household or do not live with either of their parents may face more complicated circumstances for determining income and thus eligibility for either Medicaid or subsidized private insurance in Exchanges. Analyses by McMorrow and colleagues (2012) suggest that approximately 40 million US children may face at least one complex coverage scenario under the ACA, and that, among uninsured children in the United States, 62 percent are in at least one complex coverage scenario.

For lower-income children and adults, the ACA creates new, more affordable health insurance options. At the same time, however, it also mandates that individuals obtain coverage. Although this is politically controversial, many economists feel that an individual mandate can encourage greater stability of insurance risk pools within Exchanges, and can counteract adverse selection risks created by the introduction of modified community rating and guaranteed issue insurance regulations. In 2014, individuals will be required to have health insurance or face a financial penalty. When the mandate is fully implemented in 2016, the penalty structure will equal the greater of $695 for an individual (up to three times that amount for a family) or 2.5 percent of family income. Exemptions from the coverage requirement will be available to individuals and families based on financial hardship (e.g., if the lowest-cost plan available in an Exchange is more than 8 percent of a family's income), and for those with short-term coverage gaps of less than three months, undocumented immigrants, prisoners, and those with religious objections.

As the centerpiece of the ACA, the expansion of affordable coverage to lower-income persons in conjunction with an individual mandate to encourage insurance take-up is expected to reduce the number of uninsured Americans by approximately 30 million in 2019, according to estimates published by the Congressional Budget Office in June 2012.

Burden of health care spending – underinsurance and financial burden

Another important policy issue highlighted during the legislative debate is the affordability of health insurance and medical care for US families. The extent to which health insurance and medical care are "affordable" depends on both the expenses incurred by families and their financial resources to pay for them.

Since 2001, real growth in annual US health care spending has averaged over 5 percent (Council of Economic Advisers, 2010). Estimates from the

Medical Expenditure Panel Survey Insurance Component, an annual survey of US business establishments, indicate that the average, employer-based premium for family coverage was $13,027 in 2009, while the average share of the total premium paid by families out-of-pocket was $3,474 (Agency for Healthcare Research and Quality, 2010). Premium growth in the individual insurance market has exhibited similar trends (America's Health Insurance Plans, 2011). For many families, the cost of health insurance is an important factor influencing their decision to forgo insurance altogether (Graves and Long, 2006).

To address rapidly growing premiums, many employers are making changes to workers' health benefits. Specifically, employers have increased employees' contribution requirements toward the total premium and have altered benefit designs resulting in increased cost-sharing at the point of utilizing care. For example, in 2011, the average deductible for family coverage was $1,521 for Preferred Provider Organization health plans that included deductible provisions. This contrasts with an average deductible of $679 in 2005 (Kaiser Family Foundation and Health Research and Educational Trust, 2005; 2011).Within the health services research literature, there are two common measures of affordability: underinsurance and financial burden. Underinsurance reflects whether the insurance held by a family provides adequate financial protection against health care expenditures (Bashshur, Smith, and Stiles, 1993). Underinsurance can be measured in several different ways, including expected or realized spending relative to income, insurance benefit design characteristics such as the size of the deductible or maximum out-of-pocket limit, and self-reported measures of delaying or forgoing care due to its cost. A frequently utilized measure classifies a family as being underinsured if it spends at least some percentage (e.g., 10 percent) of income on out-of-pocket costs for medical care (Blewett, Ward, and Beebe, 2006; Farley, 1985; Short and Banthin, 1995).[5] Some researchers have also adopted graduated threshold measures based on the federal poverty level, whereby lower spending thresholds (e.g., 5 percent) are used for very low income families since they have fewer financial resources to spend on health care after taking account of costs associated with basic needs, including housing, utilities, and food (Banthin et al. 2008; Cunningham, 2010).

---

[5] Pioneering work of Short (1985) and Short and Banthin (1995) examined an individual's risk of being underinsured by simulating an individual's out-of-pocket medical care expenses given a catastrophic medical event with associated costs equal to the 99th percentile of the medical care spending distribution and the individual's plan characteristics. Then by comparing these expected out-of-pocket costs to income, the authors determined whether the individual would have spent at least 10 percent of his/her income, leading them to be classified as underinsured.

Health care financial burden is another measure that is used to capture affordability. Financial burden takes into account not only out-of-pocket medical expenses, but also the out-of-pocket premiums that a family pays for its health insurance. This is similar to underinsurance, and most researchers adopt a threshold measure to classify families as having a high financial burden if they spend at least some fraction of their income on medical care and health insurance premiums.

Studies of underinsurance and financial burden for the entire US population suggest that rates have been rising over time (Banthin and Bernard, 2006; Hoffman and Schwartz, 2008; Cunningham, 2010). A subset of this literature focuses on the experiences of children and their families. For example, a study by Kogan et al. (2010) uses the 2007 National Survey of Children's Health to investigate underinsurance among US children. Their approach relies on stated responses to three questions capturing the adequacy of coverage.[6] Based on their analysis, the authors conclude that 22.7 percent of children with continuous coverage are underinsured. The authors further investigate the characteristics of underinsured children, reporting that they are more likely to be older, Hispanic, black, living in the Midwestern United States, and in poorer health status (self-reported).

There has been a considerable amount of research done on the population of children with special health care needs, including those with physical, neurological, developmental, emotional, and mental disabilities. Approximately 16 to 19 percent of US children between ages 0 and 18 have such special needs (Bethell et al., 2008; Chevarley, 2006), and they account for approximately 40 percent of the total medical costs attributed to all children (Newacheck and Kim, 2005). Many studies that have focused on this population and their caregivers stress that the children's health care costs may be financially burdensome (Allaire et al., 1992; Anderson et al., 2007; Brehaut et al., 2004; Chen and Newacheck, 2006; Chevarley, 2006; Cunningham, 1990; De Ridder and De Graeve, 2006; Galbraith et al., 2005; Newacheck and Kim, 2005; Songer et al., 1997). Moreover, the health needs of the children not only can create high medical costs, but also can affect the ability of parents' to maintain stable employment (Kogan et al., 2005).

---

[6] The questions included: (1) Does the child's health insurance offer benefits or cover services that meet his or her needs? (2) Not including premiums or costs covered by insurance, do you pay any money for the child's health care? If yes, then follow-up. (3) How often are these costs reasonable? If a parent or guardian answered "always" or "usually" to all three questions, then the child was considered to have adequate insurance coverage. If the parents or guardians answered "sometimes" or "never" to *any* of the three questions, the child was considered to be underinsured.

The ACA and burden of health care spending – underinsurance and financial burden

The anticipated effects of the ACA on out-of-pocket health care spending by families will vary across different groups within the US population based on income and insurance status. In 2014, millions of uninsured children and adults will become newly eligible for Medicaid. Since Medicaid programs do not have premiums and cost-sharing at the point of utilization is minimal, these individuals will likely face a reduction in out-of-pocket spending on health care.

Among persons who have incomes between 100 and 400 percent of FPL and lack access to affordable employer-sponsored insurance, subsidized individual coverage purchased through Exchanges has the potential to reduce their financial burden in two ways. First, children and adults will be able to obtain subsidies to offset the cost of premiums purchased within Exchanges. The value of the subsidies is tied directly to a person's family income, with lower-income families receiving larger subsidies. For higher-income persons who are uninsured, their out-of-pocket spending will increase since they will receive less help with paying the premium. However, by purchasing insurance they will have valuable financial protection in the event that they need to obtain medical care. Second, among children and adults with family incomes under 250 percent of FPL, they will also receive out-of-pocket cost-sharing subsidies. These subsidies are designed to reduce individuals' financial exposure at the point of seeking care. Like the premium assistance credits, the out-of-pocket cost-sharing subsidies are based on family income, with the most help provided for those with the lowest family incomes.

For uninsured individuals who have access to employer-sponsored insurance, but who do not take it up or have family income in excess of 400 percent of FPL, they may face additional spending in order to obtain coverage. In the United States, approximately 76.1 percent of private sector workers with an offer of employer-sponsored insurance choose to enroll (Agency for Healthcare Research and Quality, 2012). Factors including the out-of-pocket premium, income, and alternative sources of coverage (e.g., public insurance or spousal offer) have been found to be important determinants of employer-sponsored insurance take-up by workers (Abraham and Feldman, 2010). Beginning in 2014, workers who had previously turned down coverage and were uninsured may choose to take it up in order to avoid the financial penalty associated with the ACA coverage requirement. However, for a large proportion of individuals, it will require them to pay an out-of-pocket premium.

Among children and adults with family income in excess of 400 percent of FPL but who lack access to employer-sponsored coverage, they may opt to purchase coverage within the individual market, either inside or outside of Exchanges. Because their income level exceeds the threshold for obtaining premium assistance credits, they would be required to pay the full premium. This could result in significant out-of-pocket spending on premiums to obtain coverage for those who had been previously uninsured.

Within the ACA, there are also a number of provisions to regulate the market for health insurance. Implemented shortly after the ACA's passage in 2010, insurers were prohibited from imposing "unreasonable" annual limits or lifetime limits on health plans.[7] These provisions may be particularly important for families who incur very high health care costs for children with special health care needs or those who become seriously ill. In 2014, with the introduction of Exchanges, several new insurance market regulations will go into place. Specifically, the regulations call for the guaranteed issue and renewability of plans offered to individuals and small employer groups within Exchanges, and will require insurers to use modified community rating. This form of rating, as noted in the ACA language, allows insurers to modify premiums based on age, family size, geography, and tobacco status, but not health status. The expected result of this regulatory change is greater compression of the premium distribution in the individual market. Under modified community rating, healthier individuals and families are expected to pay somewhat higher premiums for insurance, while those who are in poorer health will pay less, compared to experience rating methods.

For children and adults covered by employer-sponsored insurance, the overall effects on out-of-pocket spending and financial burden are ambiguous. Provisions in the ACA are projected to affect insurance coverage and premiums in numerous ways. For example, the introduction of Exchanges is hypothesized to improve the functioning of the small employer group market. Efficiencies resulting from reductions in distribution or other administrative costs could lead to lower premiums for families whose access to coverage comes through a small employer. However, the ACA includes several changes in benefit designs that may lead to higher premiums. For example, in 2014, deductible sizes will be limited in Exchange-based plans, and certain "essential benefits," such as oral and dental care benefits for children, will be mandated (Booth, Reusch, and Touschner,

---

[7] Applicability of insurance market regulations varies by insurance market segment (individual, small group, large group) as well as whether or not it is considered to be a grandfathered plan.

2012; US Department of Health and Human Services, 2012). Therefore, the overall impact of the ACA on the out-of-pocket spending and financial burden remains ambiguous. Finally, for individuals or families that do not choose to obtain any type of health insurance, they will be required to pay a financial penalty beginning in 2014.

Consumption of medical care

Children's health outcomes are influenced by a number of factors, including their receipt of preventive and acute medical care services. Children are dependent on their parents or other caregivers to obtain access to medical care. Within the scholarly literature, several economic and noneconomic factors have been analyzed to identify associations with medical care consumption by US children.

The effect of health insurance has been found to exhibit a strong, positive correlation with children's medical care consumption. Empirical research consistently has shown that individuals with health insurance use more medical care than the uninsured (Ezzati-Rice, Rohde, and Greenblatt, 2008; Kashihara and Carper, 2009). For example, work by Cummings and colleagues (2009) finds that children with longer spells of uninsurance are less likely to receive well-child visits or flu shots, relative to those who have private or public coverage.

A literature review by Buchmueller and colleagues (2005) summarizes existing research on the relationship between health insurance and the demand for medical care by children and adults. Specifically, they summarize findings from observational studies and natural experiments of earlier state-based Medicaid or federal expansions of coverage (e.g., Children's Health Insurance Program). The authors conclude that gaining coverage leads to a higher probability of an individual having any medical care utilization as well as to a larger number of visits. See, for example, Almeida, Dubay, and Ko, 2001; Banthin and Selden, 2003; Lave et al., 1998; Long, Marquis, and Harrison, 1994; Marquis and Long, 1996.

Whether through public insurance programs such as Medicaid and the Children's Health Insurance Program (CHIP) or through private sources (employer-sponsored coverage or individual coverage), children who have insurance are more likely to receive preventive care and are more likely to receive treatment for acute conditions in a timely manner (Hoffman and Paradise, 2008; Cummings et al., 2009). Insured children are also more likely to have a usual source of care, which may be particularly important for those with chronic conditions or other special health care needs (Newacheck et al., 2000).

A related literature stream focuses on how insured children's medical care consumption is affected by their insurance benefit design and cost-sharing requirements. Perhaps the most well-known study examining this relationship is the RAND Health Insurance Experiment, whereby participants were randomized into one of five types of health plans, each having different levels of cost-sharing (RAND, 2006).[8] For child and adult participants, lower cost-sharing led to increased use of services. Other analyses have examined this relationship among insured children with specific health conditions (Hong and Shepherd, 1996; Huskamp et al., 2005). For example, recent work by Karaca-Mandic and colleagues (2012) found that increased cost-sharing for asthma medications was associated with a slight reduction in medication use among children and higher rates of asthma hospitalization among privately insured children who were between 5 and 18 years old.

Other literature has focused on documenting differences in care-seeking behavior by children as a function of their family's demographics, labor force attachment, and economic circumstances. Notably, younger parents and those with lower educational attainment predict children's delayed entry into care, lower preventive care use, and lack of compliance with recommended well-child visit schedules (Guendelman and Schwalbe, 1986; Short and Lefkowitz, 1992). Racial and ethnic disparities are also observed with respect to the number of visits received. Non-white children are less likely to have a physician visit and have fewer total physician visits than white children. Minority children are also less likely to have a usual source of care and less likely to have continuity of care (Newacheck and Halfon, 1986; 1988; Newacheck and Taylor, 1992; Tangerose Orr, Charney, and Straus, 1988; Wood et al., 1990). Other factors related to lower use of pediatric services include cultural beliefs and values as well as language or communication difficulties.

Several researchers have analyzed the effect of family structure on children's medical care utilization. At a conceptual level, parental resources are finite and each additional child represents time and energy drawn away from parents or caregivers. Thus, parental resources are diluted as the number of children in a family increases (Blake, 1989; Downey, 1995; 2001; Hauser and Kuo, 1998; Phillips, 1999; Powell and Steelman, 1990). Empirical work finds that, as family size increases, a child's propensity to utilize care declines (Chen and Escarce, 2006; Newacheck and Taylor, 1992).

Other studies have examined the relationship between the type of medical treatment received by children and family structure. For example, Rabbani

---

[8] Four of the plans had varied cost-sharing ranging from 0 to 95 percent. The fifth plan had zero cost-sharing but was a non-profit HMO-style group cooperative.

and Alexander (2009) studied children with attention deficit hyperactivity disorder (ADHD) using the National Health Interview Survey and the MEPS. They found that children from larger families were significantly more likely to be using stimulants than their counterparts. They also found that children living in large families had fewer total and office-based visits as well as lower overall use of prescriptions.

The relationship between children's medical care consumption and parental employment has also been examined. Early work by Newacheck and Halfon (1986) and Cafferata and Kasper (1985) indicates that healthy children whose mothers work outside the home are likely to have fewer ambulatory physician visits. Work by Vistnes and Hamilton (1995), using the 1987 National Medical Expenditure Survey, examined children between 0 and 15 years of age who lived with mothers during the entire survey period. They found that children with working mothers (part-time or full-time) had 22.6 percent fewer visits than children with non-working mothers. They also found a positive and significant relationship between the mother having paid sick leave as a fringe benefit and the number of sick-child visits.

Finally, several factors have been suggested as potential barriers to the receipt of medical care by children, particularly those who are uninsured. These include lack of transportation (Dutton, 1981) and lack of access to providers who are willing to see new patients (including those who lack insurance) (Gresenz, Rogowski, and Escarce, 2006).

The ACA and consumption of medical care

Several provisions within the ACA are likely to impact children's medical care consumption. Shortly after the passage of federal reform in 2010, plans were required to cover certain preventive services with zero cost-sharing. For children, some of these services include well-child visits and immunization and behavioral assessments, as well as screening for autism, obesity, and alcohol and substance abuse (in adolescents).[9]

In 2014, the expansion of health insurance through Medicaid and subsidized Exchange-based plans, as well as reductions in out-of-pocket cost sharing among families earning less than 250 percent of FPL, is expected to increase utilization of medical care by children and adults. For children, this increase is likely to be concentrated in primary care.[10]

---

[9] For a complete list, see www.healthcare.gov/news/factsheets/2010/07/preventive-services-list.html#CoveredPreventiveServicesforChildren.

[10] According to an analysis of ambulatory medical care utilization by the Centers for Disease Control and Prevention, in 2007 approximately 68.9 percent of ambulatory care visits

A recent analysis by Hofer, Abraham, and Moscovice (2011) uses the Medical Expenditure Panel Survey to estimate a multivariate regression model of annual demand for primary care visits. With the model estimates and state-level information on the number of uninsured children, the authors predict the increase in the number of primary care visits expected from the coverage expansion. Results suggest that the coverage expansion will lead to a predicted increase in the annual overall demand for primary care visits of between 2 and 4.2 million among US children 17 years of age and under by 2019. Additional research is still needed to understand the potential impact of the coverage expansion and reduced spending burden on other types of medical care, including inpatient and emergency room utilization as well as use of prescription drugs.

The anticipated increase in demand for medical care raises new concerns about the capacity of the delivery system and whether it will be able to absorb the demand shock in the short-run. For example, will there be enough nurses, physicians, and non-physician clinicians to deliver care in a timely manner? Will the mix of primary care providers and specialists be adequate? Newly insured populations will also be concentrated in particular geographic regions. In addition to aggregate supply and workforce composition issues, policymakers and other stakeholders will need to address concerns about the geographic distribution of providers to meet the increased medical care consumption resulting from the expansion of coverage.

Conclusion

The Affordable Care Act of 2010 includes numerous provisions that will modify the financing and delivery of care within the US health care system. Based on estimates by the Congressional Budget Office in July 2012, the ACA is predicted to expand coverage to 30 million Americans by 2019, an approximate 60 percent decrease in the expected number of uninsured in the US population.[11] Additionally, the legislation will reduce out-of-pocket spending and financial burden for millions of lower-income children and adults who lack access to employer-based coverage and are unable to afford individual coverage presently. With such a large-scale coverage expansion, a corresponding increase in medical care demand is expected, and with it additional pressure on providers. Among children

made by children under 15 years of age were for primary care. See Ambulatory Medical Care Utilization Estimates for 2007. Accessed at: www.cdc.gov/nchs/data/series/sr_13/sr13_169.pdf.

[11] www.cbo.gov/sites/default/files/cbofiles/attachments/43472-07-24-2012-CoverageEstimates.pdf. Accessed September 9, 2012.

and adults with higher family incomes and those with employer-based coverage, the potential financial impact of the ACA provisions is considerably more uncertain. Going forward, additional research is needed to model the ACA provisions that directly affect benefit designs, premiums, and the incentives of employers to offer coverage, before any firm conclusions can be drawn regarding the overall impact of federal health care reform on access, burden, and the utilization of medical care.

References

Abraham, J. M., DeLeire, T., and Royalty, A. B. (2009). Access to health insurance at small establishments: what can we learn from analyzing other fringe benefits? *Inquiry*, 46(3), 253–273.

Abraham, J. M., and Feldman, R. (2010). Taking up or turning down: new estimates of household demand for employer-sponsored health insurance. *Inquiry*, 47(1), 17–32.

Agency for Healthcare Research and Quality (2010). Medical Expenditure Panel Survey. Retrieved from www.meps.ahrq.gov.

(2012). *Access and cost trends: 2011 Medical Expenditure Panel Survey–insurance component*. Rockville, MD: Agency for Healthcare Research and Quality.

Allaire, S., DeNardo, B., Szer, I., Meenan, R., and Schaller, J. (1992). The economic impacts of juvenile rheumatoid arthritis. *Journal of Rheumatology*, 19(6), 952.

Almeida, R. A., Dubay, L. C., and Ko, G. (2001). Access to care and use of health services by low-income women. *Health Care Financing Review*, 22(4), 27–47.

America's Health Insurance Plans (2011). Small group health insurance in 2010: a comprehensive survey of premiums, product choices, and benefits. Seattle, WA: AHIP. Accessed at www.ahip.org/Small-Group-Report-2011.aspx on February 25, 2014.

Anderson, D., Dumont, S., Jacobs, P., and Azzaria, L. (2007). The personal costs of caring for a child with a disability: a review of the literature. *Public Health Reports*, 122(1), 3.

Banthin, J. S., and Bernard, D. M. (2006). Changes in financial burdens for health care. National estimates for the population younger than 65 years, 1996 to 2003. *Journal of the American Medical Association*, 296(22), 2712–2719.

Banthin, J. S., and Selden, T. (2003). The ABCs of children's health care: how the Medicaid expansions affected access, burdens, and coverage between 1987 and 1996. *Inquiry*, 40(2), 133–145.

Bashshur, R., Smith, D., and Stiles, R. (1993). Defining underinsurance: a conceptual framework for policy and empirical analysis. *Medical Care Review*, 50 (2), 199–218.

Bethell, C. D., Read, D., Blumberg, S. J., and Newacheck, P. W. (2008). What is the prevalence of children with special health care needs? Toward an understanding of variations in findings and methods across three national surveys. *Maternal and Child Health Journal*, 12(1), 1–14.

Blake, R. L. (1989). Integrating quantitative and qualitative methods in family research. *Family Systems Medicine*, 7(4), 411–427.

Blewett, L. A., Ward, A., and Beebe, T. J. (2006). How much health insurance is enough? Revisiting the concept of underinsurance. *Medical Care Research and Review*, 63(6), 663–700.

Booth, M., Reusch, C., and Touschner, J. (2012). *Pediatric dental benefits under the ACA*. Georgetown University Center for Children and Families.

Brehaut, J. C., Kohen, D. E., Raina, P., Walter, S. D., Russell, D. J., Swinton, M., O'Donnell, M., et al. (2004). The health of primary caregivers of children with cerebral palsy: how does it compare with that of other Canadian caregivers? *Pediatrics*, 114(2), e182.

Buchmueller, T. C., Grumbach, K., Kronick, R., and Kahn, J. G. (2005). Book review: the effect of health insurance on medical care utilization and implications for insurance expansion: a review of the literature. *Medical Care Research and Review*, 62(1), 3–30.

Cafferata, G. L., and Kasper, J. D. (1985). Family structure and children's use of ambulatory physician services. *Medical Care*, 23(4), 350–360.

Centers for Medicare and Medicaid Services. National Health Expenditure Accounts. www.cms.gov/Research-Statistics-Data-and-Systems/Statistics-Trends-and-Reports/NationalHealthExpendData/downloads/tables.pdf. Accessed February 25, 2014.

Chen, A. Y., and Escarce, J. J. (2006). Effects of family structure on children's use of ambulatory visits and prescription medications. *Health Services Research*, 41(5), 1895–1914.

Chen, A. Y., and Newacheck, P. W. (2006). Insurance coverage and financial burden for families of children with special health care needs. *Ambulatory Pediatrics*, 6(4), 204–209.

Chevarley, F. M. (2006). Utilization and expenditures for children with special health care needs. *Medical Expenditure Panel Survey Research Findings #24*.

Council of Economic Advisers (2010). *Economic Report of the President*. Washington, DC.

Cummings, J., Lavarreda, S., Rice, T., and Brown, R. E. (2009). The effects of varying periods of uninsurance on children's access to health care. *Pediatrics*, 123(3), e411–e418.

Cunningham, P. J. (1990). Medical care use and expenditures for children across stages of the family life cycle. *Journal of Marriage and Family*, 52(1), 197–207.

(2010). The growing financial burden of health care: national and state trends, 2001–2006. *Health Affairs*, 29(5), 1037–1044.

De Ridder, A., and De Graeve, D. (2006). Healthcare use, social burden and costs of children with and without ADHD in Flanders, Belgium. *Clinical Drug Investigation*, 26(2), 75–90.

DeNavas-Walt, C., Proctor, B., and Smith, J. (2011). Income, poverty, and health insurance coverage in the United States: 2010. Washington, DC: Census Bureau.

Downey, D. B. (1995). When bigger is not better: family size, parental resources, and children's educational performance. *American Sociological Review*, 60(5), 746–761. doi:10.2307/2096320

(2001). Number of siblings and intellectual development: the resource dilution explanation. *American Psychologist*, 56(6–7), 497–504. doi:10.1037/0003-066X.56.6-7.497

Dutton, D. (1981). Children's health care: the myth of equal access. *US Department of Health and Human Services.*, 357–440.

Ezzati-Rice, T. M., Rohde, F., and Greenblatt, J. (2008). *Sample design of the Medical Expenditure Panel Survey household component, 1998–2007.* US Department of Health and Human Services, Agency for Healthcare Research and Quality.

Farley, P. (1985). Who are the underinsured? *Milbank Memorial Fund Quarterly*, 63(3), 476–503.

Galbraith, A. A., Wong, S. T., Kim, S. E., and Newacheck, P. W. (2005). Out-of-pocket financial burden for low-income families with children: socioeconomic disparities and effects of insurance. *Health Services Research*, 40, 1722–1736.

Graves, J. A., and Long, S. (2006). Why do people lack health insurance? *Urban Institute*. Accessed at www.urban.org/publications/411317/html.

Gresenz, C., Rogowski, J., and Escarce, J. (2006). Dimensions of the local health care environment and use of care by uninsured children in rural and urban areas. *Pediatrics*, 117(3), e509–e517.

Guendelman, S., and Pearl, M. (2004). Children's ability to access and use health care. *Health Affairs*, 23(2), 235–244.

Guendelman, S., and Schwalbe, J. (1986). Medical care utilization by Hispanic children: how does it differ from black and white peers? *Medical Care*, 24(10), 925–940.

Hauser, R. M., and Kuo, H.-H. D. (1998). Does the gender composition of sibships affect women's educational attainment? *Journal of Human Resources*, 33 (3), 644–657.

Hofer, A., Abraham, J., and Moscovice, I. (2011). Expansion of coverage under the Patient Protection and Affordable Care Act and primary care utilization. *Milbank Quarterly*, 89(1), 69–89.

Hoffman, C., and Paradise, J. (2008). Health insurance and access to health care in the United States. *Annals of the New York Academy of Sciences*, 1136, 149–60.

Hoffman, C., and Schwartz, K. (2008). Eroding access among nonelderly US adults with chronic conditions: ten years of change. *Health Affairs*, 27, w340–w348.

Hong, S. H., and Shepherd, M. D. (1996). Outpatient prescription drug use by children enrolled in five drug benefit plans. *Clinical Therapeutics*, 18(3), 528–545.

Huskamp, H. A., Deverka, P. A., Epstein, A. M., Epstein, R. S., McGuigan, K. A., Muriel, A. C., and Frank, R. G. (2005). Impact of 3-tier formularies on drug treatment of attention-deficit/hyperactivity disorder in children. *Archives of General Psychiatry*, 62(4), 435.

Kaiser Family Foundation, and Health Research and Educational Trust (2005). Employer health benefits 2005 annual survey. *Kaiser Family Foundation*.

(2011). Employer health benefits 2011 annual survey. *Kaiser Family Foundation.*

Karaca-Mandic, P., Jena, A., Joyce, G., and Goldman, D. (2012). Out-of-pocket medication costs and use of medications and health care services among children with asthma. *Journal of the American Medical Association*, 307(12), 1284–1291.

Kashihara, D., and Carper, K. (2009). Statistical brief 272: national health care expenses in the US civilian noninstitutionalized population, 2007. *Agency for Healthcare Research and Quality.*

Kogan, M. D., Newacheck, P. W., Blumberg, S. J., Ghandour, R. M., Singh, G. K., Strickland, B. B., and van Dyck, P. C. (2010). Underinsurance among children in the United States. *New England Journal of Medicine*, 363(9), 841–851.

Kogan, M. D., Newacheck, P. W., Honberg, L., and Strickland, B. (2005). Association between underinsurance and access to care among children with special health care needs in the United States. *Pediatrics*, 116(5), 1162–1169.

Lave, J. R., Keane, C., Lin, C. J., Ricci, E. M., Amersbach, G., and LaVallee, C. P. (1998). Impact of a children's health insurance program on newly enrolled children. *Journal of the American Medical Association*, 279(22), 1820–1825.

Long, S. H., Marquis, M. S., and Harrison, E. R. (1994). The costs and financing of perinatal care in the United States. *American Journal of Public Health*, 84(9), 1473–1478.

Marquis, M. S., and Long, S. H. (1996). Reconsidering the effect of Medicaid on health care services use. *Health Services Research*, 30(6), 791–808.

McMorrow, S., Kenney, G., and Coyer, C. (2012). Addressing barriers to health insurance coverage among children: new estimates for the nation, California, New York, and Texas. May 2012. The Urban Institute Health Policy Center. www.urban.org/UploadedPDF/412561-Addressing-Barriers-to-Health-Insurance-Coverage-Among-Children.pdf. Accessed February 25, 2014.

Newacheck, P. W., and Halfon, N. (1986). The association between mother's and children's use of physician services. *Medical Care*, 24(1), 30–38.

(1988). Preventive care use by school-aged children: differences by socioeconomic status. *Pediatrics*, 82(3), 462–468.

Newacheck, P. W., and Kim, S. E. (2005). A national profile of health care utilization and expenditures for children with special health care needs. *Archives of Pediatrics and Adolescent Medicine*, 159(1), 10–17.

Newacheck, P. W., McManus, M., Fox, H. B., Hung, Y. Y., and Halfon, N. (2000). Access to health care for children with special health care needs. *Pediatrics*, 105(4), 760–766.

Newacheck, P. W., and Taylor, W. R. (1992). Childhood chronic illness: prevalence, severity, and impact. *American Journal of Public Health*, 82(3), 364–371.

OECD (2011). *Health at a Glance 2011: OECD Indicators.*

Phillips, M. (1999). Sibship size and academic achievement: what we now know and what we still need to know: comment on Guo and VanWey. *American Sociological Review*, 64(2), 188–192.

Powell, B., and Steelman, L. C. (1990). Beyond sibship size: sibling density, sex composition, and educational outcomes. *Social Forces*, 69(1), 181–206.

RAND (2006). The health insurance experiment: a classic RAND study speaks to the current health care reform debate. Retrieved from www.rand.org/content/dam/rand/pubs/research_briefs/2006/RAND_RB9174.pdf.

Rabbani, A., and Alexander, G. C. (2009). Impact of family structure on stimulant use among children with attention-deficit/hyperactivity disorder. *Health Services Research*, 44(6), 2060–2078.

Rosenbaum, S., and Westmoreland, T. M. (2012). The supreme court's surprising decision on the Medicaid expansion: how will the federal government and states proceed? *Health Affairs*, 31(8), 1663–1672.

Short, P. F. (1985). *Who are the underinsured?* Cambridge University Press for the Milbank Memorial Fund.

Short, P. F., and Banthin, J. (1995). New estimates of the underinsured younger than 65 years. *Journal of the American Medical Association*, 274(16), 1302–1306.

Short, P. F., and Lefkowitz, D. C. (1992). Encouraging preventive services for low-income children: the effect of expanding Medicaid. *Medical Care*, 30(9), 766–780.

Songer, T., LaPorte, R., Lave, J., Dorman, J., and Becker, D. (1997). Health insurance and the financial impact of IDDM in families with a child with IDDM. *Diabetes Care*, 20(4), 577.

Tangerose Orr, S., Charney, E., and Straus, J. (1988). Use of health services by black children according to payment mechanism. *Medical Care*, 26(10), 939–947.

US Department of Health and Human Services (2012). Essential Health Benefits.

Vistnes, J. P., and Hamilton, V. (1995). The time and monetary costs of outpatient care for children. *American Economic Review*, 85(2), 117–121.

Wood, D. L., Valdez, R. B., Hayashi, T., and Shen, A. (1990). Health of homeless children and housed, poor children. *Pediatrics*, 86(6), 858–866.

13   Child health and school readiness:
the significance of health literacy

Laurie T. Martin and Peggy Chen

Introduction

Many children enter kindergarten with poor health due to physical or emotional illness or limitations in their social, emotional, or physical development (High and the Committee on Early Childhood, 2008). Poor child health has both short- and long-term implications for school readiness and academic outcomes. Children with poor health have higher rates of school absenteeism, more behavior problems, difficulty concentrating, lower performance on standardized tests, increased likelihood of repeating a grade, and higher enrollment in special education services (Leslie and Jamison, 1990; Behrman, 1996; Currie, 2005). While we know that child health problems impede school readiness and performance, less attention has been paid to potential pathways for this relationship and levers such as parental health literacy and health knowledge that may be modified to improve child outcomes.

Health literacy is the "degree to which individuals have the capacity to obtain, process, and understand basic health information and services needed to make appropriate health decisions" (Ratzan and Parker, 2000). Roughly nine of every ten adults struggle to some extent with health promotion and disease prevention activities, navigating the health care system, and managing their health (DHHS, 2010). Individuals with lower health literacy have limited understanding of health risks, chronic diseases, and treatment protocols (Schillinger et al., 2002; Paasche-Orlow et al., 2005). They are also less likely to engage in screening programs (Lindau et al., 2002), follow up after abnormal test results (Lindau et al., 2006), and comply with preoperative instructions (Chew et al., 2004). Poor reading skills are associated with poor knowledge of medicines, side effects, drug interactions, and dosing instructions (Davis et al., 2006; Kripalani, Henderson et al., 2006), which may result in poorer adherence to medication regimens (Win and Schillinger, 2003; Gazmararian et al., 2006). Finally, individuals with limited literacy face significant challenges navigating the health system, from finding and entering health facilities to making health care appointments, filling out forms, and giving consent for procedures (Kirsch et al., 1993; Rudd et al., 2005).

Although the link between health literacy and health outcomes is well established in the adult literature, the impact of parental health literacy on child health has not been fully explored. Children rely on their parents to manage almost every aspect of their health. This includes preventive care (e.g., arranging for well-child visits, providing nutritious food), acute care (e.g., making treatment decisions, administering medication), chronic care (e.g., managing medication regimens, coordinating health services), and other tasks such selecting and enrolling in health insurance plans. How well parents manage and maintain their child's health is thus likely to depend on their own health literacy.

Employing a life-course framework to the issue of parental health literacy and child outcomes highlights the interdependence of the health and educational systems. Parental literacy skills and health knowledge are dependent, in part, on parents' own success in school and the development of reading, writing, science, numeracy, and communication skills. Similarly, what a child learns in school today has implications for her health literacy and the health and school readiness of her own future children. Thus, cross-systems strategies and collaborative approaches between the health and educational sectors are key to improving parental health literacy, child health, and school readiness.

Health literacy

Health literacy encompasses reading, writing, numeracy (ability to understand basic probability and numerical concepts), listening (aural language), and speaking (oral language) skills within a health context (Institute of Medicine, 2004; Paasche-Orlow et al., 2005). Distinct from general literacy, health literacy is influenced by both social and individual factors including cultural and conceptual knowledge (Institute of Medicine, 2004). The complexity of the health care system, medical jargon used by many providers (Castro et al., 2007), and exposure to novel health concepts, often while under a great deal of stress, may negatively impact health literacy even among those with adequate general literacy (Weiss, 2005). A disproportionate number of the elderly, racial and ethnic minorities, immigrants, and those with limited education lack the health literacy skills needed to meet the demands of everyday life (Weiss, 2005; DeWalt et al., 2010).

Health literacy among parents in the US is limited, with the majority of parents demonstrating inability to correctly fill out a health insurance form and nearly half of parents unable to perform at least one of two medication related tasks (Yin et al., 2009; Kumar et al., 2010). In response to the growing body of evidence of the impact of low health literacy on society, one goal of Healthy People 2020 is to "Improve the health literacy of the population" (US Department of Health and Human Services, 2010).

While individual skills and knowledge are critical components of health literacy, health literacy is also impacted by the difficulty and complexity of health information. Health literacy will be higher among all individuals if health information is presented in a way that is accurate, appropriate, understandable, and actionable. This includes communication from health care providers, pharmacies, public health agencies, media, websites, and governmental agencies (Nielsen-Bohlman et al., 2004; DHHS, 2010). Low health literacy is estimated to cost the US between 106 and 236 billion dollars annually (Vernon et al., 2007). These estimates do not consider current and future costs of children's health, school readiness, and academic success resulting from low parental health literacy, making the true costs of low health literacy much higher in practice.

Pathways by which health literacy may influence child health and school readiness

Evidence suggests that child health has significant, measurable impacts on school readiness and performance. An extensive body of research has focused on the influence of a number of parental characteristics on child health including socioeconomic status (SES), parental health, and health behaviors. Our analysis suggests that another critical factor, parental health literacy, has not been examined as part of these relationships. Figure 13.1 presents a theoretical model describing pathways for low parental health literacy to influence children's health, school readiness, and academic outcomes.

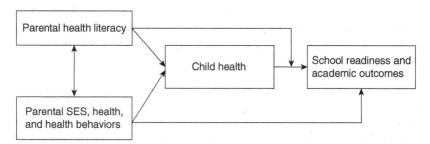

Figure 13.1 Potential pathways linking parental health literacy, child health, and school readiness.

Parental SES

The association between parental SES and child health likely begins even before birth (Bradley and Corwyn, 2002). Children from low SES families are more likely to experience poor growth *in utero*, premature birth, birth defects or disabilities (Wasserman et al., 1998; Vrijheid et al., 2000), asthma and other chronic conditions (Rosenbaum, 1992; Newacheck et al., 2004), higher blood lead levels (Starfield, 1982; Brody et al., 1994), and iron deficiency anemia (Starfield, 1989; US Department of Health and Human Services, 2000).

Little research on the association between SES and child health has included parental health literacy. However, health literacy may explain why SES indicators perform differently across cultural groups (Bradley et al., 1994; Bronfenbrenner, 1995), why consequences of health problems are often more severe for low SES children (Bradley and Corwyn, 2002; DHHS, 2008), and why social status differences in health outcomes remain within similarly insured populations (Baum et al., 1999). In fact, the American Medical Association cites poor health literacy as "a stronger predictor of a person's health than age, income, employment status, education level, and race" (Ad Hoc Committee on Health Literacy for the Council on Scientific Affairs, 1999). It follows, then, that parental health literacy may be a potential pathway by which parental SES affects child health.

Parental health

The impact of parental health on child health and well-being is well established. Children with depressed mothers, for example, are more likely to have behavior problems (O'Connor et al., 2002), attention deficit hyperactivity disorder (ADHD), and mental disorders (Cummings and Davies, 2004). Parents with severe health problems are more likely to engage in detrimental health behaviors including substance use (Swendsena and Merikangas, 2000), which may also have implications for cognitive development and school readiness, particularly for children exposed to such substances *in utero*. Parents with higher health literacy may be able to draw upon a range of skills and knowledge to more effectively manage their own health, resulting in a better control of their own health and fewer health and educational ramifications for their children.

Parental health behaviors

Many health problems in early childhood may be related to parental health behaviors. Poor maternal health behaviors, particularly during pregnancy, may have serious and long-lasting implications. Lack of prenatal care, smoking, drug use, and heavy alcohol use during pregnancy are related to child health and development both *in utero* and in early child-hood. Maternal smoking during pregnancy is associated with low birth weight (Kramer, 1987), increased likelihood of ADHD (Markussen Linnet et al., 2003), and antisocial behavior including conduct disorder and delinquency (Wakschlag et al., 2002). Parental smoking is also asso-ciated with respiratory problems in children including bronchitis and asthma (Strachan and Cook, 1998).

Parental nutritional decisions may also affect child health and academic outcomes. Children with poor nutrition (due either to lack of food or to overconsumption of non-nutritious foods) score lower on tests of cogni-tive performance and achievement (Pollitt et al., 1991), report more internalizing problems (Weinreb et al., 2002), and may be more suscep-tible to infection. One of the most prevalent nutritional problems for children, iron deficiency anemia, may also lead to shortened attention span, fatigue, and difficulty concentrating (Parker, 1989).

Parental health literacy, including proficiency in concepts such as risk and probability (i.e., numeracy), may influence their parental behaviors and those of their children. The importance of parental health literacy in the decision to smoke, for example, is highlighted in studies demonstrat-ing that smokers were more likely to underestimate their risks for serious illness due to cigarette smoking (Strecher et al., 1995). Additional evi-dence shows that both reading and numeracy skills are positively associ-ated with successful smoking cessation even after controlling for sociodemographic factors (Martin et al., 2011).

Parental health literacy may moderate the association between child health and school outcomes

With a movement toward patient centered care, parents are increasingly expected to manage their children's health in partnership with health practitioners (Nielsen-Bohlman et al., 2004). How well parents accom-plish this depends on their health literacy – their ability to access, understand, and use health related materials to make health care deci-sions, communicate with providers and other health care practitioners, and navigate the health care system to advocate for their children's health.

Parental health literacy may be critical for successfully managing a child's chronic condition (Janisse et al., 2010; Wood et al., 2010). While older children may play a role in managing their own health, younger children rely on their parents to manage their medications, communicate with health care providers, navigate the health care system, and coordinate care across multiple providers. These skills may play a role in how quickly a child's health condition is resolved or how well it is controlled. In fact,

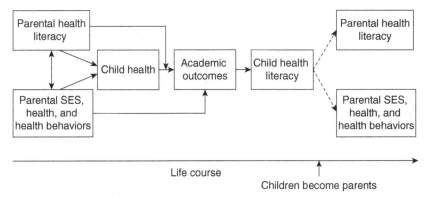

Figure 13.2 Health literacy affects well-being over the life course.

the degree of control of chronic conditions, rather than the presence of chronic conditions themselves, seems to have the greatest impact on school readiness and academic outcomes (Halterman et al., 2001; Currie, 2005).

A life-course perspective of health literacy

Life-course perspectives on health examine biological, behavioral, and psychosocial pathways that operate across an individual's life, and across generations, to influence health (Ben-Shlomo and Kuh, 2002). Figure 13.2 presents a life-course perspective of health literacy, suggesting that parental literacy skills and health knowledge are dependent, in part, on parents' own success in school and the development of reading, writing, science, numeracy, and communication skills. Similarly, the skills children learn today will influence their own health literacy and the health and school readiness of their future children. This approach supports existing work indicating that the roots of the relationship between parental literacy and child literacy begin informally in the home, with downstream effects in formal academic settings (Senechal and LeFevre, 2002; Raikes et al., 2006), and highlights the importance of both health and education fields in promoting health literacy, child health, and academic outcomes.

We will use this model as a framework to highlight current programs and strategies for improving health literacy and related outcomes. In addition, we will discuss the impact of two national initiatives that provide direction for setting goals and standards to improve health literacy through both the health and education systems. Finally, we discuss the implications for policy and make suggestions for future research directions.

Overview of current strategies to improve outcomes

Existing strategies to impact parental health literacy and child outcomes have focused on three potential intervention points: (1) the health system, (2) the education system, and (3) culture and society (Institute of Medicine, 2004). In Figure 13.3 these points of intervention are overlaid on the life-course framework of health literacy outlining the domains of influence for each intervention point. It is important to note the contexts are not mutually exclusive – the most effective strategies are likely to cut across contexts to create change on a global scale (Koh et al., 2012). Below, we highlight strategies already being employed to improve outcomes within each context. Together, they provide a multifaceted, empirical approach to improving outcomes related to limited health literacy.

Health system

A number of strategies are currently being employed within the health system, including lowering the literacy burden of health materials, improving the transfer and retention of health information, and assessing health care environments with a focus on provider communication skills.

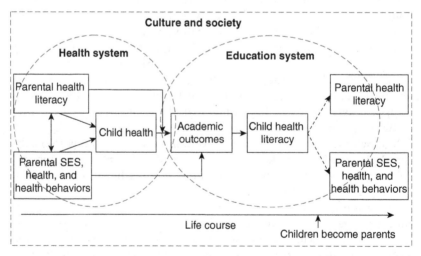

Figure 13.3 Potential points for intervention: culture and society, health system, and education system.

Lowering the literacy burden of health materials

Clear communication strategies have been shown to be effective for all individuals, not simply those with limited literacy skills (Kripalani et al., 2007). Techniques like lowering the reading level, increasing white space, using readable fonts and font sizes, avoiding medical jargon, and using short sentences and the active voice, lower the literacy burden of communication materials (Doak et al., 1996; Centers for Disease Control and Prevention, 1999).

In recent years there has also been a movement toward including members of the target audience in designing and testing communication materials. This process improves usability and health outcomes (Gustafson et al., 1999; Neuhauser, 2001). Language and culture have been additional foci of recent efforts, resulting in the development of specific Spanish language health literacy assessment tools (Yin et al., 2012) and creating culturally and community relevant health materials (Silk et al., 2010; Flecha et al., 2011).

Improving the transfer and retention of health information

A number of strategies are currently used to improve transfer and retention of health information, including interactive computer-based trainings (Blanson Henkemans et al., 2008), and tools such as pill cards, which use pictures and simple phrases to show each medicine, its purpose, how much to take, and when to take it (US Department of Health and Human Services, 2008). Other tools focus on improving the provider–patient interaction. AHRQ's *Questions Are the Answers* (US Department of Health and Human Services, 2010), The National Patient Safety Foundation's *Ask Me Three* (Partnership for Clear Health Communication, 2009), and common "teach-back" methods, where patients are asked to repeat in their own words what they need to do when they leave the provider's office, encourage active participation in managing health conditions. Because it is impossible to identify limited literacy skills without a formal assessment, many advocate a universal precautions approach (Paasche-Orlow et al., 2006) using clear communication strategies with every patient (Parker and Kreps, 2005). AHRQ's *Universal Precautions Toolkit* assesses the literacy demands of health care practices and suggests changes to help patients of all literacy levels (DeWalt et al., 2010).

Assessing health care environments

There has been increasing interest from health care facilities to assess and improve interactions with low health literacy patients. The Health Literacy Environment of Hospitals and Health Centers is a guide developed by the National Center for the Study of Adult Literacy and Learning (NCSALL/World Education, 2007) to analyze literacy related barriers to health care access and navigation. A number of self-audit tools are also being developed for health plans and primary care practices (DHHS, 2010). Finally, the AHRQ Consumer Assessment of Healthcare Providers and Systems (CAHPS) program includes a module for patients' assessments of health care providers' communication skills, including communication about health problems or concerns, medications, tests, forms, and disease self-management (US Department of Health and Human Services, 2011).

Education system

Strategies used in the education setting are not limited to the traditional school setting, but include other community-based settings as well. As such, these strategies have a broad reach, affecting children, parents, adult learners, teachers, and school staff. Three strategies are described below.

Leveraging the Coordinated School Health Program

CDC's Coordinated School Health Program (Centers for Disease Control and Prevention, 2010) is an eight-component model providing infrastructure for development and practice of health literacy in the school setting. The components include health education; physical education; nutrition services, faculty/staff wellness and health promotion; counseling and psychological services; health services; healthy school environment; and community and family involvement. Although not explicitly designed to improve health literacy, it provides a structure for a range of stakeholders to strengthen connections, increase community competence in confronting health problems, and address issues related to limited health literacy (Benham-Deal and Hodges, 2011).

Embedding health information in adult education courses

Levers for improving parental health literacy lie primarily within adult education courses, including English as a Second Language (ESL) courses, and certificate programs. Many adult education programs have sessions dedicated to functional health literacy skills such as searching for high-quality health information on the internet. Embedding health concepts in coursework provides an ideal opportunity for students to apply new skills to personal issues (Greeno, 1998; Darvin, 2006).

Capitalizing on parental involvement in early childhood education programs

There is an increasing recognition among early childhood education programs that parental health literacy is an important contributing factor to a child's health, development, and well-being. As such, several programs have begun to capitalize on the frequent contact they have with parents to affect change. As an example, the UCLA/Johnson & Johnson Health Care Institute (HCI) trains Head Start leadership to prepare and empower parents to address their children's health care needs. HCI has implemented a number of initiatives focused on topics including oral health, secondhand smoke, and building parents' knowledge and confidence in caring for minor childhood ailments, with a focus on developing parental health literacy and health knowledge (Herman and Jackson, 2010).

Culture and society

Cultural and societal factors influence how people interact with the health system and make health care decisions (Institute of Medicine, 2004). These include individual- and family-level characteristics such as SES, gender, language, race, and ethnicity, but also include broader societal-level factors such as mass media, marketing, and publicly available sources of electronic health information (Institute of Medicine, 2004).

Communicating with society

The sharing of health information is not limited to the patient–provider interaction. Rather, individuals seek health information from a variety of sources including the internet, media sources, and word of mouth. As such there is a need to ensure that principles of clear communication are implemented broadly. In acknowledgement of this, many of the more popular websites for health information, including the National Library of Medicine and WebMD, have been redesigned with clear communication principles in mind. There is also a growing interest in training journalists on health concepts, research, and health literacy to improve clear and balanced communication of health information to the public, particularly around more challenging concepts such as risk.

Identifying communities with low health literacy

Although health literacy is often thought of as an individual-level construct, it is also a public health issue (Koh et al., 2012). Poor health and limited health literacy tend to cluster based on social and societal factors. From a constrained-choice perspective (Bird and Rieker, 2008), individuals are constrained not only by the upper limits of their own health literacy but also by the health literacy of their community. An individual with limited health literacy living in an area with relatively high health literacy may benefit from the knowledge and abilities of friends and neighbors to process health and health care information. In contrast, an individual with low health literacy who lives in a community with limited health literacy may receive counter-productive information from friends and neighbors who may be less informed about appropriate health practices. Accordingly, strategies to harness community resources may leverage the effects of health literacy and health education programs (Flecha et al., 2011; Gordon et al., 2011).

The ability to identify geographic areas with large numbers of low health literacy individuals is necessary to help stakeholders such as public health practitioners, providers, and insurance companies target interventions more efficiently and cost-effectively. Some providers use educational attainment or income as a proxy for health literacy, a practice likely to produce inaccurate estimates. In fact, approximately 45 percent of high school graduates have limited health literacy (Kutner et al., 2006). To address this need, we have developed two predictive models to estimate health literacy using data from the 2003 National Assessment of Adult Literacy (NAAL) (Martin et al., 2009; Lurie et al., 2010). When applied to census data and well-defined geographic areas such as census tracts, the average health literacy of a region can be estimated and mapped, providing visual insight into community "hot spots" of lower than average health literacy (RAND Corporation, 2010; Martin et al., 2010).

National frameworks for thinking about health literacy

National Action Plan to Improve Health Literacy

In May 2010, the US Department of Health and Human Services released the *National Action Plan to Improve Health Literacy* (DHHS, 2010). This plan was developed around a vision of a society that "Provides everyone with access to accurate and actionable health information, delivers person-centered health information and services, and supports lifelong learning and skills to promote good health." The plan includes seven goals and suggests strategies, relevant for a range of disciplines, for achieving them. Specific strategies for educators and school administrators include: "Embed accurate, accessible, and actionable health information in all early childhood programs, such as Head Start and WIC"; "Connect efforts to improve children's health literacy skills with adult programs, such as adult education courses"; "Increase the amount of health education instruction in early childhood education"; and "Ensure that all students can pass National Assessment of Educational Progress (NAEP) assessments."

National Health Education Standards (NHES)

Data from the 2009 NAEP suggest that only about a third of students in fourth and eighth grade scored proficient or above in reading; 39 percent of fourth graders and 33 percent of eighth graders scored at proficient or above in math; and only 29 percent of fourth and eighth graders and 18 percent of twelfth graders scored at proficient or above in science[1] (Aud et al., 2010; US Department of Education, 2011). These findings are particularly concerning because science assessments, in addition to testing content knowledge, test one's ability to read and use charts, figures, and tables to draw conclusions. Such skills are critical components of health literacy.

The NHES standards provide a framework for teachers, administrators, and policymakers to "establish, promote, and support health-enhancing behaviors for students in all grade levels" (Centers for Disease Control and Prevention, 2010). To achieve these goals, students must develop the "capacity to obtain, interpret, and understand basic health information and services and the competence to use information in services that enhance their health" (Joint Committee on National Health Education Standards, 2007). Implementation of curriculum that meets these standards holds promise for improving students' health literacy and impacting the health and school readiness of the next generation of children.

While these frameworks are not specific to parental health literacy, they are useful for conceptualizing how health care and educational sectors can work independently and collaboratively to improve the health literacy of parents and children.

Implications for policy

Clear communication skills are critical for pediatricians, pharmacists, and other providers interacting with children and parents. Treatment plans for children can be complex, with medications and treatment plans tailored to the child's weight, age, developmental status, and competing health issues. Policy actions to improve the health literacy of, and clear communication with, both parents and children are likely to impact parental health, child health, and academic success. Below, we highlight a few high-impact policies that may improve parental and child health literacy, and thereby affect child health outcomes and school readiness.

---

[1] Based on the 2005 NAEP, the most recent year for which data on science performance are available.

Policies to improve parental health literacy

Below we summarize three potential policies relevant for parental health literacy that may positively influence child outcomes. These include: (1) implement performance incentives for the use of universal precautions, (2) standardize methods for teaching health care providers to deliver health messages using clear communication techniques, and (3) improve the delivery of accurate, accessible, and actionable health information through early childhood programs.

Implement performance incentives for the use of universal precautions

Despite evidence to suggest that close to 90 percent of the adult population lack proficient literacy skills, health care practitioners continue to communicate in ways that the majority of their patients do not fully understand. Studies have found low rates of comprehension among patients following physician visits (Crane, 1997) and low rates of parental comprehension following their children's physician visits (Grover et al., 1994). Even patients with proficient health literacy may have significant difficulty listening to and comprehending information when not feeling well or after being diagnosed with a serious illness.

Performance incentives linked to clear health communication may be an effective policy lever for improving clear communication and minimizing the mismatch between a patient's literacy skills and the literacy burden of the information he receives from his provider. Several data sources could be leveraged for such an initiative, including CAHPS data, which provide information on patients' experiences with ambulatory and facility-level care, and which is increasingly used in pay-for-performance initiatives. Given that most large health insurance companies have health literacy task forces, and that payers stand to benefit from improved health outcomes that result from clear, patient-centered communication (Stewart et al., 2000), this may be a realistic and feasible policy strategy.

Standardize methods for teaching health care providers to deliver health messages using clear communication techniques

Medical care can be intimidating for individuals with low literacy (Baker et al., 1996), and many patients with low health literacy may harbor a sense of shame, making disclosure of their low literacy more difficult (Baker et al., 1996; Institute of Medicine, 2004). It is therefore critical to utilize a universal precautions approach to employing clear communication with all patients. While the Affordable Care Act requires the inclusion of clear communication skills curricula for primary care physicians, these skills should be required for all health care providers, regardless of specialty. Existing programs within selected medical schools and residency programs teach future physicians how to communicate clearly with patients (Kripalani, Bussey-Jones et al., 2006) using clear, simple language and "teach-back" methods to assess patient comprehension of the care plans developed during each health care visit. Health care providers who have gone through such training programs demonstrate long-term retention of their skills (Moral et al., 2001; Oh et al., 2001). Despite these findings, no standardized methods exist to ensure that all health care providers meet a minimum basic standard in their ability to communicate clearly with patients.

Improve delivery of accurate, accessible, and actionable health information through early childhood programs

Staff in early childhood programs have regular, frequent interaction with parents of young children. The vast majority of these programs do not currently include programming to improve parental skills and knowledge relevant to functional health literacy. For example, the training objectives of one state's WIC in-service on the nutritional value of snack foods (Washington State Department of Health, 2009) were to explore common kids' snack foods, identify marketing strategies used to sell kids' snack foods, examine kids' snack food labels for kid-appeal, parent-appeal, and nutritional content, and practice sharing information about snack food choices. However, the program stops short of teaching staff how to share, teach, and reinforce these skills with parents, including the ability to identify high-quality information, and to read and interpret nutrition labels. Incentives and training should be provided to staff at WIC, Head Start, and other early childhood education programs to encourage and support the systematic integration of health literacy efforts into existing early childhood settings.

Policies to improve child health literacy

The policies mentioned above are likely to improve the exchange of health information between parents and providers, and foster the development of parental health literacy skills. Equally important, however, are policies focused on the development of health literacy skills among children, as development of this critical skill set not only is likely to have a positive impact on their own health as they grow and develop, but will improve the health of their own children in the future. Below we summarize four potential policies to support the development of child health literacy:

(1) implement a unified health curriculum across all schools, (2) develop effective methods of teaching health literacy across a wide range of school settings, (3) incorporate curriculum to develop health skills and knowledge across all academic subjects, and (4) promote child health literacy in health care settings.

Implement a unified health curriculum across all schools

The National Health Education Standards (NHES) provide a framework for improving health related skills and knowledge. As part of NHES, the CDC's School Health Education Resources also developed a list of characteristics defining effective health education curricula, including building personal competence, developing skills in health related communication, assessing information accuracy, decision making, planning, goal setting, and self–management (Centers for Disease Control and Prevention, 2010). Only 75 percent of states have adopted NHES or state health education standards (Benham-Deal and Hudson, 2006; Kann et al., 2007). Without a unified health curriculum for all public schools providing all students with comparable skills and knowledge, disparities in health literacy are likely to persist, and even widen over time.

Develop effective methods of teaching health literacy across a wide range of school settings

Beyond the development of a unified curriculum for teaching health literacy to children, it is also important to ensure that it is implemented consistently. Tremendous variation in school resources and priorities suggests that, without further guidance, there is likely to be significant variability in the quality and comprehensiveness of health curriculum implemented across schools. Further, children at higher risk of limited health literacy including minorities and recent immigrants are more likely to attend schools where academic priorities are focused elsewhere. Existing programs should be evaluated for suitability for scale-up and implementation across a wide range of schools (Diamond et al., 2011). Systematic methods of assessing health literacy instruction in a classroom setting should also be implemented (Marx et al., 2007).

Incorporate curriculum to develop health skills and knowledge across all academic subjects

Although it may be easier to compartmentalize health education within an existing science curriculum, health skills and knowledge should be incorporated into every academic subject. Lesson plans in language arts could use health related materials to develop reading comprehension and vocabulary; math courses could teach risk and probability in a health context; and computer classes could include instruction on navigating the internet for health related information. Embedding health related tasks, skills, and examples into other educational services including English as a Second Language (ESL) and speech and language supports would further develop relevant skills among those at the highest risk for limited health literacy and subsequent adverse outcomes. Existing research demonstrates that this integrated approach improves students' understanding and, when coupled with appropriate support for teachers, can improve their confidence teaching health and health literacy (Benham-Deal et al., 2010).

Promote child health literacy in health care settings

Health care providers have regular contact with children for both well-child exams and urgent visits. There are ongoing efforts to utilize these visits as a forum in which to promote and improve health literacy (Banister et al., 2011). Such programs deserve further investigation. Effective practices should be widely disseminated and measures to promote child health literacy in health care settings might be incorporated into provider-incentive programs.

Future research directions

Although Figures 13.1 and 13.2 present theoretical perspectives for explaining how parental health literacy may influence child health and school outcomes, quantifying these associations and examining these pathways in more detail is an important next step. A limited number of studies have started to examine the effect of parental health literacy on child outcomes; fewer have examined the longer-term and residual effects of such outcomes on school readiness and academic outcomes (Zaslow et al., 2001; Wood et al., 2010). Future studies should further elucidate this relationship and assess the long-term effects of such health outcomes on school readiness and academic outcomes.

The stability of these relationships over time also deserves further investigation. For example, if a mother's first-born child is diagnosed with type I diabetes, how does this affect her health literacy, and what implications does this have for the health and school readiness of her future children? How will the health literacy skills and knowledge she develops managing her child's diabetes affect how well she manages her second child's asthma – are the skills global, or disease specific? Early evidence indicates a dynamic model of health literacy, but future research in these areas may provide insight into additional strategies and approaches to improving parental health literacy and the health and school readiness of children.

Measures of parental health literacy should also be incorporated as a potential explanatory factor in future research on the association between SES and child outcomes. Parental literacy, for example, may help to explain why SES indicators perform differently across cultural groups (Bradley et al., 1994; Bronfenbrenner, 1995), why consequences of health problems are often more severe for low SES children (Bradley and Corwyn, 2002), and why social status differences in health outcomes remain within similarly insured populations (Baum et al., 1999).

Conclusion

Health literacy stands at the intersection of health and education policy. Taking a life-course perspective of health literacy, it becomes clear that developing relevant skills and knowledge among children helps to build and develop not only the health literacy of children, but also the health literacy of future adults and parents. Further, how effectively the health system interacts with parents has significant implications for child health. Given this natural intersection between health and education, cross-system collaborations and strategies may be particularly effective in addressing issues related to limited health literacy, child health, and academic success.

References

Ad Hoc Committee on Health Literacy for the Council on Scientific Affairs, American Medical Association (1999). Report on the Council of Scientific Affairs. *Journal of the American Medical Association*, 281, 552–557.

Aud, S., Hussar, W., et al. (2010). *The condition of education 2010*. Washington, DC: National Center for Education Statistics, Institute of Education Sciences, US Department of Education.

Baker, D. W., Parker, R., et al. (1996). The health care experience of patients with low literacy. *Archives of Family Medicine*, 5, 329–334.

Banister, E. M., Begoray, D. L., et al. (2011). Responding to adolescent women's reproductive health concerns: empowering clients through health literacy. *Health Care for Women International*, 32(4), 344–354.

Baum, A., Garofalo, J. P., et al. (1999). Socioeconomic status and chronic stress: does stress account for SES effects on health? *Annals of the New York Academy of Sciences*, 896, 131–144.

Behrman, J. R. (1996). The impact of health and nutrition on education. *World Bank Research Observer*, 11(1), 23–37.

Ben-Shlomo, Y., and Kuh, D. (2002). A life course approach to chronic disease epidemiology: conceptual models, empirical challenges and interdisciplinary perspectives. *International Journal of Epidemiology*, 31(2), 285–293.

Benham-Deal, T., and Hodges, B. (2011). Role of 21st century schools in promoting health literacy. Retrieved from www.neahin.org/healthliteracy/Images/BenhamDeal-Hodges%20Paper.pdf.

Benham-Deal, T., and Hudson, N. (2006). Are health educators in denial or facing reality? Demonstrating effectiveness within a school accountability system. *American Journal of Health Education*, 37(3), 154–158.

Benham-Deal, T., Jenkins, J. M., et al. (2010). The impact of professional development to infuse health and reading in elementary schools. *American Journal of Health Education*, 41(3), 155–166.

Bird, C., and Rieker, P., (2008). *Gender and health: the effects of constrained choices and social policies*. Cambridge University Press.

Blanson Henkemans, O. A., Rogers, W. A., et al. (2008). Usability of an adaptive computer assistant that improves self-care and health literacy of older adults. *Methods of Information in Medicine*, 47, 82–88.

Bradley, R. H., and Corwyn, R. F., (2002). Socioeconomic status and child development. *Annual Review of Psychology*, 53, 371–399.

Bradley, R. H., Whiteside-Mansell, L., et al. (1994). Early indications of resilience and their relation to experiences in the home environments of low birthweight, premature children living in poverty. *Child Development*, 65, 346–360.

Brody, D. J., Pirkle, J. L., et al. (1994). Blood lead levels in the US population. Phase 1 of the Third National Health and Nutrition Examination Survey (NHANES III, 1988 to 1991). *Journal of the American Medical Association*, 272(4), 277–283.

Bronfenbrenner, U. (1995). Developmental ecology through space and time: a future perspective. In P. Moen, G. H. Elder Jr., and K. Lüscher (eds.), *Examining lives in context: perspectives on the ecology of human development* (pp. 619–647). Washington, DC: American Psychological Association.

Castro, C. M., Wilson, C., et al. (2007). Babel babble: physicians' use of unclarified medical jargon with patients. *American Journal of Health Behavior*, 31 (Suppl. 1), 585–595.

Centers for Disease Control and Prevention (1999). *Simply Put* (2nd edn). Atlanta, GA: Office of Communication, Centers for Disease Control and Prevention.

Centers for Disease Control and Prevention (2010). Coordinated School Health Program. Retrieved September 10, 2010, from www.cdc.gov/HealthyYouth/CSHP/.

Centers for Disease Control and Prevention (2010). National Health Education Standards (NHES). Retrieved September 10, 2010, from www.cdc.gov/healthyyouth/sher/standards/index.htm.

Chew, L. D., Bradley, K. A., Flum, D. R., Cornia, P. B., and Koepsell, T. D. (2004). The impact of low health literacy on surgical practice. *American Journal of Surgery*, 188(3), 250–253.

Crane, J. A. (1997). Patient comprehension of doctor–patient communication on discharge from the emergency department. *Journal of Emergency Medicine*, 15(1), 1–7.

Cummings, M. E., and Davies, P. T. (2004). Maternal depression and child development. *Journal of Child Psychology and Psychiatry*, 35(1), 73–112.

Currie, J. (2005). Health disparities and gaps in school readiness. *Future of Children*, 15(1), 117–138.

Darvin, J. (2006). Real-world cognition doesn't end when the bell rings: literacy instruction strategies derived from situated cognition research. *Journal of Adolescent & Adult Literacy*, 49(5), 398–407.

Davis, T. C., Wolf, M. S., et al. (2006). Low literacy impairs comprehension of prescription drug warning labels. *Journal of General Internal Medicine*, 21(8), 847–851.

DeWalt, D. A., Callahan, L. F., et al. (2010). *Health Literacy Universal Precautions Toolkit*. (Prepared by North Carolina Network Consortium, The Cecil G. Sheps Center for Health Services Research, The University of North Carolina at Chapel Hill, under Contract No. HHSA290200710014.) Rockville, MD: Agency for Healthcare Research and Quality.

DHHS (2008). Healthy People 2010: Objective 11–2 data. Retrieved August 20, 2008, from http://wonder.cdc.gov/data2010/focus.htm.

(2010). *National Action Plan to Improve Health Literacy*. Washington, DC: US Government Printing Office.

Diamond, C., Saintonge, S., et al. (2011). The development of building wellness, a youth health literacy program. *Journal of Health Communication*, 16 (Suppl. 3), 103–118.

Doak, C., Doak, L., et al. (1996). *Teaching patients with low literacy skills* (2nd edn). Philadelphia: J. B. Lippincott.

Flecha, A., García, R., et al. (2011). Using health literacy in school to overcome inequalities. *European Journal of Education*, 46(2), 209–218.

Gazmararian, J. A., Kripalani, S., et al. (2006). Factors associated with medication refill adherence in cardiovascular-related diseases: a focus on health literacy. *Journal of General Internal Medicine*, 21(12), 1215–1221.

Gordon, S. C., Barry, C. D., et al. (2011). Clarifying a vision for health literacy: a holistic school-based community approach. *Holistic Nursing Practice*, 25(3), 120–126.

Greeno, J. G. (1998). The situativity of knowing, learning, and research. *American Psychologist*, 53(1), 5–26.

Grover, G., Berkowitz, C. D., et al. (1994). Parental recall after a visit to the emergency department. *Clinical Pediatrics*, 33(4), 194–201.

Gustafson, D. H., Hawkins, R., et al. (1999). Impact of a patient-centered, computer-based health information/support system. *American Journal of Preventive Medicine*, 16(1), 1–9.

Halterman, J. S., Montes, G., et al. (2001). School readiness among urban children with asthma. *Ambulatory Pediatrics*, 1(4), 201–205.

Herman, A., and Jackson, P. (2010). Empowering low-income parents with skills to reduce excess pediatric emergency room and clinic visits through a tailored low literacy training intervention. *Journal of Health Communication*, 15(8), 895–910.

High, P. C. and the Committee on Early Childhood, Adoption, and Dependent Care and Council on School Health (2008). Dependent Care and Council on School Health. *Pediatrics*, 121, e1008–e1015.

Institute of Medicine (2004). *Health literacy: a prescription to end confusion*. Washington, DC: National Academies Press.

Janisse, H. C., Naar-King, S., et al. (2010). Brief report: parent's health literacy among high-risk adolescents with insulin dependent diabetes. *Journal of Pediatric Psychology*, 35(4), 436–440.

Joint Committee on National Health Education Standards (2007). *National Health Education Standards: Achieving Excellence*. Atlanta, GA: American Cancer Society.

Kann, L., Telljohann, S., et al. (2007). Health education: results from the School Health Policies and Programs Study 2006. *Journal of School Health*, 77(8), 408–434.

Kirsch, I. S., Jungeblut, A., et al. (1993). *Adult literacy in America: a first look at the findings of the national adult literacy survey*. Washington, DC: National Center for Education Statistics, US Department of Education.

Koh, H. K., Berwick, D. M., et al. (2012). New federal policy initiatives to boost health literacy can help the nation move beyond the cycle of costly "Crisis Care." *Health Affairs*, 31(2), 434–443.

Kramer, M. S. (1987). Determinants of low birth weight: methodological assessment and meta-analysis. *Bulletin of the World Health Organization*, 65(5), 663–737.

Kripalani, S., Bussey-Jones, J., et al. (2006). A prescription for cultural competence in medical education. *Journal of General Internal Medicine*, 21(10), 1116–1120.

Kripalani, S., Henderson, L., et al. (2006). Predictors of medication self-management skill in a low-literacy population. *Journal of General Internal Medicine*, 21(8), 852–856.

Kripalani, S., Robertson, R., et al. (2007). Development of an illustrated medication schedule as a low-literacy patient education tool. *Patient Education and Counseling*, 66(3), 368–377.

Kumar, D., Sanders, L., et al. (2010). Parental understanding of infant health information: health literacy, numeracy, and the Parental Health Literacy Activities Test (PHLAT). *Academic Pediatrics*, 10(5), 309–316.

Kutner, M., Greenberg, E., et al. (2006). *The health literacy of america's adults: results from the 2003 National Assessment of Adult Literacy*. Washington, DC: National Center for Education Statistics.

Leslie, J., and Jamison, D. T. (1990). Health and nutrition considerations in education planning. 1. Educational consequences of health problems among school-age children. *Food and Nutrition Bulletin*, 12(3), 191–203.

Lindau, S., Basu, A., et al. (2006). Health literacy as a predictor of follow-up after an abnormal pap smear: a prospective study. *Journal of General Internal Medicine*, 21(8), 829–834.

Lindau, S., Tomori, C., et al. (2002). The association of health literacy with cervical cancer prevention knowledge and health behaviors in a multiethnic cohort of women. *American Journal of Obstetrics and Gynecology*, 186(5), 938–943.

Lurie, N., Martin, L. T., et al. (2010). *Estimating and mapping health literacy in the state of Missouri*. Santa Monica: RAND Corporation.

Markussen Linnet, K., Dalsgaard, S., et al. (2003). Maternal lifestyle factors in pregnancy risk of attention deficit hyperactivity disorder and associated behaviors: review of the current evidence. *American Journal of Psychiatry*, 160, 1028–1040.

Martin, L., Fremont, A., et al. (2010). *A prototype interactive mapping tool to target low health literacy in Missouri*. Santa Monica: RAND Corporation.

Martin, L. T., Ruder, T., et al. (2009). Developing predictive models of health literacy. *Journal of General Internal Medicine*, 24(11), 1211–1216.

Martin, L. T., Schonlau, M., et al. (2011). Patient activation and advocacy: which literacy skills matter most? *Journal of Health Communication*, 16 (Suppl. 3), 177–190.

Marx, E., Hudson, N., et al. (2007). Promoting health literacy through the health education assessment project. *Journal of School Health*, 77(4), 157–163.

Moral, R. R., Alamo, M. M., et al. (2001). Effectiveness of a learner-centred training programme for primary care physicians in using a patient-centred consultation style. *Family Practice*, 18(1), 60–63.

NCSALL/World Education (2007). National Center for the Study of Adult Learning and Literacy. Retrieved September 10, 2010, from www.ncsall. net/index.php?id=1163.

Neuhauser, L. (2001). Participatory design for better interactive health communication: a statewide model in the USA. *Electronic Journal of Communication/La Revue Electronique de Communications in Behavioral Biology. Part A. Original Articles* 11(3 and 4).

Newacheck, P. W., Inkelas, M., et al. (2004). Health services use and health care expenditures for children with disabilities. *Pediatrics*, 114(1), 79–85.

Nielsen-Bohlman, L., Panzer, A. M., et al. (eds.) (2004). *Health literacy: a prescription to end confusion*. Washington, DC: National Academies Press.

O'Connor, T., Heron, J., et al. (2002). Maternal antenatal anxiety and children's behavioural/emotional problems at 4 years: report from the Avon Longitudinal Study of Parents and Children. *British Journal of Psychiatry*, 180, 502–508.

Oh, J., Segal, R., et al. (2001). Retention and use of patient-centered interviewing skills after intensive training. *Academic Medicine: Journal of the Association of American Medical Colleges*, 76(6), 647–650.

Paasche-Orlow, M. K., Parker, R., et al. (2005). The prevalence of limited health literacy. *Journal of General Internal Medicine*, 20(2), 175–184.

Paasche-Orlow, M. K., Schillinger, D. G., et al. (2006). How health care systems can begin to address the challenge of limited literacy. *Journal of General Internal Medicine*, 21, 884–887.

Parker, L. (1989). *The relationship between nutrition and learning: a school employee's guide to information and action*. Washington, DC: National Education Association.

Parker, R., and Kreps, G. L. (2005). Library outreach: overcoming health literacy challenges. *Journal of the Medical Library Association*, 93(4), S81–S85.

Partnership for Clear Health Communication (2009). Ask me 3. Retrieved April 12, 2009, from www.npsf.org/askme3/index.php.

Pollitt, E., Leibel, R., et al. (1991). Brief fasting, stress, and cognition in children. *American Journal of Clinical Nutrition*, 34(August), 1526–1533.

Raikes, H., Pan, B. A., et al. (2006). Mother–child bookreading in low-income families: correlates and outcomes during the first three years of life. *Child Development*, 77(4), 924–953.

RAND Corporation (2010). Missouri Health Literacy Mapping Tool: a proto-type interactive mapping tool to target low health literacy in Missouri. Retrieved September 1, 2010, from www.rand.org/health/projects/mis souri-health-literacy/.

Ratzan, S. and Parker, R. (2000). Introduction. In C. Selden, M. Zorn, S. Ratzan, and R. Parker (eds.), *National Library of Medicine current bibliographies in medicine: health literacy*. Bethesda, MD: National Institutes of Health, US Department of Health and Human Services.

Rosenbaum, S. (1992). Child health and poor children. *American Behavioral Scientist*, 35, 275–289.

Rudd, R., Renzulli, D., Pereira, A., and Daltroy, L. (2005). Literacy demands in health care settings: the patient perspective. In J. Schwartzberg, J. VanGeest, and C. Wang (eds.), *Understanding health literacy* (pp. 69–84). Chicago: American Medical Association.

Schillinger, D., Grumbach, K., et al. (2002). Association of health literacy with diabetes outcomes. *Journal of the American Medical Association*, 288(4), 475–482.

Senechal, M. and LeFevre, J. A. (2002). Parental involvement in the development of children's reading skill: a five-year longitudinal study. *Child Development*, 73(2), 445–460.

Silk, K. J., Horodynski, M. A., et al. (2010). Strategies to increase health literacy in the infant feeding series (TIFS): a six-lesson curriculum for low-income mothers. *Health Promotion Practice*, 11(2), 226–234.

Starfield, B. (1982). Family income, ill health and medical care of US children. *Journal of Public Healthy Policy*, 3, 244–259.

(1989). Child health care and social factors: poverty, class, race. *Bulletin of the New York Academy of Medicine*, 65, 299–306.

Stewart, M., Brown, J. B., et al. (2000). The impact of patient-centered care on outcomes. *Journal of Family Practice* 49(9), 796–804.

Strachan, D. P., and Cook, D. G., (1998). Parental smoking and childhood asthma: longitudinal and case-control studies. *Thorax*, 53, 204–212.

Strecher, V., Kreuter, M., et al. (1995). Do cigarette smokers have unrealistic perceptions of their heart attack, cancer and stroke risks? *Journal of Behavioral Medicine*, 18(1), 45–54.

Swendsena, J. D., and Merikangas, K. R. (2000). The comorbidity of depression and substance use disorders. *Clinical Psychology Review*, 20(2), 173–189.

US Department of Education, National Center for Education Statistics (2011). *The nation's report card: science 2009*. Washington, DC: US Government Printing Office.

(2000). Health communication (chapter 11). *Healthy people 2010. 2nd edn. With understanding and improving health and objectives for improving health.* Washington, DC: US Government Printing Office.

(2008). How to create a pill card. Retrieved September 10, 2010, from http:// www.ahrq.gov/qual/pillcard/pillcard.htm.

US Department of Health and Human Services (2010). Did you know? The right questions to ask. Retrieved September 10, 2010, from www.ahrq.gov/ques tionsaretheanswer/.

(2010). Healthy people 2020 goals and objectives: health communication and health information technology. Retrieved from www.healthypeople.gov/2020/topicsobjectives2020/objectiveslist.aspx?topicId=18.

(2011). CAHPS item set for addressing health literacy. Retrieved from www.cahps.ahrq.gov/surveys-guidance/item-sets/health-literacy.aspx.

Vernon, J. A., Trujillo, A., et al. (2007). *Low health literacy: implications for national health policy.* University of Connecticut.

Vrijheid, M., Dolk, H., et al. (2000). Socioeconomic inequalities in risk of congenital anomaly. *Archives of Disease in Childhood,* 82, 349–352.

Wakschlag, L. S., Pickett, K. E. et al. (2002). Maternal smoking during pregnancy and severe antisocial behavior in offspring: a review. *American Journal of Public Health,* 92(6), 966–974.

Washington State Department of Health (2009). *Popular kids' snack foods: a nutrition in-service for staff.* Washington, DC.

Wasserman, C. R., Shaw, G. M., et al. (1998). Socioeconomic status, neighborhood social conditions, and neural tube defects. *American Journal of Public Health,* 88, 1674–1680.

Weinreb, L., Wehler, C., et al. (2002). Hunger: its impact on children's health and mental health. *Pediatrics,* 110(4), e41.

Weiss, B. D. (2005). Epidemiology of low health literacy. In J. Schwartzberg, J. VanGeest, and C. Wang (eds.), *Understanding Health Literacy: Implications for Medicine and Public Health* (pp. 17–40). Washington, DC: American Medical Association.

Win, K., and Schillinger, D. (2003). Understanding of warfarin therapy and stroke among ethnically diverse anticoagulation patients at a public hospital. *Journal of General Internal Medicine,* 18 (Suppl. 1), 278.

Wood, M. R., Price, J. H., et al. (2010). African American parents'/guardians' health literacy and self-efficacy and their child's level of asthma control. *Journal of Pediatric Nursing,* 25(5), 418–427.

Yin, H. S., Johnson, M., et al. (2009). The health literacy of parents in the United States: a nationally representative study. *Pediatrics,* 124 (Suppl. 3), S289–S298.

Yin, H. S., Sanders, L. M., et al. (2012). Assessment of health literacy and numeracy among spanish-speaking parents of young children: validation of the Spanish Parental Health Literacy Activities Test (PHLAT Spanish). *Academic Pediatrics,* 12(1), 68–74.

Zaslow, M. J., Hair, E. C., et al. (2001). Maternal depressive symptoms and low literacy as potential barriers to employment in a sample of families receiving welfare: are there two-generational implications? *Women & Health,* 32(3), 211–251.

14 Promoting healthy weight development in child care centers: a review of the NAP SACC program

Dianne S. Ward and Temitope O. Erinosho

Background

Childhood obesity is a serious public health problem in the United States. Since 1980, the rates of childhood obesity in the US have nearly tripled (Centers for Disease Control and Prevention, 2012a). Epidemiologic data from the 2009–10 National Health and Nutrition Examination Survey (NHANES) report that, presently, 27 percent of preschool children aged 2 to 5 years old are overweight or obese (Ogden et al., 2012), with particularly higher prevalence observed among racial and ethnic minorities (Hispanic, Mexican American, and African American children), and children from low-income families (Centers for Disease Control and Prevention, 2012b; Freedman et al., 2006; Ogden et al., 2010). Obesity in childhood is associated with a number of adverse health conditions, including the risk of developing high blood pressure, type 2 diabetes, breathing problems, fatty liver disease, and gallstones, and also becoming obese in adulthood (Centers for Disease Control and Prevention, 2012b).

Furthermore, obesity in childhood has been linked with poor educational outcomes. Studies report that overweight and obese children are more likely to have lower test scores, perceive themselves as being below average academically, report being held back a grade or year, and expect not to complete college, compared to children who are normal weight (Datar and Strum, 2006; Davis and Cooper, 2011; Falkner et al., 2001; Hollar et al., 2010; Li et al., 2012; Shore et al., 2008). This is because children who are overweight or obese tend to have lower self-esteem and poor body image, making it difficult for them to be attentive in class, and thus preventing them from learning in school (Datar and Strum, 2006). Another reason is that health problems associated with being overweight or obese may increase sick days, leading to absences from school, and consequently affecting children's performance in school (Datar and Strum, 2006; Li et al., 2012). In addition, research shows children who are obese are at greater risk of developing micronutrient deficiencies,

369

particularly iron and vitamin A deficiency, which are associated with poor learning, cognition, and school performance (Currie, 2005; Datar, Strum, and Magnabosco, 2004; Grantham-McGregor and Ani, 2001; Halterman et al., 2001; Li et al., 2008; Lozoff et al., 2000; Nead et al., 2004; Pinhas-Hamiel et al., 2006; Taras, 2005). To reduce children's risk for obesity related health problems, and limit the financial burden that may occur from children, especially racial and ethnic minorities and low-income children, who are at greatest risk for childhood obesity not attaining their highest academic potential, it is crucial that efforts to prevent obesity begin in early childhood.

Poor dietary intakes, including low intakes of fruits and vegetables and high intakes of fats and added sugars, increase the risk for childhood obesity (Anderson and Butcher, 2006; Carlson et al., 2012; te Velde et al., 2012). Physical inactivity and sedentary behaviors (e.g., television viewing, computer/video game use) are also associated with greater risk for childhood obesity (Carlson et al., 2012; Davison and Birch, 2001; te Velde et al., 2012). Children establish dietary and physical activity behaviors in early childhood (Birch and Fisher, 1998; Huston et al., 1999; Trost et al., 2003). During this critical stage of development a significant portion of young children in the US share their time between the home and child care programs. National data report that 61 percent of children aged 0 to 6 years are in some form of non-parental child care program such as child care centers, preschools, Head Start, or family child care homes on a regular basis (Forum on Child and Family Statistics, 2010). On average, children spend about 25 hours per week in these settings (Iruka and Carver, 2006). The quality and quantity of foods and beverages and of physical activity opportunities provided to children in child care settings influence children's dietary intakes and physical activity behaviors, and consequently their risk for childhood obesity.

National guidelines recommend that children consume at least one-third of their daily requirements for foods and nutrients at part-time child care programs (4–7 hours per day), and at least half to two-thirds of their daily food and nutrient requirements in full-time child care programs (≥8 hours per day) (American Dietetic Association, 2005). A few studies have evaluated menus and observed foods and beverages consumed by children in child care centers and found that they do not supply appropriate portions of children's daily requirements for many foods and nutrients (Ball, Benjamin, and Ward, 2008; Bolella et al., 1999; Briley et al., 1999; Bruening et al., 1999; Drake, 1991; Fleischhacker, Cason, and Achterberg, 2006; Oakley et al., 1995). A study of twenty child care centers in North Carolina found that although foods offered to children at mealtimes met children's requirements for fruit, milk, and sodium, foods provided were of low to average quality, providing less than children's daily requirements for vegetables, including dark green and orange vegetables and legumes, total grain and whole grain, meats and beans, and oils, and exceeding children's requirements for saturated fat, solid fats, and added sugars (Erinosho et al., 2013). Another study of forty child care centers in New York City found that between 39 percent and 48 percent of the 240 children observed consumed at least half of the daily recommended servings for milk, fruits, grains, or meat or meat alternates, while 17 percent consumed at least half of the daily recommended servings for vegetables. In terms of nutrients, at least half of the observed children consumed half of the daily recommendation for most nutrients; however, only 5 percent of the observed children consumed at least half of the daily recommendation for vitamin E (Erinosho et al., 2011). The national Early Childhood and Child Care Study found that meals offered during breakfast at child care centers that participated in the US Department of Agriculture's Child and Adult Care Food Program, a federally funded program that reimburses early care and education programs for providing meals to children, did not meet the children's requirements for protein, carbohydrate, total fat, cholesterol, vitamins A and C, calcium, and iron, provided less than children's requirement for energy (calories), and exceeded their requirement for saturated fat (US Department of Agriculture, 1997). Lunches provided at the child care centers also met children's requirements for protein, vitamins A and C, and calcium, provided less than their requirements for energy and iron, and exceeded their requirements for total fat, saturated fat, and sodium.

Studies assessing children's physical activity in child care centers also report that many children are receiving less than the 60–90 minutes of daily physical activity recommended while in such settings (Dowda et al., 2009; National Association for Sport and Physical Education, 2012; Pate et al., 2008; Pate et al., 2004; Reilly, 2010; Trost, Ward, and Senso, 2010). Pate et al. (2008) observed 3 to 5 year olds in twenty-four preschools in South Carolina (493 children, minimum of 600 thirty-second observation intervals recorded per child), and found that children participated in moderate-to-vigorous physical activities only during 3 percent of the observation intervals, but were sedentary during 87 percent of the observation intervals. In another study, Pate et al. (2004) used accelerometers to assess physical activity levels of children attending nine preschools (281 children) in South Carolina, and found that, on average, children engaged in about 8 minutes of moderate-to-vigorous physical activity per hour of school attendance, 11 minutes per hour in light activities, and 42 minutes in sedentary activities per hour of school attendance. Physical characteristics of child care centers that have been found to contribute to higher levels of moderate-to-vigorous physical activity in children include having larger playgrounds, more portable play equipment (e.g., balls, tricycles), fewer fixed items of playground equipment (e.g., jungle gyms, slides, swings), and less use of electronic media such as televisions and computers (Dowda et al., 2009).

Given the amount of time that children spend in child care programs, it is imperative that intervention efforts to address childhood obesity target such settings to ensure that children develop healthy nutrition and physical activity behaviors, and support healthy weight development early in life. However, few childhood obesity prevention interventions have been published that specifically target children under 6 years old; the majority of studies have focused on preventing obesity in school-age children (Campbell and Hesketh, 2007; Hesketh and Campbell, 2010). Of the intervention studies targeting young children, few have focused on improving nutrition and physical activity environments in child care settings in order to support healthy weight development in children (Bluford, Sherry, and Scanlon, 2007; Fitzgibbon et al., 2005; Hesketh and Campbell, 2010; Ward et al., 2008a). Given the dearth of such interventions, the Nutrition and Physical Activity Self-Assessment for Child Care (NAP SACC) program was developed for child care centers.

The NAP SACC program

Development of the NAP SACC program

The NAP SACC program is an environmental intervention for child care centers in North Carolina that was developed in 2002 (Ammerman et al., 2007). The goal of the program was to improve the nutrition and physical activity environments, practices, and policies in child care centers, and ultimately to support healthy weight gain in preschool children 3 to 5 years of age. The NAP SACC program is a theory-based intervention that utilizes constructs from Social Cognitive Theory, specifically expectancies, observational learning, self-efficacy, behavioral capability, environment, situation, reinforcement, and reciprocal determinism, against a backdrop of the Socioecological Model (Ammerman et al., 2007; Bandura, 1986; 1997; McLeroy et al., 1988; Stokols, 1996).

In designing the NAP SACC program, formative research data were collected through key informant interviews, focus group discussions, extensive literature reviews, and expert opinion. Key informant interviews with child care providers, and also focus group discussions with parents of children in child care centers, were conducted by the NAP SACC team to collect information about child care provider and parent views of the nutrition and physical activity environments in North Carolina's child care centers, evaluate their perceptions of the regulatory rating systems on nutrition and physical activity in child care settings, and identify potential opportunities to promote positive nutrition and physical activity behaviors in such settings through environmental change. An extensive literature review was conducted to gather evidence on nutrition and physical activity in child care settings, and review current guidelines, standards, and recommendations for child care programs serving children ages 2 to 5 years. State and national experts in the area of child care nutrition and physical activity were consulted to review all data gathered and identify gaps that needed to be addressed. Finally, a NAP SACC community advisory committee comprised of health professionals was convened to provide insight about the appropriateness and usability of the NAP SACC program in child care centers.

In addition to being used to design the NAP SACC program, information gathered from the comprehensive literature review, existing national standards and recommendations, expert opinion, and feedback from the NAP SACC advisory committee were used to develop best-practice recommendations for nutrition and physical activity to promote healthy weight development in preschool-aged children in child care centers (Benjamin Neelon et al., 2012; McWilliams et al., 2009). These best-practice recommendations address nine key areas of nutrition (fruits and vegetables; meats, fats, and grains; beverages; menus and variety; feeding practices; foods offered outside of regular meals and snacks; support for healthy eating; nutrition education; nutrition policy) and eight key areas of physical activity (active opportunities; fixed play environment; portable play equipment; sedentary opportunities; sedentary environment; staff behavior; physical activity training and education; physical activity policies) in child care centers. Detailed descriptions of the NAP SACC best-practice recommendations for nutrition and physical activity in child care centers are provided in Tables 14.1 and 14.2.

Components of the NAP SACC program

The NAP SACC program allows child care centers to self-assess their nutrition and physical activity environments, practices, and policies, select areas for improvement, and make environmental changes with the help of a trained NAP SACC consultant within a six-month intervention period (Ammerman et al., 2007; Benjamin et al., 2007a; NAP SACC, 2012; Ward et al., 2008a). The program is comprised of five steps: self-assessment, action planning, continuing education, technical assistance, and reassessment (Figure 14.1).

Table 14.1 *NAP SACC best-practice recommendations for nutrition in child care centers.*

Target area	NAP SACC best-practice recommendation[a]
Fruits and vegetables	Offer fruit (not juice) at least twice per day.
	Serve fruit canned in its own juice (not syrup), fresh or frozen all of the time.
	Offer vegetables (not fried) at least twice per day.
	Offer vegetables, other than potatoes, corn, or green beans, one or more times per day.
	Prepare cooked vegetables without added meat fat, margarine, or butter.
Meats, fat, and grains	Offer fried or pre-fried potatoes less than once a week or never.
	Offer fried or pre-fried meats or fish less than once a week or never.
	Offer high-fat meats less than once a week or never.
	Offer beans or lean meats at least once a day.
	Offer high-fiber, whole grain foods at least twice per day.
	Offer sweets or salty foods less than once a week or never.
Beverages	Make drinking water easily available for self-serve both indoors and outdoors.
	Offer 100 percent fruit juice twice per week or less.
	Offer sugary drinks rarely or never.
	Serve skim or 1 percent milk to children over 2 years.
	Locate soda and other vending machines off-site.
Menus and variety	Use a cycle menu of three weeks or greater that changes with seasons.
	Include a combination of new and familiar foods on weekly menus.
	Include foods from a variety of cultures on weekly menus.
Feeding practices	Staff should help children determine if they are full before removing their plate.
	Staff should help children determine if they are still hungry before serving additional food.
	Staff should gently and positively encourage children to try a new or less favorite food.
	Do not use food to encourage positive behavior.
Foods offered outside of regular meals and snacks	Provide and enforce written guidelines for healthier food brought in and served for holidays and celebrations.
	Celebrate holidays with mostly healthy foods and non-food treats.
	Fundraising should consist of selling non-food items only.
Supporting healthy eating	Staff should join children at the table for meals and consume the same food and drinks.

Table 14.1 (*cont.*)

Target area	NAP SACC best-practice recommendation[a]
	Always serve meals family style.
	Staff should rarely or never eat less healthy foods in front of children.
	Staff should talk with children about trying and enjoying healthy foods.
	Provide visible support for healthy eating in 2- to 5-year-old classrooms and common areas through use of posters, pictures, and displayed books.
Nutrition education	Provide training opportunities on nutrition (other than food safety and food program guidelines) for staff two times per year or more.
	Provide nutrition education for children through a standardized curriculum once per week or more.
	Offer nutrition education opportunities to parents two times per year or more.
Nutrition policy	Create a written policy on nutrition and food service that is available and followed. It may include items from the previous eight nutrition key areas.

[a] These best-practice recommendations were developed in 2007 as part of the initial NAP SACC program. The best practices are currently being revised to reflect the most current guidelines and recommendations for child care programs as part of the Go NAP SACC program.

Table 14.2 *NAP SACC best-practice recommendations for physical activity in child care centers.*

Target area	NAP SACC best-practice recommendation[a]
Active opportunities (Daily opportunities that may result in more physical activity)	Children provided with at least 120 min. of active playtime each day.
	Teacher-led physical activity provided to children ≥2 times per day.
	Outdoor active play provided children ≥2 times per day.
Fixed play environment (Equipment that is anchored or fixed within the center's outdoor environment)	Outdoor play space includes open, grassy areas and a track/path for wheeled toys.
	Indoor play space available for all activities, including running.
	Wide variety of fixed play equipment provided to accommodate the needs of all children.

Table 14.2 (*cont.*)

Target area	NAP SACC best-practice recommendation[a]
Portable play environment (Presence of several types of play equipment that can be transported and used in various locations)	Large variety of portable play equipment available for children to use at the same time. Outdoor portable play equipment freely available to all children at all times.
Sedentary opportunities (Daily opportunities that may result in little of no physical activity)	Television or videos rarely or never shown. Children are not seated for periods of >30 min.
Sedentary environment[b] (Items in the physical environment that may promote or discourage physical activity)	Visible support for physical activity provided in classrooms and common areas through use of posters, pictures, and displayed books. Prominent display of sedentary equipment should be limited (e.g., televisions, videos, and electronic games).
Staff behavior (Interactions between staff and children that may promote or discourage physical activity)	Staff should join children in active play. Staff should encourage children to be active. Active playtime should never be withheld as punishment. And additional active playtime should be given as a reward.
Physical activity training/education (Training and education for children, staff, and/or parents that may increase participation or knowledge related to physical activity)	Physical activity education is provided to children by using a standardized curriculum at least ≥1 time per week. Physical activity education opportunities should be offered to parents ≥2 times per year.
Physical activity policies (Child care center has written policies that address facilitation of physical activity)	Physical activity training (not including playground safety) should be provided for staff ≥2 times per year. Written policies on physical activity should be available and followed.

[a] These best-practice recommendations were developed in 2007 as part of the initial NAP SACC program. The best practices are currently being revised to reflect the most current guidelines and recommendations for child care programs as part of the Go NAP SACC program.
[b] No national recommendations were found in this area.

Self-assessment

In this phase, the child care center director, together with key center staff, completes a 44-item self-assessment tool. This tool assesses nine key areas related to nutrition (fruits and vegetables; fried foods and high-fat meats; beverages; menus and variety; meals and snacks; food items outside of

Table 14.3 *Examples of questions from the NAP SACC self-assessment tool.*

Question	1-point response[a]	2-point response	3-point response	4-point response
Milk served to children ages 2 and older is usually:	whole or regular	2 percent reduced fat	1 percent low-fat	skim or non-fat
Active play time is provided to all children:	45 minutes or less each day	46–90 minutes each day	91–120 minutes each day	more than 120 minutes each day

[a] The 1-point response is the minimal practice while the 4-point response is the best practice.

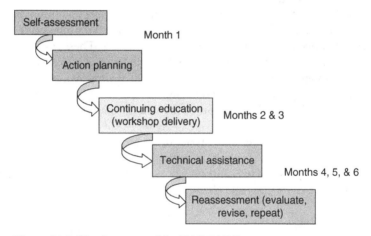

Figure 14.1 The five steps of the NAP SACC program.

regular meals and snacks; supporting healthful eating; nutrition education for young children, parents, and staff; nutrition policies) and six key areas related to physical activity (active play and inactive time; television use and viewing; play environment; supporting physical activity; physical activity education for children, parents, and staff; physical activity policies) environments, practices, and policies in child care centers. Response options on the self-assessment are scored on a four-point scale ranging from minimal practice (1 point) to best practice (4 points) (Table 14.3). Reliability and validity testing of the self-assessment indicated that the tool was an "accurate and stable" measure of the child care environment, with kappa statistics across all questions ranging from 0.20 to 1.00 for inter-rater reliability, 0.07 to 1.00 for test-retest reliability, and −0.01 to 0.79 for validity (Benjamin et al., 2007b).

Action planning

Based on the self-assessment responses, child care centers select at least three areas for improvement, and map out an action plan for making these improvements with guidance and support from the NAP SACC consultant.

Continuing education

The NAP SACC consultant delivers five continuing education workshops on childhood overweight, nutrition for children, physical activity for children, working with families, and personal health and wellness for staff, to educate staff at each child care center about the importance of healthy nutrition and physical activity environments and practices in child care centers. Additional support materials are also provided to facilitate the effective implementation of the intervention. These include a tool kit for child care centers that consists of a NAP SACC notebook, copies of educational materials for three NAP SACC workshops, and handouts for child care center staff and parents linked to each of the fifteen key areas in NAP SACC, as well as a resource manual for the NAP SACC consultant.

Targeted technical assistance

The NAP SACC consultant provides ongoing technical assistance through in-person visits and telephone calls to support the implementation of the environmental changes at the child care center.

Reassessment

Six months after implementing the NAP SACC intervention, the child care center director completes the self-assessment tool for a second time to see where improvements have or have not been made. During this phase, "Action Plans" are revised to include new goals and objectives, with ongoing technical assistance provided by the NAP SACC consultant.

Pilot-testing of the NAP SACC program

The NAP SACC program was pilot-tested in a randomized controlled trial to evaluate the feasibility and acceptability of the program (Benjamin et al., 2007a). A convenience sample of nineteen child care centers was recruited from eight counties in North Carolina. Six counties (n = 15 child care centers) were randomly assigned to the intervention arm, and two counties (n = 4 child care centers) to the control arm, matched on urban/rural status. Seventeen of the enrolled nineteen child care centers completed the self-assessment, while sixteen centers completed all components of the NAP SACC intervention, yielding an attrition rate of 16 percent. Child care centers completed the self-assessment at baseline and at the end of the six-month intervention (follow-up). Their responses on the self-assessment were scored, and total scores could range from 44 to 132 points, with the nutrition score ranging from 29 to 87 points and the physical activity score ranging from 15 to 45 points.

Findings from the pilot study showed that, between baseline and follow-up, self-assessment scores for child care centers in the intervention arm (n = 13 centers) increased an average of 12.84 points, compared to centers in the control arm (n = 4 centers), which increased an average of 7.75 points. In addition, following the intervention, centers in the intervention arm significantly ($p < .001$) improved their self-assessment scores for nutrition (median score ± standard deviation at baseline versus follow-up self-assessment = 70.08 ± 4.77 versus 77.5 ± 4.76), physical activity (median score ± standard deviation at baseline versus follow-up self-assessment = 34.23 ± 3.19 versus 41.00 ± 3.29), and nutrition and physical activity combined (median score ± standard deviation at baseline versus follow-up self-assessment = 105.31 ± 5.25 versus 118.15 ± 6.03).

In terms of the feasibility and acceptability of the NAP SACC program, child care center directors reported that the self-assessment instrument was either fairly easy to use (36 percent) or very easy to use (64 percent), a very helpful (83 percent) or somewhat helpful (17 percent) measure of their nutrition environments, and a very helpful (50 percent) or somewhat helpful (50 percent) measure of their physical activity environments. Twelve directors reported they would recommend the NAP SACC program to other child care centers. The NAP SACC consultants (n = 10) also reported on the feasibility and acceptability of the program, with most reporting that the self-assessment tool was comprehensive (80 percent agreed, 10 percent somewhat agreed, 10 percent somewhat disagreed) and easy to understand (40 percent agreed, 50 percent somewhat agreed, 10 percent disagreed). Most consultants also reported that their meetings with child care center directors were productive (70 percent agreed, 20 percent somewhat agreed, 10 percent were neutral), and felt confident in their ability to deliver the NAP SACC program (60 percent agreed, 40 percent somewhat agreed). Overall, the pilot study showed that NAP SACC was a feasible program, and was well received by both child care centers and the NAP SACC consultants. Feedback received from the child care centers and NAP SACC consultants was used to revise the self-assessment instrument.

State-wide evaluation of the NAP SACC program

Following the pilot-testing of the NAP SACC program, in 2005–6 a large, randomized controlled trial was conducted in child care centers across North Carolina to evaluate the effectiveness of the program (Ward et al., 2008a). A convenience sample of thirty child care health consultants (one consultant from each North Carolina county) who had worked with at least three child care centers but had not participated in the NAP SACC pilot study were recruited to participate in the evaluation of the NAP SACC program. The child care health consultants were randomized into either an intervention group (n = 20 consultants) or a delayed-intervention group (n = 10 consultants). Consultants in the intervention group were randomly assigned to either an in-person (n = 10 consultants) or a web-based (n = 10 consultants) training approach. In-person training sessions lasted about 3 hours (180 minutes). The web training lasted an average of 124 minutes (range = 53–363 minutes). The in-person and web-training modes were similar in content. A knowledge test administered before and after the training showed no differences in knowledge scores between consultants in both training groups (Benjamin et al., 2007c).

From the consultants' caseloads, a convenience sample of eighty-four child care centers was recruited to participate in the NAP SACC evaluation study. Two centers closed during the intervention and were excluded from the study, resulting in a total of eighty-two child care centers; that is, fifty-six child care centers in the intervention arm and twenty-six centers in the control arm. All child care centers with the same child care consultant were in the same study arm. Trained field observers who were blinded to child care center arm assignment administered the Environment and Policy Assessment and Observation (EPAO) instrument in all child care centers via one full day of direct observation in child care center classrooms and a review of child care centers documents (e.g., parent and staff handbooks, menus, classroom activity schedules) conducted before (in the fall of 2005) and immediately after (in the spring of 2006) the six-month NAP SACC intervention. The 75-item EPAO is an expanded version of the self-assessment tool that assesses nutrition and physical activity environments, practices, and policies in child care centers (Ward et al., 2008a; Ward et al., 2008b). Items on the EPAO assess eight nutrition subscales (fruits and vegetables; grains and low-fat meats; high-fat/high-sugar foods; beverages; staff behavior; nutrition environment; nutrition training and education; nutrition policy) and eight physical activity subscales (active opportunities; sedentary opportunities; sedentary environment; portable play environment; fixed play environment; staff behavior; physical activity training and education; physical activity policy). For the NAP SACC evaluation study, each item on the EPAO was converted to a 3-point scale, averaged within a given subscale, and multiplied by 10, with the average of all subscale scores representing total nutrition and physical activity scores. These scores could range from 0 to 20, with higher scores indicating that centers were closer to meeting the NAP SACC best-practice recommendations.

Findings from the NAP SACC evaluation study indicated that consultants in the intervention and control arm were similar in demographic characteristics, although median values indicated that consultants from the intervention arm were younger (32 versus 50 years old) and had a lower caseload of centers (11 versus 27 child care centers) than consultants in the control arm. Forty-one of the fifty-six child care centers in the intervention arm completed all or most aspects of the intervention. Although not statistically significant, after adjusting for consultant and baseline EPAO score, centers in the intervention arm showed an 11 percent improvement in EPAO total nutrition score between baseline and follow-up (mean score ± standard deviation at baseline versus follow-up = 8.6 ± 1.5 versus 9.5 ± 1.7; p = .06), while control centers showed no change (mean score ± standard deviation at baseline versus follow-up = 9.0 ± 1.8 versus 9.0 ± 1.7). Further exploratory analyses, excluding centers that did not implement the intervention, showed a significant difference (p = .01) in total nutrition scores between intervention and control centers at baseline and follow-up; centers in the intervention arm significantly improved their total nutrition score at follow-up (mean score ± standard deviation at baseline versus follow-up = 8.3 ± 1.4 versus 9.6 ± 1.7; p = .01). However, there was no change in total nutrition score for the control arm (mean score ± standard deviation at baseline versus follow-up = 9.0 ± 1.8 versus 9.0 ± 1.7) (Table 14.4).

For the EPAO total physical activity score, there were no significant differences between intervention and control centers in either the analysis that included all participating centers or the analysis that included only centers that completed all or most aspects of the NAP SACC intervention. However, in both analyses, a positive, although non-significant change was observed in total physical activity scores among centers in the intervention arm, compared to centers in the control arm that showed a negative change in total physical activity score. Further analyses of individual items on the EPAO showed significant improvements in mean score for the nutrition items among centers in the intervention arm (+4.3, p < .01), compared to negative changes in the control arm (−0.5). Similar findings were observed in the analyses of individual physical activity items, with mean score changes of +3.6 in the intervention arm, compared with −0.2 in the control arm (p < .05) (Table 14.4).

Table 14.4 Comparison EPAO total nutrition and physical activity scores between baseline and follow-up among centers in the intervention arm and control arm of the NAP SACC evaluation study (Ward et al., 2008a).[a]

	Intervention centers (standard deviation)			Control centers (standard deviation)			
	Baseline	Follow-up	Difference	Baseline	Follow-up	Difference	p-value
Intention to treat[b]							
Total nutrition	8.6 (1.5)	9.5 (1.7)	0.9	9.0 (1.8)	9.0 (1.7)	0.0	.06
Total physical activity	10.1 (2.4)	10.9 (2.6)	0.8	11.0 (2.8)	10.7 (1.8)	-0.3	.19
As-per-protocol[c]							
Total nutrition	8.3 (1.4)	9.6 (1.7)	1.3	9.0 (1.8)	9.0 (1.7)	0.0	.01
Total physical activity	10.1 (2.4)	11.1 (2.5)	1.0	11.0 (2.8)	10.7 (1.8)	-0.3	.15

[a] Scores range from 0–20, with higher scores closer to best-practice recommendations.

[b] Analysis that included all child care centers that participated in the NAP SACC evaluation study (n = 56 intervention centers and 26 control centers).

[c] Analysis that included only child care centers that completed all or most aspects of the NAP SACC intervention (n = 41 intervention centers and 26 control centers).

In sum, although no significant differences were found between baseline and follow-up in the analysis that included all intervention and control centers, exploratory analysis that included only child care centers that completed all or most aspects the NAP SACC program indicated that nutrition and physical activity scores for centers in the intervention arm improved following the NAP SACC intervention.

Dissemination of the NAP SACC program

Developed initially as part of the North Carolina Division of Public Health's obesity initiative, the NAP SACC program was designed to be implemented within an existing public health infrastructure and to be acceptable to child care providers. As early as 2005, interest was developing among the public health community for the NAP SACC program. When the results from the pilot study were shared, requests for access to the NAP SACC program materials increased. Because the initial funders of the program wanted liberal access, even before the evaluation was complete, NAP SACC materials were made available to the general public. Requests for training support came from several regions of the country, including New York, Arizona, and Washington State. By 2007, additional states were using the NAP SACC program including Montana, Texas, Arkansas, South Carolina, Massachusetts, Delaware, Ohio, and Pennsylvania. In 2009, Drummond and colleagues published a report about how the NAP SACC program created a "ripple" effect and influenced other components of the public health system beyond child care facilities (Drummond et al., 2009). Experience implementing the NAP SACC program has brought greater awareness of childhood obesity to a community of stakeholders, including public health professionals, child care advocates, providers, and policymakers. As of 2010, additional states that had implemented the NAP SACC program included Maine, Arizona, West Virginia, North Dakota, and Louisiana.

Because of the keen interest in the NAP SACC program, the North Carolina Center for Training and Research Translation (CTRT), with support from the Centers for Disease Control and Prevention, has made the NAP SACC program, including its web-based training (Benjamin et al., 2007c), available on their website (http://center-trt.org/). Interested individuals can log onto the website and register for training, receive training, and obtain a certificate of completion. In addition, high-quality support educational materials are available for download and distribution. This turn-key operation has greatly facilitated the dissemination and use of the NAP SACC program. Currently, about thirty-five states across the US are using the NAP SACC program.

Evidence of the impact of the NAP SACC program was noted in the "Caring for Our Children" guidelines, a joint publication by the American Academy of Pediatrics, the American Public Health Association, and the Maternal and Child Health Bureau (American Academy of Pediatrics, American Public Health Association, and National Resource Center for Health and Safety in Child Care and Early Education, 2012). Research findings and best-practice recommendations from the NAP SACC program influenced the direction of the "Caring for Our Children" standards which have the potential to impact a wide range of early care and education programs and the thousands of children in out-of-home care across the US.

NAP SACC and the Let's Move! Child Care Campaign

Further evidence of the contribution of the NAP SACC program to public health came recently by way of the White House and the release of national standards (White House Task Force, 2010). The Let's Move! campaign was started by First Lady Michelle Obama to end childhood obesity in the US. The goal of the Let's Move! initiative is to "address childhood obesity within a generation, so that children born today will develop into healthy weight adults" (Let's Move, 2012). When the campaign was announced in February 2010, attention was given to the role of early childhood and it recognized three model programs, including the NAP SACC program.

Let's Move! Child Care, a subcomponent of the Let's Move! campaign, was modeled after the NAP SACC program (Nemours, 2012). Public health researchers at the University of North Carolina at Chapel Hill who were members of the NAP SACC team played significant roles in the development and implementation of Let's Move! Child Care. The goal of Let's Move! Child Care is to encourage child care providers (i.e., child care center and family child care home providers) to strive to meet the Let's Move! Child Care best-practice recommendations for nutrition, physical activity, and screen time. The Let's Move! Child Care best-practice recommendations were developed via an extensive review of the current literature on nutrition and physical activity in early childhood and national guidelines and recommendations for early care and education programs, as well as consultations with experts in the field of nutrition, physical activity, and obesity prevention in early childhood. The Let's Move! Child Care best-practice recommendations for nutrition encourage child care providers to: provide breast milk to infants of mothers who wish to breastfeed, and welcome mothers to nurse mid-day and support parents' decisions with infant feeding; serve fruits or vegetables at every

Table 14.5 *Let's Move! Child care best-practice recommendations for child care programs.*

Target area	Let's Move! Child Care goal for child care providers
Infant feeding	Provide breast milk to infants of mothers who wish to breastfeed. Welcome mothers to nurse mid-day and support parents' decisions with infant feeding.
Food	Try to serve fruits or vegetables at every meal. Eat meals family-style whenever possible. Avoid serving fried foods.
Beverages	When possible, give water during meals and all day. Avoid sugary drinks. For children ages 2 and older, serve low- or non-fat milk and no more than 4–6 ounces of 100% fruit juice per day.
Physical activity	Provide 1–2 hours of physical activity throughout the day, including outside play when possible.
Screen time	No screen time for children under age 2. For children ages 2 and older, work to limit screen time to 30 minutes per week during child care.

meal, eat meals family-style whenever possible, and avoid serving fried foods; provide water to children at meals and throughout the day, avoid sugary beverages, and for children ages 2 and older serve low- or non-fat milk and not more than 4–6 ounces of 100 percent juice per day. The best-practice recommendations for physical activity and screen time encourage child care providers to: provide 1 to 2 hours of physical activity daily, including outside play when possible; limit screen time viewing to 30 minutes per week for children ages 2 and older, and not provide screen time viewing to children under age 2 (Table 14.5).

To participate in Let's Move! Child Care, child care providers initially sign up to register their child care program on the Let's Move! Child Care website (www.healthykidshealthyfuture.org). Upon completion of the registration, child care providers complete a Checklist Quiz to determine whether or not their child care program meets the Let's Move! Child Care best-practice recommendations. For child care providers who do not meet the best-practice recommendations, and those who seek additional information about nutrition and physical activity promotion in child care settings, educational tools and resources are provided on the Let's Move! Child Care website to aid providers in making changes that will improve the nutrition and physical activity practices in their child care program. Since its inception, the Let's Move! Child Care campaign has gained widespread acceptance. As of June 30, 2012, a total of 8,117 child care providers from all fifty states, Washington, DC, Puerto Rico, Guam, and the US Virgin Islands have registered to participate in Let's Move! Child Care.

Future directions and implications of the NAP SACC program

Although initially developed to promote healthy weight development in preschool children attending child care centers in North Carolina, the NAP SACC program has attained widespread acceptance and national recognition. The NAP SACC program is currently in use in several states across the US. In addition, the program has served as a model for other childhood obesity initiatives, including the Let's Move! Child Care campaign. While the NAP SACC program does not specifically address educational outcomes, the program has the potential to support greater academic achievement in children because of its emphasis on supporting healthy weight development in early childhood.

In terms of next steps, the NAP SACC program is moving to an interactive web-based program called Go NAP SACC. The new Go NAP SACC program will allow child care providers to follow the five basic NAP SACC steps: self-assessment, action planning, continuing education, technical assistance, and reassessment. However, in the Go NAP SACC program, child care providers may choose to implement changes in their child care program independent of the child health consultant. In addition, the program will be expanded to include recommendations for infants and toddlers, as well as family child care homes. The Go NAP SACC program website will share current research and policy updates, and barriers/promoters and success stories from the field, so that lessons learned can serve as instruction for subsequent users. The Go NAP SACC website will also offer regular webinars and trainings for child care providers and child health consultants, as well as resources and educational materials to aid child care programs in promoting nutrition and physical activity practices that support healthy weight development in early childhood. The Go NAP SACC program is currently under development and will be publicly available some time in 2014.

References

American Academy of Pediatrics, American Public Health Association, and National Resource Center for Health and Safety in Child Care and Early Education (2012). *Preventing childhood obesity in early care and education: selected standards from Caring for Our Children: national health and safety performance standards; guidelines for early care and education programs*, 3rd edn. Retrieved from http://nrckids.org/CFOC3/PDFVersion/preventing_obesity. pdf.

American Dietetic Association (2005). Position of the American Dietetic Association: benchmarks for nutrition programs in child care settings. *Journal of the American Dietetic Association*, 105(6), 979–986.

Ammerman, A. S., Ward, D. S., Benjamin, S. E., Ball, S. C., Sommers, J. K., Molloy, M., and Dodds, J. M. (2007). An intervention to promote healthy weight: Nutrition and Physical Activity Self-Assessment for Child Care (NAP SACC) theory and design. *Preventing Chronic Disease*. Retrieved from www. cdc.gov/ped/issues/2007/iui/06_0115.htm.

Anderson, P. M., and Butcher, K. E. (2006). Childhood obesity: trends and potential causes. *Future of Children*, 16(1), 19–45.

Ball, S. C., Benjamin, S. E., and Ward, D. S. (2008). Dietary intakes in North Carolina child care centers: are children meeting current recommendations. *Journal of the American Dietetic Association*, 108(4), 718–721.

Bandura, A. (1986). *Social foundations of thought and action*. Englewood Cliffs, NJ: Prentice Hall.

(1997). *Self-efficacy: the exercise of control*. New York: W. H. Freeman.

Benjamin, S. E., Ammerman, A., Sommers, J., Dodds, J., Neelon, B., Ward, D. S. (2007a). Nutrition and physical activity self-assessment for child care (NAP SACC): results from a pilot intervention. *Journal of Nutrition Education and Behavior*, 39(3), 142–149.

Benjamin, Neelon, S. E., Ball, S. C., Bangdiwala, S. I., Ammerman, A. S., and Ward, D. S. (2007b). Reliability and validity of a nutrition and physical activity environmental self-assessment for child care. *International Journal of Behavioral Nutrition and Physical Activity*.

Benjamin, S. E., Tate, D. F., Bangdiwala, S. I., Neelon, B. H., Ammerman, A. S., Dodds, J. M., and Ward, D. S. (2007c). Preparing child health consultants to address childhood overweight: a randomized controlled trial comparing web to in-person training. *Maternal and Child Health Journal*, 12(5), 662–669.

Benjamin Neelon, S. E., Vaughn, A., Ball, S. C., McWilliams, C., and Ward, D. S. (2012). Nutrition practices and mealtime environments in North Carolina child care centers. *Child Obesity*, 8(3), 215–223.

Birch, L. L., and Fisher, J. O. (1998). Development of eating behaviors among children and adolescents. *Pediatrics*, 101(3 pt. 2), 539–549.

Bluford, D. A., Sherry, B., and Scanlon, K. S. (2007). Interventions to prevent or treat obesity in preschool children: a review of evaluated programs. *Obesity (Silver Spring)*, 15(6), 1356–1372.

Bolella, M. C., Spark, A., Boccia, L. A., Nicklas, T. A., Pittman, B. P., and Williams, C. L. (1999). Nutrient intake of Head Start children: home versus school. *Journal of the American College of Nutrition*, 18(2), 108–114.

Briley, M. E., Jastrow, S., Vickers, J., and Roberts-Gray, C. (1999). Dietary intake at child-care centers and away: are parents and care providers working as partners or at cross-purposes. *Journal of the American Dietetic Association*, 99 (8), 950–954.

Bruening, K. S., Gilbride, J. A., Passanante, M. R., and McLowry, S. (1999). Dietary intakes and health outcomes among children attending 2 urban day care centers. *Journal of the American Dietetic Association*, 99(12), 1529–1535.

Campbell, K. J., and Hesketh, K. D. (2007). Strategies which aim to positively impact weight, physical activity, diet and sedentary behaviors in children from zero to five years: a systematic review of the literature. *Obesity Reviews*, 8(4), 327–338.

Carlson, J. A., Crespo, N. C., Sallis, J. F., Patterson, R. E., and Elder, J. P. (2012). Dietary-related and physical activity-related predictors of obesity in children: a 2-year prospective study. *Childhood Obesity*, 8(2), 110–115.

Centers for Disease Control and Prevention (2012a). *Basics about childhood obesity*. Retrieved from www.cdc.gov/obesity/childhood/basics.html.

(2012b). *Obesity among low-income preschool children*. Retrieved from www.cdc.gov/obesity/downloads/PedNSSFactSheet.pdf.

Currie, J. (2005). Health disparities and gaps in school readiness. *Future of Children*, 15(1), 117–137.

Datar, A., and Strum R. (2006). Childhood overweight and elementary school outcomes. *International Journal of Obesity (London)*, 30(9), 1449–1460.

Datar, A., Strum, R., and Magnabosco, J. L. (2004). Childhood overweight and academic performance: national study of kindergartners and first-graders. *Obesity Research*, 12(1), 58–68.

Davis, C. L., and Cooper, S. (2011). Fitness, fatness, cognition, behavior, and academic achievement among overweight children: do cross-sectional associations correspond to exercise trial outcomes. *Preventive Medicine*, 52(Suppl. 1), S65–S69.

Davison, K. K., and Birch, L. L. (2001). Childhood overweight: a contextual model and recommendations for future research. *Obesity Reviews*, 2(3), 159–171.

Dowda, M., Brown, W. H., McIver, K. L., Pfeiffer, K. A., O'Neill, J. R., Addy, C. L., and Pate, R. R. (2009). Policies and characteristics of the preschool environment on physical activity of young children. *Pediatrics*, 123(2), e261–e266.

Drake, A. M. (1991). Anthropometry, biochemical iron indexes and energy nutrient intake of preschool children: comparison of intake at daycare center and home. *Journal of the American Dietetic Association*, 91(12), 1587–1588.

Drummond, R. L., Staten, L. K., Sanford, M. R., Davidson, C. L., Magda Ciocazan, M., Khor, K. N., and Kaplan, F. (2009). A pebble in the pond: the ripple effect of an obesity prevention intervention targeting the child care environment. *Health Promotion and Practice*, 10(Suppl. 2), 156S–167S.

Erinosho, T. O., Ball, S. C., Hanson, P. P., Vaughn, A. E., and Ward, D. S. (2013). Assessing foods offered to children at child care centers using the Healthy Eating Index. *Journal of the Academy of Nutrition and Dietetics*, 113(8), 1084–1089.

Erinosho, T. O., Dixon, L. B., Young, C., Brotman, L. M., and Hayman, L. L. (2011). Nutrition practices and children's dietary intakes at child care centers in New York City. *Journal of the American Dietetic Association*, 111(9), 1391–1397.

Falkner, N. H., Neumark-Sztainer, D., Story, M., Jeffery, R. W., Beuhring, T., and Resnick, M. D. (2001). Social, educational, and psychological correlates of weight status in adolescents. *Obesity Research*, 9(1), 32–42.

Fitzgibbon, M. L., Stolley, M. R., Schiffer, L., Van Horn, L., Kaufer Christoffel, K., and Dyer, A. (2005). Two-year follow-up results for Hip-Hop to Health Jr.: a randomized controlled trial for overweight prevention in preschool minority children. *Journal of Pediatrics*, 146(5), 618–625.

Fleischhacker, S., Cason, K. L., and Achterberg, C. (2006). "You had peas today?": A pilot study comparing a Head Start child care center's menu with the actual food served. *Journal of the American Dietetic Association*, 106 (2), 277–280.

Forum on Child and Family Statistics (2010). America's children in brief: key national indicators of well-being, 2010. Retrieved July 25, 2012 from www. childstats.gov/pdf/ac2010/ac_10.pdf.

Freedman, D. S., Khan, L. K., Serdula, M. K., Ogden, C. L., and Dietz, W. H. (2006). Racial and ethnic differences in secular trends for childhood BMI, weight, and height. *Obesity (Silver Spring)*, 14(2), 301–308.

Grantham-McGregor, S., and Ani, C. (2001). A review of studies on the effect of iron deficiency on cognitive development in children. *Journal of Nutrition*, 131 (2S-2), 649S–668S.

Halterman, J. S., Kaczorowski, J. M., Aligne, C. A., Auinger, P., and Szilagyi, P. G. (2001). Iron deficiency and cognitive achievement among school-aged children and adolescents in the United States. *Pediatrics*, 107 (6), 1381–1386.

Hesketh, K. D., and Campbell, K. J. (2010). Interventions to prevent obesity in 0–5 year olds: an updated systematic review of the literature. *Obesity (Silver Spring)*, 18 (Suppl. 1), S27–S35.

Hollar, D., Messiah, S. E., Lopez-Mitnik, G., Hollar, L., Almon, M., and Agatston, A. S. (2010). Effect of a two-year obesity prevention intervention on percentile changes in body mass index and academic performance in low-income elementary school children. *American Journal of Public Health*, 100(4), 646–653.

Huston, A. C., Wright, J. C., Marquis, J., and Green, S. B. (1999). How young children spend their time: television and other activities. *Developmental Psychology*, 35(4), 912–925.

Iruka, I. U., and Carver, P. R. (2006). *Initial results from the 2005 NHES Early Childhood Program Participation Survey (NCES 2006–075)*. US Department of Education. Washington, DC: National Center for Education Statistics. Retrieved from http://nces.ed.gov/pubs2006/2006075.pdf.

Let's Move!. (2012). *Let's Move!: America's move to raise a healthier generation of kids*. Retrieved August 6 from www.letsmove.gov/.

Li, Y., Dai, Q., Jackson, J. C., and Zhang, J. (2008). Overweight is associated with decreased cognitive functioning among school children and adolescents. *Obesity (Silver Spring)*, 16(8), 1809–1815.

Li, Y., Raychowdhury, S., Tedders, S. H., Lyn, R., Lopez-De Fede, A., and Zhang, J. (2012). Association between increased BMI and severe school absenteeism among US children and adolescents: findings from a national survey, 2005–2008. *International Journal of Obesity (London)*, 36(4), 517–523.

Lozoff, B., Jimenez, E., Hagen, J., Mollen, E., and Wolf, A. W. (2000). Poorer behavioral and developmental outcome more than 10 years after treatment for iron deficiency in infancy. *Pediatrics*, 105(4), E51.

McLeroy, K. R., Bibeau, D., Steckler, A., and Glanz, K. (1988). An ecological perspective on health promotion programs. *Health Education Quarterly*, 15(4), 351–377.

McWillams, C., Ball, S. C., Benjamin, S. E., Hales, D., Vaughn, A., and Ward, D.S. (2009). Best practice guidelines for physical activity at child care. *Pediatrics*, 124(6): 1650–1659.

National Association for Sport and Physical Education (2012). *Active Start: a statement of physical activity guidelines for children from birth to age 5* (2nd edn.). Retrieved July 26 from www.aahperd.org/naspe/standards/national Guidelines/ActiveStart.cfm.

Nead, K. G., Halterman, J. S., Kaczorowski, J. M., Auinger, P., and Weitzman, M. (2004). Overweight children and adolescents: a risk group for iron deficiency. *Pediatrics*, 114(1): 104–108.

Nemours (2012). *Let's Move! child care*. Retrieved August 6 from www.health-ykidshealthyfuture.org/welcome.html.

Nutrition and Physical Activity Self-Assessment for Child Care (NAP SACC). (2012). *NAP SACC Home*. Retrieved August 1 from www.napsacc.org/.

Oakley, C. B., Bomba, A. K., Knight, K. B., and Byrd, S. H. (1995).Evaluation of menus planned in Mississippi child care centers participating in the Child and Adult Care Food Program. *Journal of the American Dietetic Association*, 95(7), 765–768.

Ogden, C. L., Carroll, M. D., Kit, B. K., and Flegal, K. M. (2012). Prevalence of obesity and trends in body mass index among US children and adolescents, 1999–2010. *Journal of the American Medical Association*, 307(5), 483–490.

Ogden, C. L., Lamb, M. M., Carroll, M. D., and Flegal, K. M. (2010). Obesity and socioeconomic status in children and adolescents: United States, 2005–2008. *NCHS Data Brief*, 51, 1–8.

Pate, R. R., McIver, K., Dowda, M., Brown, W. H., and Addy, C. (2008). Directly observed physical activity in preschool children. *Journal of School Health*, 78(8), 438–444.

Pate, R. R., Pfeiffer, K. A., Trost, S. G., Ziegler, P., and Dowda, M. (2004). Physical activity among children attending preschools. *Pediatrics*, 113(5), 1258–1263.

Pinhas-Hamiel, O., Doron-Panush, N., Reichman, B., Nitzan-Kaluski, D., Shalitin, S., and Geva-Lerner, L. (2006). Obese children and adolescents: a risk group for low vitamin B12 concentration. *Archives of Pediatric and Adolescent Medicine*, 160(9), 933–936.

Reilly, J. J. (2010). Low levels of objectively measured physical activity in preschoolers in child care. *Medicine and Science in Sports and Exercise*, 42(3), 502–507.

Shore, S. M., Sachs, M. L., Lidicker, J. R., Brett, S. N., Wright, A. R., and Libonati, J. R. (2008). Decrease scholastic achievement in overweight middle school students. *Obesity (Silver Spring)*, 16(7), 1535–1538.

Stokols, D. (1996). Translating social ecological theory into guidelines for community health promotion. *American Journal of Health Promotion*, 10(4), 282–298.

Taras, H. (2005). Nutrition and student performance at school. *Journal of School Health*, 75(6), 199–213.

te Velde, S. J., van Nassau, F., Uijtdewilligen, L., van Stralen, M. M., Cardon, G., De Craemer, M., Manios, Y., Brug, J., Chinapaw, M. J., and ToyBox-Study Group (2012). Energy balance-related behaviors associated with overweight and obesity in preschool children: a systematic review of prospective studies. *Obesity Reviews*, 13(Suppl. 1), 56–74.

Trost, S. G., Sirard, J. R., Dowda, M., Pfeiffer, K. A., and Pate, R. R. (2003). Physical activity in overweight and nonoverweight preschool children. *International Journal of Obesity and Related Metabolic Disorders*, 27(7), 834–839.

Trost, S. G., Ward, D. S., and Senso, M. (2010). Effects of child care policy and environment on physical activity. *Medicine and Science in Sports and Exercise*, 42(3), 520–525.

US Department of Agriculture (1997). *Early Childhood and Child Care Study*: summary of findings. Retrieved July 25, 2012 from www.fns.usda.gov/ora/menu/published/CNP/FILES/CHLDCARE.pdf.

Ward, D. S., Benjamin, S. E., Ammerman, A. S., Ball, S. C., Neelon, B. H., and Bangdiwala, S. I. (2008a). Nutrition and physical activity in child care. Results from an environmental intervention. *American Journal of Preventive Medicine*, 35(4), 352–356.

Ward, D., Hales, D., Haverly, K., Marks, J., Benjamin, S., Ball, S., and Trost, S. (2008b). An instrument to assess the obesogenic environment of child care centers. *American Journal of Health Behavior*, 32(4), 380–386.

White House Task Force (2010). *Solving the problem of childhood obesity within a generation: White House Task Force on Childhood Obesity Report to the President*. Retrieved 2012, from www.letsmove.gov/sites/letsmove.gov/files/TaskForce_on_Childhood_Obesity_May2010_FullReport.pdf.

Call to action. Human capital: challenges and opportunity

Robert H. Bruininks with Amy Susman-Stillman and Jim Thorp

An essential key to securing any economy's future is the development of human capital, or to put a more human spin on it: helping all children and youth, families, and communities reach their full potential.

Indeed the United States is no exception. A storm is coming – whipped up by two huge winds of change: one economic and one demographic. The economic trend is the steady increase in knowledge and skills necessary to succeed in the twenty-first-century global economy. The demographic trend is the rapid rise in the percentage of our population who live below the poverty line. This storm poses serious problems, because, at precisely the time when our economy will need more and more highly skilled workers and citizens than ever before, the percentages of students from backgrounds that have not historically succeeded in our education system will be at an all-time high. This trend is often referenced as the nation's growing achievement gap. If we are going to weather this perfect storm and retain our quality of life, we need to improve the academic development of all students – from early childhood through higher education and lifelong learning. We need a renewed national vision for education and the development of human capital, one that recalls our nation's great past successes (e.g., the Morrill Act, the GI Bill, the National Defense Education Act, Pell Grants), and acknowledges the changing nature of both our society and the workplace.

The foundation to such a vision is the idea that college readiness and completion must be the new standard for education in the twenty-first century.[1] Consider for a moment that the only constitutionally mandated

Robert H. Bruininks is president emeritus of the University of Minnesota and a professor in the Humphrey School of Public Affairs and the College of Eduation and Human Development. Amy Susman-Stillman is the co-director of the Center for Early Education and Development at the University of Minnesota. Jim Thorp is the communications director for the Office of Human Resources at the University of Minnesota.

[1] College readiness, in this context, is defined as the preparation and successful completion of at least two years of post-secondary education or training.

responsibility of the state of Minnesota is education. When our forefathers drafted the state constitution document in 1857, they foresaw the essential role that public education would play in the future of our young state and nation. Then, in the early twentieth century, high school was not universal, but economic changes demanded more skilled workers. As a result, we built the modern comprehensive high school. And at the end of World War II, we formulated policies such as the GI Bill to develop a higher education system that is widely accessible.

Harvard economists Claudia Goldin and Larry Katz have suggested that just as making high school education universal helped to fuel US economic growth then, access to college and lifelong learning will be key to competitiveness in the global economy of this century. College readiness, however, is not a matter of "if you build it, they will come." Academic momentum is essential. It begins with early childhood education, continues through elementary and middle school, where the foundations for college readiness and high expectations for both students and families are set, and through high school, where students must be encouraged to take a challenging curriculum to maintain their academic momentum.

Renewal of our education systems is no small feat – especially when you consider that what we increasingly refer to as P-20 education (preschool through post-secondary) is often a loose confederation of systems that collaborate when they can and sometimes compete for scarce public resources. It is difficult to underestimate the degree to which our preschool, K-12, and higher education systems in the USA are misaligned. This isn't surprising when you consider that the current model in the vast majority of communities today was designed early in the last century to send only 25–30 percent of students on to college.

Perhaps the greatest weakness today in the nation's human capital agenda is the lack of a unified vision and coordinated action in early childhood education. The adverse impact of limited opportunity to learn is particularly devastating to the educational development of children in poverty. It is estimated that at least 20 precent of young children in America are living in poverty, and the rate is increasing in the current economic climate. And these rates are higher for children of color. Poverty has a strong, negative, and long-lasting effect on young children's development, and support structures for children living in poverty are critical for improving long-term educational opportunity. The impact of poverty during early childhood is stronger than the impact of poverty later in childhood and it is experienced over the long term. Duncan et al. (2010) show that children's eventual labor market success appears to be compromised much more by poverty experienced *early*, rather than later, in childhood. The study finds that a $3,000-per-year lower family income in early childhood is associated with 17 precent lower productivity in adulthood, whereas lower income later in childhood appears to have little bearing on later productivity. Ameliorating the impacts of poverty early in life can therefore have far-reaching effects on our national prosperity. These results complement emerging neuroscience and developmental research, which tell us that serious adversity early in life can weaken the architecture of the developing brain, generating consequences that reach well into adulthood.

Past research has identified three factors in brain development – the child's relationships, learning resources, and stress – that can be adversely affected by poverty. Children develop in an environment of relationships that includes their immediate and extended families, nonfamily care-givers, neighbors, and community – and poverty can compromise those relationships. We know that brains are built from the bottom up, with simple skills and circuits forming a foundation in early childhood for more complex circuits and skills that are built later. The active ingredients that are necessary to construct a strong architecture of brain circuitry are abundant, including safe opportunities to learn and active, reciprocal relationships with adults that can be described as "serve-and-return" interactions.

When children receive few opportunities for positive serve-and-return interactions – when the responses from adults are sporadic, inappropriate, or missing entirely – they are not getting the stimulation their brains need to develop in a healthy way. Parents who are struggling to make ends meet are often less able than more affluent families to provide those experiences for their children, whether through having the choice to stay at home or by having access to high-quality child care. They are also less able to afford books, educational excursions, and other learning-related resources, which can compromise their children's cognitive development.

Perhaps the most critical impact of limited early experience is upon the development of language. Exposure to language during early childhood predicts language skills and achievement during middle childhood. Hart and Risley spent two and a half years intensely observing the language of forty-two families throughout Kansas City. Specifically, they looked at household language use in three different settings: (1) professional fam-ilies; (2) working-class families; and (3) welfare families. Hart and Risley gathered an enormous amount of data during the study and subsequent longitudinal follow-ups to formulate the often-cited 30 million-word gap between the vocabularies of welfare and professional families by age 3. This number came from the data that showed welfare children heard, on average, 616 words per hour, while children from professional families (essentially children with college educated parents) heard 2,153 words per hour. The longitudinal research in the following years demonstrated a high correlation between vocabulary size at age 3 and language test scores at ages 9 and 10 in areas of vocabulary, listening, syntax, and reading comprehension. These are the building blocks for longer-term learning. Without this foundation, the achievement gap grows with age. This study was subsequently used to fuel the fire of arguments for early childhood programs such as Head Start.

If college readiness is to become a new standard for education in the new economy, it must begin with a stronger commitment to the early years of children, especially those who experience the limited opportunities associated with poverty. Recently, Kate Wolford, president of the McKnight Foundation, and Robert Bruininks convened a group of poli-cymakers, academic researchers, and civic leaders to address the early educational needs of Minnesota's most vulnerable children. After some deliberation, this group formulated the following five-point agenda to promote preparation for school and long-term learning.

1. Strengthen outreach efforts to build greater political and public will for making our youngest children a priority in the state's investments, partic-ularly to ensure services for the most vulnerable children in Minnesota.
2. Support parents in the development of their own children and in the development and implementation of Minnesota's early childhood sys-tem, ensuring increased and inclusive parent participation at all levels.
3. Implement a Quality Rating and Improvement System for early care and education programs, linking public dollars to quality while empowering all parents to make informed decisions about early care and learning.
4. Develop a financial strategy for creating a strong system of services supporting early learning and healthy development, including the following steps:
   • identify the resources needed to expand and improve services to vulnerable children and families;
   • better leverage and align existing resources for early childhood to maximize the efficient and effective targeting and use of these funds;
   • develop new strategies for expanding the resources available for early childhood development and services.
5. Establish an organizational structure with authority and accountability for advancing healthy early childhood developmental outcomes at both the state and local levels, by:
   • carefully designing and implementing a legislatively proposed Office of Early Learning, under the guidance of the Early Childhood Advisory Council;

- identifying a means for involvement and expansion of the private sector entities and resources, and for sharing responsibilities for agreed-upon outcomes; and
- building upon existing regional and local early childhood coalitions to strengthen, coordinate, improve, and evaluate services in Minnesota communities.

Unfortunately, few communities today possess the assets to support the healthy development of young children who experience the adverse impact of poverty and limited educational opportunity. The sense of urgency felt today about the futures of our children and the results of our educational system is stronger than ever. Many of us understand that there is no better means of escaping poverty, overcoming obstacles, and achieving dreams than education. Parents and educators understand that, given appropriate resources and opportunities, everyone is born to achieve. But the path to educational achievement starts early and requires strong support from families and caring adults, and an educational system with greater focus, alignment, appropriate resources, and accountability.

It is time to move beyond rhetoric. It is time to set clear national priorities from early childhood through postsecondary education, and it is time to demonstrate the value of what we do with understandable results and measurable outcomes. We cannot accept mediocre results in the educational attainment and skills of our children. It is time to address the nation's human capital gap, renew our educational systems, restore public confidence, and create a more competitive United States position in an increasingly global economy.

As W. E. B. Du Bois once said, "Of all the civil rights for which the world has struggled and fought for 5,000 years, the right to learn is undoubtedly the most fundamental." This reality has been true throughout human history. It will be an absolute imperative to secure our future.

References

Goldin, C., and Katz, L. (2009). *The race between education and technology.* Cambridge, MA: Harvard University Press.

Duncan, G., Magnuson, K., Boyce, T., and Shonkoff, J. (2010). *The long reach of early childhood poverty: pathways and impacts.* Cammbridge, MA: Harvard Center on the Developing Child.

Hart, B., and Risley, T. http://languagefix.wordpress.com/2008/09/30/4-the-hart-risley-30-million-word-gap-study/ (The Hart-Risley 30 Million Word Gap Study – 1995 September 30, 2008 at 10:53 am | Posted in Language Acquisition).

Name index

Abraham, J., 12, 321, 340
Adams, M. J., 219
Aizer, A., 321
Alexander, G. C., 338
Almeida, R. A., 337
Amersbach, G., 337
Anderson, K., 194
Auerbach, D., 322
Ayoub, C., 10, 246

Banthin, J., 337
Barker, D. J. P., 113
Barnett, W. S., 297
Barry, C. L., 128
Bartless, J., 10
Beeber, L., 245
Beeler, T., 219
Belsky, J., 187
Berlin, L. J., 242
Braveman, P., 6, 128
Bruininks, R., 13, 395
Buchmueller, T., 320, 321, 337
Buerhaus, P., 322
Busch, S. H., 128

Cafferata, G. I., 339
Camilli, G., 297, 310
Campbell, F., 10
Card, D., 320
Chazen-Cohen, R., 10, 244
Chen, P., 12
Clements, M. A., 296
Cole, K. N., 297
Crawford, A., 9
Cummings, E. M., 240, 337
Cunha, F., 4, 55
Currie, J., 320, 322, 323

Dale, P. S., 297
Daniels, D., 297
Day, M., 295

Decker, S., 322, 323
Dobkin, C., 320
D'Onise, K., 9, 10
Drummond, R. L., 383
Du Bois, W. E. B., 396
Dubay, L. C., 337
Duncan, G., 9, 57–60, 128, 393

Egerter, S., 6
Englund, M., 10
Epstein, A., 321
Erinosho, T., 12–13

Feiler, R., 297
Foorman, B. R., 219
Frick, K., 9
Frisvold, D., 189

Gaynor, M., 322
Georgieff, M., 9
Gest, S. D., 10
Golbeck, S. L., 296
Goldin, C., 393
Graue, E., 296, 298, 301
Greenberg, M. T., 220
Gruber, J., 320, 322
Grumbach, K., 337
Guendelman, S., 330
Guyer, B., 9

Haas, J., 321
Halfon, N., 339
Hamilton, V., 339
Hammond, M., 126
Hanratty, M., 321
Harrison, E. R., 337
Hart, B., 394–395
Hayakawa, M., 11
Heckman, J., 4, 13, 55
Hofer, A., 321, 340

Subject index

Entries for figures and tables are in bold typeface.